The Popisl
A study in the his
reign of Charles II

John Pollock

Alpha Editions

This edition published in 2024

ISBN 9789357945479

Design and Setting By

Alpha Editions

www.alphaedis.com

Email - info@alphaedis.com

Contents

PREFACE

When I first undertook the study of the Popish Plot the late Lord Acton wrote to me: "There are three quite unravelled mysteries;—what was going on between Coleman and Père la Chaize; how Oates got hold of the wrong story; and who killed Godfrey." The following book is an attempt to answer these questions and to elucidate points of obscurity connected with them.

In the course of the work I have received much kind help from Dr. Jackson and Mr. Stanley Leathes of this college, from the Rev. J. N. Figgis of St. Catharine's College, and from my father; and Mr. C. H. Firth of All Souls' College has been exceedingly generous in giving the assistance of his invaluable learning and experience to a novice attacking problems which have been left too long untouched by those better fitted for the task.

It is only as a mark of the deep gratitude I bear him that I have ventured to dedicate this book to the memory of the illustrious man whose death has deprived it of its sternest critic. Few can know so well as myself how far its attainment falls short of the standard which he set up. With that standard before me I can justify myself only by the thought that I have tried to follow strictly the injunction: Nothing extenuate, nor set down aught in malice.

J. P.

TRINITY COLLEGE, CAMBRIDGE, 1903.

TABLE OF SOME EVENTS OCCURRING IN THE HISTORY OF THE POPISH PLOT

1677. Ash Wednesday	Titus Oates converted to the Church of Rome.
April	Enters the English Jesuit college at Valladolid.
October 30	Expelled from the college at Valladolid.
December 10	Enters the English Jesuit college at St. Omers.
1678. April 24	Jesuit congregation held at St. James' Palace.
June 23	Oates expelled from the college at St. Omers
June 27	and returns to London.
August 13	Christopher Kirkby informs the king of a plot against his life.
August 14	Kirkby and Dr. Tonge examined by the Earl of Danby.
	The king goes to Windsor.
August 31	The forged letters sent to Bedingfield at Windsor.
September 2	Tonge introduces Oates to Kirkby at his lodgings at Vauxhall.
September 6	Oates swears to the truth of his information before Sir Edmund Berry Godfrey.
September 27	Oates and Tonge summoned before the Privy Council.
September 28	Oates swears again to the truth of his information before Godfrey and leaves a copy with him.
	Oates examined at length by the council. Search for Jesuits begun that night.
	Edward Coleman pays a secret visit to Godfrey.

September 29	Sir George Wakeman before the council.
	Oates again examined by the council and continues the search for Jesuits at night.
	Warrant issued for the arrest of Coleman and seizure of his papers.
September 30	Coleman surrenders to the warrant against him and is placed in charge of an officer. His house searched and his papers seized.
	Oates examined twice by the council and again searches for Jesuits.
October 1	The king goes to Newmarket.
	Coleman's papers examined by a committee of the council.
	Coleman committed to Newgate.
October 12	Sir Edmund Berry Godfrey missing.
October 15	News of his disappearance published.
October 17	His body found in a field at the foot of Primrose Hill.
October 18, 19	An inquest held.
October 20	Reward of £500 offered for the discovery of Godfrey's murderers.
October 21	Meeting of Parliament (seventeenth session of Charles II's second or Long Parliament).
October 23	Oates at the bar of the House of Commons.
October 24	Assurance of protection added to the reward offered for the discovery of Godfrey's murderers.
October 25–31	The Earl of Powis, Viscount Stafford, Lord Petre, Lord Bellasis, and Lord Arundel of Wardour surrender to the warrants out against them as being, on Oates' information, concerned in the Plot.

October 28	Test Act passes the Commons.
October 30, 31	Oates at the bar of the House of Lords.
November 1	Resolution of both Houses of Parliament with regard to the Plot.
	Funeral of Godfrey.
	Proclamation commanding Popish recusants to depart ten miles from London.
	Arrest of Samuel Atkins.
November 5	Bedloe surrenders himself at Bristol.
November 7	Bedloe comes to town and is examined by the king and secretaries. Examination of Coleman in Newgate.
November 10, 18	Bedloe at the bar of the House of Commons
November 12	and at the bar of the House of Lords.
November 20	Test Act passed, but with a proviso exempting the Duke of York.
November 21	Trial and conviction of William Staley for high treason.
November 24	Oates accuses the queen in examination by Secretary Coventry.
November 26	Staley executed at Tyburn, denying his guilt.
November 27	Trial and conviction of Coleman for high treason. Bedloe accuses the queen.
November 28	Oates accuses the queen at the bar of the House of Commons. He is confined by the king and his papers are seized.
November 30	The king refuses to pass the Militia bill, even for half an hour.
December 3	Execution of Coleman.

December 5	The five Popish Lords impeached.
December 16	Supply granted for disbanding the army.
December 17	Trial and conviction of Ireland, Pickering, and Grove for high treason.
December 19	Montagu's papers seized. He produces Danby's letters to the Commons, revealing the secret treaty with Louis XIV.
December 21	Miles Prance arrested and recognised by Bedloe. Impeachment of Danby.
December 23	Prance confesses and accuses Green, Berry, and Hill of being Godfrey's murderers.
December 28	Dugdale comes forward as a witness.
December 29	Prance recants.
December 30	Parliament prorogued till February 4.
1679. January 11	Prance retracts his recantation.
January 24	Long Parliament dissolved.
	Ireland and Grove executed; Pickering respited till May 25.
February 5	Trial and conviction of Green, Berry, and Hill for Godfrey's murder.
February 8	Atkins is acquitted of the same murder.
February 21	Execution of Green and Hill.
February 28	Execution of Berry.
March 3	The king declares that he was never married to any woman but Queen Catherine.
March 4	The Duke of York leaves for Brussels by command of the king.
March 6	The king repeats his declaration.
	The third Parliament meets. Edward Seymour

chosen Speaker, and is rejected by the king.

March 13	Parliament prorogued for two days.
March 15	Serjeant Gregory chosen Speaker.
March 21	Parliament votes the Plot to be read. Prance's examination read to the Lords.
March 22	The Commons resolve to proceed with Danby's impeachment.
March 24	Danby takes refuge at Whitehall.
March 25	Speech on Scotland by Shaftesbury.
April 1	Bill of attainder voted against Danby.
April 15	Bill of attainder passed.
April 16	Danby surrenders himself and is committed to the Tower.
	A supply voted and appropriated for the disbandment of the army.
April 21	The king declares a new privy council, devised by Sir William Temple.
April 24	Trial and conviction of Reading.
April 27	Resolution of Parliament against the Duke of York.
April 30	The king's speech concerning the succession.
May 3	Sharp, Archbishop of St. Andrews, murdered.
May 11	The Exclusion bill voted by the Commons.
May 15	The Exclusion bill read for the first time.
May 23, 24	The Commons attack the system of secret service money.
May 26	The Habeas Corpus Act passed. The Parliament prorogued to August 14, and afterwards dissolved against the advice of the whole council.

May 29	Outbreak of the Bothwell Brigg rebellion. The Covenant proclaimed in the west of Scotland.
June 1	Claverhouse defeated at Drumclog.
June	Publication of "An Appeal from the City to the Country."
June 13	Trial and conviction of Whitebread, Fenwick, Harcourt, Gavan, and Turner (the five Jesuits) for high treason.
June 14	Trial and conviction of Richard Langhorn for high treason.
June 15	Monmouth starts to suppress the rebellion.
June 20	Execution of the Five Jesuits.
June 22	The Covenanters routed by Monmouth at Bothwell Brigg.
July 9	Samuel Pepys and Sir Anthony Deane, in prison on account of the Plot, admitted to bail by Scroggs.
July 14	Execution of Langhorn.
July 17	Sir Thomas Gascoigne committed to the Tower on a charge of high treason.
July 18	Sir George Wakeman, Marshall, Romney, and Corker tried for high treason and acquitted.
August	Executions in the provinces of priests on account of their orders.
August 22	The king ill at Windsor.
August 23	The Duke of York summoned from Brussels.
August 29	The Duke sets out from Brussels
September 2	and reaches Windsor.
September 12	The Duke of Monmouth removed from his commission of Lord General.

September 24	Monmouth leaves for Holland.
September 27	James leaves for Brussels, thence to Scotland.
October 7	The new Parliament, meeting, is prorogued by successive stages to October 1680.
October 15	Shaftesbury dismissed from his place at the council board.
October 20	Dangerfield searches Col. Mansell's lodgings and is arrested.
October 27	Dangerfield committed to prison on charge of high treason.
October 29	Papers found in Mrs. Cellier's meal tub.
November 9	Dangerfield pardoned.
November 17	First great Pope Burning, organised by the Green Ribbon Club.
November 19	Laurence Hyde appointed First Commissioner of the Treasury.
November 25	Trial and conviction of Knox and Lane.
November 27	Monmouth returns to England without leave.
December 6	Archbishop Plunket committed to the castle at Dublin.
December 9	Petition of seventeen Whig peers for the sitting of Parliament marks the beginning of the practice of petitioning.
December 11	Proclamation against petitioning.
1680. January 6	Mowbray and Bolron pardoned.
January 9	Mrs. Cellier accuses Sir Robert Peyton of high treason.
January 21	Oates and Bedloe exhibit articles against Lord Chief Justice Scroggs.

January 31	Lord Russell, Lord Cavendish, Sir Henry Capel, and Mr. Powle resign their places on the council.
February 5	Benjamin Harris tried and convicted for a libel in publishing "An Appeal from the City to the Country."
February 11	Sir Thomas Gascoigne tried for high treason and acquitted.
February 24	The Duke of York returns from Scotland.
February 26	Declaration of the Scottish Privy Council of their abhorrence of tumultuous petitions published in the *Gazette* marks the beginning of the "abhorrers'" addresses.
March 8	The king and the Duke of York entertained at a banquet by the Lord Mayor.
March 30	Thomas Dare of Taunton fined for seditious and dangerous words.
April 15	Assault on Arnold.
April 26 and June 7	Declarations published in the *Gazette* denying all truth in the rumour of the Black Box.
May 11	Indictment of high treason, on Dangerfield's evidence, against the Countess of Powis ignored by the grand jury of Middlesex.
May 13	The king ill at Windsor.
May 15	"A Letter to a Person of Honour concerning the Black Box" published.
May 24	Trial and conviction of Tasborough and Price.
June 10	Conclusion of a treaty between England and Spain to maintain the peace of Nymeguen.
June 11	Mrs. Cellier tried for high treason and acquitted.
June 23	The Earl of Castlemaine tried for high treason and acquitted.

June 26	Shaftesbury, with Titus Oates and fourteen peers and commoners, presents the Duke of York as a popish recusant.
July 14	Trial and conviction of Giles for an attempt to murder Arnold.
July 28, 29	Trials for high treason at York. Lady Tempest, Sir Miles Stapleton, and Mary Pressicks acquitted, but Thwing, a priest, convicted.
August–October	Western progress of the Duke of Monmouth.
August 20	Death of Bedloe at Bristol.
September 11	Trial and conviction of Mrs. Cellier for writing and publishing a libel.
October 20	The Duke of York leaves London for Edinburgh.
October 21	Meeting of Charles II's fourth Parliament.
October 26	Dangerfield at the bar of the House of Commons.
October 28	Bedloe's deathbed deposition read to the House of Commons. Two members of the Commons expelled for discrediting the Plot.
October 30	Archbishop Plunket brought to London and committed to the Tower.
November 2	The Exclusion bill voted.
November 10	Lord Stafford's trial resolved on by the Commons.
November 11	Third reading of the Exclusion bill in the House of Commons.
November 15	The Exclusion bill rejected by the House of Lords owing to Lord Halifax.
November 16	Halifax proposes the banishment of the Duke of York.
November 17	Second great Pope Burning.
	The House of Commons proceed against Halifax.

November 24	The Commons vote the impeachment of Lord Chief Justice North.
November 30–December 7	Trial and conviction of Lord Stafford for high treason.
December 15	Sir Robert Peyton expelled from the House of Commons.
December 29	Execution of Stafford.
1681. January 5	The Commons vote the impeachment of Lord Chief Justice Scroggs and other judges.
January 7, 10	The Commons pass resolutions against the Duke of York, against such as shall lend money to the crown, against a prorogation.
January 10	Parliament prorogued
January 18	and suddenly dissolved.
January 25	Sixteen Whig peers present a petition against a parliament being held at Oxford.
February 28	Edward Fitzharris arrested for writing a treasonable libel.
March 14	The king concludes a secret verbal treaty with Louis XIV and sets out for Oxford.
March 17	Shaftesbury and other Whig leaders set out for Oxford with an armed escort.
March 21	Meeting of Charles II's fifth and last Parliament at Oxford.
March 25	The Commons impeach Fitzharris.
March 26	The Exclusion bill voted.
	The Lords refuse to proceed on Fitzharris' impeachment.
March 28	The Exclusion bill read the first time in the House of Commons. Parliament suddenly dissolved.

May	The king's declaration justifying the dissolution answered by "A Just and Modest Vindication of the Proceedings of the two Last Parliaments."
May 3	Trial and conviction of Archbishop Plunket for high treason.
June 9	Trial and conviction of Fitzharris for high treason.
July 1	Execution of Plunket and Fitzharris.

DESIGNS OF THE ROMAN CATHOLICS

CHAPTER I

TITUS OATES

TITUS OATES has justly been considered one of the world's great impostors. By birth he was an Anabaptist, by prudence a clergyman, by profession a perjurer. From an obscure and beggarly existence he raised himself to opulence and an influence more than episcopal, and, when he fell, it was with the fame of having survived the finest flogging ever inflicted. De Quincey considered the murder of Godfrey to be the most artistic performance of the seventeenth century. It was far surpassed by the products of Oates' roving imagination. To the connoisseur of murder the mystery of Godfrey's death may be more exhilarating, but in the field of broad humour Oates bears the palm. There is, after all, something laughable about the rascal. His gross personality had in it a comic strain. He could not only invent but, when unexpected events occurred, adapt them on the instant to his own end. His coarse tongue was not without a kind of wit. Whenever he appears on the scene, as has been said of Jeffreys, we may be sure of good sport. Yet to his victims he was an emblem of tragic injustice. Very serious were his lies to the fifteen men whom he brought to death. The world was greedy of horrors, and Oates sounded the alarm at the crucial moment. In the game he went on to play the masterstrokes were his. Those who would reduce him to a subordinate of his associate Dr. Tonge, the hare-brained parson whose quarterly denunciations of Rome failed to arouse the interest of Protestant London, have strangely misunderstood his character. Tonge was a necessary go-between, but Oates the supreme mover of diabolical purpose.

In the year of the execution of King Charles the First Titus Oates was born at Oakham in the county of Rutland. His father, Samuel Oates, son of the rector of Marsham in Norfolk, had graduated from Corpus College, Cambridge, and received orders from the hands of the Bishop of Norwich. On the advent of the Puritan Revolution he turned Anabaptist, and achieved fame in the eastern counties as a Dipper of energy and sanctity. In 1650 he became chaplain to Colonel Pride's regiment, and four years later had the distinction of being arrested by Monk for seditious practices in Scotland. The Restoration returned him to the bosom of the established church, and in 1666 he was presented by Sir Richard Barker to the rectory of All Saints' at Hastings. Shortly before, his son Titus went his ways to seek education and a livelihood in the world as a scholar. Ejected in turn from Merchant Taylors' School and Gonville and Caius, Cambridge, he found a refuge at St. John's College, and some three years later was instituted to the vicarage of Bobbing in Kent. "By the same token," it was remarked, "the plague and he visited Cambridge at the same time."

Oates was a bird of passage. He obtained a license not to reside in his parish, and went to visit his father at Hastings. Long time did not pass before he took wing again. He had already once been indicted for perjury, though no further proceedings were taken in the case.[1] Now he conspired with his father to bring an odious charge against the schoolmaster of Hastings, who had incurred his enmity. The charge fell to the ground, Oates' abominable evidence was proved to be false, and he was thrown into gaol pending an action for a thousand pounds damages.[2] Escape from prison saved him from disaster, and he fled to London. As far as is known, no attempt was made to prosecute him. The men of Hastings were probably rejoiced at his disappearance. There was no profit to be made out of such a culprit as Oates. If he were caught, it would only bring expense and trouble to the authorities. It was the business of no one else to pursue the matter. So Oates went free. Without employment, he managed to obtain the post of chaplain on board a vessel in the Royal Navy. The calling was rather more disreputable than that of the Fleet parson of later times. Discipline on board the king's ships was chiefly manifest by its absence; under the captaincy of favourites from court the efficiency of the service was maintained only by the rude ability of men who had been bred in it; and the standard expected from the chaplain was "damnably low." Nevertheless Oates failed to achieve the required measure of respectability. He was expelled upon the same grounds as he had formerly urged against the fortunate schoolmaster.[3]

The mischance marked the beginning of his rise. Again adrift in London, the tide threw him upon William Smith, his former master at Merchant Taylors' School. It was Bartholomew-tide in the year 1676. With Smith was Matthew Medburne, a player from the Duke of York's theatre, and by creed a Roman Catholic. The two made friends with Oates, and on Medburne's introduction he became a member of a club which met twice a week at the Pheasant Inn in Fuller's Rents. The club contained both Catholics and Protestants, discussion of religion and politics being prohibited under penalty of a fine.[4] Here Oates made his first acquaintance with those of the religion which he was afterwards to turn to a source of so great profit. The rule which forbade controversy applied only to the meetings of the club, and beyond its limits discussion between members seems to have been free. It was perhaps by the agency of some of these that in the winter of the same year Oates was admitted as chaplain into the service of the Duke of Norfolk.[5] Testimony to character on the engagement of a servant in the seventeenth century was probably not severely examined.

In the house of the great Catholic noble Oates found himself in the company of priests of the forbidden church. Conversation turned on the subject of religion, and Oates lent ear to the addresses of the other side. Though he wore the gown of an English minister, his faith sat light upon him, and he did not scruple to change it for advantage. On Ash Wednesday 1677 he was formally reconciled to the Church of Rome.[6] The instrument for the salvation of the strayed lamb was one Berry, alias Hutchinson, a Jesuit whom Oates had afterwards the grace to describe as "a saintlike man, one that was religious for religion's sake." By others the instrument was thought to be somewhat weak-minded; at a later date he seceded to the Protestant faith and became curate in the city, later still to be welcomed back into the bosom of his previous church; withal a very pious person, removed from politics, and much given to making converts. Neither conversion nor piety alone was an end to Oates. He soon made his way to Father Richard Strange, provincial of the Society of Jesus, and notified him of a desire for admission into the order. Consulting with his fellows, Strange gave consent to the proposal, and before the end of April, Oates was shipped on a Bilboa merchantman with letters to the English Jesuit seminary at Valladolid.[7]

There was little that Oates could hope from a career as an English parson. Almost any other calling, especially one that took him abroad, offered better chances. He probably believed that Jesuit emissaries led a merry life and a licentious. Perhaps it is true that, as he said, vague talk in the Duke of Norfolk's household of the glorious future for Catholicism had come to his ears. At least the times must make him credulous of Catholic machinations. To his sanguine mind the future would present unbounded possibilities. On the other side, stout recruits for the Catholic cause were not to be despised. Oates' character was tough, and he was not the man to shrink from dirty work. Had they known him well, his new patrons would hardly have welcomed him as a convert. The plausible humility he aired was the outcome of a discretion which rarely lasted longer than to save him from starvation. By nature he was a bully, brutal, sensual, avaricious, and gifted with a greed of adulation which, in a man of less impudence, would have caused his speedy ruin. From earliest youth he was a liar. Yet he was shrewd enough, and shrewdness and promptitude were qualities not without a certain value. His vices had not yet grown to be notorious. So he was taken to serve masters who generally succeeded in giving their pupils at least the outward stamp of piety. In person Oates was hideous. His body was short, his shoulders broad. He was bull-necked and bow-legged. Under a low forehead his eyes were set small and deep. His countenance was large and moon-like. So monstrous was his length of chin that the wide slit mouth seemed almost to bisect his purple face. His voice rasped inharmoniously, and he could tune it at will to the true Puritan whine or to scold on terms with such a master of abuse as Jeffreys. The pen of Dryden has drawn a matchless portrait of the man—

Sunk were his eyes, his voice was harsh and loud,

Sure signs he neither choleric was nor proud:

His long chin proved his wit, his saint-like grace

A church vermilion and a Moses' face.[8]

This was the tender being whom the Colegio de los Ingleses took to nurse into a Jesuit.

The project failed of its mark. Five short months completed Oates' stay amid the new surroundings. On October 30, 1677 he was expelled the college and shipped home, reaching London in November.[9] The sojourn was in after days utilised to elevate him to the dignity of doctor of divinity. He had obtained the degree at Salamanca, he said. The truth was more accurately expressed in the lines—

The spirit caught him up, the Lord knows where,

And gave him his Rabbinical degree

Unknown to foreign university;[10]

for none but priests were admitted by the Catholic Church to the doctorate, Oates was never a priest, and was never at Salamanca in his life.[11] Though Valladolid had proved no great success, Oates was unabashed. He returned to Strange and the Jesuits in London. Protestations were renewed, and the eagerness of the expelled novice was not to be withstood. The Jesuits afterwards professed that they simply desired to keep Oates out of the way. Whatever their motive, he was given a new trial. The society furnished a new suit of clothes and a periwig, put four pounds into his pocket, and sent him to complete his education at St. Omers. On December 10 he was admitted into the seminary.[12] For one ambitious of an ecclesiastical career the venture was not fruitful. Long evidence was given at a later date descriptive of Oates' course in the college. In important points it lies under strong suspicion,[13] but the picture of his daily doings may be taken as faithful. Oates was not a congenial companion to his fellows. Though a separate table was provided for him at meals, he went to school with the rest and attempted to gain their intimacy. He was the source of continual quarrels, spoiled sport, tried to play the bully, and sometimes met with the retribution that falls on bullies. He was reader in the sodality, and enlivened more serious works, such as Father Worsley's *Controversies*, with interludes from that most entertaining book, *The Contempt of the Clergy*.[14] He had a pan broken over his head for insisting at a play by the novices on sitting in the place reserved for the musicians. On another occasion he excited the amusement of the college by allowing himself to be beaten up and down by a lad with a fox's brush. Still nobler was an effort in the pulpit, where he preached "a pleasant sermon," expounding his belief that "King Charles the Second halted between two opinions and a stream of Popery went between his legs."[15] Lurid tales of Oates' conduct were afterwards published by the Jesuit fathers.[16] What is more certainly true is the fact that his presence in the seminary rapidly became embarrassing. On June 23, 1678 he was turned out of doors, and shook the dust of St. Omers from his feet. On the 27th he reached London.[17]

When Oates formed his alliance with Dr. Ezrael Tonge, rector of St. Michael's in Wood Street, is uncertain. The point is not without importance. If Oates came first to Tonge in the summer of 1678, the fact would be so far in his favour that he may have sought a good market for wares which he believed to be in some degree sound. If he took directions from Tonge before his visit to the Jesuit seminaries, the chance of his sincerity would be much diminished. Simpson Tonge, the rector's son, afterwards composed a journal of these events. Unhappily his statements are without value. Hoping for reward at one time from Oates, at another from his enemies, Tonge contradicted himself flatly, urging for the informer that Oates had sought his father only after the return from St. Omers; against him, that the two had, during an intimacy of two years, designed the Popish Plot before ever Oates went abroad.[18] Judgment must therefore be suspended; but it is notable that King Charles thought the evidence as to the intrigue between Oates and Tonge unworthy of credence. Simpson Tonge was taken to Windsor in the summer of 1680 to reveal his knowledge. He left there papers in which evidence of the facts was contained. Charles examined them, and told Sydney Godolphin that "he found them very slight and immaterial," and refused to see Tonge again.[19] At whatever point co-operation began, acquaintance between the two men was likely enough of long standing. Tonge had been presented to his living by Sir Richard Barker, the ancient patron of Samuel Oates. A natural tie thus existed, now to be developed by circumstances into strong union. The doctor was an assiduous labourer in the Protestant vineyard. His fear of Popery amounted to mania. Volumes poured from his pen in denunciation of Catholic conspiracies. A catalogue was afterwards made of Tonge's library. Its character may be judged from the titles of the following works:—*Massacres threatened to Prevent, Temple and Tabernacle, Arguments to suppress Popery*.[20] He had co-operated with John Evelyn in translating *The Mystery of Jesuitism*, a work which King Charles said he had carried for two days in his pocket and read; "at which," writes Evelyn, "I did not a little wonder."[21] When fame overtook him, Tonge raised the ghost of Habernfeld's Plot and spent some ingenuity in turning the name of Sir Edmund Berry Godfrey to *Dy'd by Rome's reveng'd fury*, that of Edward Coleman to *Lo a damned crew*. Now he passed a bashful and disappointed life. Needy and full of silly notions, he divided his time between the detection of Jesuitry and the study of obscure sciences. Here was beyond doubt the man to interest himself in Oates. For Oates had brought back from beyond seas a prodigious tale, calculated to set the most unpractical alarmist in action.

The scope of the disclosure was vast. Written at length and with the promise of more to come, Oates' *True and Exact Narrative of the Horrid Plot and Conspiracy of the Popish Party against the life of His Sacred Majesty, the Government, and the Protestant Religion* filled a folio pamphlet of sixty-eight pages. The Pope, said Oates, had declared himself lord of the kingdoms of England and Ireland. To the work of their reduction and government the Jesuits were commissioned by papal briefs and instructed by orders from the general of the society. Jesuit agents were at work fomenting rebellion in Scotland and Ireland. Money had been raised and arms collected. The hour had only to strike for an Irish port to be opened to a French force in aid of the great scheme. The Papists had burned down London once and tried to burn it again. A third attempt would be no less successful than the first. Chief of all, a "consult" of the English Jesuits had been held on April 24, 1678 at the White Horse tavern in the Strand, to concert means for the king's assassination. Charles was a bastard and an excommunicated heretic. He deserved death, and the deed was necessary for the Catholic cause. Want of variety in the instruments chosen should not save him. He was to be poisoned by the queen's physician. He was to be shot with silver bullets in St. James' Park. Four Irish ruffians were hired to dispatch him at Windsor. A Jesuit named Coniers had consecrated a knife a foot in length to stab him. Great sums of money were promised by French and Spanish Jesuits and by the Benedictine prior to whoever should do the work. If the Duke of York did not consent to the king's death, the same fate lay in store for him. In all this Oates had been a confidential messenger and an active agent. It was only due to the fact that he had been appointed for the task of killing Dr. Tonge that the scheme thus carefully prepared was not put to the test; for Tonge had moved him to exchange the trade of murderer and incendiary for that of informer. Thus the great plot was divulged, together with the names of ninety-nine persons concerned, as well as those nominated for offices under the prospective Jesuit government, of whom the most prominent were the Lords Arundel of Wardour, Powis, Petre, Stafford, Bellasis, Sir William Godolphin, Sir George Wakeman, and Mr. Edward Coleman. The falsehood of all this has been conclusively demonstrated. Not only did Oates bear all the marks of the liar and never produce the slightest evidence for what he announced, but much of his story is contradicted by the actual conditions of politics at the time. The fact of his conviction for perjury is widely known and its justice unquestioned. To rebut his accusations singly would be fruitless, because unnecessary. Their general untruth has long been known. Much time was occupied by Oates and Tonge in reducing their bulk to the shape, first of forty-three, then of eighty-one articles. Oates took a lodging in Vauxhall, near Sir Richard Barker's house, where Tonge dwelt. Together they drafted and copied until all was prepared. Nothing lacked but a proper flourish for the introduction of so grand an event.

For this a pretty little comedy was arranged. Oates was to keep behind the scenes while Tonge rang up the curtain. Nor did Tonge wish to expose himself too soon to vulgar light. He procured an acquaintance, Mr. Christopher Kirkby, to act as prologue. Kirkby was a poor gentleman of good family, interested in chemistry, and holding some small appointment in the royal laboratory. Their common taste for science probably accounted for his relation with Tonge; and since he was known to the king, he could now do the doctor good service. On August 11, 1678 Oates thrust a copy of the precious manuscript under the wainscot of a gallery in Sir Richard Barker's house. There Tonge found it, and on the following day read it to Kirkby, who declared in horror at the contents that the king should be informed. He would take this part upon himself, he said. Accordingly on August 13, as Charles was starting for his accustomed walk in St. James' Park, Kirkby slipped a note into his hand begging for a short audience on a matter of vital importance. The king read it and called Kirkby to ask what he meant. "Sire," returned the other, "your enemies have a design against your life. Keep within the company, for I know not but you may be in danger in this very walk." "How may that be?" asked the king. "By being shot at," answered Kirkby, and desired to give fuller information in some more private spot. Charles bade him wait in his closet, and finished his stroll with composure.[22]

CHAPTER II

THE NATURE OF THE DESIGNS

FOR contemporaries the Popish Plot provided a noble field of battle. Between its supporters and its assailants controversy raged hotly. Hosts of writers in England and abroad proved incontestably either its truth or its falsehood.[23] With which of the two the victory lay is hard to determine. Discredit presently fell on the Plot, but the balance was restored by the Revolution, when Oates' release, pardon, and pension gave again the stamp of authority to his revelations. From this high estate its reputation quickly fell. Hume pronounced belief in it to be the touchstone for a hopelessly prejudiced Whig, Fox declared the evidence offered "impossible to be true," and before the end of the eighteenth century Dalrymple accused Shaftesbury of having contrived and managed the whole affair. Since that time little serious criticism, with the notable exception of Ranke's luminous account, has been attempted. Historians have generally contented themselves with relying on the informers' certain mendacity to prove the entire falsehood of the plot which they denounced. The argument is patently unsound. As Charles II himself declared, the fact that Oates and his followers were liars of the first order does not warrant the conclusion that all they said was untrue and that the plot was wholly of the imagination.[24] The grounds upon which judgment must be based deserve to be more closely considered.

On November 8, 1675 a remarkable debate took place in the House of Commons. Mr. Russell and Sir Henry Goodrick informed the House of an outrage said to have been committed by a Jesuit upon a recent convert from Roman Catholicism. Amid keen excitement they related that one Luzancy, a Frenchman, who, having lately come over to the Church of England, had in the French chapel at the Savoy preached a hot sermon against the errors of Rome, had been compelled at peril of his life to retract all he had said and sign a recantation of his faith. The man guilty of this deed was Dr. Burnet, commonly known as Father St. Germain, a Jesuit belonging to the household of the Duchess of York.[25] The Commons were highly enraged. "This goes beyond all precedents," cried Sir Charles Harbord, "to persuade not only with arguments but poignards!" He never heard the like way before. Assurance was given by Mr. Secretary Williamson that strict inquiry was being made. The king was busy with the matter. Luzancy had been examined on oath before the council, and a special meeting was now summoned. A warrant was out for St. Germain, but the Jesuit had fled. The House expressed its feeling by moving that the

Lord Chief Justice be requested to issue a second warrant for St. Germain's arrest, and yet another in general terms "to search for and apprehend all priests and Jesuits whatsoever."[26] It was a strange story that Luzancy told. By Protestants he was said to have been a learned Jesuit, by Catholics a rascally bastard of a disreputable French actress.[27] The two accounts are perhaps not irreconcilable. At least he was a convert and had preached. Thereupon St. Germain, as he said, threatened him and forced a recantation. Before resorting to this extreme the Jesuit had tried persuasion. The Duke of York, he told Luzancy, was a confessed Roman Catholic. At heart the king himself belonged to the same faith and would approve of all he did. Schemes were afoot to procure an act for liberty of conscience for the Catholics. That granted, within two years most of the nation would acknowledge the Pope. It was sometimes good to force people to heaven; and there were in London many priests and Jesuits doing God very great service. Others besides Luzancy had been threatened with tales of Protestant blood flowing in the London streets; and these, being summoned to the council, attested that the fact was so. Lord Halifax rose and told the king that, if his Majesty would allow that course to Protestants for the conversion of Papists, he did not question but in a very short time it should be effected.[28] Two days later a proclamation was issued signifying that Luzancy was taken into the royal protection, and St. Germain, with a price of £200 on his head, fled to France, there to become one of the most active of Jesuit intriguers.[29] Though the brandished dagger was likely enough an embellishment of Luzancy's invention, it is probable that his story was in substance true. In December St. Germain found himself in Paris and in close correspondence with Edward Coleman, the Duchess of York's secretary. Such a man writing within a month from the catastrophe would certainly, had he been falsely charged, be loud in vindication of his innocence and denunciation of the villain who had worked his ruin. St. Germain merely wrote that his leaving London in this fashion troubled him much. He had done all that a man of honesty and honour could; an ambiguous phrase. It was absolutely necessary, more for his companions and the Catholics' sake than for his own, that his conduct should be justified.[30] Evidently St. Germain was less troubled at the injustice of the charge against him than incensed at its results. What he wanted was not that his character might be cleared from a false accusation, but that the tables might be turned on his accuser.[31]

The conduct of St. Germain illustrates well the aims of the Roman Catholic party in England about the year 1675. Their policy, already undergoing modification, had root deep in the history of the times.

For the first thirteen years of his reign Catholics looked for the advancement of their cause to the king. During the Civil War none had shown a more steadfast loyalty than they, and none hailed the Restoration with greater eagerness. Half a century earlier a considerable number of the squires of England had been Catholic. They were a class bound closely to the royal cause both by tradition and by personal inclination, and though the operation of the penal laws effectively prevented their ranks from swelling, they rendered conspicuous service to the crown in the day of trouble. With their strength further diminished by death and by confiscation of estates under the Commonwealth government, their hopes rose higher at the king's return. There was much justification for their sanguine view. The promise of religious liberty contained in the declaration of Breda was known to be in accord with Charles' own desires. He was the son of a Catholic mother and of a father suspected, however unjustly, of Catholic tendencies. He was himself not free from the same suspicion. He was under the deepest obligations to his Catholic subjects. They had risked their persons and squandered their fortunes for him. They had fought and intrigued for him, and succoured him in distress. He owed them life and liberty. They had done so much for him that it was not unreasonable to hope that, as it was not averse to his wishes, he would do something for them.

The disappointment of the Catholic expectations was not long delayed. Whatever promises Charles had made, and whatever hopes he had fostered, were dependent upon others, and not upon himself, for fulfilment. The Restoration was a national work, and it was not in the power of the king to act openly in opposition to the nation that had restored him. Since he was not a Catholic, he was impelled to run no great risk for the interest of those who were. And it became increasingly clear that by far the greater part of the nation was in no mind to tolerate any change which would make for freedom of life and opinion for the maintainers of a religion which was feared and fiercely hated by the governing classes and by the church which aspired to govern in England. Fear of Roman Catholicism was a legacy of the dreadful days of Queen Mary and of her sister's Protestant triumph. That legacy was a possession not of one sect or of one party alone. Cavaliers and Roundheads, Puritans and high churchmen shared it alike. So long as the Church of Rome was of a warring disposition, it was vain to expect that the English people would see in it other than an enemy. The Protestant religion was too insecurely established in the land and the memory of sudden changes and violent assaults too recent for Englishmen to harbour a spirit of liberal charity towards those who disagreed from them in matters of faith. The Catholic, who cried for present relief from an odious tyranny, appeared in their eyes as one who, were relief granted, would seize any future chance to play the tyrant himself.

No less than twelve penal statutes, of tremendous force, existed to prevent Roman Catholics from exercising influence in the state.[32] Had they been strictly executed, the Catholic religion must have been crushed out of England; but they were generally allowed to remain dormant. Even so they were a constant menace and an occasional source of more or less annoyance, varying infinitely according to time and place and the will of the authorities from an insulting reminder of Catholic inferiority to cruel and deliberate persecution. The tenor of these laws was so stringent that among moderate Protestants there were many who believed that the more obnoxious and unjust might be removed without placing a weapon of serious strength in the hands of their opponents. In the House of Lords a party was formed in favour of the Catholic and Presbyterian claims and opposed to the arrogant pretensions of the Earl of Clarendon and his followers. Clarendon's wish was for the supremacy of his own church, but there were already not a few who had begun to view his position with jealousy. In June 1661 a committee of prominent Catholics met at Arundel House to consider their position. They presented a petition to the Lords protesting against the penalties on the refusal of Catholics to take the oaths of allegiance and supremacy, but after several debates and the lapse of more than eighteen months it was resolved that "nothing had been offered to move their lordships to alter anything in the oaths." Nevertheless Colonel Tuke of Cressing Temple was admitted to the bar and heard against the "sanguinary laws," and papers on the subject were laid on the table of the House. The petitioners disclaimed the Pope's temporal authority and offered to swear "to oppose with their lives and fortunes the pontiff himself, if he should ever attempt to execute that pretended power, and to obey their sovereign in opposition to all foreign and domestic power whatsoever, without restriction." A committee was appointed to deal with the matter, and acting on its report the Lords resolved to abolish the writ *de haeretico inquirendo* and the statutes making it treason to take orders in the Roman Church, as well as those making it felony to harbour Catholic priests and præmunire to maintain the authority of the Bishop of Rome.

At this point, when all seemed going well, misfortune intervened and the hopes of success were dashed to the ground. It was suggested that on account of its known activity and powers of intrigue the Society of Jesus should be excepted from the scope of the proposed measure. A heated controversy was instantly aroused. While Protestants and many Catholics demanded that the Jesuits should accept the situation and retire gracefully to win advantages for their brothers in religion, members of the society retorted that a conspiracy was on foot to divide the body Catholic against itself, and that it was not for the general good to accept favours at the price of sacrificing the most able and flourishing order of the church. It soon became evident that the Jesuits were not to be moved. Their struggle in

England had been hard. Their position among English Catholics was one of great importance. They would not now surrender it for the sake of a partial and problematical success from the enjoyment of which they were themselves to be excluded. The time when affairs were still unsettled was rather one at which they should be spurred to greater efforts.

Without the compliance of the Jesuits the moderate Catholics could do nothing. A feeling of disgust at the selfish policy of the society found free expression. It seemed that its members would never consider the interest of others before their own. Nevertheless there was no remedy; the committee at Arundel House was dissolved; at the request of the Catholic peers the progress of the bill of relief in the House of Lords was suspended, and it was never resumed.[33]

No better fate attended the king's efforts to make good the promises he had given at Breda. With the assurance of support from the Independents and Presbyterians he had issued late in the year 1662 a Declaration of Indulgence, suspending all penal laws against dissenters, Catholic as well as others, by virtue of the power which he considered inherent in the crown.[34] The move called forth a storm of opposition, both against the dispensing power and against the object for which it was used. To appease the Commons, Lord Ashley, afterwards Earl of Shaftesbury, brought in a bill to define and legalise the royal power to dispense with laws requiring oaths and subscription to the doctrines of the established church. The answer of the Commons was an address against the Declaration,[35] in the House of Lords Ashley's bill was defeated by Clarendon and the bishops, and on March 31, 1663 Parliament addressed the king for a proclamation ordering all Catholic priests to leave the realm. Charles never forgave his minister, but he was powerless to resist. On April 2 he recanted his declaration by issuing the desired order. A bill to check the growth of popery and nonconformity passed quickly through the House of Commons, but was stopped by the influence of the Catholic peers, and an address for the execution of all laws against dissenters was voted in its place.[36]

Thus the penal laws were retained in their full vigour. And if the enactments against the Catholics were not removed from the statute book, still less were the causes which had produced them removed from men's minds. Only the establishment of general confidence that the Catholic religion lacked power to menace the cause of Protestantism in England and to invade the rights which were dear to Englishmen could be effective in this; and confidence, so far from becoming general, shrank to limits that became ever narrower. In the years that followed, fear of the advance of Catholicism only increased. Fresh laws were passed to check it. The House of Commons voted address after address that the old might be put in action, petition after petition for the banishment of priests and Jesuits from court and capital. To their alarm and chagrin it appeared that all efforts were in vain, and belief spread that the failure was chiefly due to opposition emanating from the highest quarters. Instead of aiding in the accomplishment of the desired object, the influence of the crown seemed to be directed absolutely to prevent it. For the king's policy was one which could only inspire the nation with a sense of growing distrust.[37]

Though Charles II had ascended the throne on a wave of popular enthusiasm, his ideas were widely removed from those of his subjects. By birth and education his mind was drawn towards the aims and methods of French politics, and he leaned away from the Church of England. With this bias he inherited for Puritanism and the Presbyterians a dislike strengthened by personal experience. Coming into England without knowledge of parliamentary government, his first trial of it was far from encouraging. He found Parliament intolerant, suspicious, unstatesman-like. The Commons fenced in the Anglican Church with severe penal laws against dissent, and gave the king an income less than the annual expenses of government and the services by half a million pounds. Charles had been restored to a bankrupt inheritance, and with every good intention the Commons failed completely to render it solvent. Soon their good-will ceased. They were jealous of the royal expenditure. They did not perceive the royal wants. They destroyed the existing financial arrangements and did not replace them with better.[38] They desired to carry the Protestant and Parliamentary system to its logical end in controlling the King's foreign policy and directing it against the influence of the Roman Catholic Church. To Charles this was intolerable. To be forced to act at the bidding of Parliament was odious to him. He would be no crowned do-nothing. And here the fortunes of England touched on those of France. The schemes of Louis XIV for the expansion and consolidation of the French kingdom made it imperative that he should obtain for their prosecution the neutrality, if not the assistance, of England. He could not devote his energy to the settlement of his north-east frontier and the maintenance of his claims on the Spanish empire with a Protestant country ever ready to strike at his back. He was therefore always ready to pay for the concurrence of Charles and with him of England.[39] The establishment of the Roman Catholic religion, could it be effected, would be of material assistance to him. Especially on the religious side of his policy it would be a powerful support. Charles, on the other hand, desired to free himself from the financial control of Parliament and to grant toleration to the Catholics. He was therefore always ready to be bought. He was all the better pleased since co-operation with France brought him into conflict with the Dutch republic, which he disliked upon commercial and detested upon dynastic grounds. Toleration Charles found to be impossible, and he was subjected to constant annoyance by the attempts of the Commons to control his dealings. Thus his aims crystallised into a policy of making the crown supreme in the constitution and establishing the Roman Catholic faith as the state religion upon the approved model in France.[40]

The plan undertaken in concert with his great ally was not the first effort of Charles to give his ideas effect. During his exile on the continent various tenders had been made for papal support; Charles promised in return conversion and favour to his Catholic subjects; and within a few years of the Restoration a serious negotiation was started with Pope Alexander VII. In 1663 Sir Richard Bellings was sent on a mission to Rome to beg the bestowal of a cardinal's hat on the Abbé d'Aubigny, almoner to the newly-married queen, and cousin to the king. Charles took the opportunity to propose through Bellings the formation of an Anglican Roman Church in England. He was to announce his conversion, the Archbishop of Canterbury was to be patriarch of the three realms, and liberty of conscience should be assured to remaining Protestants. Roman Catholicism would become the state religion and Rome gain the whole strength of the English hierarchy.[41] An understanding was impracticable and the scheme fell through; but the renewed solicitations of the English court on Aubigny's behalf were successful. In November 1665 he was nominated Cardinal, and died almost immediately after. To the hopes of the Catholics his death was a terrible blow. "The clouds," wrote the general of the Jesuits on hearing of it, "which are gathering over Holland, Poland, and Constantinople are so dense that every prudent man must see reason to apprehend enormous catastrophes and storms that will not be ended without irreparable disasters. But in my mind all these coming evils are overshadowed by the death of the Abbé Aubigny, which deprives the Church, for a time at least, of the joy of beholding an English cardinal of such illustrious blood, created at the public instances of two queens, and at the secret request of a king, a prodigy which would, without doubt have confounded heresy and inaugurated bright fortunes to the unhappy Catholics."

Three years later a still more remarkable embassy than Bellings' took place. It is not even in our own day commonly known that the Duke of Monmouth, reputed the eldest of the sons of Charles II, had an elder brother. So well was the secret kept, that during the long struggle to save the Protestant succession and to exclude the Duke of York from the throne, no man ever discovered that there was another whose claims were better than those of the popular favourite, and who had of his free will preferred the gown of an obscure clerk to the brilliant prospect of favour at court and the chance of wearing the English crown. For this son, born to the king in the Isle of Jersey at the age of sixteen or seventeen years, the child of a lady of one of the noblest families in his dominions, was named by his father James Stuart, and urged to be at hand to maintain his rights should both the royal brothers die without male heirs. He set the dazzling fortune aside and resolved to live and die a Jesuit. In the year 1668, then being some four and twenty years old, he entered the house of novices of the Jesuits at Rome under the name of James de la Cloche. Towards the end of the same year Charles wrote to Johannes Oliva, the general, desiring that his son might be sent to England to discuss matters of religion. Assuming the name of Henri de Rohan, La Cloche made for England. He was received by the queen and the queen mother, and by them secretly taken to the king. What passed between father and son has never transpired. La Cloche was sent back to Rome by the king as his "secret ambassador to the Father General," charged with an oral commission and orders to return to England as soon as it was fulfilled. The nature of that mission is unknown, and whether or no the young man returned to England. Trace of embassy and ambassador alike is lost, and the young prince disappears from history. Yet it may be that his figure can be descried again, flitting mysteriously across the life of his father. At the height of the turmoil of the Popish Plot a certain gentleman was employed to bring privately from beyond seas a Roman Catholic priest, with whom the king had secret business to transact. The king and the priest stayed long closeted together. At length the priest came out with signs of horror and fear on his face. Charles had been seized with a fit and, when the priest would have called for help, to preserve their secret summoned strength to hold him till the attack had passed. On Charles' death two papers on religion were found in his cabinet and published in a translation by his brother. The originals were in French, in the form of an argument addressed by one person to another, and it is suggested, not without reason, that their author was the same man as the king's questionable visitor, and none other than his own son, who had forgotten his native tongue and had surrendered fame and country for the good of his soul and of the Catholic Church.[42]

One more negotiation was undertaken directly with Rome. By command of the pope the papal internuncio at Brussels came to England. He had sent a confidant to prepare the way, and was assured of welcome at court. The Venetian envoy offered the hospitality of his house to the visitor, and arranged an interview with the king. The queen, the Duke of York, and Lord Arlington were also present, and the nuncio received promises of the king's good intentions towards the Catholics.[43] The fruits of this undertaking, had there been any, were spoiled before the gathering by the intrigue into which Charles had already entered with Louis XIV. Only under a Catholic constitution, said Charles, might a King of England hope to be absolute. He was to live to see the prophecy falsified, and by his own unaided effort to accomplish what he believed impossible, but now he showed the courage of his convictions by attempting to make England

Catholic. The scheme was afoot in the summer of 1669. Nearly a year passed in its completion, and on June 1, 1670 "le Traité de Madame" was signed at Dover. Arlington, Clifford, Arundel, and Sir Richard Bellings signed for England, and Colbert for France; and Henrietta of Orleans, to whose skilful management success was due, returned to her husband's home to die, leaving a potent influence to carry on her work—Louise de Kéroualle. Louis' object in the treaty was to break the Triple Alliance and carry the war to a successful conclusion; that of Charles to make himself master of England once again under the Catholic banner. The two kings were to aid each other in men and money. "It was in reality," says Lord Acton, "a plot under cover of Catholicism to introduce absolute monarchy and to make England a dependency of France, not only by the acceptance of French money, but by submission to a French army."[44] Charles was to declare himself a Catholic when he thought fit. In the event of resistance from his subjects he was to receive from Louis the sum of £150,000 and a force of 6000 men to bring his country under the yoke. Lauderdale held an army 20,000 strong in Scotland, bound to serve anywhere within British dominions. Ireland under Lord Berkeley was steeped in Catholic and loyal sentiment. The garrisons and ports of England were being placed in safe hands. If the scheme succeeded, the Anglican Church would be overthrown, Parliamentary government would be rendered futile, and Charles would be left at the head of a Catholic state and master of his realm.

Success however was so far from attainment that no attempt was made to put "la grande affaire" into effect. It was decided that Charles' declaration of Catholicism should be preceded by his attack in concert with Louis on the Dutch. War was declared on March 17, 1672. Two days before, the Declaration of Indulgence, suspending all penal laws against dissenters, was issued. It sprang from the desire to obtain the support of dissent for the war and to pave the way for a successful issue of the Catholic policy at its close. Arms alone could determine victory or defeat. If Charles thereafter found himself in a position to dictate to Parliament, the rest might not prove difficult. Otherwise there would be little hope of success. But the war did not justify Charles' expectations. Dutch tenacity and the growing hostility in England to the alliance with France made it certain that the chief objects for which Charles had sealed the Dover treaty could not be achieved. When on February 19, 1674 he concluded peace with the Republic for 800,000 crowns, the honour of the flag northward from Cape Finisterre, and the retention of all his conquests outside Europe, the king seemed to have emerged successfully from the struggle. In fact he had failed to reach the goal. Unless he gained a commanding position at home by military success abroad, he could not hope to put into practice the English part of the programme drawn up at Dover. It was something that his nephew the Prince of Orange had ousted the odious republican faction from power in Holland, and much that the Republic had been for ever detached from its alliance with France; but even this was hardly sufficient compensation to Charles for the abandonment of his policy in England. He had planned to restore the monarchy to its ancient estate by means of Roman Catholicism. He had failed, and now he turned his back finally upon Catholicism as a political power. He had already been compelled to cancel the Declaration of Indulgence, and on March 29, 1673 clearly marked the change by giving the royal assent to the Test Act. A return to the policy of Anglican Royalism, which in some ways approached that of Clarendon, was shaped. The Cabal had been dissipated, the plans of its Catholic members ruined, its Protestant members driven into opposition. Charles, guiding foreign policy himself, and Danby as Lord Treasurer managing affairs at home, determined to draw all stable elements in the kingdom round the Church and the Crown, and to offer a united opposition to the factions and the dissenters. The famous Non-Resisting Test was the result.[45] Here again Charles failed. The opposition of Shaftesbury rendered abortive the second line of policy by which the king attempted to restore the full majesty of the crown. There was nothing left him now but a policy of resistance. The next move in the game must come from his opponents. Thus the three following years were spent by Charles intriguing first with Louis, then with William, seeming to be on the brink of war and a Protestant policy and always drawing back. No decisive step could be taken until the panic of the Popish Plot gave to the country party an opportunity, which after a three years' struggle the king turned to his own account with signal triumph.

From the moment when he revoked the Declaration of Indulgence the Catholics had nothing to hope from Charles. Up to that time Roman Catholic policy in England looked to him; thereafter he stood apart from it. Throughout his reign the king had been studying to rise to absolute sovereignty on the ladder of Catholicism. By the treaty of Dover he was actively concerned in a conspiracy to overturn the established church and again to introduce the Roman Catholic religion into England. He had undoubtedly been guilty of an act which in a subject would have been high treason. Although he now dissociated himself from his former policy, it was not abandoned by others. The Catholics had been deceived by Charles. They now fixed their hopes upon his brother, the Duke of York. Since the king would no longer join with the Jesuit party, it was determined to go without him. From that time James became the centre of their intrigues and negotiations. He was the point round which their hopes revolved.

The foundation of the intrigue was laid in the summer of 1673. Some eighteen months before the duke had made known to a small circle his conversion to the Roman Catholic Church.[46] The step was taken in the deepest secrecy, and even at Rome was not recognised as final until some years afterwards, for although James laid down his office of Lord High Admiral in consequence of the Test Act, he still continued to attend service in the royal chapel.[47] But despite all caution, enough suspicion was aroused by James' marriage at the suggestion of the French court with a Roman Catholic princess, Mary of Modena. It was a definite sign of his attachment to the French and Catholic interest, and paved the way for the correspondence which was afterwards so nearly to procure his downfall. The duke had for secretary a young man named Edward Coleman, whom mysterious doings and a tragic fate have invested with not unmerited interest. Coleman was the son of an English clergyman. At an early age he was converted to the Catholic faith and educated by the Jesuits, and to the furtherance of their schemes devoted the rest of his life. To the good cause he brought glowing ardour and varied talents. He was noted as a keen controversialist and a successful fisherman of souls. The confidence of three ambassadors from the court of France argues versatile ability in the man. With Ruvigny Coleman enjoyed some intimacy; Courtin found him of the greatest assistance; he discussed with Barillon subjects of delicacy on his master's behalf. The ambassadors found him a man of spirit, adept in intrigue, with fingers on the wires by which parties were pulled. And they valued him accordingly. For Coleman undertook the difficult task of agent between Louis XIV and the mercenary Whigs. More than three thousand pounds can be traced passing through his hands. The leaders of the opposition had their price at some five hundred guineas; but these took their money direct from the ambassador. Coleman dealt with the rank and file, and here the gold, which among the more exalted would have soon been exhausted, probably went far. He kept a sumptuous table for his friends and laid up for himself what he gained by way of commission. Knowledge of foreign languages, a ready pen, and his Jesuit connection marked Coleman as the man for the duke's service. He had all the talents for the post save one. James' want of discretion was reflected in his secretary. Twice Coleman was dismissed; the dismissal was apparent only, and he continued work as busily as before. He had occupied himself in writing seditious letters to rouse discontent in the provinces against the government. Complaint was made. Coleman was discharged from his place by the duke. He was immediately taken into the service of the duchess in the same capacity. Some years later his zeal brought him into collision with the Bishop of London. Compton went to the king and obtained an order to the duke to dismiss his wife's secretary. The French ambassador was much perturbed and pressed James to afford protection, Coleman received his dismissal and took ship to Calais. His Jesuit friends sent the news sadly one to another. His very talents, it was said, had destroyed him. He was too much in the duke's counsels. His enemies could not countenance the presence of a man of such parts. The duchess chose a new secretary. Within a fortnight Coleman returned, and in secret resumed his office. He was in the duke's confidence and necessary to him.[48] Altogether Coleman was not quite the innocent lamb that he has often been painted.

At the outbreak of the second Dutch war an English cavalry regiment was sent for the French service under the command of Lord Duras. Among the officers was Sir William Throckmorton, an intimate of Coleman and converted by him to the Catholic faith. Throckmorton left the regiment and settled in Paris as his friend's agent. The two corresponded at length, and by Throckmorton's means Coleman was put in communication with Père Ferrier, Louis XIV's Jesuit confessor. Ferrier was assured by Coleman that parliament would force Charles II to break with France and make peace with the Dutch. The accuracy of his prophecy gained the confessor's confidence. Letters were exchanged and the means to advance the Duke of York and the Catholic cause in England debated. Ferrier was the first of Louis' confessors to play an important part in politics, and his alliance was an achievement to be counted to the duke.[49] Coleman proceeded to extend his connection in other quarters. Under the assumed name of Rice the Earl of Berkshire was in communication with him, urging with doleful foreboding the overthrow of parliament and the Protestant party.[50] Berkshire was Coleman's sole correspondent known in England, but on the continent others took up the thread. In France the Jesuit Sheldon was high in praise of Coleman and his design. From Brussels the papal internuncio Albani discussed it somewhat coolly. Meanwhile Coleman's relations with Paris had undergone a change. In May 1675 Sir William Throckmorton died disreputably of a wound received in the course of his too eager courtship of a certain Lady Brown, while his wife yet lived,[51] and in December St. Germain, banished from England, took up his place. More important was the death of Père Ferrier in September of the same year, for Louis XIV chose as his confessor Père de la Chaize, the famous Jesuit whose dealings with Coleman subsequently formed the heaviest part of the proof against the unlucky intriguer.[52] Finally to the list of his political correspondents whose names are known Coleman added that of Cardinal Howard, better known as Cardinal Norfolk, at the Roman court.[53]

Of this correspondence nearly two hundred letters have been preserved. The insight which they give into the minds and intentions of their writers is invaluable. They throw a strong light upon the undercurrent of political movement at a time when politics were perhaps more complicated and their undercurrents more potent than at any time before or after. From them might be detailed the tenor of the designs undertaken by a great religious party during a period of fierce struggle. Such reconstruction from a fragmentary correspondence must always be difficult. In the case of the Coleman correspondence the difficulty would be great. That the letters can be read at all is due to the fact that the key to the cipher in which they are written was found with them. Not only were they written in an arbitrary cipher, not to be elucidated without the key, but in such guarded and metaphorical language that the meaning can often be caught only by chance or conjecture.[54] Parables can easily be understood after the events to the arrangements for which they refer; but when no effect follows, the drift is more obscure. When before the Spanish Armada an English agent writes from Spain that bales of wool are being stored in large quantities, muniments of war may be read between the lines. When Jacobites give notice to their exiled king that Mr. Jackson need only appear in Westminster Hall to recover his estate, or that a cargo of the right sort, now in great demand, must be shipped at once, their meaning is transparent. But to the obscure terms used by Coleman and his friends after events afford a slighter clue. No notion discussed by them was ever tested as a practicable scheme in action. Neither success nor exposure sheds light whereby to read their letters. Whatever is in them must be painfully read as intention alone, and as intention abandoned. The general ideas however are plain, and an admirable exposition by Coleman himself saves the necessity of piecing them together from small fragments.

On September 29, 1675 he wrote a long letter to Père de la Chaize relating in some detail the history of the intrigues of the previous years.[55] Catholic ascendency in England and a general peace in favour of France were the objects for which he had worked. For these the dissolution of Parliament and money were necessary, money both to dissolve Parliament and to supply the king's wants. Next to Parliament Lord Arlington was the Duke of York's greatest enemy; for Arlington was the supporter, if not the promoter of the Test Act.[56] In response to this beginning Père Ferrier had sent a note to the duke through Sir William Throckmorton. In agreement with James it was Louis XIV's opinion that Arlington and the Parliament formed a great obstacle to their joint interest; and if the duke could succeed in dissolving the present Parliament, he would lend the assistance of his power and purse to procure another better suited to their purpose. The duke replied to Ferrier in person, and Coleman answered too. Their letters were to the same effect. The French king's offer was most generous and highly gratifying, but money was needed at the moment as urgently as thereafter, for without money a dissolution could not be obtained, and without a dissolution everything done so far would be nugatory. So far as money went it was possible to consult Ruvigny, the ambassador in England; further not, for Ruvigny was a Protestant. Eulogies of Throckmorton and Coleman passed from Ferrier to James and back, each expressing to the other his confidence in their agents.[57] At this time, said

Coleman, Charles II was undecided and felt the arguments for and against dissolution equally strong. But if a large sum such as £300,000 had been offered to him on condition that Parliament should be dissolved, he would certainly have accepted both money and condition. Peace would then be assured, with other advantages to follow. Logic built upon money, wrote Coleman, had more charms at the court of St. James than any other form of reasoning.[58] To obtain this money Coleman and his associates had worked hard. Not only did Coleman write to Ferrier about it and talk to Ruvigny about it in London, but he made Throckmorton press for it in Paris, and press Pomponne, the French secretary of state, as well as the confessor. Twice Throckmorton persuaded Pomponne to speak particularly to Louis on the subject, and once he sent a memoir for the king's perusal. Louis returned it with expressions of great interest in the duke's cause and the message "that he should always be ready to join and work with him." Also Pomponne was bidden to say that he had orders to direct Ruvigny "that he should take measures and directions from the duke," especially in what concerned the dissolution of Parliament, Louis, he said, was most sensible of the need for energy and caution and gave the greatest consideration to the matter.[59] At the same time Sheldon was pressing the French king's confessor.[60] Still the money did not come. One excuse after another was made. Pomponne declared that so great a sum as that demanded could not possibly be spared by Louis; and Throckmorton believed that this was so; but he was compelled to admit that another campaign would cost perhaps ten times as much. The foreign secretary also complained that the duke did not appear sufficiently in the movement himself. He was answered by Coleman that James had ceased negotiating with the ambassador as Ruvigny gave so little help, but he was in communication with Ferrier. Coleman thought that Ruvigny's backwardness was deliberate. Sheldon and Throckmorton were of the same opinion, and Throckmorton suggested as an alternative that a subscription should be raised from the Catholics; £50,000 he thought might be promised from France, and he hoped for twice that sum in England.[61]

While Coleman was begging from the French court and declaring his exclusive devotion to the interests of France, he was at the same time urging the papal nuncio to obtain money from the Pope and the Emperor and renouncing all designs except that of forwarding the Catholic cause in the Pope's behalf. Albani was moderately enthusiastic. The Emperor commanded him to assure the Duke of York of the passionate zeal he entertained for his service and the Catholic cause. The Pope too would assist in matters in which he might properly appear. But James must himself point the direction of the assistance to be granted. Coleman replied that he had already shewn the way. Money alone was needed to procure the dissolution of Parliament. Dissolution would mean peace abroad and

Catholic ascendency in England to the great advantage of the Pope, the Emperor, and the whole Church. It was incumbent on the Emperor and more especially on the Pope to open wide the purse for so fair a prospect.[62] The nuncio was not however to be carried away by emotion. Money could not be expended by the Pope upon such vague expectation. He had others to think of in greater straits than the English Catholics. Before the matter could be submitted to Rome more definite guarantees must be given that the Catholic cause would really be served. In any case what the Pope could afford would be nothing in comparison to what was needed.[63] Coleman continued to press, even to the point of Albani's annoyance.[64] Repetition of the same arguments merely met the same reply; and when by command of the Duke of York Coleman paid a secret visit to Brussels to interview the nuncio, the result was no better.[65]

So the shuttlecock was beaten backwards and forwards between London, Paris, and Brussels. Writing to La Chaize Coleman naturally made no mention of his correspondence with the nuncio. Different arguments had to be used in the two quarters. To Albani Coleman vowed his undying affection for the Pope, to the Jesuit an extremity of devotion for French interests. Neither the one nor the other had the desired effect. Advice and encouragement were forthcoming, but not pistoles. The bashfulness of Coleman's correspondents is not hard to understand. Albani gave his reasons brutally enough. Those at the court of Versailles were probably of the same nature. And here they had additional force, for if on general grounds the French were unlikely to pay, they were still less likely to support the Duke of York with doubtful advantages at a time when they could obtain their chief object by subsidising his brother the king. No one of business habits would pour his gold into English pockets without reasonable expectation of a proportionate return. The English pocket had the appearance of being constructed upon a principle contrary to that of Fortunatus' purse.

The scheme for which support was thus begged from whoever seemed likely to give was not promising to any but an enthusiast. Money was wanted certainly to bring Charles to the dissolution of Parliament, an idea which was constantly in the air at court. The Cavalier Parliament was an uncompromising opponent of Popery, and the Catholics bore it a heavy grudge. But dissolution in itself would hardly improve their own position. The design reached considerably farther than that. It was no less than to bribe the king to issue another declaration of indulgence, appoint the Duke of York again to the office of Lord High Admiral, and leave the whole management of affairs to his hands.[66] In the course of the next year a new parliament should be assembled, bribed to support the French and Catholic interest, and the Catholic position in England would be assured. James was an able and popular officer and enjoyed great authority in the navy. Supposing the stroke could be effected, he would occupy a position not only of dignity but of power to meet any attack that might be made upon his new state. The scheme was so far advanced that Coleman drew up a declaration for the king to issue setting forth his reasons for a dissolution, and solemnly protesting his intention to stand by the Protestant religion and the decisions of the next parliament. That was to be before the end of February 1675.[67]

Although Coleman wrote to the nuncio that the Catholics had never before had so favourable an opportunity, the design was shortly modified and deferred.[68] In its present shape the possibility of putting it to the test depended upon the good-will of the ministers. After the dissolution of Parliament their assistance would be necessary. Without it nothing could be done. If Parliament were dissolved and the ministers stopped the execution of all that was to follow, the last state would be worse than the first. And it now became evident that matters were in just that case. Whatever the Cabal might have done, it was certain that those who followed would have no hand in exalting the Duke of York's power. Danby, whose watchword was Monarchy and No Toleration, was now firmly fixed in authority. Early in February a proclamation was issued ordering the execution of the penal laws, whetted against Roman Catholics by the promise of reward to informers; young men were to be recalled from Catholic seminaries abroad, subjects were forbidden to hear mass in the chapels of foreign ambassadors, all English priests were banished from the kingdom.[69] The effect of the proclamation was chiefly moral; but the worst consequences might be expected from the Non-Resistance bill, now in active preparation for the April session. Should this be passed, Catholic, Presbyterian, and Whig alike would be excluded from all part in the management of affairs, and the royal Church of England would triumph. The Duke of York's party veered round and adopted the cause of parliament as a bulwark for themselves against the ministerial attack. The moment was critical for all concerned. A golden age seemed to have arrived for the Commons. Money was showered lavishly on them. Fortune rained every coinage in Europe. Danby, the Bishops, the Dutch, and the Spanish ambassador did battle with their rouleaux against the Catholics, the Nonconformists, the French ambassador and theirs. The scenes in Parliament were unprecedented, and have since scarcely been surpassed. Swords were drawn and members spat across the floor of the House. In the House of Lords the king appeared regularly at the debates to exert a personal influence on his peers, and was likened to the sun, scorching his opponents. Here Charles and Danby had the advantage, and after seventeen days the bill was sent down to the Commons; but Shaftesbury, who had fought with the utmost resolution, seized his opportunity to foment the old dispute between the Houses as to the right of appeal to the Lords, with such success that the session had to be closed before the bill could be introduced, Parliament was prorogued, and the Test vanished for ever.[70] Coleman and his friends breathed again and proceeded to adapt their programme to the new situation. Since dissolution would not help them, they would mould Parliament to their design. At the moment the Duke of York's position was as precarious as before; but, wrote Coleman to La Chaize, "if he could gain any considerable new addition of power, all would come over to him as the only steady centre of our government, and nobody would contend with him further. Then would Catholics be at rest and his most Christian Majesty's interest be secured with us in England beyond all apprehensions whatsoever. In order to this we have two great designs to attempt the next sessions. First, that which we were about before, viz. to put Parliament upon making it their humble request to the king that the fleet may be put in his royal highness' care.[71] Secondly, to get an act for general liberty of conscience." Coleman had already spoken to Ruvigny on the subject; the ambassador was not enthusiastic, but he admitted the advantages that would ensue to France. Twenty thousand pounds, thought Coleman, would ensure success; and success would be "the greatest blow to the Protestant religion here that ever it received since its birth."[72] La Chaize answered briefly, promising to give the matter consideration and desiring to hear more from his correspondent.[73] Coleman rejoined in his last letter to the confessor that has been preserved. He engaged to write whenever occasion arose, and sent La Chaize a cipher for use between themselves; and for greater security he would write between lines of trivial import in lemon juice, legible when held to the fire. Only that part of the business not relating to religion could be discussed with Ruvigny, continued Coleman; and then, coming to the point, "We have here a mighty work upon our hands, no less then the conversion of three kingdoms, and by that perhaps the subduing of a pestilent heresy, which has domineered over great part of this northern world a long time; there were never such hopes of success since the death of Queen Mary as now in our days, when God has given us a prince who is become (may I say, a miracle) zealous of being the author and instrument of so glorious a work.... That which we rely upon most, next to God Almighty's providence and the favour of my master the duke, is the mighty mind of his most Christian Majesty."[74]

The significance of this is beyond doubt. It has been the custom of historians, quoting the last passage alone, to belittle its importance as the exaggerated outpouring of a zealot's fancy. Taken with the context it is seen to be something very different. The words only express more clearly what was often hinted at and half outspoken in the correspondence which led up to this point. Jesuit agents and the Duke of York's confidential secretary, for such in fact Coleman was, had something more to do than to entertain themselves by writing at length and in cipher to all parts of Europe with no other intention than to express their hopes for the propagation of the Catholic faith in a manner quite detached from politics, or to discuss political schemes as matters of speculative interest; such things are not done for amusement. Coleman's phrases are pregnant with real meaning. They are to be understood literally. The design which his letters sketch was in substance the same as that afterwards put into practice when the Duke of York ascended the throne as James II. Under the guise of a demand for liberty of worship, it was a design to turn England into a Roman Catholic state in the interest of France and the Jesuits, and by the aid of French money. The remark of Halifax that dissenters only plead for conscience to obtain power was eminently true of his own time. No less true was it that those who separated themselves from the religion of the state aimed at the subversion of it.[75]

High treason, be it remarked, is the only crime known to the law in which the intention and not the act constitutes the offence. The famous statute of Edward III had defined as the most important treasons the compassing or imagining of the king's death, the levying of war against the king, and adherence to the king's enemies within the realm or without.[76] An act passed at the height of power of one of the most powerful monarchs who have reigned in England was insufficient for the needs of those whose position was less secure. The severity of repeated enactments under Henry VIII to create new treasons, and perhaps the difficulty of meeting attempts against the crown by statutory definition, rendered this method of supplying the want unpopular and unsatisfactory. So in the reign of Queen Elizabeth the extension of the statute of Edward III by construction became the settled mode of procedure. With the lapse of time the scope of constructive treason was extended. Coke laid down that an overt act witnessing the intention to depose or imprison the king or to place him in the power of another was sufficient to prove the compassing and imagining his death. Conspiracy with a foreign prince to invade the realm by open hostility, declared by an overt act, is evidence of the same.[77] Hale held conspiracy, the logical end of which must be the death or deposition of the king, even though this were not the direct intention, to be an act of high treason. To levy war against the king is an overt act of treason; conspiracy to levy war is thus an overt act of treason by compassing the king's death. To restrain the king by force, to compel him to yield certain demands, to extort legislation by terror and a strong hand, in fact all movements tending to deprive him of his kingly government, whether of the nature of personal pressure or of riot and disturbance in the country, are acts of treason. To collect arms, to gather company, to write letters are evidence of the intention of the same.[78] Treason by adherence to the king's enemies was equally expansive. Thus it has been held, says Sir James Stephen, "that to imagine the king's death means to intend anything whatever which under any circumstances may possibly have a tendency, however remote, to expose the king to personal danger or to the forcible deprivation of any part of the authority incidental to his office."[79] In 1678 a question was put to the judges by the Attorney-General: "Whether it be not high treason to endeavour to extirpate the religion established in this country, and to introduce the Pope's authority by combination and assistance of foreign power?" The judges were unanimous in their opinion that it was treason.[80] And in the case of Lord Preston in 1691 it was held that taking a boat at Surrey Stairs in Middlesex in order to board a ship off the coast of Kent, and convey to the French king papers containing information on the naval and military state of England, with the purpose of helping him to invade the realm, was an overt act of treason by compassing and imagining the death of the king.[81]

Doubt cannot exist as to the dangerous consequence of the correspondence carried on by Coleman. Under the most favourable interpretation it reveals a design to accomplish again by means of bribery what the English nation had already rejected as illegal and unconstitutional, a deed which was said to have broken forty acts of Parliament,[82] to give the sanction of authority to a religion which was banned and to priests who were under doom of high treason. And the most favourable interpretation is certainly not the most just. Those "great designs ... to the utter ruin of the Protestant party," which should "drive away the Parliament and the Protestants ... and settle in their employments the Catholics," refuse such a colouring.[83] At Coleman's subsequent trial the Lord Chief Justice told him, "Your design was to bring in Popery into England and to promote the interest of the French king in this place.... Our religion was to be subverted, Popery established, and the three kingdoms to be converted";[84] and what the Chief Justice said was true. Coleman and the party to which he belonged had designed "to extirpate the religion established in this country" by the assistance of money given by a foreign power. Such an endeavour could not be undertaken without the commission of high treason. By the theory of the constitution the king can do no wrong. Much less can he do wrong to himself. He cannot be persuaded to perform an act directed against his own person. Great persuasion or importunity addressed to the king, says Hale, cannot be held an act of treason, since an intention must be manifested to restrain or influence him by force.[85] But the king cannot be supposed of his free will to undertake measures having their end, according to the construction of the statute, in the compassing of his own death. Nor can he be supposed to be persuaded to such measures, for both cases involve a contradiction of himself. No king can be guilty of high treason. Except by Act of Parliament none in England can divest his office of any of the full authority pertaining thereto. Persuasion of the king to do so is by the nature of the case impossible, whether it be in the form of money or other. Any one who plans a fundamental change of the constitution, to be effected by money or other means except by the constitutional action of Parliament, falls under the penalty for treason none the less because he may hope for assistance from the man who is king, since the king cannot be considered to assist an unconstitutional change. Any one planning such a change, though he intends to obtain the king's assistance, acts against the king's authority as much as if he did not so intend, and is therefore guilty of high treason. Of such possible changes the overthrow of the Church of England is one, for the king cannot otherwise than constitutionally join in the subversion of the church of which he is head, and which he has sworn to maintain. If he is successfully persuaded to take part in such an act, the persuasion must be regarded as tantamount to force, for persuasion of the king to commit treason against himself is absurd. And the position of a man declaring his intention to accomplish this change is exactly that of Coleman and the Jesuit party in England. There can be no doubt that the subjects who took part with Charles II in the treaty of Dover were guilty of high treason, none the less because the man who was king acted in concert with them. And similarly, none the less because they expressed the intention of bribing the king to assist their design, no doubt can exist that Coleman and his associates were brought by their schemes under the penalty of the same crime.

Such was the state of the Roman Catholic designs—the real Popish Plot—in England at the close of the year 1675. The direction in which they turned during the next three years is now to seek. At the outset the chief part of the evidence fails. Until his arrest in September 1678 Coleman continued his foreign correspondence,[86] but in comparison with the letters of earlier date the portion of it preserved is meagre indeed. Above all, no such exposition of his schemes as Coleman sent to La Chaize exists to afford a clue to the tangled and mysterious allusions with which his letters abound. The only two of Coleman's later correspondents whose letters are extant were St. Germain and Cardinal Howard. The last written by St. Germain from Paris bears the date October 15, 1678, but with this exception all his letters belong to the year 1676. They are partly occupied with business of slight connection with politics. A scheme of the Duchess of York for the increase of an English Carmelite convent at Antwerp was pressed upon the French court. Rambling intrigues undertaken for the purpose finally succeeded in breaking down Louis XIV's reluctance, the convent was allowed to plant colonies in the French Netherlands, and the irritation caused to the duchess by the delay was allayed by a splendid present of diamonds made her in secret by the King of France.[87] St. Germain's letters also show that intrigues were being ceaselessly carried on in the French and Jesuit interest throughout the year 1676 by Coleman and his party. They do not show at all clearly of what nature those intrigues were. After the failure in England caused by his indiscretion Coleman probably did not accord him full confidence. St. Germain's complaints of his treatment were constant; and he was always in want of money.[88] Nor does the Italian correspondence throw much greater light. Cardinal Howard's letters extend with somewhat longer intervals from January 1676 to the end of the following year. They tell still less of the political intrigues. The business passing through Howard's hands was considerable. He was concerned with the difficult business of keeping the Duke of York on good terms with the Pope. Coleman's endeavours to keep up the pretence that James was not engaged to French schemes were not uniformly successful, and on the death of Clement X Howard received definite orders from home to vote in the conclave with the French party. Yet the task was accomplished with some adroitness. Howard was able to persuade the Pope that the marriage of Mary of York to the Prince of Orange was not due to her father's fault, and on another occasion obtained a letter from James to Innocent XI of such sweetness that "the good man in reading it could not abstain from tears." Sinister rumours were afloat at Rome of the duke's Jesuit connection, and repeated warnings were sent that, if they proved true, his cause would be ruined. There were even grave doubts as to the genuine character of his faith. For some time the troublesome conduct of an English Protestant agent at Florence occupied Howard's attention. The Inquisition bestirred itself in the matter. A triangular correspondence between Howard, Coleman, and Lord Arundel resulted in the man's recall and led them to debate the possibility of a match between the Princess Anne and the son of the Duke of Florence. Another source of continual trouble was Prince Rinaldo d'Este in his quest for a cardinal's hat. While his niece, the Duchess of York, backed by a special envoy from the court of Modena, was worrying the French ambassador in London for Louis XIV's support, Coleman applied directly to Howard at Rome. Promises of consideration for the matter were all that could be obtained. The prince, who had no claims other than those of family, afterwards gained his object by constant importunity. Courtin had information that the Spanish ambassador had offered the Duke of York the whole credit of Spain for the prosecution of Rinaldo's suit if he would quit the French interest, and therefore could not risk the result of a definite refusal; but neither Paris nor Rome manifested at this time the slightest intention to support the Modenese pretensions.[89] Cardinal Howard was in fact the official correspondent of the English Catholic party at Rome, and beyond the general business of helping in the amelioration of Catholic conditions and the improvement of the relations between different sections of the party, had little to do with particular schemes that might be fostered by one or another. Thus the literary evidence on the development of Roman Catholic policy in England is of the slightest. Accessible documents give little information. Nothing can be known exactly. The course of events between the years 1675 and 1678 cannot be elucidated by aid of the evidence of those who shaped it. The argument must be from the known to the unknown.

To start with, it is known that Coleman's correspondence did not cease, as he stated, in the year 1675. On the contrary, it was maintained down to the day of his arrest and even beyond.[90] Among others it is almost certain that he continued his negotiation with Père de la Chaize.[91] The subject of this later correspondence is debatable. It may have been concerned with a design again to establish the Roman Catholic religion in England. Or it may not; and in this case Coleman's letters may have been filled with matters of less importance, such as are to be found in those of Cardinal Howard. This alternative however is hardly tenable. Not only are there allusions in St. Germain's letters inexplicable except on the supposition that they refer to the hopes of the Catholics for the re-establishment of their religion, but the position of Coleman and the Jesuits rendered a continuance of their schemes virtually necessary. Early in 1676 St. Germain wrote that he had urged on La Chaize the absolute necessity of "vigorous counsels ... to produce success in the traffic of the Catholics"; in these, he said, the Duke of York took the lead, and that by the inspiration of Coleman. A month later he added that Coleman was incurring reproof at Paris on account of the violent measures he was said to advocate. The secretary of the English ambassador tried to ingratiate himself with the Jesuit by professing great zeal for the duke; was he sincere, asked St. Germain, and "has the duke all along trusted him with the secret of his affair"? On Ruvigny's return to Paris from his embassy St. Germain had an interview with him. Ruvigny expressed the opinion that the intrigues of Coleman and the Jesuits would prove fatal to James. Their conduct was detestable not only to Protestants and the government, but to a certain section of the Catholics also, "because," said the ambassador, "they would introduce an authority without limits and push Mr. Coleman to make such strange steps which must precipitate them into destruction."[92] Had the policy of which St. Germain was an agent been wholly without reproach, it would be hard to ascribe an adequate meaning to expressions like these. Coleman's anxiety to deny his correspondence would be equally difficult of explanation. Curious too would be the comment of Pomponne, the French minister for foreign affairs; for he undertook to prove the absurdity of the charges against Coleman by remarking in ridicule that he had even been accused of intriguing with Père de la Chaize, a fact the truth of which was perfectly known to him.[93] The situation of affairs argues with still greater force. The Jesuits were beyond all others the most militant order of the church. They formed the advance guard in the march against heresy. They had already borne, and were again to bear, the brunt of the battle. It was their particular business to carry war into the enemy's camp, for this was the reason as well as the excuse for their existence. They must work, fight, intrigue against the heretic and the heretic state, or leave their mission unfulfilled. And Coleman was in the same position. He was a pupil of the Jesuits, and under the guise of secretary to the Duchess of York maintained an active correspondence with agents abroad in the interest of their chief hope, the duke. Intrigue was his business, and his conduct of it was made more eager by the keenness of a convert. No one in the least acquainted with the history of the Jesuits and with the writings of their apologists can believe that their method of procedure was by conversion of individuals alone. The society has always been in its essence political, and in the troubled times of the seventeenth century political action of the exiled, the feared, the reputed traitor was seldom calculated to avoid the retribution of the laws by which those against whom it was directed were fenced. The penal laws were harsh, but harshness was of necessity; and the very necessity of their harshness begot retaliation; while retaliation completed the circle by driving into conflict with the law many who would have been glad to obey in peace and nurse conscience in quiet.

The class of Catholics whom Ruvigny found opposed to the Jesuit policy was large. At the close of the seventeenth century it probably comprised a majority of Roman Catholics in England. These were they who would take the oath of allegiance to their sovereign, holding it no bar to their faith, the followers of Blackloe, of Peter Walsh, of John Sergeant, the men who thought it no shame to liberalise belief by divorcing it from statecraft, the adherents of the church but not of the court of Rome.[94] The Jesuits had already once in the reign of Charles II interposed to prevent Roman Catholics in England from bettering their position, and when persecution fell on these in the evil days of Oates' grandeur, they showed to the astonishment of the society that it had earned small gratitude from them.[95] On the question of the oath of allegiance the English Catholic body was divided throughout the century. Catholics were willing to prove their loyalty by taking the oath, but this proof they were not allowed to give. The fruitless concessions offered by Charles I showed conclusively that despite all protestations the papal party would not abandon the deposing power. Whenever the movement in favour of the oath seemed to be gaining strength, the whole weight of the papal court and of the Society of Jesus was thrown into the scale against it. It was probably the only point upon which the two were at this time in agreement. The Earls of Bristol, Berkshire, Cardigan, Lord Stafford, and Lord Petre actually took the oath, and of these, horrid thought to the Jesuits, two had for their confessors Benedictines; Lord Arundel, and for a time the Duke of York, stood firm in refusal.[96] The division between the Catholics was purely political; it marked those on whose loyalty reliance could be placed from those who must be suspected of disloyalty; and the former class suffered for what the latter alone undertook. The line lay between the Catholic and the Jesuit parties, between those who would be satisfied with liberty of conscience and those who would not. Undoubtedly the Catholic body in England was much weakened thereby, and government owed not a little to the moderate Catholics; but however much the execution of Catholic policy was hampered, its direction was not diverted. Abstinence from political action was the basis of the pure Catholic position. The Jesuits held the wires of politics in their hands and directed the policy. They too affirmed purity of faith to be their motive. "Prosecution for matters of conscience," remarks Halifax, "is very unjust; but great care ought to be taken that private conscience is not pleaded against the security of the public constitution. For when private conscience comes to be a justifiable rule of action, a man may be a traitor to the state and plead conscience for treason."[97]

Thus it may be accepted that Coleman's correspondence between the years 1675 and 1678 was not of an entirely innocent character, but was concerned with matters of perilous import for the prosperity of the government and of the Church of England. Since it was not dropped, the negotiation must have proceeded either in the same line as that in which it lay at the end of 1675 or in another. Did the design drag on a weary course in the feeble hope of finding a parliament congenial to Roman Catholic ideas and of obtaining the king's support in return for a substantial sum of money: or did the Catholic politicians change their tactics to discover a better opening? If the argument is thus far sound, answer can be made without hesitation. Early in that year Coleman and his party had found that in the event of a dissolution of Parliament they could not hope for a third declaration of indulgence and the reappointment of the Duke of York to the offices which he had formerly held. The design was thereupon altered to a scheme for bribing the existing parliament to petition for the recall to office of James, and to pass an act for general liberty of conscience. Coleman's ideas were based on two miscalculations. He understood neither the temper of the English people nor the character of Charles II. The king was to him an amiable debauchee, caring only for his pleasures and his pocket. A sufficient present of money would induce him to retire from the management of affairs and console himself with his mistresses, leaving the reins of power for his brother to handle. As most men of his own and after times have thought the same, Coleman's mistake is perhaps excusable. Nothing could be further from the truth. Not money, but power was what Charles wanted, and in the use of power, not of money, he was skilled. Any plan grounded upon this conception of his character was foredoomed to failure. Equally grave was the other miscalculation, and in this too Coleman was not peculiar. A man looking back on the history of the seventeenth century, and guided by the story of the Revolution, can say with assurance that any attempt in its latter half to restore Catholicism in England must have been hopeless of success. The nation which drove out James II would have driven out another for the like cause. Charles himself had learnt this in the best of schools. The fact may have been plain to clear-sighted statesmen, but to the mass a restoration of the old religion was looked on as among events that were more than possible. Here was the root of the deep hatred of Catholicism cherished by the English nation. Not only was the event hoped by the one side, but it was feared by the other. And the hopeful party had more reason to hope than the fearful to fear. Englishmen might with justice anticipate intrigues and even plots, but never their success. But the Jesuit, whose education was continental and whose ideas were traditional, was unaware of the change that had passed over England. He was still inspired by the genius and followed the example of the dead Robert Parsons. His mind was filled with the great instances of past times. Henry VIII, Edward, Mary, and Elizabeth had drawn their subjects with them like sheep from one church into another. Within the memory of man a wave of Puritanism had swept over the country, tottered, and broken. There followed a loyal reaction and a court in which strong elements were Catholic. The people who had so willingly followed their leaders before might be expected to do so again. The hope of rebuilding the ruins of Jerusalem was strong in the belief of its possibility.[98] Such notions render the undertaking of Coleman and his party intelligible. But they were not blinded by prejudice to the obvious meaning of facts passing within range of their own observation. One scheme had already been abandoned: the second was to be abandoned now. For if the former had proved impracticable, much more so was the latter. To ask the House of Commons in the year 1676 to pass an act of religious toleration and to petition in favour of the Duke of York was to suggest that it should contradict its nature. The strongest characteristic of the Cavalier Parliament was its hatred of Roman Catholicism. It had already forced the retractation of two declarations of indulgence, and had on several occasions instituted proceedings against the Catholics. Coleman's experience perhaps led him to ascribe an undue importance to the influence of money. Dishonest members of the country party might accept bribes from the French king when the course which they were asked to take would be to the embarrassment of government, but not all the gold of France would induce them to put a weapon of such strength into the grasp of the court as to petition for what they had repeatedly prevented it from accomplishing. Popery and tyranny, it was said, went hand in hand. It must soon have been seen by the Catholic managers that such a policy was hopeless. If this was not evident at first, it must have become more than plain when early in April 1676 the Duke of York took the momentous step of ceasing to go to the royal chapel, and all England knew that he was a Catholic. It was the first occasion for a long time on which he had acted not in consonance with the ideas of France. Rome was delighted and recognised him as a true son, but elsewhere the news was not hailed with such joy. James had obtained his brother's consent only with difficulty. Pomponne marked the withdrawal of the declaration of indulgence as the beginning of the troubles that crowded on the royal authority in England. The duke's declaration created a notable addition. The effect of his move was instantaneous. Throughout the country the feeling roused was intense, the penal laws were once more put into execution, and Charles told the French ambassador that if he were to die the duke would not be allowed to remain in the country eight days.[99] It is perhaps to this time that the abandonment of the second scheme sketched by Coleman to La Chaize should be referred.[100] There can at all events be no doubt that its impracticable nature soon became manifest. It was therefore along another line that the design proceeded from the summer of 1676 onwards.

Since the year 1670 various ways of procuring success for the Catholic religion have thus been considered, adopted, and abandoned. The policy of the Dover treaty had been led by Charles. Had it been successful he would have been left at the head of a Catholic state, controlled and compact. That had been blown to the winds. The declaration of indulgence, faint resemblance of the plan which was to have been put into execution, was the direct result of royal authority. With its failure the king's leadership in the last movement of the counter-reformation ceased. Then followed the two schemes which Coleman related to La Chaize. In the one the motive power was to be the king, backed by the ministers and Parliament; in the other Parliament, working on the king and supported by him. When these were deserted, practically every arrangement in which the king could figure as chief had been tried. The game of the Dover treaty had been opened by the king, backed by French force; that of the declaration by the king's move alone; Coleman had suggested action by the king and Parliament, by Parliament and the king. Unless one of these moves was made again, Charles would stand in the background of the game; none would be made again, for each had been proved ineffective. Even by the last two the object had been to raise the authority not of the king, but of the Duke of York. The only remaining possibility was that the duke should be not only the object, but the leader of the game. He was the piece with which the move had to be made.

In what direction then could the move be made? So far from being an assistance to the Catholic movement, Charles was now a direct hindrance to it. He had abandoned the Catholic interest as a political weapon, and had engaged in a policy of Anglican predominance. Undoubtedly the design must be conducted behind his back, but it was impossible not to take count of his position and influence in the state. Three courses were left open to the managers of the movement. The king might be forced to take action on their side, or he might be thrust away from it, or he might be gradually elbowed into a position where his personal action would be negligible. The last course had already been considered. During the winter of 1674 and spring of the next year Lord Berkshire and Sir William Throckmorton had submitted the advisability of adopting a platform, the chief planks in which should be the debauchery and political profligacy of the king and the sobriety and ability of the Duke of York. By this means they hoped that all the supporters of order and moderation would be drawn to the duke, James would be surrounded by a compact and influential party composed of Catholics and Protestants alike, the whole management of affairs would eventually fall into his hands, and the king would be left beyond the range of politics, ousted from their control, contented with the otiose life of a peaceful rake.[101] This however had been discarded for the plans submitted by Coleman to Père de la Chaize, in turn to be relegated to the domain of untried political suggestion. The scope for the design was therefore reduced to the alternatives: Charles must either be thrust on one side or be compelled to take action in it himself. As he had already been tried as a leader and had failed, the latter course would mean that the plan should run without him, until at the moment of success he should be forced by the necessity of events to throw in his lot with the movement. In the former case the course of events would be exactly similar, save that the king would not be taken into the scheme at any point, and the movement would be carried to completion without him. That both of these courses involved treasonable schemes is hardly open to doubt. The logical end of the negotiations in either case was a *coup d'état*, in whatever degree, a revolutionary measure.

In March of the year 1679 the Earl of Berkshire lay dying in Paris. A month later a man passing under the name of John Johnson landed at Folkestone, and was arrested at Dover on his way to London. He was a certain Colonel John Scott, for whose arrival the authorities had been on the watch for some time past. Whether or no he was the same Colonel Scott who acted as an English spy in Holland during the second Dutch war it is impossible to say. Latterly he had been attached to the household of the Prince de Condé, and had commanded a troop of horse in the French service.[102] Subsequent events make it seem likely that orders for the Colonel's apprehension were issued by the secretary of state, owing to the belief that he had information of value to impart. To the officers at Dover he ascribed his return to England to a desire to see his native country, but when he reached London he told a different tale. As the Earl of Berkshire lay on his deathbed, he sent for Colonel Scott, who had vainly called a famous physician to his aid, and bade him take a message to the king. There had been a foolish and an ill design carried on in England, he said. He was a good Roman Catholic, and in the Catholic religion he was minded to die; but some of his faith were swayed by a giddy madness, and this he blamed. He was neither a contriver nor a great supporter of the business. He would not have had a hand in it but that Lord Arundel, Coleman, and others had told him that it could not miscarry, and that, if he did not stand with them, evil would be thought of him. That he ought long before to have disclosed what he knew he was well aware; personal duty and the allegiance of every man to his sovereign should have constrained him to speak; there were bad men in the matter, Lord Bellasis and others, who spoke ill of the king and very irreverently. But to his knowledge there was never talk of killing the king; if there had been, he would have spoken out. Then Colonel Scott asked who those others were; but Lord Berkshire begged for no questions, repeating, "If I had known of approaching dangers to the king, I should have told him." Presently the sick man began to sigh and to weep. "Friend," said he, "I see things will go as you will. For God's sake promise me you will find some way to tell the king every word I say, and that though some passages in letters of mine may look a little oddly, I would have run any hazard rather than have suffered any injury to have been done to his Majesty's person. 'Tis true I would have been glad to see all England Catholic, but not by the way of some ill men." Let the king have nothing to do with those he had named, nor with Stafford, nor Powis, nor Petre. Yet he hoped and believed that matter would not be found against them to take away their lives.[103] If Colonel Scott spoke truth, then the foregoing argument is certainly not quite baseless. And reason may be given for supposing this to be the case. At the time when Scott gave his information the fact of Berkshire's correspondence with Coleman was not publicly known. Coleman had already been tried and executed, and at the trial a number of his letters were read as evidence against him, but among them none from Lord Berkshire. Until the publication of the correspondence by order of the House of Commons this was the only channel by which particular knowledge of it reached the world at large. The other letters were not published until December 1680. It must therefore be supposed that Scott obtained his knowledge of the earl's correspondence privately. The only persons who had private knowledge on the subject were Lord Berkshire, the officials in whose custody the letters lay, and Coleman. Coleman was dead before Colonel Scott came into England, and the secretary of state by whom he was examined would have been most unlikely to furnish him with materials. It must therefore have been from Lord Berkshire himself that he obtained his information. But, it may be suggested, Scott may have drawn his bow at a venture, knowing merely that Berkshire was a prominent Catholic, and using his name as likely to gain credence for his story. The weight against this suggestion is heavy. If Scott had been for all he knew inventing the letters of which he spoke, he would surely have said more about them than he did. To mention them in so casual a manner would have been useless. The simplicity and directness of his relation points in this matter to its substantial truth. Another proof of genuineness has still greater force, the extreme moderation of the whole narrative. A scoundrel following in the track of Oates and Bedloe would never have concocted such a story. So far from being to his advantage, what Scott said might actually put him into a most unpleasant predicament. The chief point of the plot which Oates had discovered was the king's assassination. The chief agents in it were said to be the Jesuits. All the informers who came after spoke to the same effect and tried to spice their tales still more highly. Scott said not a word about the Jesuits. He stated on his sole authority, one of the men who might be expected to know, that no harm was intended to the king. To some extent what he said is borne out by Berkshire's letters. Passages in them must certainly have looked "a little oddly" to the government, and perhaps contained matters technically treasonable, but in nothing do they suggest any personal danger to the king. No one looking for the rewards of a professional informer would have acted as Colonel Scott. Nor did he ever seek these. He never came forward to give evidence against those condemned for the Plot. His name does not appear in the list of secret service money, doled out to the shameless witnesses for the crown. Nothing more is known of him.[104] His information may be accepted as genuine. Clearly then there was some truth in the discovery of a Roman Catholic conspiracy in the year 1678. What Lord Berkshire said sketches its essence. Oates was not after all aiming shafts entirely at random. During his stay in the Jesuit seminaries in Spain and Flanders he must have obtained an inkling of what was in the air, and proceeded to act upon the information to his best advantage. That the whole truth had little resemblance to his tale of fire and massacre is certain, but the tale was not wholly devoid of truth. His vast superstructure of lies was not without a slight basis of solid fact.

This conclusion can in some degree be supported from other sources. Any attempt to reconstruct the part played by the Catholic reformation in the years preceding the appearance of Oates must be chiefly conjectural. Scarcely any evidence on the subject is known, but what more comes to hand points in the same direction. In December 1680, as he lay in the Tower under sentence for high treason, Lord Stafford sent a message by Dr. Burnet and the Earl of Carlisle to the House of Lords that he would confess all he knew of the Catholic intrigues. He was admitted to speak from the bar of the House. Unfortunately his statement does not refer at all to the later years of the movement, for when he came to describe the project debated between Shaftesbury and the Duke of York for a coalition between the Catholic and country parties to obtain a dissolution of Parliament and general toleration, Stafford was stopped hastily at the mention of the great Whig leader's name. To a few more questions put he simply answered no, and was presently sent back to the Tower. Cut short as it was, his account is of some value. He admitted that he had endeavoured to alter the established faith, and gave some details of the meeting held early in Charles II's reign at the Earl of Bristol's house to discuss the oath of allegiance. He had always disapproved the policy of the declarations of indulgence, and marked them as causes of the downfall of his religion. At one time he almost decided to leave England and live beyond sea. Others however were not of his opinion. The Papists and Jesuits had been far too open in their conduct, he said, and he had even seen a priest in the House of Lords standing below the bar. All his fellow peers, excepting the Earl of Bristol, were in favour of toleration for the Catholics. There was even talk of a restitution of the church lands, but Stafford warned the Duke of York that they were in so many hands as to render any attempt of the kind impracticable.[105] All this does not amount to much; nevertheless it shows a drift in one direction. Other straws are floated down the same stream. In the summer of 1678, when it was doubtful whether or no England would declare war on Louis XIV, Catholics in Ireland were discussing the chances in that event of a rebellion in their country aided by France. Calculations were made on the strength of the French navy, and there was talk of a rising in Scotland as well.[106] There were Jesuit missioners in Scotland, poor and hard worked, and it is possible that Jesuit influence had been concerned in organising the rebellion there in the year 1666;[107] while in 1679 there was serious consideration of a movement in Ireland under Colonel Fitzpatrick, who crossed to Brussels during the Duke of York's exile there to consult with him.[108] More definite information can be obtained from the case of Père de la Colombière. The celebrated Jesuit preacher, famed for his propagation of the cult of the Sacred Heart, was living in England at the time of the Popish Plot panic, and acting as confessor to the Duchess of York, Two Frenchmen, Olivier du Fiquet or Figuère and Francois Verdier, accused him to the House of Lords of extraordinary activity in spreading the Catholic religion. La Colombière had concealed himself, but was discovered, arrested, and shipped out of the country. Besides the general charge of caring for the growth of his faith, he was accused of a close connection with Coleman and Père de la Chaize. In attempting the conversion of Fiquet, who was a Protestant, he had used as an argument that the Duke of York was openly, and the king in secret, Catholic by faith. Parliament, he said, should not always be master; in a short time all England would be changed.[109] Supposing that these men had wished to make their accusation a source of gain, they would have charged the confessor with being a party to the king's assassination, or at least to the plot in general. Since they did not, their statements may be taken as true. Nothing dishonourable was alleged against La Colombière, but he plainly harboured the expectation of seeing England before long Catholic. His hope was shared by others; for in advising on the establishment of a nunnery by the Yorkshire baronet, Sir Thomas Gascoigne, the Jesuit John Pracid wrote on June 9, 1678 to suggest the insertion of a clause in the deed, depending on the condition: "If England be converted."[110] At most the evidence is slight, but it seems clear that the Jesuit party was indulging in hopes considerably more active than they could naturally have been if wholly unsupported by any plan of action.

While the schemes of which these traces are to be found were in the air, Oates was studying and being expelled from Valladolid and St. Omers. There were in Flanders twenty-seven English Roman Catholic seminaries; five belonged to the Jesuits, and of these the establishment at St. Omers was the largest. It contained some thirty professed fathers and a hundred and twenty scholars.[111] Probably the best education in Europe was provided for the boys, and life there was comfortable; but to the unwilling the seminary became a prison. Pressure was put upon them to become priests, and communication with the outside world was carefully restricted. In a letter preserved from this time a Welsh boy, placed in the college by a wicked uncle, wrote secretly to his father begging piteously to redeem him from his great captivity.[112] Here, unless he made a prodigious guess, the most fortunate in history, Oates must have acquired hints dropped on the subject of the movement in England. It is not very profitable to speculate on the question exactly how much truth his vivid imagination concealed. Possibly a demonstration of force was suggested, organised by the great Catholic nobles and relying on support for the Duke of York to be gained in the navy. The fleet was at the moment being strengthened by the addition of several capital ships, and in the spring of 1678 was at full strength in sea service, with complete stores for six months.[113] If this were the case, if Arundel, Bellasis, and Stafford were implicated in the affair, but nothing definitely arranged so soon as the autumn of 1678, Oates' diffident denunciation of these peers and the evident falsehoods which he, Bedloe, and Dugdale afterwards told in their statements regarding the Popish army, would be sufficiently accounted for. Or again, it is possible that the design included help from France in money, and perhaps the use of the English regiments employed in the French service. Many of their officers were Irishmen, and most Catholics.[114] For this it would be necessary to wait until peace was definitely concluded in order that both men and money might be liberated from the calls on them. Such a supposition would go some way to explain the "dark, suspicious letter" seized at Coleman's house after his arrest, and bearing the date September 18, 1678. The writer, posting from Paris, informed Coleman that the peace had broken all their plans, for the

French pretended that since its conclusion they had no need of his party. Yet there was hope from another quarter. Let an agent known to him be sent over. "To put our traffic afoot," continues the letter, "it's absolutely necessary that my friend come speedily over to you, to converse with you and our other friends, because his measures are so well taken in Italy, that we can't miss to establish this commodity better from those parts than from any here at present, tho' hereafter we may find means and helps from hence too. But it's most certain, now is the time or never to put things in order to establish it with you."[115] The letter seems to point to hopes of early aid from France, since disappointed. In this case Père de la Chaize, or whoever managed the affair in France, may have thought that the gold of French Catholics could be put to better purpose than to assist their fellows of the faith in England in a forlorn hope. The likelihood of such a desertion is to some extent supported by the refusal of the French government in November 1678 to take any steps to assist the Duke of York or his party.[116] But from the scraps of evidence obtainable it is plain that the design, supposing it to have been such as is here sketched, had not advanced beyond the stage of negotiation, ready to be construed into immediate action.

According to the information which Lord Berkshire gave to Colonel Scott, no harm was intended to the king; at least he knew of none. This may well have been; but at the same time it is necessary to remember that Charles was at the moment the greatest impediment to the chance of Catholic success. He was little older than his brother, and enjoyed far better health. As far as could be judged, he was by no means likely to be the first to die. He had definitely adopted a policy adverse to the Catholics. If he were to die, the charge of revolutionary dealing would lie at the door of those who should attempt to keep the Duke of York from the throne. So long as he lived, any attempt to restore the Roman Catholic religion in England, certainly any attempt made behind his back, would be a matter of high treason and against the interests of peace and established order. This much only can be said with safety, that the brothers hated each other,[117] that the death of the king was talked of in Jesuit seminaries on the continent,[118] and that James was not above tolerating, if he did not direct, an attempt to murder the husband of his daughter.[119]

CHAPTER III

OATES AGAIN

THUS the Popish Plot was introduced to the world, "a transaction which had its root in hell and its branches among the clouds."[120] While Charles proceeded on his walk, Chiffinch, his confidential valet, refused Kirkby admittance into the royal bedchamber, not knowing his business. Kirkby therefore waited in the gallery till Charles returned and summoned him to ask the grounds of such loyal fears. Kirkby replied that two men, by name Pickering and Grove, were watching for an opportunity to shoot him, and that should they fail, Sir George Wakeman, the queen's physician, was employed to use poison.[121] Oates and Tonge had committed this piece of information to paper for him the day before. Asked how he knew this, Kirkby answered that he had the news from a friend, who was ready to appear with his papers whenever the king should command. He had waited to give his warning the day before, but had failed. Charles ordered him to return with his friend in the evening. Accordingly between eight and nine o'clock Kirkby escorted Dr. Tonge to Whitehall. The doctor brought with him a copy of the forty-three articles and solemnly presented it to the king, with a humble request for its safe keeping. He entreated that only the "most private cabinet" should be acquainted with the contents; otherwise the secret would leak out, full discovery of the plot would be prevented, and the lives of the discoverers put in hazard. But if under the guise of chemical students they might have access to his Majesty until seizure of the conspirators' letters showed beyond doubt the truth of their story, all would be well. Tonge afterwards complained that full discovery was rendered impossible because the king did not take his advice. Charles was too busy or too apathetic to attend to the matter himself. He was going to Windsor on the morrow, he said, and would leave the inquiry to Lord Treasurer Danby, on whose ability and honour he placed all reliance.[122] Whence did the papers come to Tonge? he asked. The doctor returned he had found them under the wainscot in Sir Richard Barker's house; he did not know the author, but suspected him to be a man who had once or twice been there in his absence and had formerly discoursed with him on such matters as appeared in the articles. Of his condition too Tonge was uncertain, but thought he had been among the Jesuits; perhaps, he suggested, the man had been set on by secular priests or the Jansenists.[123] Much the same story was told next day to the Earl of Danby. Tonge and Kirkby called on him in the afternoon, and Kirkby, introducing the doctor, was requested to leave. The Lord Treasurer had read the information overnight and proceeded to examine Tonge on the subject. Were the papers originals? No, they were copies of the doctor's writing, the originals being in his custody. He did not know the author, but guessed who he was. Did he know where to find this man? No, but he had lately seen him two or three times in the street and thought it likely they might meet again before long.[124] Many were Dr. Tonge's falsehoods in order to raise an air of sufficient mystery. Three or four days later he returned to Danby with the information that his guess at the authorship of the papers was correct; nevertheless for secrecy's sake he was not to give the name, since if the fact were to become known the informer would be murdered by the Papists. Danby asked some more particulars. Did the doctor know Pickering and honest William, as Oates had called Grove, who were named as the king's assassins? Certainly; he could point them out waiting their murderous chance in St. James' Park. He did not know their lodging, but would find it out and inform the earl; for Danby insisted that they should be arrested forthwith. Leaving a gentleman of his household in London in communication with Tonge, Danby drove down to Windsor and told the king all that had passed. He urged that one of the secretaries of state should issue a warrant for the apprehension of the dangerous persons and that the whole matter should be brought before the council, but Charles would not hear of it. On the contrary, he commanded Danby not even to mention the affair to the Duke of York, only saying that he would take great care of himself till more was known. The Treasurer left Windsor for his house at Wimbledon and sent directions that Lloyd, the gentleman whom he had trusted, should bring him whatever news occurred.[125] Meanwhile Oates was consorting with his Jesuit acquaintances, and even obtained supplies from them; somewhat to their discredit, seeing that he had twice been expelled from Jesuit colleges.[126] In the intervals he concocted additional information, which Tonge took to Kirkby to copy and Kirkby gave to Lloyd for Danby's perusal.

Despite Tonge's assurance that Pickering and Grove might be captured in St. James' Park with their guns, the inquiry seemed as far from reaching solid ground as ever. All that the doctor could do was to point out Pickering to Lloyd in the chapel at Somerset House. It was offered as an excuse for Grove's absence that he had a cold. Something better than this was obviously required. So one night Tonge went to Wimbledon himself and informed Danby that the assassins were bound for Windsor the next morning; he would arrange for Lloyd to travel in the same coach with them and procure their arrest on arrival. The Treasurer started at once and slept that night at Windsor, laying his plans for the capture; but when the coach drove in, lo! Danby's gentleman stepped out alone. The others had been prevented from coming by an unforeseen accident. Within two days at furthest however, as Lloyd brought word from Tonge, they would be sure to come. Curiously enough the ruffians failed a second time. On this occasion they were riding and one of the horses had hurt his shoulder. The most that Tonge could manage was by way of addition to the information already lodged. Although Pickering and Grove had been stopped from attacking the king at Windsor, they had all but made the attempt in London. Unfortunately the flint of Pickering's pistol was loose and he dared not fire: and for this he suffered a penance of thirty lashes. The story was afterwards improved, for Pickering had missed a rare chance not only once, but three times. Now his flint was loose, on another occasion he had no powder in the pan, on a third he had loaded with bullets only and no powder. It might be suspected too that the discovery of the plot was no longer a secret; for Oates, going one day to see Whitebread, the Jesuit provincial, had been met with abuse as a traitor and even with blows. Clearly the Duke of York, who had seen Kirkby come from his first interview with the king, had mistaken him for Oates and told his confessor of the accident.[127] The doctor's efforts were vain. By no device could Charles be moved to take interest in the matter. Danby was alarmed by the idea that he was the only man beside his master to whom Tonge's disclosures were known, thinking perhaps that if ill came it might go hard with himself, and urged that they might be communicated to others; but the king had already come to the conclusion that the conspiracy was fictitious, and after the ridiculous excuses offered by Tonge for the absence of the supposed assassins was all the more positive in his refusal to order a formal inquiry. He should alarm all England, he said, and put thoughts of killing him into the minds of people who had no such notions before.[128]

Oates and Tonge now planned a bolder stroke. On August 30 Danby received news from Tonge, for Oates was at this time still unknown to him, that letters telling of treasonable designs had been sent to Father Bedingfield, the Duke of York's Jesuit confessor, and might be intercepted at the Windsor post-office. Danby instantly returned to Windsor and showed Tonge's letter to the king. He was met by the announcement that Bedingfield had already been at the post-office. The confessor had found a packet awaiting him. It contained four letters, ostensibly from priests of his order known to him but not in their hands, and a fifth in the same style. All were apparently of dangerous concern, full of mysterious phrases which seemed of no good meaning. Bedingfield took the letters to the duke, who showed them to the king. Thus when Danby arrived at Windsor his news was stale. Charles believed still less in the existence of a real plot. The letters were transparent forgeries. Purporting to be written by different persons, from different places, at different dates, they bore a curious likeness one to another. The paper on which they were written bore the same watermark and appeared to have been cut from one sheet. In every case the name signed was misspelt. Throughout, the writing was disfigured by the same blemishes of style and spelling. Only one of the letters contained a single stop, and that seemed to have been made accidentally. Oates professed afterwards that the handwriting was disguised and that the writers made mistakes on purpose, should the letters be intercepted, to lull the reader to false security. A Jesuit in London, who scented the discovery of the plot, had sent warning to Bedingfield, and the confessor had handed his letters to the duke with the express intention of showing them to be counterfeit and himself to be innocent. Thus, declared the informer with indignation, they had been made to appear the work of forgery. So far as the last goes, Oates spoke the truth. They were patently the composition of himself and his confederate. A tribute to the unscrupulous energy of those who adopted the plot for political purposes is paid by the fact that these letters were suppressed and never brought forward as evidence, although three of the men who were supposed to have written them were afterwards tried for treasons of which, had they been genuine, the letters would have afforded strong proof. Oates met the rebuff by going at Kirkby's instigation to swear to the truth of his story before a London magistrate. But at court the intriguers were badly received. Kirkby and Tonge called several times on the Treasurer, only to be refused admittance, and when Charles met his old acquaintance he passed by him without word or look.[129]

At this moment a sudden move of the Duke of York threw the game into the hands of Oates. With his usual want of tact James demanded an inquiry into the matter by the privy council. What difference this actually made to the course of subsequent events it is hard to calculate, for Oates was clever enough to place himself in a position not wholly dependent on the action of government, but at least it smoothed his way at the moment. The act of the duke was that of applying the bellows to the seed of a mighty conflagration. At the meeting of Parliament Danby was accused of having tried to stifle the plot; unjustly, for he too had urged investigation. For some time Charles withstood their instance. Danby alone he could have resisted, but when James, whose occasions for importunity were better than those of the Treasurer, added his demand, the king gave way and, against his better judgment, consented. Oates was still occupied in enlarging and copying his information when on the evening of September 27 Kirkby brought word from Lloyd that Tonge was summoned to go with him to the council. The council had already risen and their appearance was postponed till the next morning. Tonge asserted that he would have been better pleased had the inquiry been longer delayed that yet more of the plot might have been discovered. His feelings must really have been of some relief at the opportunity afforded, tempered with suspicion of the council's intention towards himself. Taking the precaution to place his information beyond reach of danger by leaving a sworn copy with the magistrate who had attested his oath, Oates accompanied his friend to Whitehall. Some ten days earlier Charles had been made acquainted with the informer's name. The opinion of the government was that Tonge had no other end in view than to obtain a deanery. That notion must have been rudely dispelled by Oates' appearance at the council board.[130]

Dr. Tonge was the first to enter and, kneeling, handed a petition for pardon for himself and Oates, together with a list of the plotters and their lodging. He was asked who Oates was. An acquaintance of short standing, he answered. He had been a chaplain in the navy on board Sir Richard Ruth's ship, but having given information of some miscarriages had received hard dealing from the privy council. In point of fact this was the occasion when he had been summarily ejected from the service. As Tonge begged excuse from reciting what he knew further of the plot, an abstract he had made of Oates' information was read. Oates was called and examined on the contents of the papers. The council sat long, and he was heard at length. His statements were of so general a character that little criticism could be made, but the board was sufficiently satisfied to authorise the informer to search for the men he had named as conspirators. As night fell, he issued forth armed with warrants and officers. Before morning Father Ireland, procurator of the province of the Society of Jesus, Fenwick, agent for the college at St. Omers, Pickering, and other Jesuits were in Newgate. Oates returned to the council on the morning of Sunday, being Michaelmas day, to continue his examination. This time the king was present. Oates was made to repeat all he had said the day before. He had named in his narrative Don John of Austria as not only cognizant of the plot, but active in it. What was he like? asked Charles. Tall and graceful, with fair hair, Oates replied promptly. Charles had seen Don John and knew him to be short, fat, and dark. Oates said that he had seen Père de la Chaize pay in Paris ten thousand pounds as the price for the king's death. The victim now asked in what part of Paris. In the Jesuits' house close to the Louvre, was the answer. Again Oates had committed himself, for there was no such house in that position. The letters sent to Bedingfield at Windsor were produced. Oates skated over the thin ice as best he could, declaring that Jesuits used to make their letters appear foolish to conceal their meaning. He pursued his tale with unbroken confidence. Arundel and Bellasis were mentioned. Charles remarked that those lords had served him faithfully, and that without clear proof he would not credit anything against them. Oates protested to God that he would accuse none falsely; he did not say that they were partners in the plot, only that they were to have been acquainted with it. His whole behaviour was of a piece with this. Loud in general accusations, he refused to bring particular charges against persons who might appear to contradict him successfully. Whenever he was pressed, he drew back and hedged. The king ended the meeting by exclaiming that he was a most lying knave.[131]

Oates' credit was rudely shaken. Nevertheless the matter could not be dropped without further investigation. The informer managed to cover his mistakes by the suggestion that he had himself been deceived. He had misspelt the name of Louis XIV's confessor, calling him Le Shee; but in an age of loose spelling, when Barillon wrote of Shaftesbury as Schasberi, and Cardinal Howard's name was spelt Huart by a papal nuncio, this was not of great weight. Oates had evidently lied, but perhaps he had spoken some truth. His assurance and readiness had been such as to amaze the council. Charles himself was taken aback, and though he gave no credence to the informer's story, felt that great care was necessary for the discovery of the truth. Falsehood has not been unknown in the seventeenth and other centuries as a prop to even a good cause. At all events persons, against whom serious charges, not disproved, had been made, could not be allowed to remain at large. So on the second night in succession Oates was sent his rounds with a guard, sleepless and defying the stormy weather. Before dawn most of the Jesuits of eminence in London lay in gaol. At one point the party encountered a check. Oates led his men to arrest Whitebread, the provincial, at the residence of the Spanish ambassador. The ambassador's servants resisted the intrusion, and the next day Count Egmont and the Marquis Bourgemayne lodged a complaint with the secretary of state. Material compensation was not to be had, but an ample apology; and the soldiers with Oates were said to have been drunk and were punished.[132] Of greater importance than persons was a find of papers. A warrant had been signed at the council board for the arrest of Coleman. When the meeting rose the Earl of Danby noticed that direction for seizing his papers had been omitted. He hastily caused another warrant for this purpose to be drawn, and obtained the five requisite signatures just in time that a messenger might be dispatched the same evening. Coleman's house was searched, and, besides others, a deal box containing the most important of his letters was found in a secret recess behind a chimney. Danby could boast with justice, when he was accused of having acted in the French and papist interest, that but for his action the chief evidence of the schemes of both in England might never have come to hand. The Duke of York, against whom they told heavily, would never forgive him, he said. Coleman surrendered himself on Monday morning, and was put under the charge of a messenger with only Oates' accusation against him. He managed to send word to the French ambassador that nothing would be found in his papers to embarrass him. A cruel awakening from the dream was not long delayed. When his letters came to be read, the lords of the council looked grave and signed a warrant for his commitment. Coleman disappeared into Newgate.[133]

On Monday, September 30, Oates was again examined before the council, and again coursed London for Jesuits. The town was by this time thoroughly alarmed. Coleman's papers were regarded by the council as of high importance. They shewed at any rate that Oates had known of his correspondence with La Chaize, and seemed evidence of a serious state of affairs. In the streets they were taken as proof of his every statement. Catholics who had sneered at the disclosure began to realise that the charges against Coleman were heavy and that he was in danger of his life.[134] The Protestant mob of London was convinced that the charges against all accused were true. The Duchess of York started on a visit to the Princess of Orange in Holland. It was said that she was smuggling guilty priests out of the country. A fever seemed to be in men's minds. Freedom of speech vanished. To doubt the truth of the discovery was dangerous. Opinions favourable to the Catholics were not to be uttered without risk. The household of the Duke of York was in consternation, and James himself gloomy and disquiet. Orders were sent into the country to search the houses of Catholics for weapons. Sir John Reresby hurried to town with his family to be on the scene of a ferment the greatness whereof none but an eye-witness could conceive. "In fine," wrote Lord Peterborough, "hell was let loose; malice, revenge, and ambition were supported by all that falsehood and perjury could contrive; and lastly, it was the most deplorable time that was ever seen in England." Oates was hailed as the saviour of the nation and was lodged with Dr. Tonge in Whitehall under a guard. "One might," exclaimed North, "have denied Christ with less contest than the Plot." To add to the general confusion the king left for the races at Newmarket, scandalising all by his indecent levity. During his absence Dr. Burnet paid Tonge a visit in his lodgings at Whitehall. He found the poor man so much uplifted that he seemed to have lost the little sense he ever had. Oates appeared and was introduced. He had already received a visit from Evelyn. The courtier found him "furiously indiscreet." Burnet received the flattering intelligence that he had been specially marked by the Jesuits for death; the same had been said of Stillingfleet; but the divines thought the compliment cheap when they found that it had been paid also to Ezrael Tonge. The informer burst into a torrent of fury against the Jesuits and swore he would have their blood. Disliking the strain, Burnet turned the conversation to ask what arguments had prevailed upon him to join the Church of Rome. Whereupon Oates stood up and, laying his hands on his breast, declared: God and his holy angels knew that he had never changed, but that he had gone over to the Roman Catholics to betray them.[135] The perjurer might well triumph. The days of his glory were beginning. On October 21 Parliament met. Before that time Godfrey, the magistrate before whom Oates had sworn to the truth of his deposition, was dead amid circumstances of horror and suspicion, and the future of the informer with his hideous accusations was assured.

SIR EDMUND BERRY GODFREY

CHAPTER I

SIR EDMUND BERRY GODFREY

THE death of Sir Edmund Berry Godfrey has passed for one of the most remarkable mysteries in English history. The profound sensation which it caused, the momentous consequences which it produced, the extreme difficulty of discovering the truth, have rendered Godfrey's figure fascinating to historians. Opinion as to the nature of his end has been widely different. To the minds of Kennet, Oldmixon, and Christie the Catholics were responsible. North declared that he was murdered by the patrons of Oates, to give currency to the belief in the Plot. Sir James Fitzjames Stephen hazards that Oates himself was the murderer, and is supported by Mr. Traill and Mr. Sidney Lee. L'Estrange was positive that he committed suicide. Lingard and Sir George Sitwell have given the same verdict. Ralph, Hallam, Macaulay, Ranke, and Klopp pronounce the problem unsolved. Hume has pronounced it insoluble. All have admitted the intricacy of the case and its importance. None has been able without fear of contradiction to answer the question, "What was the fate of Sir Edmund Godfrey?" On the answer to this question depends to a great extent the nature of the final judgment to be passed upon the Popish Plot. If Godfrey met his death at the hands of political assassins, the weight of the fact is obvious. If he was murdered by the Roman Catholics, much of the censure which has been poured on the Protestant party misses the mark; if by Protestant agents, that censure must be redoubled before the demands of justice are satisfied. If he committed suicide, or was done to death in a private cause, the criminal folly of many and the detestable crime of a few who in the cause of religious intolerance fastened his death upon the innocent were so black as to deserve almost the same penalty.

Scarcely ever has a fact so problematical been attended by such weighty results. Sir Edmund Godfrey left his house on October 12, 1678. On October 17 his corpse was found in the fields at the foot of Primrose Hill. From that moment belief in the Popish Plot was rooted in the mind of the nation. The excitement throughout the country rose to the mark of frenzy. Godfrey's death seemed clear evidence of the truth of Oates' sanguinary tales, and the prelude to a general massacre of Protestants. It became an article of faith that he had been murdered by the Catholics. To deny it was to incur the most awkward suspicion. No man thought himself safe from the same fate. Every householder laid in a stock of arms. Posts and chains barricaded the streets of the city. Night after night the Trained Bands stood to arms and paraded the town as if an insurrection were expected before morning. During the winter which followed, wrote Shaftesbury, "the soberest and most peaceable of the people have, either in town or country, hardly slept for fear of fire or massacring by the Papists." Alderman Sir Thomas Player declared that when he went to bed "he did not know but the next morning they might all rise with their throats cut." And this state of things continued, as sober Calamy remarked, "not for a few weeks or months only, but for a great while together." It was regarded as most fortunate that the Protestants did not seek to avenge Godfrey and anticipate their own doom by exterminating the Roman Catholics.[136]

Upon the death of a London magistrate was grounded the firm conviction of the reality of the Popish Plot, under cover of which the Whig party was all but successful in deranging the legitimate succession to the throne, and even perhaps in overturning the monarchy itself. Of the instruments by which Shaftesbury turned the Plot to this end, none was more powerful than the belief in Godfrey's murder. In one connection or another that event appeared in almost all the state trials of the two following years, in the debates in Parliament, in the pulpit, on the stage.[137] The part which it played in the electioneering methods of the Whigs was still more formidable, and Godfrey's corpse was a central figure in the grand annual ceremonies of Pope Burning, which were arranged by the Green Ribbon Club.[138] Without the mystery of Godfrey's death it is possible that the agitation of the plot would have burnt itself out in the course of a few months. As it was, the fuel was fanned into a blaze of unexampled fierceness, which did not die down until nearly three momentous years in English history had passed.

No one undertaking the study of this problem is likely to underrate the difficulty of the task. To find a solution is obviously a matter of great importance; but it is also a matter in which small success may reasonably be expected. The door of the secret has remained unopened for so long. The door is not one which can be forced, and the key is missing. It would be worse than sanguine to hope for its discovery after a light search. Nevertheless there is some hope. "When a door-key is missing," says Dr. Gardiner, "the householder does not lose time in deploring the intricacy of the lock; he tries every key at his disposal to see whether it will fit the wards, and only sends for the locksmith when he finds that his own keys are useless. So it is with historical inquiry.... Try, if need be, one hypothesis after another.... Apply them to the evidence, and when one fails to unlock the secret, try another. Only when all imaginable keys have failed, have you a right to call the public to witness your avowal of incompetence to solve the riddle."[139] In the case of the Gunpowder Plot Dr. Gardiner tried the key afforded by the traditional story and found that it fitted the lock. With the secret of Sir Edmund Godfrey's death the method must be different.

There is no traditional story to test. What seems more remarkable is that no determined attempt has been made to construct a consistent theory to fill the empty place. Contemporaries who approached the question answered it according to their prejudice, and selected only such evidence as would support their preconceptions. Later historians who have answered definitely have arrived at their conclusions by considering the balance of general probability in the matter, and have supported them from the contemporaries whose evidence lies on the side to which the balance seems to them to fall. No one has formed a hypothesis to explain the facts and tested it by all the evidence, in whatever direction it seems to point. The following study is an attempt to accomplish this. It would be impertinent to suppose that it offers a perfect key to fit the lock. But it offers a key with which trial may be made, and which may not be found altogether of the wrong size and shape. There is at least a hypothesis to be tested. If it jars with established fact, this will be detected. If the test reveals assumptions which are beyond the scope of legitimate imagination, it must be discarded. At least its abandonment will be because it has been shown to be inconsistent with the facts of the case. It will then leave the way clear for the same test to be applied to another theory.

Sir Edmund Berry—and not Edmundbury—Godfrey was a justice of the peace for the county of Middlesex and the city of Westminster. He came of a Kentish family of some wealth and of good repute in the county. His elder brother, father, and grandfather had all been justices of the peace before him, and he was popularly said himself to be "the best justice of the peace in England." He had been educated at Westminster and Christ Church, Oxford, had spent some time in travelling abroad, was a member of Gray's Inn, and owned a prosperous business as merchant of wood and coal in Hartshorn Lane, near Charing Cross.[140] To the public he had long been known. During the ghastly year when London was in the grip of the plague and all who could fled to the pure air of the country, Godfrey stayed at his post in town. London was given up to the dying, the dead, and their plunderers. In the midst of the chaos Godfrey went about his duties with redoubled energy and conspicuous gallantry. Numerous thefts from corpses were traced to a notorious ruffian. A warrant was issued for his apprehension. The wretch took refuge in the pest-house, whither none would follow him. Godfrey himself entered the forbidden spot and took the man alone. As an appropriate punishment he sentenced him to be whipped round the churchyard which he had robbed. It was of this time that his friend Dr. Lloyd spoke: "He was the man (shall I say the only man of his place?) that stayed to do good, and did the good he stayed for.... His house was not only the seat of justice, but an hospital of charity."[141] The king was not slow to recognise good service, especially when the recognition was not expensive. Charles gave Godfrey a knighthood and a silver tankard, inscribed with an eulogy of the service which he had done during the plague and the great fire.[142] Three years later Godfrey roused sentiments of a less grateful character in his sovereign. Sir Alexander Frazier, the king's physician, owed the justice £30 for firewood. Godfrey issued a writ against the debtor; but Frazier took the matter before the king, the bailiffs were arrested, and together with the magistrate were committed to the porter's lodge at Whitehall. Charles was so much angered at the interference with his servant that he had the bailiffs flogged, and was scarcely restrained from ordering the infliction of the same punishment on Godfrey himself. "The justice," writes Pepys, "do lie and justify his act, and says he will suffer in the cause for the people, and do refuse to receive almost any nutriment." To the great wrath of the king, Godfrey was supported by the Lord Chief Justice and several of the judges. After an imprisonment of six days Charles was forced to set the magistrate at liberty and to restore him to the commission of the peace from which his name had been struck off.[143]

A portrait of Godfrey belongs to the parish of St. Martin in the Fields.[144] It shows the bust of a spare man, dressed in a close-fitting coat of dark material, a high lace collar, and a full-bottomed wig. The head is large, the forehead wide and high, the nose hooked, the chin strong and prominent. The frank eyes and pleasant expression of the firm lips belie the idea of melancholy. Godfrey's height was exceptional, and his appearance made more striking by a pronounced stoop. He commonly wore a broad-brimmed hat with a gold band, and in walking fixed his eyes on the ground, as though in deep thought. Now and again he wiped his mouth with a handkerchief. "He was a man," writes Roger North, "so remarkable in person and garb, that, described at Wapping, he could not be mistaken at Westminster."[145] Godfrey moved in good society. He numbered the Earl of Danby among his acquaintance, was on terms of friendship with Sir William Jones and the Lord Chancellor, and counted Gilbert Burnet and Dr. Lloyd among his intimates.

Early in 1678 he was ordered to the south of France for the benefit of his health. He stayed for some months at Montpellier, and there admired the construction of the great canal which Louis XIV was undertaking to connect the Mediterranean and the Atlantic.[146] Late in the summer Godfrey returned to England and resumed his magisterial duties in London. It was scarcely beyond the ordinary scope of these when on September 6 three men entered his office and desired him to swear one of them to the truth of certain information which he had committed to writing. The three were Titus Oates, Dr. Tonge, and Christopher Kirkby. The paper contained Oates' famous information drawn up in forty-three articles. Oates made affidavit to the truth of the contents, and his oath was witnessed by his two friends and attested by Godfrey. They refused however to allow the magistrate to read the information in detail, "telling him that his Majesty had already a true copy thereof, and that it was not convenient that it should be yet communicated to anybody else, only acquainting him in general that it contained matter of treason and felony and other high crimes." Godfrey was satisfied, and the three men departed without more ado.[147] Oates professed afterwards to have taken this course as a safeguard for himself and his discovery from the vengeance of the Jesuits. His motive was far more probably to form a connection apart from the court, where he had been poorly received. At this point, so far as Godfrey was concerned, the matter rested. He was relieved of responsibility by the fact that the information had been forwarded to the king, and there were no steps for him to take. But on the morning of Saturday, September 28, Oates appeared before him again. Kirkby and Tonge had been summoned to the council the previous evening, but before they could be fetched the council had risen after giving orders that they should attend the next day. During the last three weeks the informer and his allies had felt their distrust of the council become more acute. While Oates had been engaged in writing copies of his information, Tonge had on several occasions been refused admittance to the Lord Treasurer. They believed that the discovery was neglected, and probably suspected that the summons to Whitehall was the prelude to discredit and imprisonment. To guard against this they determined to remove the matter from the discretion of the council. Two copies of the information, now in the form of eighty-three articles, were laid before Godfrey, who attested Oates' oath to the truth of their contents. One Godfrey retained in his possession, the other was taken by Oates to the council at Whitehall.[148]

Godfrey was now in the centre of the intrigue. His eminence and reputation for the fearless performance of his duty had no doubt directed Oates to select him as the recipient of the discovery. The fact that he was known to have resisted pressure from court with success on a former occasion made it likely that he would not submit to be bullied or cajoled into suppressing the information if, as Oates feared, the court had determined on this. He would certainly insist upon making the facts public and would force an inquiry into the matter. As a matter of fact Oates and Tonge were mistaken, for the council proposed to investigate the case thoroughly. Even so, it was from their point of view a good move to lay the information before Godfrey. It would appear to be evidence of Oates' desire to act in a straightforward manner and frankly according to the law. But in doing so they introduced a complication of which they were probably unaware. Godfrey was not only remarkable for his ability as justice of the peace, but for the tolerance with which he dealt between the parties and creeds with which the business of every magistrate lay. He was credited with sound principles in church and state, but he did not find it inconsistent with these to allow his vigilance to sleep on occasion. The penal laws against dissenters were not to his mind, and he refrained from their strict execution. He "was not apt to search for priests or mass-houses: so that few men of his zeal lived upon better terms with the papists than he did." Dr. Lloyd put the matter in his funeral sermon: "The compassion that he had for all men that did amiss extended itself to all manner of dissenters, and amongst them he had a kindness for the persons of many Roman Catholics." Among these was Edward Coleman, secretary of the Duchess of York, who was now accused by Oates of high treason.[149] The intimacy between the two men exercised a profound influence upon the course of after events, which Oates could not have foreseen. After Godfrey's disappearance his connection with Coleman became known; but at the time it was only apparent that Godfrey was an energetic magistrate who possessed the somewhat rare quality of being impervious to court influence. That he was upon friendly terms with the Roman Catholics was, for the informer's purpose, of little moment. Oates was in search of support outside the council-chamber, and Godfrey offered exactly what he wanted. In case the government wished to suppress the discovery of the plot, Godfrey was not the man to acquiesce in such a design on account of private considerations.

On Saturday, October 12, Sir Edmund Godfrey left his house in Hartshorn Lane between nine and ten o'clock in the morning. That night he did not return home. The next day Godfrey's clerk sent to inquire at his mother's house in Hammersmith. Obtaining no news there, the clerk communicated with his master's two brothers, who lived in the city. They sent word that they would come to Hartshorn Lane later in the day, and enjoined the clerk meanwhile to keep Godfrey's absence secret. In the evening Mr. Michael and Mr. Benjamin Godfrey appeared at their brother's house, and set out in company with the clerk upon a round of inquiry. That night and all Monday they continued the search, but could nowhere obtain tidings of the missing man. On Tuesday the brothers laid information of Godfrey's absence before the Lord Chancellor, and in the afternoon of the same day the clerk publicly announced his disappearance at a crowded funeral.[150] Up to this time the fact was unknown except to Godfrey's household and near relatives. It was afterwards asserted by those who wished to prove his suicide that the secret had been kept in order to prevent discovery of the manner of his death. The law directed that the estate of a person dying by his own hand should be forfeited to the crown, and to prevent the forfeiture Godfrey's family concealed the fact. Sir Roger L'Estrange devoted some effort to establish this.[151] He was however so unwise as immediately to demolish his case by collecting evidence to show that the dead man's brothers had approached the Lord Chancellor, "to beg his lordship's assistance to secure their brother's estate, in case he should be found to have made himself away."[152] Certainly, if the Godfreys had known his suicide and had been moved to conceal it in order to save his estate, the last person in the world to whom they would have admitted their motive was the Lord Chancellor. L'Estrange's sense of the contradictory was small. Not only did he commit this blunder, but he was at considerable pains to show that the fact of Godfrey's disappearance was never concealed at all; on the contrary, the news was bruited about the town as early as the afternoon of the day on which Sir Edmund left his house, in order to raise a cry that he had been murdered by the Roman Catholics.[153] He did not consider that, as the only persons who had first-hand news of Godfrey's absence were members of his family, the rumour must have emanated from themselves; whereas he persisted at the same time that their one object was to keep the fact secret. There was good reason why the family should be unwilling to publish Sir Edmund's disappearance until they had, if possible, some clue to his whereabouts or his fate. A man of his prominence and consideration could not vanish from the scene without giving rise to reports of an unpleasant nature. When for expedience sake his brothers announced that he was missing and brought the matter to the notice of government, there sprang into being tales which any persons of repute would have been glad to avoid, none the less because they perhaps believed that some of them might be true. On the Wednesday and Thursday following stories of Godfrey's adventures were rife. He had chosen to disappear to escape creditors, to whom he owed large sums of money. As no creditors appeared this notion was exploded.[154] He had been suddenly married in scandalous circumstances to a lady of fortune. He had been traced to a house of ill repute, now in one part of the town, now in another, and there found in the midst of a debauch. With one of these last stories the Duke of Norfolk went armed to Whitehall, and was so ill-advised as to announce it for a fact. But gradually, as none of them gained support, the rumour spread that Godfrey had been murdered. It was reported that he had been last seen at the Cock-pit, the Earl of Danby's house; then at the Duke of Norfolk's residence, Arundel House; then at St. James', the Duke of York's palace; even Whitehall, it was said, was not spared.[155] The general belief was, "the Papists have made away with him." Everywhere the missing magistrate afforded the main topic of conversation. The government was occupied with the case. Michael and Benjamin Godfrey were summoned before the council, and there was talk of a proclamation on the subject.[156]

Before further steps could be taken definite news came to hand. On Thursday, October 17, a man, who could never afterwards be found, came into the shop of a London bookseller in the afternoon with the information that Sir Edmund Berry Godfrey had been found dead near St. Pancras' Church with a sword thrust through his body. A Scotch minister and his friend were in the shop and carried the news to Burnet.[157] The report was correct. At two o'clock in the afternoon two men were walking across the fields at the foot of Primrose Hill, when they saw, lying at the edge of a ditch, a stick, a scabbard, a belt, and a pair of gloves. Pushing aside the brambles, they found a man's corpse in the ditch, head downwards. With this discovery they proceeded to the Whitehouse Inn, which stood in a lane not far off. John Rawson, the innkeeper, offered them a shilling to fetch the articles which they had seen on the bank, but rain had begun to fall, and they decided to wait till it should cease. By five o'clock the rain had stopped, and Rawson, with a constable and several of his neighbours, set out, guided by the men who had brought the news. They found the body at the bottom of the ditch resting in a crooked position; "the left hand under the head upon the bottom of the ditch; the right hand a little stretched out, and touching the bank on the right side; the knees touching the bottom of the ditch, and the feet not touching the ground, but resting upon the brambles": through the body, which hung transversely, a sword had been driven with such force that its point had pierced the back and protruded for the length of two hand-breadths. In the ditch lay the dead man's hat and periwig. The constable called the company to notice particularly the details of the situation. They then hoisted the corpse out of the ditch, and to facilitate the carriage withdrew the sword; it was "somewhat hard in the drawing, and crashed upon the bone in the plucking of it forth." The body was set upon two watchmen's staves and carried to the Whitehouse Inn, where it was placed upon a table. As they came into the light the men recognised, what they had already guessed, that the dead man was Sir Edmund Berry Godfrey. A note of the articles found was taken. Besides those brought from the bank and the ditch, a large sum of money was found in the pockets.[158] On the fingers were three rings. Leaving two watchmen to guard the body, the constable and half a dozen others rode off to Hartshorn Lane. There they found Godfrey's brothers and his brother-in-law, Mr. Plucknet. Towards ten o'clock at night the constable returned to the inn with Plucknet, who formally identified the body. Rawson and Brown, the constable, then took him to view the place where it had been found, by the light of a lantern. The same night the brothers Godfrey sent to Whitehall to notify what had passed, and a warrant was issued for the summons of a jury to take the inquest.[159]

On the following morning a jury of eighteen men and Mr. Cooper, coroner of Middlesex, met at the Whitehouse. At the instance of some officious tradesmen the coroner of Westminster offered his services also, but they were properly refused.[160] The jury sat all day, and as the evidence was unfinished, adjourned in the evening. On Saturday, October 19, the inquest was continued at the Rose and Crown in St. Giles' in the Fields, and late at night the verdict was returned: "That certain persons to the jurors unknown, a certain piece of linen cloth of no value, about the neck of Sir Edmundbury Godfrey, then and there, feloniously, wilfully, and of their malice aforethought, did tie and fasten; and therewith the said Sir Edmundbury Godfrey, feloniously, wilfully, and of their malice aforethought, did suffocate and strangle, of which suffocation and strangling he, the said Sir Edmundbury Godfrey, then and there instantly died."[161] Stripped of its cumbrous verbiage the jury gave a verdict of murder by strangling against some person or persons unknown. They were determined in this chiefly by the medical evidence.[162] Testimony was given at great length on the position and appearance of the corpse in the ditch. A number of people had examined the body and the spot where it was found. Five surgeons and two of the king's apothecaries formed professional opinions on the subject. At the inquest only two of the surgeons gave evidence, but the testimony of the others, taken at a later date, entirely supported their judgment. To points of fact there was no lack of witnesses.

Godfrey's movements were traced to one o'clock on the afternoon of Saturday, October 12. At nine o'clock in the morning one of the jurymen had seen him talking to a milk-woman near Paddington; at eleven another had seen him returning from Paddington to London; at one Radcliffe, an oilman, had seen him pass his house in the Strand, near Charing Cross.[163] It was proved that on Tuesday there had been nothing in the ditch where Godfrey's corpse was found two days later.[164] Further evidence of this was given at the trial of Thompson, Pain, and Farwell in 1682 for a libel "importing that Sir Edmund Bury Godfrey murdered himself," Mr. Robert Forset was then subpœnaed to appear as a witness, but was not called. He deposed before the Lord Mayor that on Tuesday, October 15, 1678 he had hunted a pack of harriers over the field where the body was found, and that his friend Mr. Harwood, lately deceased, had on the next day hunted the hounds over the same place and along the ditch itself; on neither occasion was anything to be seen of cane, gloves, or corpse.[165] An examination of the body revealed remarkable peculiarities. From the neck to the top of the stomach the flesh was much bruised, and seemed to have been stamped with a man's feet or beaten with some blunt weapon.[166] Below the left ear was a contused swelling, as if a hard knot had been tied underneath. Round the neck was a mark indented in the flesh, merging above and below into thick purple creases. The mark was not visible until the collar had been unbuttoned. The surgeons' opinion was unanimous to the effect that it had been caused by a cloth or handkerchief tightly tied, and that the collar had been fastened over it.[167] The neck was dislocated.[168] The body was lissom, and in spots on the face and the bruised part of the chest showed signs of putrefaction. Two wounds had been inflicted on the breast. One pierced as far as a rib, by which the sword had been stopped. From the other, which was under the left breast, the sword had been extracted by the constable; it had been driven through the cavity of the heart and had transfixed the body.[169] These facts were suggestive, but the point which deservedly attracted most attention was the striking absence of blood from the clothes of the dead man and the place where his corpse had been found. In spite of the rain the ditch, which was thickly protected by brambles and bushes, was dry, and would certainly have shewn marks of blood if any had been there. The evidence is positive that there was none. Brown, the constable, Rawson, and Mr. Plucknet examined the spot with lanterns on the night of Thursday, October 17. Early the next morning the ditch was searched by several other persons. At no time did it contain traces of any blood whatever. A few yards to the side of the ditch the grass was stained with blood and serum which had oozed from the wound in the back after the withdrawal of the sword. Some stumps, over which the men carrying the body to the inn had stumbled, were stained in the same way. As they had entered the house the body had been jerked against the doorpost; similar marks were found there; and when it was set on the table there was a further effusion of blood and serum which dripped upon the floor of the inn parlour. With the exception of the part of the shirt which covered the wound at the back, the clothes of the dead man were without any stain of blood.[170] The importance of this is obvious. A sword driven through the living heart must produce a great discharge of blood. The clothes of a man thus killed would be saturated with blood. The ground on which he lay would be covered with it. Only in one case would this not happen. If the sword plugged the orifice of the wound in such a way as wholly to stop the flow of blood from it, the quantity which escaped would be inconsiderable. In the case of Sir Edmund Godfrey this could not have taken place. L'Estrange says: "The sword stopped the fore part of the wound, as tight as a tap."[171] But the only manner in which he could suggest that Godfrey committed suicide was by resting his sword on the edge of the bank beyond the ditch and falling forward on it.[172] It is impossible to believe that if he had killed himself in this manner the sword should not have been disturbed or twisted by his fall. As he fell, it must have been violently wrenched, the wound would have been torn, and the ensuing rush of blood have flooded the ditch and his body lying in it.[173] Apart from L'Estrange's bare word, there is no reason to believe that the wound was plugged by the blade of the sword. This would have been in itself a remarkable circumstance; and the fact that there is no evidence to the point, when every other detail was so carefully noted, raises a presumption that the statement was untrue. Even if it had been the case, the second wound would still afford matter for consideration. It would be sufficiently strange that a man wishing to end his life should bethink himself of falling on his sword only after bungling over the easier way of suicide by stabbing himself. But it is hardly credible that a considerable flesh wound should be made and the weapon withdrawn from it without some flow of blood resulting; and there was no blood at all on the front of Godfrey's body or on the clothes covering the two wounds. The surgeons and the jury who trusted them were perfectly right in their conclusion. There can be no substantial doubt that the wounds found on Godfrey's body were not the cause of his death, but were inflicted at some time after the event. As a dead man cannot be supposed to thrust a sword through his own corpse, he had certainly been murdered. When this point was reached, the nature of his end was evident. The neck was dislocated and showed signs of strangulation. Clearly the magistrate had been throttled in a violent struggle, during which his neck was broken and his body hideously bruised. The clerk proved that when his master went out on the morning of October 12 "he had then a laced band about his neck." When the body was found, this had disappeared. Presumably it was with this that the act had been accomplished.

That the murder was not for vulgar ends of robbery was proved by the valuables found upon the body. Another fact of importance which came to light at the inquest shewed as clearly that it was dictated by some deeper motive. The lanes leading to the fields surrounding Primrose Hill were deep and miry. If Godfrey had walked thither to commit suicide, his shoes would have told a tale of the ground over which he had come. When his body was found the shoes were clean.[174] Upon this was based the conclusion that Godfrey had not walked to Primrose Hill on that day at all. It was clear that he had been murdered in some other place, that the murderers had then conveyed his body to Primrose Hill, had transfixed it with his sword, and thrown it into the ditch, that the dead man might seem to have taken his own life.

The result of the inquest was confirmed by what passed some years later. In the course of the year 1681 a series of letters were published in the *Loyal Protestant Intelligencer*, purporting to prove that Sir Edmund Godfrey had committed suicide. Thompson, Pain, and Farwell, the publisher and authors of the letters, were tried before Chief Justice Pemberton on June 20, 1682 for libel and misdemeanour. The accused attempted to justify their action, but the witnesses whom they called gave evidence which only established still more firmly the facts elicited at the inquest. Belief in the Popish Plot was at this time on the wane throughout the country, and at court was almost a sign of disloyalty. The men were tried in the fairest manner possible, and upon full evidence were convicted. Thompson and Farwell were pilloried and fined £100 each, and Pain, whose share in the business had been less than theirs, escaped with a fine.[175] None but those who were willing to accept L'Estrange's bad testimony, assertions, and insinuations could refrain from believing that Godfrey's death was a cold-blooded murder. Even some who would have been glad to credit his suicide were convinced. The king certainly could not be suspected of a desire to establish belief in the murder. When news of the discovery of the body first reached him, he thought that Godfrey had killed himself.[176] But when Dr. Lloyd, who went with Burnet to view the body at the Whitehouse Inn, brought word of what they had seen, Charles was, to outward appearance at all events, convinced that this could not have been the case. He was open enough in his raillery at the witnesses of the plot, but he never used his witty tongue to turn Godfrey's murder into a suicide.[177]

The rumours which had before connected the magistrate's disappearance with the Roman Catholics were now redoubled in vigour.[178] Conviction of their truth became general. The Whig party under the lead of Shaftesbury boomed the case. Portrait medals of Godfrey were struck representing the Pope as directing his murder. Ballads were composed in Godfrey's memory. Sermons were preached on the subject. Dr. Stillingfleet's effusion ran into two editions in as many days, and ten thousand copies were sold in less than a month.[179] An enterprising cutler made a special "Godfrey" dagger and sold three thousand in one day. On one side of the blade was graven: Remember the murder of Edmond Bury Godfrey; on the other: Remember religion. One, ornamented with a gilt handle, was sent to the Duke of York. Ladies of high degree carried these daggers about their persons and slept with them beneath their pillows, to guard themselves from a similar doom. Others as timid followed the lead of the Countess of Shaftesbury, who had a set of pocket pistols made for her muff.[180] The corpse of the murdered magistrate was brought to London in state, and lay exposed in the street for two days. A continual procession of people who came to gaze on the sight passed up and down. Few who came departed without rage, terror, and revenge rooted in their hearts. On October 31 the body was borne to burial at St. Martin's in the Fields. Seventy-two clergymen walked before; above a thousand persons of distinction followed after. The church was crowded. Dr. Lloyd, afterwards Dean of Bangor and Bishop of St. Asaph, himself a friend of Godfrey, preached a funeral sermon from the text: "Died Abner as a fool dieth?" It consisted of an elaborate eulogy of the dead man and an inflammatory attack upon the Roman Catholics. To crown the theatrical pomp of this parade, there mounted the pulpit beside the preacher two able-bodied divines, to guard his life from the attack which it was confidently expected would be made. "A most portentous spectacle, sure," exclaims North. "Three parsons in one pulpit! Enough of itself, on a less occasion, to excite terror in the audience."[181] There was one thing still lacking. As yet no evidence had appeared to connect any one with the crime. On October 21 a committee of secrecy was appointed by the House of Commons to inquire into the Popish Plot and the murder of Sir Edmund Berry Godfrey. On the 23rd a similar committee was established by the House of Lords.[182]

The secretaries of state and the privy council were already overwhelmed with work which the investigation of the plot had thrown upon their shoulders. For ten days the committees laboured at the inquiry, and examined some dozens of witnesses without drawing nearer to the desired end. Nothing appeared to throw light upon the subject. Every clue which was taken up vanished in a haze of rumour and uncertainty. There seemed every probability that the murderers would escape detection. But information was soon to be forthcoming to shed a ray of light upon the scene.

CHAPTER II

BEDLOE AND ATKINS

ON October 20 a proclamation was published offering a pardon and the reward of £500 to any one whose evidence should lead to the apprehension and conviction of the murderers. Four days later a second proclamation was issued containing in addition to these a promise of protection to the discoverer of the culprits. It is easy to point out that this course offered temptations to perjury and to sneer at the motives of the government, but it must be remembered that in the days when the police were a force of the future it was only by obtaining an accomplice in the crime to give evidence that criminals could in many cases be brought to justice. The proclamations took effect. At five o'clock in the afternoon of Friday, November 1, Samuel Atkins was arrested at the offices of the Admiralty in Derby House for being concerned in the murder of Sir Edmund Godfrey. Atkins was clerk to Samuel Pepys, the secretary of the navy board. He was arrested on the evidence of a certain Captain Charles Atkins. The two men were not related by blood, but were acquaintances, and "for name-sake have been called cousins." Captain Atkins had laid information before Henry Coventry on October 27.[183] Three days later he made the same relation to the privy council, and on Friday, November 1, swore to his statement before Sir Philip Howard, justice of the peace for the county of Middlesex. He deposed: "That in Derby-house, being in discourse with Samuel Atkins (clerk of Mr. Pepys, secretary of the Admiralty), the said Samuel did say that Sir Edmundbury Godfrey had very much vilified his master, and that if he lived long would be the ruin of him; upon which the said Samuel did ask this examinant whether he did think Child to be a man of courage and secrecy; to which this examinant did reply that the said Child had been at sea, and had behaved himself very well, as he had been informed; upon which the said Samuel bid this examinant send the said Child to his master, Mr. Pepys, but not to him the said Samuel, for that he would not be seen to know anything of it. This examinant did endeavour to find out the said Child, but did not meet with him till the day after the discourse had happened between him and Samuel Atkins, at the Three Tobacco Pipes in Holborn, where this examinant did tell Child that Secretary Pepys would speak with him; and the next time that this examinant did see the said Child (after he had given him that direction) he, the said Child, did endeavour to engage the said examinant to join him in the murder of a man."[184] The quarrel between Pepys and Godfrey, he said further, was occasioned by the discovery of the Popish Plot.[185]

Samuel Atkins was immediately carried before the committee of inquiry of the House of Lords. The conduct of the committee reflected anything but credit upon its members. An account of the proceedings in his case was afterwards drawn up by Atkins for Mr. Pepys.[186] In the course of them he had been subjected to great annoyance and ill-treatment; he had been imprisoned for a considerable length of time, and had been tried for his life. Every motive was present to induce him to be unfair towards the instigators of his prosecution. Even if he were perfectly honest in drawing up his account, it could hardly be an accurate relation of what took place. The careful literary form in which it is written shows that he arranged it elaborately and revised it often. Since his papers were twice taken from him in prison, he must have composed it afterwards from memory.[187] But after full allowance is made for this, the statement probably represents with considerable truth what took place. It was not written for publication as a controversial pamphlet, but for Pepys' private information. Atkins was likely therefore to attempt as far as possible to tell the truth. Moreover the conclusions to be drawn from it are supported by a consideration of the evidence produced in the case and the trial in which it ended.[188]

Atkins indignantly denied the whole story. He was several times called before the committee, and received considerable attention from the Earl of Shaftesbury himself, its most prominent member. Noble lords and reverend bishops alternately coaxed him to confess and threatened him with the awful consequences of a refusal. Plain hints were given to him that both he and his master must certainly be papists, and that he had only to admit their complicity in Godfrey's murder to gain liberty, pardon, and prosperity. In the intervals he was remanded to Newgate to reflect upon the best means of getting out of it. Before he knew what reception his revelations would find with the parties, Oates had taken care to exonerate the Duke of York from all concern in the plot. It would be a fine stroke for Shaftesbury, with whose schemes this did not at all accord, if he could implicate the duke in the murder. If only Atkins could be brought to accuse Pepys, the duke, under whom he had worked for many years at the Admiralty, would offer an easy mark.

That this was Shaftesbury's real object can hardly be doubted. Captain Atkins was known to be a person of disreputable character, and gave his evidence in the most suspicious manner.[189] When the man Child was produced he did not know Samuel Atkins by sight, and was unable to say anything about the matter.[190] The captain was treated by the committee with consideration. Although some show was made of pressing him in examination on his statements, the pressure was removed as soon as it appeared that his embarrassment was likely to lead to awkward consequences to his patrons.[191] He was sent to interview his namesake in

Newgate in the hope of extorting admissions in the course of conversation, and seemed to have been posted with fresh charges against Pepys and the Duke. He was evidently prepared to spice and expand his evidence in this direction whenever it seemed desirable.[192] But before the time arrived for this, a new witness appeared upon the scene.

On Wednesday, October 30, a man named William Bedloe wrote from Bristol to Henry Coventry, secretary of state, signifying that he had information to give concerning the murder of Sir Edmund Godfrey, and desiring aid and protection in coming to London. The next day he wrote in a similar strain to Secretary Sir Joseph Williamson. Both the secretaries answered him. To make sure that he should not think better of his project and escape, Williamson wrote to the mayor of Bristol enclosing a communication for Bedloe, while Coventry addressed his reply to Bedloe and enclosed a letter to the mayor with orders to give whatever assistance might be necessary.[193] Bedloe gave himself up forthwith to the mayor and was sent post-haste to town. On November 7 he made a deposition before the council and was examined in the presence of the king; on the 8th he was examined by the Lords' committee and made a statement at the bar of the House.[194] It has constantly been said that at his first examination Bedloe denied all knowledge of the Popish Plot, and after professing to speak only to Godfrey's murder, the next day expanded his information to embrace more general topics; and it is told that the king on hearing this exclaimed, "Surely this man has received a new lesson during the last twenty-four hours.[195]" The story is a mere fiction. In his first deposition he "acquainted the Lords that he had several things to communicate to them which related to the plot, and that he was able to confirm several passages which Mr. Oates had discovered concerning the plot."[196] Examined on this, he gave a long account of the military operations to be taken by the Roman Catholics; Chepstow Castle was to be surrendered to Lord Powis, who was to command an army of twenty thousand "religious men" shipped from Spain; a similar number were to sail from Flanders to join Lord Bellasis at Bridlington Bay. He had known this for four years, and had been employed by the Jesuits in London to carry letters to Douay, Paris, and Madrid.[197] As far as Bedloe's character is concerned the matter is immaterial, for another lie from his mouth would scarcely add weight to the scale of his perjury; but it is important not to exaggerate the folly and credulity of the government, and here at least it has been maligned. This was little more than a support for Oates' story in general. The more remarkable part of Bedloe's information dealt with the murder of Sir Edmund Godfrey. All that need be extracted from it at this point is his evidence against Atkins. Godfrey, he swore, had been murdered on Saturday, October 12, in Somerset House, the queen's palace. He was himself to have been one of the party to do the deed, but failed to come at the right time. Soon after nine o'clock on Monday night he had been taken by one of the murderers to see the dead body in the room where it had been laid. There, in a small company, he saw by the light of a dark lantern, standing near the corpse, two men "who owned themselves, the one to be Lord Bellasis' servant, and the other to be Mr. Atkins, Pepys' clerk."[198] The account which was communicated to the Lords concludes: "The same time Mr. Atkins being called in before Mr. Bedloe, Mr. Bedloe saith that he is in all things very like the person he saw in the room with Sir Edmundbury Godfrey's dead body; and he doth verily believe it was him that owned himself to be Pepys' clerk; but because he never saw him before that time, he cannot positively swear it, but he doth verily believe him to be that man."[199] According to Atkins' own account Bedloe's charge against him at this meeting was still more vague. Bedloe was asked if he knew the accused. Turning to Atkins he said, "I believe, Sir, I have seen you somewhere, I think, but I cannot tell where; I don't indeed remember your face." "Is this the man, Mr. Bedloe?" asked the Duke of Buckingham. "My Lord," returned the informer, "I can't swear this is he; 'twas a young man, and he told me his name was Atkins, a clerk, belonging to Derby House; but I cannot swear this is the same person."[200]

Bedloe was a man of evil character. He had been in the service of Lord Bellasis, and had subsequently held a commission as lieutenant in a foot company in Flanders.[201] He was of a type not uncommon in the seventeenth century, one of the vast crowd who lived a roving life of poverty and dishonesty, travelling from one country to another, in many services and under many names, living upon their own wits and other people's money, men for whom no falsehood was too black, no crime too gross to be turned to profit, men without truth, without shame, without fear of God or man. Bedloe was afterwards known to be notorious throughout Europe. He had been imprisoned in Spain for obtaining money under false pretences. He had been imprisoned in the Marshalsea for debt. He had been sentenced to death for robbery in Normandy, but had escaped from prison. When the agitation of the Popish Plot broke out he had only lately been released from Newgate. He had passed himself off on the continent as a nobleman, and had swindled his way from Dunkirk to Madrid. In Flanders his name was Lord Newport, in France he called himself Lord Cornwallis, in Spain Lord Gerard.[202] When he was examined before the House of Lords he denied without reservation that he knew Titus Oates.[203] The government made inquiries behind his back. His mother, his sister, and a friend were examined by the Bishop of Llandaff on Bedloe's behaviour between November 2 and 5, when he had stayed at his mother's house at Chepstow. It appeared that he had discoursed to them about the plot, and had announced his intention of discovering the murderers of Godfrey; but he also told them that he had known Oates intimately when they were together in Spain.[204] This might have led to unfortunate consequences. Bedloe attempted to recover the slip by saying that he had known Oates personally, but not by that name, since at Valladolid he had called himself Ambrose. Oates supported him by the statement that he had been acquainted with Bedloe in Spain under the name of Williams.[205] The recovery was not sufficient, for Bedloe had told his family that he had known Oates by the same name; but the unsystematic method of examination came to the informer's aid, and the fact passed at the time unnoticed. His denial of Oates' name and recognition of his person took place before the House of Lords, while the facts which proved his perjury in this only came to the notice of the privy council. When examinations of the same persons on the same or different points might be conducted by the secretaries of state, by the privy council, at the bar of the House of Lords, at the bar of the House of Commons, or before the secret committee of either one house or the other, and when it was the business of nobody to dissect and digest the results of this mass of raw evidence, it can hardly be a matter of surprise that contradictions went undetected and lying statements unrebuked.

In spite of this false step Bedloe was a man of some ingenuity and even moderation. In his evidence against Atkins he had left the way open to advance, if possible, and charge Pepys' clerk more fully with being implicated in the murder, or to retreat, if necessary, and protest with a profusion of sincerity that he had been hoaxed. He was far too careful to run the risk of definitely accusing any one with having been in a certain place at a certain time until he was sure that his reputation would not be ruined by running upon an alibi. The tactics which he employed were justified by their success. After the examination of Friday, November 8, Atkins was sent back to Newgate and heavily ironed. On the following Monday Captain Atkins was again sent to him in prison and exhorted him to be cheerful and confess his guilt. This interview was the prelude to a visit on the next day from four members of the House of Commons, headed by Sacheverell and Birch. They went over the whole case to the prisoner, pointed out the extreme danger in which he was situated, urged him with every argument to confess, and declared that his refusal would be held to aggravate the crime of the murder. Atkins remained obdurate, and the four left him with serious countenances, Sacheverell saying as he went away that the prisoner was "one of the most ingenious men to say nothing" whom he had ever met.[206] Since nothing was to be gained in this fashion it was determined to bring Atkins to trial. The date seems to have been fixed for Wednesday, November 20, the day before the conviction of Staley. When the day came the case was postponed. Atkins remained in Newgate, and was allowed pen, ink, and paper to compose his defence. The fact was that the committee had received intelligence that Atkins could produce good evidence of an alibi for the evening of October 14, the only point at which the evidence of Bedloe touched him. He had in the meantime by the help of his friends collected witnesses, and the crown was unable to face the trial without knowing what statements they would make. When Atkins had committed enough to writing, his papers were seized, and gave to the prosecution detailed information on the subject.[207] On December 13 his witnesses were summoned before the committee of the House of Lords. They proved to be Captain Vittells of the yacht *Catherine* and five of his men. They were examined at length. On Monday, October 14, Atkins had sent word to Captain Vittells that he would bring two gentlewomen, his friends, to see the yacht. At half-past four o'clock in the afternoon they appeared at Greenwich, where the vessel lay, and came aboard. The captain took them to his cabin, and they drank a glass of wine. The wine was good, the company pleasant, and they stayed drinking till seven o'clock. Atkins then sent away his boat and returned to supper. After supper they drank again, and the gentlemen toasted the ladies, and the ladies toasted the gentlemen, till night had fallen and the clock pointed to half-past ten. By this time they were all, said the captain, pretty fresh, and Mr. Atkins very much fuddled. Captain Vittells put his guests, with a Dutch cheese and half a dozen bottles of wine as a parting gift, into a boat belonging to the yacht and sent them to land. The tide flowed so strongly that the men rowing the wherry could not make London Bridge, but set Atkins and the two ladies ashore at Billingsgate at half-past eleven o'clock, and assisted them into a coach. "Atkins," said one of the sailors, "was much in drink, and slept most of the way up."[208] He must have blessed the fate that led him to joviality and intoxication on that evening. It was obvious that he could not have been soberly watching Sir Edmund Godfrey's corpse at Somerset House when he was at the time named by Bedloe, and for two hours after, first hilarious and then somnolent at Greenwich. The evidence was unimpeachable. The only fact revealed by a somewhat sharp examination was that some of the sailors had signed a paper for the information of Mr. Pepys stating at what time they had left Atkins. One of them admitted that he could not read, but added immediately that he was a Protestant. In the seventeenth century sound religious principles covered a want of many letters.

At this point the case rested. A true bill had already been found against Atkins by the grand jury, but it was not until Tuesday, February 11, 1679 that he could obtain a trial.[209] Important developments had in the meantime taken place, and Atkins was no longer the game at which the plot-hunters drove. On the day before he was brought to the bar three men were convicted of the same murder for which he was indicted on two counts, both as principal and as accessory. The former of these was now dropped, and Atkins was tried only as an accessory to the murder of Sir Edmund Godfrey. The centre of interest in the case had moved away from him and

Mr. Pepys and the Duke of York, and the same evidence originally preferred against him was produced in court without addition. The case for the prosecution was lamentably weak. Captain Atkins swore to his previous story at greater length, but without any new statement of importance.[210] Bedloe followed with the story of the man who gave his name as Atkins at the meeting over Godfrey's corpse; but whereas he had formerly seemed willing to recognise Atkins without much difficulty, he now professed himself entirely unable to swear to his identity. "There was a very little light," he said, "and the man was one I was not acquainted with.... So that it is hard for me to swear that this is he. And now I am upon one gentleman's life, I would not be guilty of a falsehood to take away another's. I do not remember that he was such a person as the prisoner is; as far as I can remember he had a more manly face than he hath, and a beard."[211] The crown evidence was so feeble that it was never even proposed to call the man Child. An attempt was made to show that Atkins was a Roman Catholic, but failed ignominiously.[212] The prisoner called Captain Vittells and one of his men, who proved an alibi in the most decisive manner; the Attorney-General threw up his case, and the jury without leaving the bar returned a verdict of not guilty.[213] Sir William Jones was anxious that no one should go away with the opinion that the king's evidence had been disproved. The Lord Chief Justice supported him. He pointed out that Bedloe had not been contradicted, and that every one who appeared at the trial might speak the truth and the prisoner yet be perfectly innocent.[214] What he did not say, and what neither he nor many others thought, was that Bedloe might equally be telling the grossest falsehoods.

CHAPTER III

BEDLOE AND PRANCE

THE change in the situation had been caused by the appearance of a witness whose evidence about the murder was of the greatest weight, and whose position in the intrigues of the Popish Plot has always been of some obscurity. Bedloe's information was already of a startling character. It was as follows. Early in October he had been offered by two Jesuits, Walsh and Le Fevre, the sum of £4000 to assist in killing a man "that was a great obstacle to their designs." He gave his word that he would do so, but when on Friday, October 11, Le Fevre told him to be ready at four o'clock the next day to do the business, he became nervous and failed to be at the place of meeting. On Sunday he met Le Fevre by accident in Fleet Street, and by appointment joined him between 8 and 9 o'clock P.M. the next day in the court of Somerset House. Le Fevre told Bedloe that the man whom he had been engaged to kill was dead and his corpse lying in the building at that moment. Bedloe was taken into a small room to see the body. Besides himself and Le Fevre there were also present Walsh, the man who called himself Atkins, a gentleman in the household of Lord Bellasis, and a person whom he took to be one of the attendants in the queen's chapel. A cloth was thrown off the body, and by the light of a dark lantern he recognised the features of Sir Edmund Berry Godfrey. It was agreed to carry the corpse to Clarendon House, and to take it thence by coach to the fields at the foot of Primrose Hill. Bedloe promised to return at eleven o'clock to assist, but went away intending to meddle with the business no more. The next day he happened to meet Le Fevre in Lincoln's Inn Fields. Le Fevre began to rebuke him for breaking his word. Bedloe answered that he had been unwilling to come because he had recognised the dead man. Le Fevre bound him to secrecy and then proceeded to tell him how the murder had been committed. Under pretence of making a further discovery of the plot, the two Jesuits and Lord Bellasis' gentleman had persuaded Godfrey to come into Somerset House with him. They then set upon him and with two others dragged him into a room in the corner of the court. A pistol was held to his head and he was threatened with death unless he would surrender the examinations which he had taken concerning the plot. If they could obtain these, said Le Fevre, fresh examinations would have to be taken, the originals could then be produced, and the contradictions which would certainly appear between the two would exonerate the plotters and convict the informers of falsehood in the eyes of the world. Godfrey refused, saying that he had sent the papers to Whitehall. Upon this they seized him, held a pillow over the face until he was nearly stifled, and then strangled him with a long cravat. On Monday night, after Bedloe had gone away, the murderers carried the body out into the fields and placed it where it was found with the sword run through it.[215]

Bedloe's evidence varied greatly on points of detail. The amount of the reward which he was offered varied from two guineas to four thousand pounds; the time at which Godfrey was killed from two o'clock to five; the day on which his corpse was removed from Monday to Wednesday. Sometimes he was stifled with one, at others with two pillows. Once Bedloe said that the body was placed in the room where the Duke of Albemarle lay in state, while according to another statement it was hidden in the queen's chapel. When his evidence was heard in court, a multitude of further alterations was introduced. In all the different versions of his story however there appeared with but little variation the statement that Godfrey had been murdered in Somerset House in the course of the afternoon on Saturday, October 12, by the means or at the direction of three Jesuits, Walsh, Pritchard, and Le Fevre, and that on the night of the following Monday he had seen the body lying in Somerset House in the presence of these three, and of a man whom he thought to be a waiter in the queen's chapel.

Of all those mentioned only one fish had been netted, and it was certain that even he could not be brought to land. At the trial of Atkins the Attorney-General darkly hinted that had it not been for the conviction on the previous day, the prisoner would have been indicted as a principal in Godfrey's murder, and would probably have been condemned.[216] But it may be doubted that this was more than a piece of bravado. The evidence of Captain Atkins was worth nothing; that of Bedloe little more. If the informers had expanded and defined their information to an extent unparalleled even in the history of the Popish Plot, where such things were not rare, it would hardly have produced much effect. The evidence produced for Atkins' alibi was too strong to be seriously shaken. By the middle of November the investigation into the murder had thus come to a halt. Proclamations were out for the rest of the men accused by Bedloe, but there seemed to be every probability that they would escape. If Atkins were brought to trial and acquitted, consequences which would be serious to the policy of the Whigs on the committees of secrecy might ensue. Consequences almost as serious were to be expected in the event of his being released without a trial. In either one case or the other the failure to obtain a conviction for the murder of Godfrey would be damaging to their cause. They had staked much on the cards, and it seemed as if the game was going against them. Unless fortune came to their aid, the murder of which there had been so much talk would go unpunished, and the sensation which it created would die down.

Meanwhile the public mind was occupied on other points. The trials of Staley, Coleman, and Ireland for high treason filled the greater part of one excited month.[217] Almost till Christmas the great murder case made no progress. Just then, when it must have seemed less than likely after the lapse of eight weeks and after the only hopeful trail had disappeared that any substantial advance should be gained, an extraordinary incident occurred. There was living in Covent Garden a Roman Catholic silversmith, by name Miles Prance, who did a fair business with those of his own religion and was occasionally employed by the queen. He was a friend of the Jesuits who had been imprisoned on account of the plot and, being in liquor one day at a tavern, had declared loudly "that they were very honest men." Suspicion was aroused, and on inquiry it was found that he had slept away from his house for three nights about the time of Godfrey's disappearance. In point of fact this had been before the date of the murder, and Prance's subsequent connection with the case was due to this initial mistake. His landlord laid information, and on Saturday, December 21, Prance was arrested for being concerned in Godfrey's murder. He was taken into the lobby of the House of Commons and was there waiting until the committee was ready to examine him, when Bedloe happened to pass through. His eye fell upon Prance and he cried out without hesitation, "This is one of the rogues that I saw with a dark lantern about the body of Sir Edmond Bury Godfrey, but he was then in a periwig."[218] Prance was taken before the committee of the House of Lords and strictly examined. He denied knowing Walsh, Pritchard, or Le Fevre. He denied that he was guilty of Sir Edmund Godfrey's death and that he had assisted in removing his body. When he spoke of Fenwick and Ireland in the coffee-house he was drunk. He had not worn a periwig once in the last ten years, but he owned one at home which had been made twelve months since from his wife's hair. He had not been to the queen's chapel at Somerset House once a month. After denying that he had received money from Grove, he confessed that Grove had paid him for some work. He first denied, but afterwards admitted that he had hired a horse to ride out of town. He had intended to leave London to escape the oaths administered to Roman Catholics, but had in the meantime been arrested.[219] Prance was committed a close prisoner to Newgate, and was lodged in the cell known as the condemned hole. There he remained during the nights of December 21 and 22. On the morning of Monday, December 23, he sent a message to the committee of inquiry offering on the assurance of pardon to confess. By order of the House of Lords the Duke of Buckingham and other noblemen were sent to Newgate with the promise of pardon and to take his examination.[220] At the same time the Commons ordered that the committee of secrecy or any three of them should examine Prance in prison, and acquaint his fellow-prisoners in Newgate with the king's assurance of pardon consequent on discoveries relating to the plot.[221] Prance confessed that he had been engaged in the murder and had much information to give on the subject. He was examined by the lords, and on the next day repeated his deposition before the privy council. At the beginning of October one Gerald, or Fitzgerald, an Irish priest belonging to the household of the Venetian ambassador, had approached him on the subject of putting out of the way a man whose name was not divulged. About a week later he learned that this was Sir Edmund Godfrey. Two other men were also concerned in the matter. Green, a cushion-layer in the chapel at Somerset House, and Laurence Hill, servant to Dr. Gauden, the treasurer of the queen's chapel. They told him that Godfrey was to be killed, "for that he was a great enemy to the queen or her servants, and that he had used some Irishmen ill." Lord Bellasis, said Gerald, had promised a reward. Prance consented to their proposals, the more readily because he had a private grudge against the magistrate. During the next week they watched for an opportunity to waylay Godfrey, and on Saturday, October 12, "did dodge him from his house that morning to all the places he went to until he came to his death."[222] The same day the king ordered the Duke of Monmouth and the Earl of Ossory to accompany Prance to Somerset House and examine him on the spot where he said that the murder had taken place. There he entered into a detailed account of the crime. At about nine o'clock at night[223] Godfrey was coming from St. Clement Danes down the Strand, followed by Hill, Green, and Gerald. Hill walked on ahead, and as Godfrey came opposite the water-gate of Somerset House begged him to come into the court and put an end to a quarrel between two men who were fighting. The magistrate turned in through the wicket, with Hill, Green, and Gerald following them. Prance, who was waiting inside, came to the gate to keep watch. The others went down the court until they came to a bench in the right-hand corner close to the stable-rails, where Berry, the porter of Somerset House, and an Irishman, whose name Prance did not know, were sitting. Green crept up close behind, and when they had reached the bench threw a large twisted handkerchief round Godfrey's neck and pulled it tight. The three other men set upon him and dragged him down into the corner behind the bench. Green knelt upon his chest and pounded it, and then wrung his neck round until it was broken. This, said Prance, Green had told him a quarter of an hour afterwards when he came down from the gate to see what had happened. The body was carried across the court, through a door in the left-hand corner, from which a flight of stairs led to a long gallery. From the gallery a door opened on to a flight of eight steps, leading into Hill's lodgings. In a small room to the right of the entrance the body was set on the floor, leaning against the bed.

There it remained for two days. On Monday night at nine or ten o'clock the same men removed the corpse to another part of Somerset House, "into some room towards the garden." As it lay there Prance was taken by Hill to see it. He could not say if he had seen Bedloe there, but Gerald and Green were present. Thence twenty-four hours later the body was taken back, first to a room near Hill's lodging, and on Wednesday evening to the same room in which it had been at first. At midnight Hill procured a sedan chair, and Godfrey's corpse was put inside. Berry opened the gate of the court, and Prance, Gerald, Green, and the Irishman carried the chair as far as the new Grecian Church in Soho. There Hill met them with a horse, upon which the body was set. Sitting behind the body. Hill rode off in company with Green and Gerald, and deposited it where it was found, having first transfixed it with the sword.

Having taken his examination, Monmouth and Ossory bade Prance guide them to the places he had mentioned. Without hesitation he led the way to the bench, and described with assurance the manner in which the murder had been committed. Then he shewed the room in which the body had first been laid, and conducted his examiners to every spot of which he had spoken with unerring direction. To this process there was one exception. Prance could not find the room in which he said the corpse had been placed on the night of Monday 14. The three passed up and down, into the corner of the piazza, down a flight of steps, up again, across the great court which lay towards the river, into and out of several rooms, but without success. The room could not be found. Finally Prance desisted from the search, "saying that he had never been there but that once, when Hill conveyed him thither with a dark lantern, but that it was some chamber towards the garden." Monmouth and Ossory returned to the council-chamber with the report of Prance's examination, upon which the council made a note, "that the said particulars were very consonant to what he had spoken at the board in the morning, before his going."[224] The council sat again in the afternoon. Green, Hill, and Berry were summoned. All denied with emphasis the charges which Prance had made against them, and denied that they knew Sir Edmund Godfrey. Green and Hill admitted knowing Father Gerald, and Green identified the Irishman mentioned by Prance as a priest named Kelly. In one point Hill confirmed Prance's evidence. While they had been in his lodgings that morning, Monmouth and Ossory had examined Mrs. Broadstreet, the housekeeper of his master, Dr. Gauden. She affirmed that Hill left the lodgings at Michaelmas to move into a house of his own in Stanhope Street. When Prance said she was mistaken, since Hill had not left his rooms in Somerset House until a fortnight after Michaelmas, Mrs. Broadstreet contradicted him angrily. Hill now declared that in the middle of October he had been busy making arrangements for the move; on the day of Godfrey's disappearance he was still occupied with his landlord in drawing up terms of agreement, and the agreement was not concluded until the Wednesday following.[225]

In addition to his evidence about Godfrey's murder, Prance made a statement concerning the plot. Fenwick, Ireland, and Grove, he said, had told him that "Lord Petre, Lord Bellasis, the Earl of Powis, and Lord Arundell were to command the army." As more decisive evidence had already been given against all these, his information was of little consequence. He also desired to be set at liberty, that he might be able to discover some persons connected with the plot whose names were unknown to him. The request was naturally refused, but Prance was removed from the dungeon and Hill was confined there in his place.[226] Within forty-eight hours from this time Prance had recanted his whole story. On the evening of Sunday, December 29, Captain Richardson, the keeper of Newgate, received an order of council to bring Prance before the Lords' committee for examination. Prance was in a state of great agitation and begged to be taken to see the king. Charles received him in the presence of Richardson and Chiffinch, his confidential valet. Prance fell upon his knees and declared that the whole of his evidence had been false, that he was innocent of the murder, and the men whom he had accused as far as he knew were innocent too. The next day he was taken before the council and persisted that he knew no more of Godfrey's murder than was known to the world. He was asked if any one had been tampering with him and answered, No. Hardly had he been taken back to Newgate when he begged Captain Richardson to return to the king and say that all his evidence had been true, and his recantation false.[227] From this he again departed and reaffirmed his recantation. He was heavily ironed and a second time imprisoned in the condemned hole. Here he remained until January 11, 1679, when to complete the cycle of his contradictions he once more retracted his recantation and declared that the whole of his original confession was true.

On February 10, 1679 Green, Berry, and Hill were brought to the bar of the Court of King's Bench to be tried upon an indictment for the murder of Sir Edmund Berry Godfrey. The prosecution began by evidence to shew that for some days before his disappearance Godfrey had been in a state of alarm. Oates swore that Godfrey had complained to him of the treatment he had received in consequence of having taken his deposition; on the one hand those who wished to accelerate the discovery of the plot had blamed him for not being sufficiently eager in its prosecution; those, on the other, who were endangered by Oates' revelations had threatened the magistrate for the action which he had taken. Godfrey told Oates that "he went in fear of his life by the popish party, and that he had been dogged several days." The testimony of Oates carries no greater weight on this than on any other occasion, but he was supported by another and a more respectable witness. Mr. Robinson, chief protonotary of the court of common pleas, gave evidence of Godfrey's disturbance of mind. The two had met on October 7, and Robinson questioned the magistrate about the depositions which he had taken. Godfrey replied that he wished that another had been in his place, for he would have small thanks for his pains; the bottom of the matter had not yet been reached, he said; and then, turning to Robinson, exclaimed, "Upon my conscience I believe I shall be the first martyr,"[228] This was the prelude by which the evidence of Prance and Bedloe was introduced. Bedloe retold the story to which he had treated the council, the committee, and the House of Lords. This time it differed in almost every point of detail from the statements which he had previously made. The Jesuits who tempted him into the murder had sent him about a week before to effect an acquaintance with Godfrey. There were several separate schemes on foot to dispatch the justice. After seeing the body upon Monday night he had gone away and never seen the murderers again. The Jesuits told him that Godfrey had been strangled, but how he did not know. His account of his many interviews with Le Fevre were hopelessly at variance with what he had said about them before.[229] But as the rules of legal procedure did not admit as evidence depositions and reports of testimony given elsewhere, it was impossible to convict the witness of these alterations. Bedloe's evidence too shewed striking points of difference from that of Prance, who preceded him, even after he had toned it into better accord. The prisoners, excited and ignorant, unused to sifting evidence and wholly unskilled in examining witnesses, failed altogether to detect and point out the discrepancies.

The evidence given by Prance was, on the contrary, remarkably consistent with the information which he had furnished on other occasions. He went through all the incidents which he had detailed first to the council and then on the spot to the Duke of Monmouth and the Earl of Ossory. He described each point with perfect decision and answered the questions put to him without hesitation. The only point on which he showed uncertainty was when he was asked to describe the room in which the body lay on the night of October 14. He said frankly, "I am not certain of the room, and so cannot describe it." In one particular alone did a statement vary from his previous evidence. He had told the council that on the morning of the fatal Saturday Green had called at Godfrey's house and inquired if he was at home.[230] Now he said that he could not be certain whether it was Green or Hill who went to Hartshorn Lane.[231] His motive in altering the distinct statement is not far to seek. Elizabeth Curtis, who had been maid at Godfrey's house, was called as a witness. She testified that on the morning of October 12 Hill came to see her master and had conversation with him for several minutes. He wore the same clothes, she said, in which he appeared in court; and Hill admitted that he had been dressed in the same way on that day. Green had come to Hartshorn Lane about a fortnight before to ask for Godfrey, but on the date of his disappearance Hill was there alone.[232] The suspicion is difficult to stifle that Prance had some knowledge of the evidence which the maid would give, and altered his own in order not to contradict it. When he afterwards published his *True Narrative and Discovery of several Remarkable Passages relating to the Horrid Popish Plot*, he simply stated in accordance with the evidence of Curtis that it was Hill who spoke with Godfrey on that morning.[233] In some other points Prance's evidence was supported by independent witnesses. He had spoken of meetings held by Gerald, Kelly, the prisoners, and himself at a tavern with the sign of the Plow, where he was enticed to be a party to the murder. The fact that they were frequenters of the Plow was proved by the landlord of the inn and his servant.[234] About a fortnight after the murder Prance had entertained a small party at the Queen's Head Inn at Bow. Gerald was there, and a priest named Leweson, and one Mr. Vernatt, who was described as being in service to Lord Bellasis. They were joined by a friend of Vernatt, named Dethick, and dined on flounders and a barrel of oysters. According to Prance's statement Vernatt should have been present at the murder, but as he had been prevented, Gerald furnished the company with an account of the manner in which it had been accomplished. While the talk ran thus, Prance heard a noise outside the door. Opening it suddenly, he caught the drawer eavesdropping and sent him off with threats of a kicking.[235] This was confirmed by the evidence of the drawer. He had listened at the door and heard Godfrey's name mentioned, and one of the party had threatened to kick him downstairs.[236] Several important witnesses were called for the defence. Mary Tilden, the niece of Dr. Gauden, and his housekeeper, Mrs. Broadstreet, gave evidence that Hill was at home on the evening of the murder and the following nights, when he was accused of being busy with the body, and that the corpse was never brought to their lodgings. The judges continually bullied and sneered at the witnesses. The room in which Prance said the body was laid was described by Sir Robert Southwell as "an extraordinary little place." Mrs. Broadstreet said that it was impossible for a corpse to be placed there without their knowledge. On this Mr. Justice Wild told her that it was very suspicious, and Dolben remarked, "It is well you are not indicted." The hostile attitude of the court was not mollified when it appeared that there was some confusion in the evidence of both witnesses. Mary Tilden stated that during the time when they were in town she had never been out of the lodgings after eight o'clock in the evening. "When were you out of town?" asked Mr. Justice Jones. "In October," the witness answered. The judge pointed out that October was just the month in question. Mistress Tilden said that she had made a mistake; she had meant to say that they were out of town in September. She said too that there was only one key to the door of the lodgings; but Prance declared, and was not contradicted, that in her examination before the Duke of Monmouth, Mrs. Broadstreet had admitted that there were several. The latter made the mistake of saying that Hill occupied the rooms until a fortnight after Michaelmas, whereas she had before sworn, as Sir Robert Southwell testified, that he left them in the first week in October.[237] The workman who had been employed at Hill's new house in Stanhope Street proved that he had been in Hill's company from nine to two in the afternoon of Saturday, October 12, and a neighbour that Hill had been at his house from five to seven o'clock on the same evening.[238] Green called for his defence his maid, his landlord, and the landlord's wife. The maid testified that Green was always at home before nine o'clock at night; James Warrier and his wife that he was within doors in their company till after ten o'clock on the night of October 12. Mrs. Warrier however made the mistake of saying that this was a fortnight after Michaelmas day, which it was not, and so raised a doubt that the evidence was directed to a time a week later than the date in question.[239] The most weighty evidence for the defence was produced by Berry in the persons of the sentries who had kept guard at the gate of Somerset House on the night of Wednesday, October 16. On that night Prance swore that Berry had opened the gate to let the sedan chair containing Godfrey's corpse pass out. From seven to ten o'clock Nicholas Trollop had kept guard, Nicholas Wright from ten to one, from one to four Gabriel Hasket. During the first watch a chair had been carried into Somerset House, but all three men were confident that none had been carried out. They were equally positive that at no time had they left the beat to drink at Berry's house or with any one else. If the gate had been opened and a sedan taken through, it would certainly have been seen by the soldier on duty. Berry's maid also testified that her master had come in that evening at dusk and had remained at home until he went to bed at midnight.[240] The only part of the evidence for the prisoners to which the Lord Chief Justice devoted attention in his summing up was the testimony of the sentries. He remarked to the jury that it was a dark night and that the soldier might not have seen the gate opened, or, having seen, might have forgotten, Scroggs went over the evidence of Bedloe briefly and of Prance at length, and delivered a harangue on the horrors of the Plot, of which Godfrey's murder, he said, was "a monstrous evidence." After a short deliberation the jury returned a verdict of guilty against all the prisoners. The Chief Justice declared if it were the last word he had to speak in this world he should have pronounced the same verdict, and the spectators in court met his announcement with a shout of applause.[241]

On February 11 Green, Berry, and Hill came up to receive sentence, and ten days later Green and Hill were hanged at Tyburn, denying their guilt to the last. Berry, who was distinguished from them by being a Protestant, was granted a week's respite. To the indignation of Protestant politicians he made no confession, and when he was executed on February 28, declaring his innocence to the end, a rumour was spread that the court party had gained him to a false conversion in order to give the Roman Catholics the chance of saying that he at least could not have lied in hope of salvation.[242] It was afterwards remembered that by an extraordinary coincidence Primrose Hill, at the foot of which Godfrey's body was found, had in former days borne the name of Greenberry Hill.[243]

CHAPTER IV

PRANCE AND BEDLOE

AT this point the atmosphere begins somewhat to clear. Two trials have been discussed, and the result is seen that the two chief witnesses at them were guilty of wilful perjury. Bedloe contradicted himself beyond belief. Although it was by no means clear at the time, the men convicted upon the evidence of Prance were certainly innocent. This has since been universally recognised. Yet the verdict against them was not perverse, and small blame attaches to the judges and jury who acted on the evidence of Prance. For all they knew he was speaking the truth. The witnesses for the defence were uncertain in points of time to which they spoke, and Prance was to a certain extent corroborated by independent evidence. On the case which came into court the conviction was certainly justifiable. It is now possible to see that the verdict was wrong. The motive which Prance alleged for the crime was weak in the extreme, and his subsequent conduct supports the fact of his perjury. Although an absolute alibi was not proved for any of the accused at the time of the murder, a considerable body of evidence came near the point, and an alibi was proved both for Green and for Hill at the time when Prance stated that each was engaged in dogging Sir Edmund Godfrey to his death. The sentries proved that the body had not been removed in the manner which Prance described. The evidence of the inmates of Hill's house proved that it had not been placed where Prance affirmed. Green, Berry, and Hill were wrongfully put to death.

From this point it is necessary to start upon the pursuit of the truth, and before starting it is well to take a view of the situation. Sir Edmund Berry Godfrey disappeared on Saturday, October 12. Five days later his body was found in a field near Primrose Hill. He had been murdered, and the crime was committed for some motive which was not that of robbery. He was murdered moreover not where his corpse was found, but in some other place from which it had afterwards been conveyed thither. Whoever was the criminal had placed the body in such a way that those who found it might attribute the magistrate's death to suicide. Two witnesses appeared to give evidence to the fact of the murder. These two were the only men who ever professed to have direct knowledge on the subject. They both accused innocent men, told elaborate falsehoods, and contradicted one another. Their stories were so unlike, and yet had so much in common, that the fact must be explained by supposing either that there was some truth in what they said, or that one swore falsely to support the perjury of the other. The relation between the two is the point to which attention must be devoted in order to trace the interaction of their motives and to determine whether both or neither or one and not the other knew anything about the murder of Sir Edmund Godfrey.

Nearly eight years after these events, in the second year of the reign of King James the Second, Miles Prance pleaded guilty to an indictment of wilful perjury for having sworn falsely at the trial of Green, Berry, and Hill.[244] Later, when L'Estrange was writing his work on *The Mystery of Sir E. B. Godfrey Unfolded,* Prance sent to him an account of the manner in which his evidence had been procured. He was, he said, wholly innocent and wholly ignorant of the murder. Before his arrest he knew no more of Godfrey, Bedloe, or any one else concerned than was known to the world at large. His arrest took place upon Saturday, December 21. During the nights of Saturday and Sunday he lay in irons in the dungeon in Newgate. Early on the Sunday morning he was disturbed by the entrance of a man, who, as Prance declared, laid a sheet of paper beside him and went out. Soon after another entered, set down a candle, and went out. By the light of the candle Prance read the paper; "wherein," says L'Estrange, "he found the substance of these following minutes. So many Popish lords to be mentioned by name; fifty thousand men to be raised; commissions given out; officers appointed. Ireland was acquainted with the design; and Bedloe's evidence against Godfrey was summed up and abstracted in it too. There were suggestions in it that Prance must undoubtedly be privy to the plot, with words to this purpose, you had better confess than be hanged." In the evening of the same day he was taken to Shaftesbury's house and examined by the earl. The Whig leader threatened him with hanging if he would not confess and acquiesce in what had been suggested to him in the paper. He could resist no longer, he said, "and so framed a pretended discovery in part, with a promise to speak out more at large if he might have his pardon." A paper containing this was given him to sign, and he was sent back to Newgate, where he made a formal confession the next day. Clearly, thought Prance, the men who came into his cell, and left instructions for the evidence which he was to give and a light by which to read them, had acted under orders from Shaftesbury.[245] This is what Prance and L'Estrange had to say about this first confession. Before examining it further it will be proper to consider Prance's condition between that time and the date when after numerous manœuvres he finally returned to it. On December 30 he appeared before the council and recanted his confession. For nine days there seems to have been no development. Prance lay in the dungeon and adhered to his last statement. But on January 8 Captain Richardson, the keeper of Newgate, and his servant, Charles Cooper, appeared before a committee of the privy council with information that Prance was feigning madness. When he was fettered he behaved the more sensibly. It was ordered accordingly that he should be kept in irons and that Dr. Lloyd, the

Dean of Bangor, should be asked to visit and converse with him.[246] On January 10 a similar order was given for the admittance of William Boyce, an old friend of Prance, to be with him in prison. Cooper passed two nights with the prisoner. His sleep was irregular, and he spent long periods raving and crying out that "it was not he murdered him, but they killed him." In spite of his wild talk Prance seemed to behave rather as if he wished to be thought mad than as if he actually were so; he ate heartily, used a bed and blankets which had been given him, and adjusted his dress with care.[247] Boyce also visited him, and found him sometimes reasonable, at others apparently out of his senses. Once he found him lying at full length on the boards of his cell and crying, "Guilty, guilty; not guilty, not guilty; no murder"; but when he first went to the prison Prance met him quietly and said, "Here am I in prison, and I am like to be hanged. I am falsely accused." Shaftesbury's threats had terrified him for the safety of his life, but he was anxious to learn that Green, Berry, and Hill had not been set at liberty, and in a conversation of January 11 told Boyce "that he would confess all if he were sure of his pardon."[248] On Friday, January 10, Dr. Lloyd visited Newgate and found Prance in a very wretched condition. The weather was intensely cold, and the prisoner suffered severely from it, despite the covering with which he had been provided. He was very weak and denied his guilt sullenly, but after a time begged Lloyd to come again the next day, when he would tell everything that he knew.[249] Accordingly on the evening of January 11 the dean returned, and Prance was brought to him by the hall fire. For some time he remained stupefied by the cold; he was without a pulse and seemed almost dead; but after warming himself at the fire threw off the lethargy and conversed with Lloyd briskly and with freedom. The dean reported to the council: "He appeared very well composed and in good humour, saying that he had confessed honestly before, and had not wronged any of those he had accused." He proceeded further to tell of a plot to murder the Earl of Shaftesbury, and said that a servant of Lord Arundel, one Messenger, had undertaken to kill the king. Lloyd warned him to be careful of speaking the truth; Prance protested that he would do nothing else. When he had finished his confession he asked to be lodged in a warmer room and to have the irons knocked off.[250] From that time onward he remained steadfast to his first confession. Writing many years later, when everybody connected with the Plot had fallen into discredit and Prance had pleaded guilty to the charge of perjury, Lloyd assured L'Estrange that he had never believed the informer's evidence. In this he was deceived by his after opinions, for at the time he told Burnet that it was impossible for him to doubt Prance's sincerity.[251] Lloyd did not escape the calumny which pursued every one who refused to be an uncompromising supporter of all the evidence offered in the investigation of the Plot. He expressed himself doubtful as to the guilt of Berry and thought that Prance might have made a mistake of identity. It was immediately said that Berry had made horrible confessions to him, and that he had been pressed at court not to divulge them.[252]

Prison life in the seventeenth century was hard. Prisoners were treated in a way that would now be considered shameful, and Prance did not escape his share of ill-treatment. He was kept in the cell reserved for felons and murderers. According to the general practice he was heavily ironed. Until his life was thought in danger he had nothing but the boards on which to lie. The greatest hardship arose from the cold, against which there was no real provision. But there is no evidence that Prance more hardly used than his fellow gaol-birds. A detestable attempt was afterwards made to prove that he had been tortured in prison to extract confessions from him. In the course of the year 1680 Mrs. Cellier, the Roman Catholic midwife of otherwise dubious reputation, published a pamphlet entitled "Malice Defeated; or a Brief Relation of the Accusation and Deliverance of Elizabeth Cellier." The work was an attack upon the prosecutors of the Popish Plot, conducted with all the coarse weapons of seventeenth-century controversy. Incidentally she called the crown witnesses "hangman's hounds for weekly pensions." On September 11 she was indicted for a malicious libel and tried before Baron Weston and the Lord Mayor. The libel lay in her open declaration that Prance was put on the rack in Newgate and that Francis Corral, who had been imprisoned on suspicion of complicity in Godfrey's murder, was subjected to intolerably ill treatment and active torture in Newgate in order to make him confess his guilt.[253] The charges which Mrs. Cellier made were not only outrageous but ridiculous, and were so improbable as not to deserve detailed discussion. Witnesses were called for the prosecution who proved their complete falsity, and Mrs. Cellier's counsel virtually threw up his brief. Not only did the keeper of Newgate deny everything in the publication relating to himself, but the parties who had been mentioned in it were summoned as witnesses and gave decisive evidence. Prance denied the whole story and, what was of greater value than his word, made the pertinent remark that, had he been used in such a way as Mrs. Cellier suggested, Dr. Lloyd must certainly have known about it. The man Corral had been kept out of court by the defence, but he had already denied all Mrs. Cellier's allegations in a deposition made before the Lord Mayor. His wife had made a similar deposition and, being now called as a witness, wholly refused to support the statements of the accused. Her husband had been treated hardly, as were all prisoners, but Mrs. Cellier's charges of torture and brutality were false. She had been allowed to see her husband occasionally and to send him food constantly, and he had been given a charcoal fire in his cell to protect him from the cold weather. Mrs. Cellier had offered to support them both, apparently on the understanding that they should acquiesce in what she had said.[254]

Another important witness proved the falsehood of many statements made in the publication, and after a lengthy summing up of the evidence by Baron Weston the jury without difficulty returned a verdict of guilty against the prisoner. Mrs. Cellier was sentenced to stand three times on the pillory, to a fine of a thousand pounds, and to imprisonment until the fine was paid.[255] Eight years later the same charges were repeated by Sir Roger L'Estrange and were supported by Prance, to whose objects this line of conduct was now better suited. The evidence which L'Estrange collected was exactly similar to that which Mrs. Cellier had obtained, and equally worthless. Not only the result of the trial, but the essential improbability of the facts alleged makes it certain that these allegations were absolutely devoid of truth.[256] Dr. Lloyd, who was well acquainted with the hard treatment accorded to Prance, saw no evidence that it exceeded the common practice of the prison, and disbelieved the gruesome stories which were industriously spread abroad.[257]

Whether or no Prance was subjected to illegitimate and illegal pressure after his recantation in order to secure his adherence to the earlier confession is a question of less importance than how that confession was obtained. Prance's subsequent account has already been given. It remains to be considered whether that was true or false. Apart from the rest of the evidence produced at the trials of the Popish Plot, that of Prance exhibited one remarkable peculiarity. All the other witnesses altered and rearranged their stories with constant facility to suit the conditions in which they found themselves at any moment. Among this rout of shifting informations the evidence of Prance offers an exception to the rule of self-contradiction. In all but a few particulars it remained constant. Other witnesses invariably put out feelers to try in what direction they had best develop their tales. The methods of Oates, Atkins, and Bedloe are notorious instances of this. Prance produced the flower of his full-blown. Its bouquet was as strong when it first met the air as at any later time. The evidence which he gave to Godfrey's murder in his first confession was as decisive and consistent in form as after constant repetition, recantation, and renewed asseverance. Almost all the other witnesses at their first appearance told stories which were loose, haphazard, inconsequent. Prance's story was from the beginning minute and elaborate. He spoke of places in great detail and afterwards pointed them out. He gave a coherent account of what had happened at each spot. On these points he did not contradict himself. The evidence which he proceeded to give about the Plot in general throws his account of Godfrey's death into high relief. His later information was exactly similar in character to that offered by all the other witnesses. It was vague and incoherent and full of absurdities. The contrast to the elaboration and detail of his previous evidence is striking.

Compared with Bedloe's account of the murder the testimony of Prance shows another noteworthy feature. The evidence of the two men hardly covers the same ground at all. In almost every particular it offers remarkable points of difference. Up to the date of October 12 the two stories run in different lines altogether. According to Prance two priests, named Gerald and Kelly, had, by means of menace and abstract arguments, induced him to join with them and four others, Green, Hill, Berry, and Vernatt, in the murder of Sir Edmund Berry Godfrey, on the score that "he was a busy man and going about to ruin all the Catholics in England."[258] One Leweson, a priest, was also to have a hand in the business. Bedloe's tale on the contrary was that Le Fevre, Pritchard, Keynes, and Walsh, four Jesuits, had employed him to effect an introduction to Godfrey for them. Le Fevre afterwards offered him £4000, to be paid by Lord Bellasis through Coleman, if he would undertake to kill "a very material man" in order to obtain some incriminating papers in his possession, without which "the business would be so obstructed and go near to be discovered" that the great Plot would come to grief.[259] At this point the stories begin to converge, and at the same time retain strikingly different features. Prance's account ran that on October 12 Gerald, Green, and Hill decoyed Godfrey as he came down the Strand from St. Clement's into Somerset House at about 9 o'clock in the evening under pretence of a quarrel. Green, Gerald, Hill, and Kelly then attacked him. Green strangled him with a twisted handkerchief, knelt with all his force upon his chest and "wrung his neck round," while Berry and Prance kept watch.[260] On the nights of Saturday and Sunday the body was left in Hill's lodgings in Somerset House, and on Monday was removed to another room across the court. There Hill shewed it to Prance by the light of a dark lantern at past 10 o'clock at night: "Gerald and Hill and Kelly and all were there."[261] Prance had no knowledge of seeing Bedloe in the room. At midnight on Wednesday, October 16, the corpse was placed in a sedan chair and carried, as Prance said, by Gerald, Green, Kelly, and himself as far as Soho Church. Hill met them there with a horse, on which he put the body and rode with it to Primrose Hill.[262] Bedloe's finished account gave a picture very unlike this. He stated that on Monday, October 14, between 9 and 10 o'clock P.M. Le Fevre took him to a room in Somerset House and showed him the body of the murdered man lying under a cloak. He recognised the body to be that of Sir Edmund Godfrey. Besides Le Fevre he only saw in the room Walsh, a servant of Lord Bellasis, the supposed Atkins, and another man whom he had often seen in the chapel and afterwards recognised as Prance.[263] The next day Le Fevre described the murder to him in detail. Before 5 o'clock in the afternoon of October 12 Le Fevre, Walsh, and Lord Bellasis' gentleman had brought Godfrey from the King's Head Inn in the Strand to Somerset House under the pretext of taking him to capture some conspirators near

St. Clement's Church. They took him into a room and, holding a pistol to his head, demanded the informations which he had taken. On his refusal they stifled him with a pillow and then strangled him with his cravat.[264] On Monday night the murderers agreed with Bedloe "to carry the body in a chair to the corner of Clarendon House, and there to put him in a coach to carry him to the place where he was found."[265] Two accounts of the same facts could hardly be imagined to differ more from one another than the stories of Prance and Bedloe. To state the matter briefly, Bedloe swore that Godfrey was murdered in one place, at one time, in one manner, for one motive, by one set of men; Prance swore that he was murdered in another place, at another time, in another manner, for another motive, by another set of men. Both Prance and Bedloe swore that they had seen the body of Sir Edmund Godfrey at nearly the same time in a room in Somerset House on the night of Monday, October 14, but Prance swore only to the presence of the men whom he had named as the murderers, while Bedloe swore only to the presence of the men whom he had named, with the addition of "the other person he saw often in the chapel," whom he afterwards recognised to be Prance.

What then becomes of Prance's statement that the only source of his information was the paper introduced into his cell on the morning of December 22, and containing the substance of Bedloe's evidence? He professed that it was solely from this that his elaborate confession of December 23 and 24 was drawn, and that it was arranged not only by the connivance, but absolutely at the direction of the Earl of Shaftesbury. Nor was this all. He told L'Estrange further that after he had been forced to retract his recantation his friend Boyce had acted as agent of Bedloe and Shaftesbury in bringing his evidence into line with that of Bedloe. On one point he refused to yield; he would not own that he had worn the periwig of which Bedloe had spoken; but for the rest, according to his own account, he made no difficulty.[266] The story is glaringly inconsistent with the facts. So far from agreeing first or last with Bedloe, Prance contradicted him in almost every possible point. If it was true that, as he said, he was wholly ignorant of the murder and concocted his confession from minutes of Bedloe's evidence which were given to him, the confession would have worn a very different colour. His only object was to save his neck and get out of Newgate. He would certainly have taken the material with which he was provided, and have simply repeated Bedloe's tale with so much alteration as was necessary to make himself a partner in the murder. He had no motive to do anything else. Even alone he could hardly have missed the point, and by his own statement did not. Under the astute guidance of Shaftesbury there could be no possible danger of bungling. Instead of this being the case he acted in a fashion which, if he spoke the truth, would have been inconceivable. Not only did he not tell the same story as that which he professed was his only guide, but he told a tale so entirely different that neither Bedloe's name nor the name of a single man given by Bedloe was mentioned in it at all. The idea of collusion between the informers in this way must be discarded. It is impossible that it should be true.

The story was adorned with another flourish which Prance did not himself venture to adopt. On his arrest he was met by Bedloe in the lobby of the House of Commons and there charged by him with complicity in the murder. L'Estrange declared that Bedloe had first made inquiries about him and had seized the opportunity to take a good view of him under the guidance of Sir William Waller.[267] But it would be little good to Bedloe to act in this way in accusing a man who might for all he knew refuse to give evidence, or give evidence which would not corroborate his own. The more definitely he accused Prance, the more difficult would be his own position if Prance should not support him. He must certainly have assured himself beforehand that Prance would make a good witness. Assurance might have been gained either by arranging that Prance should be informed of what was expected before his arrest, or by the knowledge that Shaftesbury would see to the matter afterwards. Both conjectures are in the same case. The latter has been shewn to be wide of the mark. For the same reasons the former must be thought equally inaccurate. Further than this the comparison between the evidence of Prance and Bedloe shows conclusively that the two did not arrange beforehand to give false evidence about the murder. Perjurers may be as stupid as other men, and an awkward muddle might have ensued; but two men arranging a profitable piece of perjury would hardly be at the pains to contradict each other's evidence in every particular. Also, between the date of Bedloe's first information and Prance's confession there intervened a period of seven long weeks. If there had been previous collusion between the two. Prance would have come forward far sooner than four days before Christmas.

Out of the total number of possible hypotheses which may be advanced to account for the relation between Prance and Bedloe two are thus disposed of. The witnesses did not arrange together to give evidence of Godfrey's murder. Nor was Prance furnished with the information which he was wanted to give and then subjected to such pressure that he was compelled to acquiesce in it. What then are the remaining explanations which may be put forward? The notion that Bedloe, on seeing Prance in custody on December 21, proceeded to denounce him at a venture in the bare hope of getting some support from him may be dismissed briefly. It would in any one have been a mad action to expose himself to the risk that Prance could prove an alibi, but for Bedloe to take such a course would have been more than improbable. When at a former date he accused Atkins of complicity in the murder, he used the greatest caution to obviate this risk. Until he knew whether or no Atkins could prove an alibi he would make no positive charge at all. The fact that his caution was justified would only make him more careful to avoid being caught in a trap similar to that which he had only just avoided. A more probable supposition is that Bedloe had made sufficient inquiries to be sure that Prance could not prove an alibi, and then denounced him, as if on the spur of the moment. This is a theory which has likelihood in its favour and deserves to be well weighed. Bedloe, it is supposed, had given entirely false information about the murder. After his failure to secure the conviction of Atkins he was compelled to turn in another direction. Looking round, his eye fell upon Prance as a suitable tool. He made careful inquiries as to his opportunity and ability to bear false witness, found that Prance would be unable to make out an alibi, and denounced him dramatically at Westminster. Prance was clapped into prison and, without having any notes of Bedloe's evidence given him, was so terrified by the two nights which he spent in the dungeon in Newgate that he concocted a false story and then made confession of it. There is certainly something to be said in favour of this view. It was common talk that Godfrey had been murdered in Somerset House, and Bedloe was well known to have said as much. Prance was well acquainted with the place and the people belonging to it. He had at least as fair a chance as another of making a plausible account of the murder. He was in considerable danger and in great discomfort. He had already lost his liberty and bade fair to lose his life for speaking the truth. It was natural enough that he should renounce his honesty and spin a tale to save his skin. He could make use of knowledge which would render it unlikely that he should be caught tripping. He had heard Bedloe say that he saw him on the Monday night standing by the body with a dark lantern, so that he could place this incident in his story without hesitation. The publicity of the manner of Godfrey's death would enable him to speak with equal certainty as to the actual murder.

Here is a plausible enough theory of the relation between the witnesses and the manner in which Prance's evidence was procured. Unfortunately there are considerable difficulties in the way of its acceptance. If Prance was enabled by the words which he heard Bedloe speak to place the incident of October 14 in his narrative, he was also enabled to make a connection with Bedloe himself at that point. As according to the hypothesis this was his only knowledge of the details of Bedloe's information, he would have been eager to make the most of it. It would have been the first point for him to clutch. On the contrary, Prance did nothing of the kind. He did not mention Bedloe's name at all. The question why he did not is, if this theory be true, unanswerable. Bedloe too went to the trouble of spending four valuable weeks in his search for a suitable instrument to bear out his story.

If that was the case it is surely strange that he should not have attempted to make certain that the man whom he obtained at last should be more or less acquainted with the tale which he was to corroborate. To do this after the arrest would probably be very difficult, but as a previous step it would be by no means so hard. Oates and Bedloe had many disreputable friends, by profession Roman Catholics, who could have easily effected an introduction to Prance and have held conversation the meaning of which would after his arrest be plain. Instead of this Bedloe on the hypothesis preferred to run the risk of having his whole story contradicted. These are objections of weight; but a still greater lies in the nature of the evidence which Prance gave on his confession. He had been in a very cold dungeon for thirty-six hours at most, from the evening of December 21 to the morning of December 23. If he was unprepared for Bedloe's charge, his mind must have been in a turmoil of conflicting emotions. Yet within this time he evolved a story so detailed, elaborate, connected, and consistent that he never afterwards found the need to alter it materially. For such a task phenomenal powers of memory, imagination, and coolness would be demanded. A man of Prance's station, suddenly thrown into a horrible prison on a false charge, cannot be supposed to have been endowed with such a wealth of mental equipment. If he had possessed a tithe of the powers which in this case would have been necessary, he would have made sure of cementing a firm connection in his narrative between himself and Bedloe.

This consideration then has reached the result that the relation between the two men is not only inexplicable on the theory just discussed, but that it is inexplicable except upon the ground that there was more in Prance's evidence than a work of mere fancy. Within the space of thirty-six hours, and with every condition adverse to clear and connected thought, he could not have produced the evidence which he gave on December 23 and 24 unless it had been based upon some reality in fact. On December 24 he was taken to all the places of which he had spoken, and went to each, describing the transaction on the spot in a manner perfectly consonant with what he had said under examination elsewhere. The consistence of his story, its readiness, the minuteness of its detail point to the certainty that he was speaking, not of incidents manufactured to order, but of facts within his knowledge. Prance was in fact a party to the murder.[268] From this it is a sure deduction that when Bedloe denounced him in the lobby of the House of Commons he was not, as L'Estrange asserted, making a move in a game which had been arranged beforehand, but had on the contrary really recognised the man and on the instant made an accusation not wholly devoid of truth. Bedloe too must therefore have known something about the murder. It would be an unbelievable coincidence that, if Bedloe were wholly ignorant, he should chance to choose, out of all London, one of the few who were not.

It now becomes evident what part of Prance's evidence was true and what false. The three men whose conviction for the murder he procured were certainly innocent. Almost with equal certainty it can be said that he was not speaking at random. The truth of what he affirmed lay therefore in the facts and the manner of the transaction which he described. The murder had taken place at Somerset House in the way which he related, but he fastened the crime upon men who were guiltless of Godfrey's death. The extent of Bedloe's information also can be calculated. On every point of time and place he had prevaricated and contradicted himself beyond measure. On none of these is his testimony of the slightest value. Nevertheless he was possessed of enough knowledge to accuse definitely a man who was actively concerned in the crime and could relate the facts as they happened. Clearly he had become acquainted with the persons who were guilty of the murder. The probability then is that those whose names he first gave directly were the culprits. Prance he did not know by name, but by sight alone. From the beginning he had always spoken of "the waiter in the queen's chapel," or of the man whom "he saw often in the chapel." If this had been a chance shot, he would afterwards have identified this man with Green, who actually answered to the description. Instead of this he recognised him in the person of Prance. As he only mentioned the fact incidentally and did not insist upon it as a circumstance in his favour, his word on the point is the more deserving of credit. If Prance himself was a party to the murder he must have known the real authors of it. He must have accused the innocent not from necessity but from choice, and in order to conceal the guilty. As he was expected and supposed to corroborate Bedloe's evidence, his most natural course was to introduce into his story all those whom Bedloe had named. He carefully avoided mentioning any of them. No other reason is conceivable except that he knew Bedloe to have exposed the real murderers, and that he wished to shield them. What then was the motive of the crime, and how did this extraordinary complication arise?

CHAPTER V

THE SECRET

SIR EDMUND BERRY GODFREY was an intimate friend of Edward Coleman, secretary to the Duchess of York. At the time of the murder Coleman lay in Newgate under an accusation of treason, and had so lain for a fortnight. He was therefore never examined on the subject of his friend's death. The omission was unfortunate, for Coleman could probably have thrown some light upon the nature of the magistrate's end.[269] It was constantly said, and the statement has often been repeated, that when Oates left a copy of his information with Godfrey on September 27, Godfrey at once wrote to Coleman an account of the charges contained in it to give the Duke of York warning of the coming storm.[270] The story was extensively used by those who wished to prove that Godfrey had been murdered by the supporters of the Plot, or that he had committed suicide from fear of a parliamentary inquiry into his conduct. He had not only this reason for fear, urged L'Estrange, but he had concealed the fact of Oates' discovery to him for nearly a whole month; this was the meaning of Godfrey's enigmatical expressions of apprehension, and his fear, combined with constitutional melancholy, drove him to take his own life.[271] Whether or no he suffered from depression is not a question of importance, since it has been proved that he did not commit suicide, but was murdered. The rest of the argument is equally unsound. When Godfrey took Oates' first deposition on September 6, he had no copy of the information left with him and knew that it had already been communicated to the government.[272] As for the fact that Godfrey had sent an account of Oates' revelations to the Duke of York, it would be absurd to suppose that plans of vengeance were harboured against him on this score, for the duke had been acquainted with the matter since August 31, when the forged letters were sent to Bedingfield at Windsor, so that the information he received from Godfrey was unimportant.[273] As this was a fact of which the Lord Treasurer was perfectly aware, the suggestions of North and Warner, the Jesuit provincial, that Godfrey had been threatened and finally dispatched by order of Danby, on account of his officiousness in making a communication to the duke, fall to the ground at the same time.[274] Taken in this sense the words in which Godfrey foreshadowed his doom are meaningless. He had assured Mr. Robinson that he believed he should be the first martyr. "I do not fear them," he added, "if they come fairly, and I shall not part with my life tamely." He declared to Burnet his belief that he would be knocked on the head. To his sister-in-law he said, "If any danger be, I shall be the first shall suffer." He had told one Mr. Wynnel that he was master of a dangerous secret, which would be fatal to him. "Oates," he said, "is sworn and is perjured."[275] Clearly Godfrey was labouring under an apprehension of quite definite character. He was in possession of secret information concerning Oates' discovery and believed that it would cost him his life. What this secret was is now to seek. The nature of it must show why danger was to be apprehended and from what quarter.

The statement that Godfrey wrote to Coleman to acquaint him with Oates' accusations is not quite correct. Burnet notes: "It was generally believed that Coleman and he were long in a private conversation, between the time of his (Coleman's) being put in the messenger's hands and his being made a close prisoner."[276] Such a conversation in fact took place, though it was earlier than Burnet thought. Coleman surrendered to the warrant against him on Monday, September 30.[277] Two days before he came to the house of Mr. George Welden, a common friend of himself and the magistrate. Welden sent his servant to Godfrey's house with the message that one Clarke wanted to speak to him. It was the form arranged between them for use when Godfrey was in company and Coleman wished to see him. Godfrey went to Mr. Welden's and there had an interview with Coleman. "When Mr. Coleman and Sir Edmondbury were together at my house," said Welden, "they were reading papers."[278] It can hardly be doubted what these papers were. The date was Saturday, September 28, the day on which Godfrey had taken Oates' deposition. In that Oates had made charges of the most serious nature against Coleman; and Coleman was Godfrey's friend. The papers can scarcely have been other than Godfrey's copy of the deposition. Godfrey had probably sent at once to Coleman to tell him what had passed. This much may be gathered from the reports of letters which he was said to have sent to Coleman and the Duke of York. Coleman then met him at Welden's house, and together they went through Oates' information, "Oates," said Godfrey, "is sworn and is perjured." This alone was hardly a secret so dangerous as to make him fear for his life. Many believed it. It was not an uncommon thing to say. The most grievous consequence that could ensue would be to gain the reputation of a "bloody papist," and possibly to be threatened with implication in the Plot. Such an opinion could not conceivably lead to fears of assaults by night and secret assassination. But there was one particular in which knowledge of Oates' perjury might be very dangerous indeed. No doubt Coleman pointed out Oates' long tale of lies through many articles of his deposition. There was one which he certainly would not omit. The cardinal point in the Plot, according to Oates' revelation, was a Jesuit congregation held on April 24, 1678 at the White Horse Tavern in the Strand, where means were concerted for the king's assassination. At all the trials of the Jesuits Oates came forward to give evidence to this point. It was of the first importance.

Oates' statement was false. No congregation had met on that day at the White Horse Tavern. His perjury is more easy to prove here than in most other particulars, for it is certain that the Jesuit congregation was held on April 24 in a different place. It was held at St. James' Palace, the residence of the Duke of York. More than five years afterwards James II let out the secret to Sir John Reresby.[279] Up to that time it had been well guarded. It was of the utmost consequence that the fact should not be known. Had it been discovered, the discredit into which Oates would have fallen would have been of little moment compared to the extent of the gain to the Whig and Protestant party. To Shaftesbury the knowledge would have meant everything. Witnesses of the fact would certainly have been forthcoming, and James' reception of the Jesuits in his home was a formal act of high treason. The Exclusion bill would have been unnecessary. James would have been successfully impeached and would have been lucky to escape with his head upon his shoulders. Charles would hardly have been able to withstand the outcry for the recognition of the Protestant duke as heir to the throne, the Revolution would never have come to pass, and the English throne might to this day support a bastard Stuart line instead of the legitimate Hanoverian dynasty. Besides the Duke of York and the Jesuit party one man only was acquainted with this stupendous fact. It is hardly credible that Godfrey met Coleman on September 28, 1678 with any other object than to discuss with him the charges made by Oates. Still less is it credible that Coleman failed to point out Oates' perjury in this matter. It need not be supposed that a definite statement passed from him. A hint would have sufficed. In some way, it may be conjectured, Coleman disclosed to the magistrate that which he should have concealed. Such understandings are abrupt in origin but swift in growth. Beyond doubt the secret, the shadow of which Godfrey saw stretching across the line of his life, was that the Jesuit congregation of April 24 had been held in the house and under the patronage of the Duke of York.[280]

And hence arose the perplexity and depression of mind from which he is said to have suffered during the last days of his life. He was possessed of information which, if published, would infallibly ruin the cause of the Duke of York and of the Catholics, to whom he was friendly. It had come to him in private from his friend, and to use it might seem an act almost of treachery. Yet with these sentiments Godfrey's duty as a magistrate was in absolute conflict. It was undoubtedly his business at once to communicate his knowledge to the government. Not only was it illegal not to do so, and highly important that such a weighty fact should not escape detection, but Godfrey found himself at the centre of the investigation of Oates' discovery, and to reveal his news was probably the only way of exposing Oates' perjury. Nor did Godfrey underestimate the danger into which this knowledge brought him. He feared that he would be assassinated. The

Jesuits were confronted with the fact that a secret of unbounded value to their enemies had come into the hands of just one of the men who could not afford, however much he might wish, to retain it. Godfrey was, by virtue of his position as justice of the peace, a government official. He might take time to approach the point of revealing his information, but sooner or later he would assuredly reveal it. All the tremendous consequences which would ensue could not then be prevented or palliated. The only possible remedy was to take from Godfrey the power of divulging the secret. His silence must be secured, and it could only be made certain by the grave. To the suggestion that the motive to the crime was not sufficient, it need only be answered that at least nine men preferred to die a horrible and ignominious death rather than prove their innocence and purchase life by telling the facts.[281] Godfrey's death was no ludicrous act of stupid revenge, but a clear-headed piece of business. It was a move in the game which was played in England between parties and religions, and which dealt with issues graver than those of life and death.

So far the matter is clear. Sir Edmund Godfrey was an intolerable obstacle to the Jesuit party. He was in possession of a secret the disclosure of which would utterly ruin them. He recognised himself that his life was in danger and went in expectation of being assassinated. His murder was, like Charles the First's execution, a cruel necessity. Two men gave evidence as to his death. The one, Bedloe, contradicted himself beyond belief. Nevertheless he was able to recognise and accuse the other, Prance, whose minute and consistent descriptions of time and place mark him as a partner in the crime. The inference therefore is sound that, as Bedloe accused correctly a man whom he knew by sight and not by name, some of the men whose names he gave directly in his account of the murder were probably the real criminals. These were Le Fevre, the Jesuit confessor of the queen, Charles Walsh, a Jesuit attached to the household of Lord Bellasis, and Charles Pritchard, a third member of the Society of Jesus. With them were associated the Roman Catholic silversmith, Miles Prance, whom Bedloe recognised as the man whom he had taken for a waiter in the queen's chapel, and a servant of Lord Bellasis, whom he named as Mr. Robert Dent.[282] Strictly, it is only a matter of conjecture that these men undertook the deed, but it is supported by considerable probability. They were singularly unfitted for the task. Godfrey had to be killed and his corpse to be disposed in such a way that the crime might not be traced to its true source. The men to do this were not professional criminals. They did not know, what constant experience has demonstrated, that the most apparently simple crimes are the hardest to bring home to their authors. Their proper course was to waylay the magistrate in the darkness of a narrow street, strip his body of every article of value, and leave it to be supposed that the murder had been committed for a vulgar robbery.

Instead of this they determined to dispose the corpse in such a way that Godfrey might be thought to have committed suicide. The disposal would need time, and to gain the time necessary it was needful that they should choose a spot to which they could have free access, and where they would be undisturbed. As the most secret spot known to them they chose exactly that which they should have most avoided, the queen's palace, Somerset House. To decoy Godfrey was not difficult, for, contrary to the practice of the day, he went abroad habitually without a servant.[283] The court of Somerset House was not, as the Duke of York afterwards declared in his memoirs, crowded with people; on the contrary, it was understood that the queen was private, and orders were given that visitors were not to be admitted in their coaches.[284] The queen's confessor and his friends however could doubtless secure an entrance. Here Godfrey was murdered, and in Somerset House his body remained for four nights. In what place it was kept cannot be decided. Hill's lodgings were certainly not used. Perhaps the spot chosen was the room in the same passage where Prance said that the body had lain during one night.[285] The drops of white wax which Burnet afterwards saw must have here been spilt upon the dead man's clothes. Godfrey himself never used wax candles.[286] On Wednesday night the body was removed from Somerset House and carried to the field in which it was found. That it was not taken through the gate is made certain by the sentries' evidence. It must therefore have been carried through a private door. Thence it was taken in a carriage to the foot of Primrose Hill; marks of coach wheels were seen in the ground leading towards the spot in a place where coaches were not used to be driven.[287] Godfrey's sword was driven through his body, and the corpse was left lying in the ditch, where it was found next day.

In lodgings near Wild House lived four men. Two of them were Le Fevre and Walsh, parties to the murder of Sir Edmund Godfrey; the others were Captain William Bedloe, "the discoverer of the Popish Plot," and his coadjutor, Charles Atkins. Atkins had declared before the secretary of state that he lodged at Holborn, but Bedloe let the truth appear in his examination. As it was a slip, which he immediately tried to cover, and he was far from bringing it forward as a point in his favour, his statement may be accepted.[288] Bedloe was thus in daily contact with two of the criminals. He was on terms of intimacy with them. They went about in his company and confided in him enough to allow him to be present at secret celebration of the mass.[289] From this quarter Bedloe's information was derived. It is easy to conjecture how he could have obtained it. Walsh and Le Fevre were absent from their lodgings for a considerable part of the nights of Saturday and Wednesday, October 12 and 16. Bedloe's suspicions must have been aroused, and either by threats or cajolery he wormed part of the secret out of his friends. He obtained a general idea of the way in which the murder had been committed and of the persons concerned in it. One of these was a frequenter of the queen's chapel whom he knew by sight. He thought him to be a subordinate official there. If he went afterwards to the chapel to discover him he must have been disappointed, for the man occupied no office. He had failed to learn his name. It was only by accident that nearly two months later he met Prance and recognised him as the man he wanted. As he had no knowledge himself of the murder and could not profess to have been present at it, he devised the story that he had been shewn the body as it lay in a room in Somerset House on the night of October 14. At this point he introduced the name of Samuel Atkins. Le Fevre and Walsh had in the meantime disappeared, and Bedloe was left without any fish in his net. Doubtless the fact that Charles Atkins was his fellow-lodger suggested the idea of implicating Pepys' clerk. Samuel Atkins was well known to his namesake and had in times past given him considerable assistance.[290] Charles Atkins now shewed his gratitude by arranging with Bedloe to accuse his benefactor of complicity in Godfrey's murder.

Prance's conduct is now easy to explain. He was denounced by a man who, as he had good reason to know, was not a party to the crime and could have no certain knowledge of it. If he could shew a bold front and stoutly maintain his perfect innocence all might be well. But to do this meant to expose himself to the danger of being hanged. Bedloe had moreover named other of the real criminals. They might yet be taken and the secret be dragged from them. This at any cost must be prevented. So Prance determined to pose as the repentant convert and to shield the real culprits by bringing to death men whom he knew to be innocent. His knowledge of the crime enabled him to describe its details in the most convincing manner, while his acquaintance with the circle of Somerset House enabled him to fit the wrong persons to the facts. No doubt, when he was once out of the condemned cell, he felt that he would prefer to keep free of the business altogether. Perhaps too he was not without shame and horror at the idea of accusing innocent men. He recanted. A recantation moreover, if he could persevere in it, might succeed in shattering Bedloe's credit as well as his own and in diverting the line of inquiry from Somerset House. Pressure was immediately put upon him, he was forced to retract and to return to his original course of action. In this he was perfectly successful. Not only was the investigation removed from a quarter unpleasantly near to the Duke of York, but Prance manipulated his evidence so cleverly that even the keen inquisitors who sat on the parliamentary committees never for a moment suspected that the germ of truth for which they were seeking was not contained in his but in Bedloe's information. After the appearance of Prance that was relegated to a secondary position; but as Bedloe gained the reward of £500 offered for the discovery of the murder, was lodged in apartments at Whitehall, and received a weekly pension of ten pounds from the secret service fund, he had no reason to be dissatisfied with the result. Prance too received a bounty of fifty pounds "in respect of his services about the plot."[291] The fact that the murder was sworn to have taken place in Somerset House was not without danger to the queen herself. At Bedloe's first information she acted a prudent part. She sent a message to the House of Lords expressing her grief at the thought that such a crime could have taken place in her residence, and offered to do anything in her power that might contribute to the discovery of the murderers. When an order was given to search the palace, she threw open the rooms and in every way facilitated the process. The course which she adopted was most wise. The Lords were touched by her confidence and voted thanks for her message.[292] Her confessor, who had been accused by Bedloe, was not charged by Prance. In spite of the libels which assailed her she was never again molested on the matter.[293]

Prance's attitude as it has here been sketched accorded entirely with the rest of his evidence. In his examination before the council he began his story; "On a certain Monday."[294] When he was taken by Monmouth and Ossory to Somerset House he said "that it was either at the latter end or the beginning of the week" that Godfrey had met his death.[295] The significance of this is clear. No one wishing to construct a false account of the murder could possibly have made these statements. It was notorious that Godfrey had disappeared upon Saturday, October 12. To postpone the date of the murder would be to add a ludicrous difficulty to the story. This is exactly what Prance wanted to do. If only he could be branded as a liar and thrust ignominiously out of the circle of inquiry, his dearest object would be accomplished. Other statements in his information make it certain that this was the case. After naming Monday night as the time of the murder, he went on to say to the council that the body lay in Somerset House for four days, and was then carried away on the night of Wednesday. Reckoning at the shortest, the fourth day from Monday night was Friday, twenty-four hours after Godfrey's body was found. Reckoning backwards from Wednesday, the fourth day was Saturday, when Godfrey was missed. Prance was therefore deliberately falsifying his evidence in point of time when he named Monday. A similar result is obtained from his examination by the Duke of Monmouth. In that he said that the day of the murder was either at the latter end or the beginning of the week. He further said "that the body lay in Somerset House about six or seven days before it was carried out." Counting the week-end from Friday to Tuesday, six days from either of those or the intermediate points brings the calculation at least to Thursday. At the same time Prance declared that the body was removed at midnight on Wednesday. It is evident that he was trying to throw dust in the eyes of the investigators. These tactics were in vain, and he was forced to tell the story in point of time truthfully. As for the fictitious view of the body on the night of October 14, Prance simply told Bedloe's story with as little variation as possible, with the exception that he did not mention Bedloe at all. Bedloe had landed himself in hopeless confusion when he was taken to Somerset House to shew the room where it had taken place.[296] Prance did not attempt to point it out.

Prance did not stop at his evidence on the subject of the murder, but went on to give information as to the Plot. Unless he had done so he could hardly have hoped to escape from prison, for it would seem incredible to the authorities that he should know so much and yet not know more. Perhaps too he was bitten with the excitement and glory of an informer's life. His evidence was not however calculated to assist materially the party whose interest it was to prosecute the plot. He had already aroused annoyance by contradicting Bedloe's evidence concerning the murder.[297] He now proceeded to spin out a string of utterly ridiculous stories about the Jesuits and other Roman Catholics. All that was important in his evidence was hearsay or directed against men who had already to contend against weightier accusations. He declared that Fenwick, Ireland, and Grove had told him that four of the five Popish lords were "to command the army."[298] They had for some time past been in prison in the Tower on far more direct charges. At the trial of Ireland and Grove Prance was not produced as a witness at all. At the trial of Whitbread, Fenwick, and Harcourt he made the same statement. Fenwick had told him also that he need not fear to lose his trade in the case of civil war, for he should have plenty of work to do in making church ornaments.[299] These stories were again retailed at the trials of Langhorn and Wakeman.[300] When he was summoned as a witness against Lord Stafford he could say no more than that one Singleton, a priest, had told him "that he would make no more to stab forty parliament men than to eat his dinner."[301] Much of his evidence about the Plot was so ludicrous that it could never be brought into court at all. Four men were to kill the Earl of Shaftesbury and went continually with pistols in their pockets. One Bradshaw, an upholsterer, had said openly in a tavern that it was no more sin to kill a Protestant than to kill a dog, and that "he was resolved to kill some of the busy lords." It was the commonest talk among Roman Catholics that the king and Lord Shaftesbury were to be murdered. It was equally an ordinary subject of conversation that a great army was to be raised for the extirpation of heretics. A surgeon, named Ridley, had often told him "that he hoped to be chirurgeon to the Catholic army in England"; and when he complimented one Moore, a servant of the Duke of Norfolk, upon "a very brave horse" which he was riding, "Moore wished that he had ten thousand of them, and hoped in a short time that they might have them for the Catholic cause." In his publication Prance added to this a disquisition on the immorality of the secular priests, among whom he had at the time two brothers.[302] So tangled and nonsensical a tale could be a source of strength to no prosecution. Dr. Lloyd was alarmed at the extent and facility of Prance's new information.[303] Bishop Burnet thought, "It looked very strange, and added no credit to his other evidence that the papists should thus be talking of killing the king as if it had been a common piece of news.[304] And Warner, the Jesuit provincial, characterised Prance's later evidence as of little scope and less weight."[305]

To how many persons Prance's real position in the tortuous intrigues which circled round the murder of Sir Edmund Godfrey was known is a question very difficult to answer. By the Jesuit writers on the Plot his character is treated with a moderation foreign to their attacks on the other informers. He is to them "a silversmith of no obscurity," and "by far less guilty than the rest in the crimes of their past lives."[306] It is hard to think that some of them were not acquainted with the part which he had played. There are stronger indications that within a select circle his true character was appreciated. When James II came to the throne Prance was brought to trial for perjury, and on June 15, 1686 pleaded guilty to the charge. The court treated him to a lecture in which his conduct was compared favourably to that of Oates, who had remained hardened to the end, and promised to have compassion on a true penitent. He was sentenced to pay a fine of a hundred pounds, to be three times pilloried for the space of an hour, and to be whipped from Newgate to Tyburn. The last and heaviest part of the punishment, the flogging, under which Oates' iron frame had nearly sunk, was remitted by the king's command.[307] There is considerable reason to believe that the trial was collusive and the result prearranged. That Prance should confess himself perjured is easy to understand: to understand why Prance's sentence was lightened, unless it was in reward for good service done, would be very difficult. All the reasons which had worked before for the exculpation of the Roman Catholics from the guilt of Godfrey's murder were now redoubled in force. Oates had already suffered for his crimes. The Popish Plot, as Sir John Reresby told James, was not only dead, but buried. To overthrow the Protestant story of Godfrey's death would be to throw the last sod upon its grave. This was much; but James was not the man to forego without reason the sweetest part of his vengeance upon the witness who had set up that story. The rancour with which he pursued Oates and Dangerfield seemed to have completely vanished when the turn came to Prance. Prance had certainly diverted the investigation from James' personal neighbourhood; but Oates had been saved nothing of his terrible punishment by the fact that he had cleared the Duke of York in his first revelation of the plot. The harm done by Dangerfield to the Catholic cause was nothing compared to that accomplished by Prance, if the surface of events told a true tale. Dangerfield was whipped, if not to death, at least to a point near it. But Prance was let off the lash. Without the flogging his sentence was trifling. James had no love for light sentences in themselves.

His action is only explicable on the ground that he was acquainted with the truth, and knew how valuable an instrument Prance had proved himself.

One man at least could have told him the facts: Father John Warner, late provincial of the Jesuits in England and confessor of the king. Less than three years later, when the storm of revolution burst over the Catholic court and drove its supporters to seek a penurious refuge on the continent, a shipload of these was setting out from Gravesend in mid December. They were bound for Dunkirk with as many valuables as they could carry with them. Before they could set sail, information was laid and an active man, aided by the officers of the harbour, boarded the vessel. The last passengers were being rowed out from shore. They were arrested in the boat and carried back with the others seized on the ship. They were Father Warner and Miles Prance. While the officers were busy in caring for the captured property, their prisoners escaped. Warner made his way to Maidstone and by means of a forged passport crossed the Channel. Prance was soon after retaken in the attempt to follow under a false name. The vessel on board which he was found was seized, but those on her were discharged, and Prance was probably successful in his third endeavour to reach the continent.[308] Supposing that Prance had been the Protestant puppet which he has been believed, this was queer company in which to find him. He had attacked Warner's religion, accused his friends, and brought to death those of his faith by false oaths. His confession of perjury would hardly weigh down the scale against this. At least he was not the man whom Warner would choose as a travelling companion on a journey in which detection might at any moment mean imprisonment and even death. The risk that Prance would turn coat again and denounce him was not inconsiderable. Prance's conduct too was remarkable. Why should he fly from the Revolution? True, he had confessed that his accusations of the Catholics were false, and he could not expect great gratitude from the party in power; but he had only to retract his words once more, on the plea that his confession had been extorted against his will, to live in safety, at any rate, if not with prosperity. Away from England, surrounded by those whom he had wronged, the future before him was hopeless.

The supposition cannot be supported. Prance's position in the politics of the plot is not easy to set in a clear light. The attempt made here to do so at least offers a hypothesis by which some of the difficulties are explained. The last phase of the informer's career, at all events, becomes intelligible. Prance had been throughout one of the most astute and audacious of the Jesuit agents, and Warner must have been perfectly aware of the fact.

The success of Godfrey's murder as a political move is indubitable. The Duke of York was the pivot of the Roman Catholic schemes in England,[309] and Godfrey's death saved both from utter ruin. Nevertheless it was attended by gravely adverse consequences. If the fact of the Jesuit congregation at St. James' Palace had become known, nothing could have saved the duke. But the crime which prevented this gave an impetus to the pursuit of the Plot and a strength to the Whig party, so great that it all but succeeded in barring him from the throne and establishing a Protestant dynasty. Godfrey's fame rose almost to the height of legend. On a Sunday in the February after his murder a great darkness overspread the face of the sky of London. The atmosphere was so murky that in many churches service could not be continued without the aid of candles. It was said that in the midst of the gloom in the queen's chapel at Somerset House, even while mass was being said, the figure of Sir Edmund Berry Godfrey appeared above the altar. Thereafter the place went by the name of Godfrey Hall.[310]

POLITICS OF THE PLOT

CHAPTER I

THE GOVERNMENT

"THE English nation are a sober people," wrote Charles I to his abler son, "however at present infatuated." Charles II had greater right than ever his father to believe that his subjects were mad. The appearance of Oates and the death of Godfrey heralded an outburst of feeling as monstrous as the obscure events which were its cause. From the sense of proportion they had displayed in the Civil War the English people seemed now divorced and, while they affected to judge those of "less happier lands" fickle and tempest-tossed, let the tide of insobriety mount to the point of complete abandonment. Public opinion was formed without reason. The accumulated suspicion and hatred of years swelled into an overpowering volume of tumultuous emotion. Scarcely the most sane escaped the prevailing contagion of prejudice and terror. None could tell where the spread would stop.

The times were in a ferment when Parliament met on October 21, 1678. In his speech from the throne the king gave notice to the Houses that information had been laid of a Jesuit conspiracy against his life, and he and the Lord Chancellor following promised a strict inquiry. The government wished to keep the investigation clear of Westminster, recognising the danger of parliamentary interference;[311] but the Commons were of another mind. They returned to their house, and business was begun by members of the privy council. Motions were made to take the king's speech into consideration, for the keep of the army, and the court party tried first to turn the attention of the house to the need for money. The question was about to be put, while country members sat in amazement. Suddenly one rose to his feet and in a speech of fire brought to debate the subject that was in the mind of every man present. He admired, he said, that none of those gentlemen who had spoken nor any others of the house who held great places at court should speak one word of the Plot, though his Majesty's life and government were exposed to manifest danger; the property, liberty, lives, and, yet dearer, the religion of all were embarked in the same bottom; that neither an army nor money, in however vast sums, could protect a prince from the knife of a villain the murder of two Kings of France testified; and was the prisoner Coleman, so inconsiderable a person, to be thought the chief agent in a design of such importance, of such deep intrigues and tortuous ways But a few days before Sir Edmund Godfrey had been done to death. Were a spaniel lost, inquiry was made in the *Gazette*: now a worthy gentleman had been barbarously murdered in discharge of his duty, and no search was undertaken for the criminals. The privy council, declared the speaker, was cold in its pursuit; let the great council of the land proceed with greater vigour.[312] Parliament threw itself into the case with immediate determination. Committees were appointed to consider ways and means for the preservation of the king's person, to inquire into the Plot and Godfrey's murder, a bill was prepared to disable papists from sitting in either house of Parliament, addresses were made for the removal of all popish recusants from London and for a day of solemn fast, which was accordingly appointed by proclamation for November 13. Oates and Bedloe were heard with their expansive tales at the bars of both houses, and on the 1st of November a joint resolution was voted that "there hath been and still is a damnable and hellish Plot, contrived and carried on by Popish Recusants, for the assassinating and murdering the King and rooting out and destroying the Protestant religion."[313]

Consternation was not expressed in debate alone. Gallant members were in alarm as well for themselves as for their sovereign. Sir Edward Rich informed the Lords' committee of an apprehension he had for some time felt that both houses of Parliament were to be blown up. A beggar at the Great Door was arrested on suspicion that he was an Irish earl's son. Great knocking had been heard underground in the night hours. Sir John Cotton, who owned a cellar beneath the Painted Chamber, was requested to have his coals and faggots removed from so dangerous a spot, and the Duke of Monmouth generously lent guards to stand watch until a strict examination could be made. Accompanied by the Masters of the Ordnance and an expert builder. Sir Christopher Wren and Sir Jonas Moore conducted the inspection. They reported the lower structure of the house to be in an extremely dangerous state. The walls were mostly seven feet thick and contained many secret places. Vaults ran all the way from the Thames under Westminster Hall. By the help of neighbours who owned the cellars any one could introduce a store of gunpowder within four and twenty hours. Without a guard their lordships could have no security. Orders were given for the adjoining houses and vaults to be cleared, for the cellars to be opened one into another, and sentinels to patrol them night and day under command of a trusty officer. It was even doubted whether Parliament had not better remove to Northumberland House. Still as neither knocking nor the beggar were seen to produce ill effects, nothing further was done, and Sir Edward Rich found himself derided as a lunatic.[314] Beyond Westminster the terror ran no less high. A report came to town that St. John's College, Cambridge, had been burnt down and three priests taken with fireballs in their possession. The new prison at Clerkenwell was fired and some priests immured there hailed as the obvious incendiaries. Somerset House was searched by Lord Ossory, who was promptly said to have found a hundred thousand fireballs and hand-grenades, A poor Venetian soapmaker was thrown into prison on the charge of manufacturing similar infernal machines; but on examination his wares turned out to be merely balls of scent. Dread of fire seemed to have touched the limit when Sir William Jones sent an express from Hampstead with orders to move his store of firewood from the front to the back cellar of his house in London that it might be less near the malign hands of Jesuits. And from Flanders came the disquieting rumour that if, as was expected, the Catholics in England were destroyed in the turmoil, the burghers of Bruges had prepared the same fate for English Protestants in their town.[315]

Into the midst of so fierce a storm Charles II and his government were thus suddenly thrown. It had broken over their heads almost without warning. September had passed with a clear sky; October was not out before the elements had massed their forces against the king's devoted servants and were threatening to overwhelm the land with a gigantic catastrophe. In August Charles had at his control a formidable army and in his pocket the sum of £800,000, with the added satisfaction of seeing removed by the general peace a fruitful opportunity for his political opponents: before December the throne on which he sat seemed tottering to its fall. The servants of the crown faced the situation with admirable fortitude. English statecraft of the Restoration period was a haphazard school. Since the fall of Clarendon integrity of dealing had ceased to be an ideal for English politicians. Common honesty, the saving grace of party principle, fled from a scene where could be witnessed the sight of offices bought and sold with cheerful frankness and votes bidden for as at an auction without shame. The king's chief minister lent himself to a policy of which he heartily disapproved. The king's mistresses were notable pieces in the game played at court. A quarrel between them might be expected to influence the fate of incalculable futures. General want of method reduced the public services to chaos. The salaries of ambassadors fell into long arrear; clerks in the offices of the secretaries of state petitioned vehemently for their wages; the very gentlemen waiters were forced to urge that either their diet or money in its stead should not be denied them.[316] Nevertheless the nation throve on a habit of inspired disorder. Lord Treasurer Danby increased the royal revenue wonderfully. The Stop of the Exchequer, a breach of faith which convulsed the city, scarcely sufficed to shock the national credit. The growth of trade and commerce was completely changing the aspect of England, and wealth increased rapidly. Able and painstaking men such as Sir Joseph Williamson, Sir William Temple, Henry Coventry, Sir Leoline Jenkins, and in a lesser degree Samuel Pepys and the Earl of Conway, conducted the changeful administration of affairs with industry and circumspection. Want of order did not disturb them, for they were used to none; and secretaries of state were accustomed to pursue their royal master with business in bed, at his after-dinner dose, and even to still more remote places of retreat.[317] A continual shifting of the horizon prepared them for unexpected events. Without brilliant parts they learned to confront steadily situations of difficulty and danger. That which now met them was not without precedent. It had become almost a tradition of Charles' government to expect the worst without ceasing to hope for the best. From the Restoration onwards alarms had been frequent and a spirit of revolt, even of revolution, in the air. Venner's insurrection and the trouble in Scotland served during the earlier years to make plain that stability was not assured, and it was not only events on the surface that denoted uneasiness. In 1673 and the following year attention was occupied by a mysterious affair, never probed to the bottom, in which Edmund Everard, later perjured as an informer at the time of the Popish Plot, was charged with a design to poison the Duke of Monmouth and other persons of quality, and himself confessed his ill intention, having apparently been tutored by some of the experts in that art who flourished across the channel; with the result that he was thrown into the Tower, and was able four years after to boast of having been the first to discover the Plot and to charge the authorities with stifling it in his person.[318] Other problems trod upon the heels of this in quick succession. Throughout the years 1675 and 1676 the government shewed anxiety lest a fresh sectarian movement was on foot. A great riot made in the former year by the London prentices drew watchful eyes upon reputed fanatics. Considerable information was collected in the provinces, and judges on circuit earned golden praise by proving their attachment in word and deed to the established church. At Worcester a man of notorious opinions stood his trial for treason, but the jury acquitted him on the ground of madness, and despite plain speaking from the bench held to their verdict. Dark hints reached the government that on the first meeting of Parliament after the long prorogation an attempt would be made to seize the king and his brother and "order all things securely." Somewhat later Compton, Bishop of London, furnished the Lord Treasurer with particulars of conventicles held by Anabaptists and other dangerous dissenters in the city and in Southwark, amounting to the number of sixteen, and for the most part frequented by between one and three hundred persons; while from another source Danby learned that the total of a few of the London congregations rose to over four thousand souls.[319]

At the same time other adversaries of the church were not neglected. Already in the spring of 1676 report was rife of papists laying in supplies of arms, and a gentleman of Hereford was charged by a number of witnesses with having declared that, had a recent account of the king's sickness or death continued but one day longer, the Duke of York would have been proclaimed, and rather than allow the duke to want men he would have raised a troop of horse at his own expense. Orders were sent to the deputy lieutenant of the county to keep stricter watch over the Roman Catholics of whom such tales were told.[320] Repeated proclamations against the bold and open repair to the chapels of foreign ambassadors for the purpose of hearing mass and of the maintenance by them of English priests were doubtless caused by political need, but the same reason cannot account for private directions given by the king to Secretary Coventry to obtain information as to the extent and nature of the correspondence carried on with foreign parts by Edward Coleman. Instructions were issued for his letters to be intercepted, and some dozen were seized, but among them, unfortunately for all concerned, none of high importance. Although no find was made, the fact that search should have been thought necessary denotes in the government a real sense of the working underground.[321] Shortly before, Danby had caused the bishops to make returns of the proportion of Roman Catholics and other dissenters to conformists in their several dioceses, and that from the Bishop of Winchester is preserved. Dr. Morley had been advised that the motive was a fear of the result should the laws against conventicles be fully executed, as it was suspected that the number of those to be suppressed exceeded that of the suppressors. He was delighted to reply that the fear was groundless. Out of nearly 160,000 inhabitants in the diocese of Winchester 140,000 conformed to the Church of England, and of the remainder only 968 were classed as popish recusants; while the bishop's pious belief that the odds in favour of his side would be equally great elsewhere was confirmed by an abstract of the returns for the whole province of Canterbury setting down the complete number of papists at 11,870. Other accounts gave the number of Catholics in London alone as 30,000, and their real strength in England remains unknown; but Danby had to admit to the French ambassador, when he spoke of the alarm caused by the Duke of York's conduct, that they did not muster in all more than twelve thousand.[322] Though he did not lose sight of Catholic movements and provided himself with detailed accounts of their less known leaders in London,[323] the Lord Treasurer clearly entertained keener fears of danger from the other side.

So corrupt and able a statesman as the Earl of Danby could not fail of being an object of attack when the panic of the Popish Plot swept over the country. The one party accused him of having contrived the whole affair to sustain his credit by a persecution of the Catholics and an increase of the army, the other of stifling it to save the Duke of York, his former patron.[324] In truth he had done neither the one nor the other. When Tonge's information first came to hand he had regarded it carefully and wished to sift the matter with caution. As likelihood grew stronger that the doctor was a liar, Danby became cooler towards him; so cool indeed that Tonge and his associates fell into a fright for the prosperity of their future and sought help elsewhere. Yet he realised the necessity for watchfulness, and it was due to his energy that Coleman's papers were seized.[325] This attitude was hardly changed by the meeting of Parliament. The Lord Treasurer was a consistent opponent of the French and Roman Catholic interest. His constant endeavour was to draw Charles into union with Parliament and foreign Protestant powers against the pretensions of Louis XIV, and he thought that unless the king obtained foreign aid and set himself to a regular conquest of his country this was the only way to avoid complete division and debility at home;[326] but though these were his hopes, he was ready at the very moment of urging them to support his master's private policy abroad in a wholly contrary spirit, and so caused his own fall; for when Charles wrote to Paris for money from the French king, Danby executed his orders, thus leaving his handwriting to be produced against him. The fate that forced the Lord Treasurer to act on instructions he detested was bitter. Nevertheless he was not prepared to sacrifice office for principle. He continued to obey orders and to hold his place. Retribution fell on him. The immoral character of his conduct reaped a full reward; but it must be remembered that at a time when the king was master of his servants as well in fact as in name, there was something in Danby's plea that the monarch's command in matters of peace and war and foreign policy was absolute to his minister, and not open to question. Immoral or not, the danger of Danby's course was obvious, for powerful enemies at home and abroad were eagerly waiting the moment to hurl the forerunners of prime ministers from his eminent seat.

The opportunity had at last arrived. Feared and hated by the opposition for his policy of Anglican predominance at home, by the French government as a chief supporter of Protestant resistance on the continent, by both for the army which might be used against either, Danby found himself assailed by a combination of the Whig leaders and the French ambassador. He had refused the place of secretary of state to Ralph Montagu, ambassador in Paris, and the latter was now recalled from his post by Charles owing to a discreditable intrigue he had formed with the Duchess of Cleveland, abandoned and living in France. Nor did the disgrace end there, for Montagu's name was struck off the list of the privy council. With him he brought back to England letters written by Danby to demand subsidies from Louis. His intentions could not yet be foreseen, but the indications of public events were enough to cause the Treasurer grave anxiety. An atmosphere of plot and disturbance surrounded the court, and while information poured in, little exact evidence could be extracted from it. Money either to pay or to disband the army there was none; the fleet was equally without provision, and Parliament was tender of voting supplies lest they should be misused. The Commons had imprisoned Secretary Williamson for issuing commissions to popish recusants, and were highly incensed when on the next day Charles calmly released him: worst of all, they were preparing a bill to raise the militia of the whole kingdom without possibility of its disbandment for a period of six weeks. Danby believed that under cover of the universal excitement sinister designs against the Duke of York and himself were in the air. Many were of opinion, he wrote to Sir William Temple, that those who called for inquiry into the Plot had objects nearer their hearts that they were pursuing under its cover. Yet he was so overwhelmed with business that he hardly had time to review the situation in his mind and consider the best course to pursue.[327]

Suddenly the bolt fell as if from the blue. Danby was warned by Sir John Reresby of danger impending from Montagu's side. He had in vain attempted to manage the ambassador's exclusion from Parliament; Montagu was defeated at Grinstead by the Treasurer's candidate, and narrowly won a seat for Northampton on a contested election. Had he failed he could scarcely have dared fortune, but privilege of Parliament secured him from the enmity of the powers. Roused to immediate action, the minister attempted a counterstroke. Montagu had held unauthorised communication with the papal nuncio at Paris, and Danby charged him before the council with his malpractice, swiftly sending a warrant to seize his papers. But here the adroit statesman met more than his match. In the midst of the disturbance caused to the Commons by the king's message on the subject, Montagu quietly remarked that he believed the search a design by abstracting evidence to conceal the misconduct of a great minister of which he had knowledge. He had in fact removed the documents from his other papers and placed them in safe keeping; and on the following day they were triumphantly produced to the House as evidence of Danby's popery, treachery, and subservience to the interests of the King of France. For Montagu had been bought by Barillon and Shaftesbury, and promised Louis XIV for a hundred thousand crowns to procure the Treasurer's ruin within six months. At a moment when all Protestants in the realm were crying in horror at the danger threatening their religion, the spectacle was exhibited of the king's chief minister hurled from power by the French ambassador in conjunction with the leaders of the Protestant party for his too powerful support of the Protestant cause and the Anglican constitution. The man who had reorganised the royal finance, and had persistently advocated a national policy in the cause of English commerce and the English crown, vanished from the scene, accused of treachery to all three and under the stigma of having robbed his master and left twenty-two shillings and ten pence in an exchequer which, after payment for a vast addition to the navy, was actually stocked with over a hundred thousand pounds.[328] Charged with plotting, the Treasurer was himself the victim of a plot as base and planned by men as unscrupulous as are known to the annals of English politics. The rest of the story is thrice-told; how Danby was impeached and defended himself, pardoned and raised to a marquisate, how he lay hid in Whitehall while the bill of attainder was being passed, how he saved his head by surrendering four days before the attaint had force, and passed from the intrigues of the Popish Plot to an imprisonment of five years in the Tower, whence he was released in the day of his master's triumph. Many years after, when Danby published his letters, he took occasion to prove himself no less unscrupulous than his enemies by judiciously altering the words, "I approve of this letter," which stood in the king's writing at the foot of the most incriminating sheet, to those which in their yet more exonerating form have become famous; "This letter is writ by my order—C. R." Meanwhile his opponents triumphed, and Montagu was even successful in obtaining from the French king as much as half the reward promised for his perfidy.[329]

The fall of the Lord Treasurer swelled the difficulties of the government without disconcerting its policy. Though the opposition could score so great a success, there was no thought of giving up the main issue. The scheme of the militia bill was struck to the ground, for Charles declared that he would not comply with it for so much as the space of half an hour; he had not forgotten that the home forces might be used against other than foreign enemies. The Whig party was inspired with rage. Ten days before it had met with a still more serious rebuff. On November 20 the bill disabling Roman Catholics from sitting in Parliament was passed by the Lords, but with a proviso excepting the Duke of York by name from its action. James had won his point only by tears and incredible exertion, and the opposition expected confidently to throw the proviso out in the Commons. A furious debate took place. Supporters of the duke were assailed with cries of "Coleman's letters! Coleman's letters!" High words were bandied across the floor of the House, and Sir Jonathan Trelawny, on the court side, was committed to the Tower for boxing the ears of Mr. Ash, a country member, and calling him a rascal. Yet to the bitter disappointment of its opponents the government was successful, and the saving clause passed by a majority of two votes. The French ambassador thought that James could have hardly escaped from a greater danger.[330] Another was already looming darkly against him out of the cloudy future. Early in the session of Parliament Shaftesbury, supported by Halifax, Essex, and Barlow, now Bishop of London, had demanded the Duke of York's dismissal from the king's presence and counsels. Lord Russell moved an address to the same effect in the Commons. In the debate which followed Sacheverell, acting on the report of Coleman's examination that he had himself drawn up, gave the first direct hint of the memorable project of the Exclusion bill. Might not the king and Parliament, he asked, dispose of the succession to the crown of England?[331] The idea struck immediate root. It was the obvious point to which all that had gone before tended. The exclusion of James was to be the touchstone of English politics for two years, and the lines on which parties were to be divided by it showed themselves at once. King

Charles did not delay to make his view of the situation plain. He told Danby in private that he would not object to pare the nails of a popish successor, but that nothing should induce him to see his brother's right suffer injury; and with more dignified language and thanks for the care manifested for his personal safety informed Parliament of his readiness to join in all possible ways and means to establish the Protestant religion in firm security. Subjects might be assured that he would assent to any bills presented to safeguard them during the reign of his successor, with this ominous condition only, that none should diminish the just powers of the throne or tend to impeach the right of succession and the descent of the crown in the true line.[332] On the other side the Whig lords, with whom Halifax was still at this time allied, had adopted the notion and persuaded Barillon that an attack upon the duke was the best way to attain his end. The ambassador was not wholly convinced but, since the resistance he could make to their plan would be useless, went the way of his friends and lent them judicious assistance. At least the Frenchman's policy proved successful. His objects were to overthrow Danby and force Charles to disband the army which might perhaps be used against France. Danby fell; and on the very day when the warrant was sent to seize Montagu's papers, the Commons voted a supply for the purpose of paying off all the troops raised in the course of the preceding year. A month later, as a last attempt to save his minister, Charles dissolved the Cavalier Parliament after an unbroken existence of eighteen years.

The elections for the new parliament were fought amid intense excitement and with peculiar energy. Both parties exerted their utmost powers to gain the day. The contest was the sole subject of conversation. Purse and pen and all other imaginable means of influence were employed without stint to elevate the intelligence and debase the morals of the electors of England. At this time began the ingenious practice of splitting freeholds to multiply votes. Under the guidance of Shaftesbury pamphlets urging the Exclusion as the only means of safety for the nation flooded the country. Lord Russell, one of the most honest of his party, was elected for two counties. Drunkenness and bribery were everywhere notorious. At Norwich "a strange consumption of beer" was noted by Sir Thomas Browne. Sir William Waller, a magistrate famed for his success in priest-hunting, won a seat at Westminster at no less a cost, as those on his own side reported, than of a thousand pounds. At the Bedfordshire polls the same interest carried the day for six times that sum. Everywhere the Whigs were victorious. When the result came to be known, it was found that the government could rely upon a mere handful of twenty or thirty votes in the new parliament as against a hundred and fifty in the old.[333]

Notwithstanding the disastrous complexion of affairs Charles began the session on March 6, 1679 with considerable success. Outside the circle of politicians the chief cause of alarm to the nation was the continued existence of the army. The king had decided to remove the ground of fear by undertaking the actual disbandment of his troops. To this end he demanded from the Commons the accomplishment of the offer made by the last parliament. On April 16 a supply of over £206,000 was voted and appropriated for the purpose, and the disbandment began at once.[334] Before many months had passed a source of apparent strength and real weakness to the government was thus removed. Accusations of arbitrary rule lost much of their force; for those who now indulged in the charge were not only open to the retort, which could be levelled at them before, that their insistance was insincere, but found themselves in a far less good position to reply. It was perhaps with more personal pleasure that Charles defeated the Commons in an altercation that took place at the opening of Parliament over their choice of a Speaker, Edward Seymour, a wealthy and profligate Devonshire landowner, who had served in the chair in the late House of Commons, was noted for an able opponent of the court and in particular of Lord Danby. The government determined to effect a change, and named for Speaker Sir Thomas Meres, a member of the Whig party, as less likely to give offence than one from the court side. The Commons however elected Seymour again, and he, having wind of the king's intention to grant the formal request made by all Speakers to be relieved of their dignity, on his presentation omitted the customary words; but the Lord Chancellor replied for Charles that he could not allow such talent to be wasted on the post, having other employment for him, and sent Seymour and the rest of the Commons back to choose another. High was the indignation of the House, which sat for a whole week headless, combative, and remonstrating. One ardent member declared: "This is gagging the Commons of England and, like an Italian revenge, damning the soul first, then killing the body." A representation was made to the king, protesting that his action was without precedent and the Commons only within their rights, and a second to justify the first, which Charles had told them was mere waste of time. In answer the king prorogued Parliament for two days. When it again assembled, the matter was allowed to drop. Neither Seymour nor Meres was proposed, but Serjeant Gregory, of a more neutral disposition, who was elected and approved without difficulty.[335] Though the Commons professed to be satisfied, since they had established their right to a free choice, the honours lay in reality with Charles, who had successfully rejected a freely chosen candidate objectionable to himself.

The beginning of the parliament was prophetic of what was to come. At the time no cause could seem lower than that of the court. The Whigs had swept the country at the elections. Everything at Whitehall, at the exchequer, in the services, was in disorder and disrepair. The royal household still clamoured for unpaid wages. The whole nation was in a ferment. Men's minds were painfully divided by the project of exclusion. Innumerable cabals, intriguing one against another, troubled the surface of politics and clouded the depths. No one could tell what designs and what dangers any moment might bring forth. Above all no one could gauge the king's intentions. Uncertainty reigned everywhere, and it seemed as if the opposing forces had but to make one push and thrust aside the resistance of government, order England as they would, and reign in peace.[336] A somewhat different light is shed by after events on "the very melancholy aspect" which Sir John Reresby noted in the kingdom. In spite of the clamour raised on all sides against feebleness and irresolution, the government had marshalled its strength with some adroitness. Danby was in the Tower. The army was in the act of being disbanded. The treasury was put into commission, and the Earl of Essex, whose austerity and popular sympathies could not but inspire some measure of confidence, named as first commissioner. Before Parliament assembled the Duke of York at his brother's command had left the kingdom, and was watching events with wrath and foreboding, but with little influence, from across the Channel. Nothing that could betoken a conciliatory spirit in the court had been omitted. There followed a move still more important as a check to the unbridled Commons. The committee of secrecy had just been instructed to consider methods of impeachment of the five Popish lords, when on April 21 the king announced to Parliament that he had chosen a new privy council. The scheme he went on to outline, though attributed at the time to divers other heads, had its origin in the elegant fancy of Sir William Temple.[337] That excellent ambassador and gardener, returning from a mission to the Hague, found the turbulence of the state and the dangers surrounding the king such that he promptly set to considering how he might devise some advantage to his master's service. Diplomatic experience and a natural bent to theoretical statesmanship were more prominent in his mind than knowledge of the practical expedients which must temper the keenness of political ideas in action. He saw Parliament daily encroaching, as it seemed to him, on the royal prerogative; he saw the king drawing apart from his people; he feared an open rupture which might throw the state into convulsion. On these considerations he evolved the notion of a third authority, which, standing midway between the two, should act at the same time as a cushion and as a link. The instrument he found in the privy council. By reducing the number from fifty to thirty Temple hoped that business would be discussed by the whole board, cabals and secret understandings avoided. Members were no longer to be of one party only, or allied in ambition; on the contrary, fifteen places should go to officers of state, fifteen to popular leaders from both houses of Parliament; and since he observed authority to follow land, Temple arranged that the total income of the several members should amount to £300,000, a sum to be compared not unfavourably with that of the House of Commons, which was estimated at a third as much again. By such a council the king's policy would be ably regulated. Its composition would give confidence even to the most hostile parliament. Neither by Parliament nor by king could its authority be lightly disregarded. In the event of a breach between the two the council would be rich enough to assist the finances of the state. At the same time the king could be certain, by means of the votes of his fifteen officers, that he would not be forced to act against his own interests. The project won instant approval. Essex considered that it pointed a return to the happy days of the Restoration; Lord Sunderland, now secretary of state in place of Sir Joseph Williamson, was favourably impressed; the Lord Chancellor declared it was as a thing from heaven fallen into his majesty's breast. The Chancellor's remark had an unwitting point. Though the scheme was of Temple's conception, Charles made it his own by a characteristic touch. He consented to the inclusion of Halifax in the new council only after some pressure, for he disliked and perhaps feared the great Trimmer. It was therefore with amazement that his advisers heard the king name Lord Shaftesbury. Still more amazing, Charles positively insisted on the earl's inclusion as an extraordinary member of the council and its president. Temple was compelled to submit, not without protest. It was an act which should have given pause to optimists. None the less the news of the scheme was hailed with general applause. Bonfires were lighted in the city, the East India Company's stock rose rapidly, Barillon did not conceal his mortification, and the Dutch republic marked the occasion by the appointment of one of its most able ministers as ambassador to St. James'; only the House of Commons viewed the matter in an unexpected light and with dissatisfaction. While the French feared a bond of union between the hostile parties in England and old Cavaliers that the king had delivered himself into the hands of his enemies, the Whigs held sullenly aloof from rejoicing, or proclaimed that they were being led into a trap. The Earl of Essex had already lost credit with his friends by serving on the commission for the treasury, and those of the party who took places on the council found that glances were cast askance at them as betrayers of their trust.[338]

To most eyes the situation as affected by the change of council was far from clear. The king himself held the key to it. Whether or no Temple's scheme was really practicable, Charles did not intend to try. He had gained a point by dissolving his old council, which was filled with friends of Danby.[339] Another and a greater advantage was that signified by the choice of Shaftesbury as president of the new. His friends thought the king guilty of a lamentable piece of feebleness. Had the council been meant to consult it would perhaps have been so. But this was far from Charles' design.

"God's fish!" he said to an intimate, "they have put a set of men about me, but they shall know nothing, and this keep to yourself." Evidently the diplomatic constitution had no grand future before it. And so it proved. Within a short time the author was actively disregarding his own principle by forming one of a cabinet of four with Sunderland, Essex, and Halifax, to arrange matters before they came before the council and Parliament; while Charles, as good as his word, kept his own counsel and acted without the advice either of them or of the board at large, on one notable occasion against its will and to the great displeasure of the popular members. In Parliament the Whig councillors continued their opposition as fiercely as ever, but at the council board they had little influence. The position rapidly became impossible. It can hardly be doubted that this was Charles' exact intention. He had achieved a double success. He had seemed to give the Whig leaders a chance of reforming the government, while in fact he had only driven them to greater exasperation. In the eyes of the nation he had offered a compromise, secure in the knowledge that it would not be accepted. The trick which the Commons feared had been played to a nicety. For this their chiefs had only to thank themselves. Had they acted on their suspicion and refused places on the council, their conduct would in this have been faultless. But the bait was too tempting to be rejected. They accepted the offer of office, intending from this new post of vantage to pursue their old plans. Their duplicity gained nothing. The king had provided for the result, and their failure could only seem due to the deceit and intolerance with which they had repulsed his good intentions. On October 15, 1679 Shaftesbury was dismissed from the council in consequence of his agitation against the Duke of York, and three months later Russell, Cavendish, Capel, and Powle, his four most prominent allies on the board, tendered their resignation by his advice. Charles accepted it in the words, "With all my heart." The famous scheme was thus finally abandoned. Temple withdrew from politics to his garden and his library. Essex quitted the treasury and openly joined the opposition. Only Halifax, after retirement to the country, remained in the king's service.[340]

Meanwhile the tide in Parliament ran high against the government. The new constitution had hardly begun its career before the Commons on April 27 settled to consider how they might best preserve his Majesty's person from the attacks of papists. Impotent attempts made by members in the court interest to divert the debate only increased its keenness, and the House passed from stage to stage of fiery enthusiasm until on Mr. Hampden's motion it was unanimously declared that "the Duke of York being a papist and the hopes of his coming such to the crown have given the greatest countenance and encouragement to the present conspiracies and designs of papists against the king and the Protestant religion." With the addition that James had been the unwilling cause of the Plot, the House of Lords adopted the motion as it stood. This was the prelude to the piece to come. On Sunday, May 11, when daylight had gone out with talk, a resolution was carried, those against it refusing to have their votes taken, "that a bill be brought in to disable the Duke of York to inherit the Imperial Crown of this realm." It was followed by the ferocious declaration of the Commons that they would stand by his Majesty with their lives and fortunes and, should he come to any violent death (which God forbid!), revenge it to the utmost upon the Roman Catholics. Four days later the Exclusion bill was introduced and read for the first time. On May 21 it passed the second reading and was committed. The threatening aspect of these events could not be mistaken. The Commons were fierce and pertinacious. Danby's discomfiture was followed by an attack on Lauderdale and by another, still more violent, on the system of secret service money. "Extraordinary heats" broke out on the question whether bishops had or having should retain their right to sit in judgment upon peers arraigned on a capital charge, for the trial of the five Popish lords was expected, and the strength of the spiritual peers was a matter of grave consideration to those who hoped for an adverse verdict. Many were the indecencies, records Burnet, that arose on this occasion both in town and in country. Shaftesbury was expecting an easy triumph. Suddenly all came to an end. The king had information that the common council of the city was about to offer public assistance to the Commons in their efforts for the preservation of the Protestant faith, and that an inflammatory remonstrance on the subject of the Plot lay ready for presentation in the House. His mind was made up. With the cheerfulness characteristic of him he seemed to be thinking of nothing, when on May 26 he summoned the Commons to his presence and without warning declared a prorogation of three months. Eight weeks later Charles dissolved the Little Parliament of Westminster against the advice of almost the whole of his council. The blow fell with crushing effect upon the Whig party. Shaftesbury swore openly that he would have the heads of those who had counselled it.[341] Yet this uproarious session produced one good thing. Before proroguing Parliament the king gave his assent to the Habeas Corpus Act, its solitary record on the statute book. How near that sheet was to being blank may be told by the fact that this measure, of weighty importance in the history of England, only passed its third reading in the House of Lords because the Whig teller in joke counted one very fat lord as ten.[342]

Neither Parliament nor the privy council as a whole can properly be said at this time to have been the government of the country. Under the old system the council was a large and chiefly honorary body, the business of which was regularly transacted by a few of its members. By Sir William Temple's construction it became a miniature of the House of Commons as in the days when the government could count upon about half the votes with an occasional majority. Though those who carried on affairs might be privy councillors, there were also many councillors who made it their chief business to prevent them from doing so. The parliament of 1679 was still less to be classed with the government than its predecessor. Here the Commons hardly disguised an overmastering wish to obstruct the administration by others until it fell wholly into their own hands, and to force on the government a policy framed in the country and strongly disapproved at court. The humour of the Commons seemed to infect the Lords also. The alarm and activity of the upper house throughout the panic of the Plot almost equalled those of the Commons; and it was by great exertion alone that the court could carry the day even when the gravest interests were at stake. The English state presented at the moment a striking appearance. Since the beginning of the modern world government in England has been with scant exception by consent, not only in the sense that in every case force is ultimately on the side of the governed, but by virtue of the fact that the English government has had nothing on which to rely but the consent of the nation. Two famous examples had already shown how hard of execution other methods must be. Mutual agreement between parts of the frame was necessary to its usefulness. But now it seemed as if this was no more. Variance had sprung up and silently grown until it became direct opposition. Government and governed were divided by an openly contrary spirit. It was a question how far Charles' government could allow the division to widen without being engulfed in it. On the one side were ranged the forcible and callous statesmen who had organised the country party in the old Cavalier Parliament and transformed its soul to Whiggism; the country gentlemen, formerly staunchest adherents of the government, the class from whom now its keen opponents were drawn; religious dissenters; high-principled republicans; malcontents of every kind; the squirearchy, the magistracy, the Church of England.[343] On the other there met this formidable array a mere handful of men, dependents of the court or trained officials zealous to perform their duty and to uphold the traditions of English politics. The government was formed of the king and his servants, chief among them the secretaries of state. Apart from these support for the king's policy was meagre indeed.

The work which fell on the secretaries' shoulders was immense. Throughout the winter which followed Oates' revelations a perpetual stream of reports, warnings, informations poured into their offices. From all quarters came disturbing news. Alarms of armed men exercising in bands at night were constant. Spanish forces were said to have landed in Ireland and the French in Scotland. Tynemouth Castle was reported blown up by gunpowder. Five thousand Spaniards were in Wales. A combined French and Spanish fleet was only prevented by a storm from landing at Milford Haven. The king's ships at Chatham and elsewhere were to be burnt and thus facilitate the passage of troops from Dunkirk, while Hull and other seaports were ready to receive the invaders. Gentlemen rode up from Yorkshire with wild tales of "the crack and noise" in those parts, and in the West Riding the militia was called out against imaginary foes. Vast fears came from Cheshire of strange persons and a private post, denoting no good intentions. An English doctor wrote from Amsterdam telling how he had overheard conspirators planning the king's destruction for the month of April, and had barely escaped being murdered for his indiscretion.[344] All this and a vast mass of the same description demanded instant attention, decision, and answer. Frivolous accusations against reputed papists and plotters were innumerable. A well-wisher sent from Vienna as a present to the king an antidote of astonishing excellence against possible poisons. A still more ingenious correspondent forwarded a scheme to turn the tables on the pope by "assaulting the city of Rome on that side where the Vatican palace stands and bringing away the library."[345] In Ireland, where the Duke of Ormonde's sober government preserved admirable order, long reports were drawn up for the instruction of the secretaries at Whitehall, and these too had to be perused.[346] London alone, apart from the turmoil caused by Godfrey's death, provided heavy work. Order had to be taken for safeguarding the palace; twenty doors leading into St. James' Park were blocked and a sewer grated. Protestants and Catholics posted mutual accusations to Whitehall until the secretaries were at their wits' end how to deal with them. On the prorogation of Parliament in May, bills were distributed urging the prentices to take arms and demand the trial of the lords in the Tower. The guards at the palace were doubled, strong watches posted, and every precaution taken. A few weeks before it had been thought necessary to send two companies of dragoons to Portsmouth,[347] The whole country seemed on the verge of insurrection. In December Charles thought he saw signs of a rebellion brewing. A few months later Danby drew up a memorandum in the Tower which clearly shewed that he was of the same opinion. He suggested that the king should take up his residence out of London and call Parliament to meet him away from the capital, the stronghold of his opponents' power. Touch should be kept with the troops disbanded. All who had served against the king in the Civil War could be forced to register their names. The navy might be officered by men who would have influence on the sailors. Lastly and most significant, the Tower should be secured.[348]

Such and so multifarious were the doings of members of the government. Yet they were members only. The head was the king's, the policy his, and to him its ultimate failure or success must be ascribed.

CHAPTER II

THE CATHOLICS

OF the five hundred Cavalier gentlemen who fell in the Civil War more than one-third were Catholics,[349] The remnant of the class that had once been the most dignified and the wealthiest in England was thrown by the Popish Plot into the fiercest persecution known to its history. For the first time a real attempt was made to put the penal laws into full force. All over the country the prisons were filled, houses of Roman Catholics searched for arms, their estates confiscated. Fourteen men were executed for high treason in the Plot, three for Godfrey's murder. Eight Catholic priests suffered on account of their orders under the statute of Queen Elizabeth which made it treason for a subject to take orders from the Church of Rome and, returning to England, to remain there upwards of forty days. Five died in prison. Thirty more were condemned to death, but were reprieved, and of these sixteen died in confinement.[350] The actual figures are enough, but they do not complete the tale of suffering. Nothing is told by them of the persecution less than to death, the harrying of men and women for conscience' sake, the cruel blight fallen on the lives of hundreds because of the crimes and follies of intriguers who turned religion to be an affair of politics. The odour of mystery and the fear of foreign assault which Catholic designs had for years aggravated had worked in the minds of Englishmen with so strong a ferment that, were there much or little of truth in the Plot, it needed only an opportunity for hardly concealed terror and hatred finally to burst restraint.[351] On all sides the lot of Catholics was pitiable. Those in London who were not imprisoned were banished from the capital. As many as thirty thousand were said to have fled. In the country fresh persecution awaited them. Justices of the peace had orders to execute strictly the laws against recusants, the Lord Chancellor to weed the commission of those who did not. Popish books and relics were diligently sought out, seized, and burnt. The library, papers, and vestments of Father Harcourt, rector of the Jesuit College in London, went to make a public bonfire. Wild House, the residence of the Weld family near the Strand, and a noted resort of Roman Catholics, was ransacked and twenty-seven chests of goods haled from a grotto in the garden. Houses of eminent Catholics all over the kingdom were searched and searched again, and sometimes almost destroyed by the efforts of officers to find hidden priests. Catholic merchants found themselves bankrupt. Everywhere Catholics were driven from home and livelihood, reduced to beggary. Only the Penderels, Huddlestone the priest, and others who had helped the king in his flight from Worcester escaped the general fate. Charles' gratitude procured for them exemption from the action of the laws.[352] For the rest only good fortune could mitigate the horrors of that time. Those in prison had nothing on which to subsist but the charity of friends. Seized at inns, in secret retreats, on beds of sickness, they were hurried through rain or snow to dreadful cells without money or a sufficient supply of clothes. The Duke and Duchess of York, Lord Castlemaine, and other noble Catholics made great efforts for their fellows in religion. Yet to relieve the vast mass of suffering no private aid could suffice. Many were reduced to the greatest distress. Some even died of want. Priests, hunted from one to another more painful hiding-place, were put to every shift to evade capture. For days they lay, cramped and hungry, in holes within walls, behind chimneys, even fastened up beneath tables, while their pursuers tore up the floors, broke down the walls, dug up the garden walks within a few yards of them. When they ventured forth to escape, it was in the depth of winter, through ice and mud, and in the teeth of midnight storms. Nor were the pious alone objects of attack. The most irreligious of their religion were not spared. Long-stored enmity and an insatiable desire for novelty caught at victims of whatever character. The Duchesse Mazarin, who lived only for play and her light loves, was accused of being a party to the Plot. Where the end would come no man could say. All the Catholics in the service of the royal family who could took ship for the continent. The Duchess of York wrote to her brother that she could not describe the hundredth part of the trouble into which they were plunged. Many abjured their faith or at least took the condemned oaths of allegiance and supremacy. Pilate and Herod, wrote the Jesuit Warner to his general, were banded with the heretic priests against his society and the Catholics. A few weeks later he added: "Hope itself is scarce left us."[353]

In no part of the country was persecution more bitter than in Yorkshire. Even before the time of the Popish Plot Catholics in the country had been subjected to considerable annoyance, and when "the great crack and noise" of the event burst on the astonished ears of the world they became at once the object of vehement attack. Inquisition was made in all parts for priests and recusants. The cells of York Castle, of which the condition was notorious in an age of notorious prisons, were filled. To priests and their relatives particular attention was paid. Soon two scoundrels, by name Mowbray and Bolron, came forward to give evidence of the preparations of papists to aid in the grand design discovered by Oates. Bolron had been manager of coal-pits on the estate of Sir Thomas Gascoigne, an aged baronet and representative of the ancient family of Barnbow Hall in the West Riding, and, being suspected of fraud, was threatened with a prosecution for felony by Lady Tempest, the baronet's daughter. Mowbray was a servant in the same family discharged on suspicion of theft. Thus the two had every reason to plot revenge. Bolron swore that Sir Thomas, together with his daughter, Sir Miles Stapleton, several other gentlemen, and his nephew, a priest named Thwing, had signed a resolution to kill the king and had offered a thousand pounds to whoever should do the deed. Mowbray added that they had intended to burn London and York to the ground. The Yorkshire magistrates refused to act on the information of known criminals, but Bolron went to town and found in Shaftesbury an inquisitor who would not consent to see the matter dropped.[354] Sir Thomas was tried at Westminster, but acquitted by a jury of Yorkshire gentlemen. Sir Miles Stapleton and Lady Tempest stood their trial at York. They also were acquitted, but upon the same discreditable evidence Thwing was convicted and on October 23, 1680 suffered the penalty for high treason. In spite of the fact that three juries had disbelieved his word Bolron was able by permission of the House of Commons to produce an ingenious forgery, entitled "The Papists' Bloody Oath of Secrecy and Litany of Intercession," which after repeated exposure and the lapse of more than two centuries is still sometimes taken for true by his more gullible, if less malignant, successors. For the moment the acquittal of Gascoigne and his friends stayed the flow of blood, but the Yorkshire Protestants shewed effectively by their conduct at the Revolution that their feelings remained unchanged.[355]

While persecution fell indiscriminately on those who confessed the creed of the Roman Church, it was not to be expected that all should view their troubles alike. The lead given in the speech from the throne was freely followed. It was a Jesuit plot, said the king. It was a Jesuit plot, cried Catholics who were not under the influence of the order. The society has seldom drawn the affection of many outside its own ranks in any age, and in the seventeenth century incurred the hatred of almost all parts of the English Catholic body. Constant intrigues set the secular priests, members of the other orders, and, it can hardly be doubted, a large number of laymen against its restless and selfish policy. The result was plain. For the doings of the society every one had now to suffer. In the midst of fierce trouble it was not against the government but against the Jesuits that Catholic resentment was shewn. Jesuits were everywhere scouted, railed at for their pernicious principles, scarce treated civilly in the company they sought. There was even rejoicing at their downfall. At last old scores would be paid off; at last all the juggles and intrigues at court would find their due reward in public shame. The Jesuit historian sighs with meek grief at the additional burden the society was compelled to bear.[356] It was perhaps not only political intrigues that roused the displeasure of laymen. Though many of the priesthood were men of saintly temper and bore affliction with constancy and admirable effort on behalf of their brethren, there were also black sheep among them. Scandal caused by priests who thronged the court was of long standing. In the opinion of the more discreet their behaviour was such as to cause harm rather than good to the Catholic religion in England.[357] The case of St. Germain was notorious. Great disrepute was brought on the Society of Jesus by the story of Godfrey's murder: had the real facts been known they would have been more damaging still. Yet more unfortunate, since it brought laughter with it, was the case of Father John Gavan, the famous martyr and Jesuit who was likened to "an angel of God" and his voice in preaching to "a silver trumpet"; for, having done battle in youth with the lust of the flesh, he was seized at the height of his reputation in the stables of the Imperial ambassador, where he was hiding with a woman who passed as his wife and their son.[358]

It was the distressing fate of so prized a member of the society to be a cause of dissension and scandal. Even his death at Tyburn did not make an end. The no less famous Dr. John Sergeant, who had passed a long career in controversy against Jesuit and Protestant divines, came forward to blacken Gavan's memory. Sergeant had already given trouble to the Roman officials by his teaching on the oath of allegiance.[359] With the prosecution of the Popish Plot the movement in favour of the oath naturally grew in strength among moderate Catholics; the formula had been many times condemned at Rome; and it was heard with dismay at the curia that the Duke of Norfolk had flouted authority and taken the oath, presumably to obtain more easily a pass to go beyond seas.[360] With others of his order Gavan had written against the oath and, though he pronounced in his speech from the gallows against the notion that kings might be killed at the pope's command, would not surrender the theory of the deposing power.[361] Soon after his execution Sergeant came to Henry Sidney, ambassador at the Hague. He knew nothing of the Plot, but offered to prove that according to the teaching of a certain Jesuit the queen might lawfully kill the king for his unfaithfulness. Sidney brought the priest to London, where on October 31, 1679 he was examined by the king in council. A few months later the council again received his information and that of another priest, David Morris, who had been educated at St. Omers and the English Jesuit College in Rome. The Jesuit of whom they spoke was Gavan. It seemed that he had expressed the opinion complained of to a lady living in Brussels. By order of the House of Commons the depositions were printed and obtained a wide circulation. The spectacle of two priests informing against a brother in orders was calculated to afford grave scandal to Catholics and equal satisfaction to Protestants. Considerable pains were taken by the Jesuits to upset the credit of the story, and the rector of the college at Liège wrote an account containing a denial of the fact by the lady in question; but the compiler of the *Annual Letters* for the year 1680 was unfortunate in choosing to cast doubt upon her credibility, thus leaving the matter as much open to question as before.[362] The division in the Catholic body of which this was a symptom was a source of undoubted weakness: all the efforts to crush those in favour of the oath were unavailing, and lively agitation was caused by the certain news that the Duke of York himself had pledged his allegiance by it, seduced thereto by the example of so many born Catholics who upheld its lawfulness.[363] However much it might be denied in public controversy, the refusal to allow the oath to Catholics was indissolubly bound up with the claim to the papal power of deposition. About the same time a priest whose name is given as Forstal maintained that the king might be deposed at the command or at least with the participation of the pope. James questioned the nuncio at Brussels on the subject, and received answer that the error lay not in the opinion held, but in the choice of so inopportune a moment to express it, since the worst consequences might be expected. No doubt the matter was in debate, but the meaning to be drawn from the prelate's reply was obvious, for he did not think it worth while to argue the point further. The priest guilty of such rashness was induced to withdraw for a time to a monastery in Westphalia. Prudence was above all things necessary in the cause of the church.[364]

The Catholic body was thus divided within itself when the odium into which it had fallen was enhanced by the obscure intrigue known as the Meal Tub Plot. It was a time when Catholics could afford to take few risks in their conduct. Besides direct charges against them they lay under the imputation of more than one attempt to confound their accusers by means as base as those used against themselves; two brothers of Prance, who was not distinguished by the world from other informers, were secular priests; Jennison, a follower in the train of Oates, had a brother in the Society of Jesus, who lay dying in Newgate, and was thought to be a wealthy country gentleman appearing for honesty's sake to enlighten his fellow-countrymen; strong suspicion attached to witnesses who came to speak for the Jesuits at their trials.[365] It might therefore be expected that the more Catholics loved their religion, the more carefully would they refrain from adding to the frightful hostility already shewn against it. Nevertheless it was at this moment that some of their leaders, not without influence or repute, undertook to retaliate on their enemies by weapons of more than questionable worth. Whether they were the first movers in the affair or entered it on the invitation of others was the question.

In March 1679 a young man of infamous character who went by the name sometimes of Willoughby, sometimes of Dangerfield, lay in the debtor's side of Newgate. Having been in gaol for the best part of a year, he began to turn his thoughts to means of getting out, and proceeded to draw articles of complaint against Captain Richardson, the keeper of Newgate, for his treatment of prisoners. This came to the ears of another gaol-bird, Mrs. White, who, fancying Dangerfield's ability, on her discharge imparted the fact to a friend on the look-out for an assistant of talent. Her friend was Mrs. Cellier, whose name and character have become notorious in a swarm of pamphlets and reports of trials of the time. She was the wife of a French merchant and pursued the profession of midwife, and assuredly of something else, within a circle of Roman Catholic notables. She was employed to collect alms for the relief of those of her religion in prison for the Plot. She had been concerned in the unsavoury case of Knox and Lane, who were put up to defame Oates' character.[366] When witnesses were sent over from St. Omers to give evidence at the trials, it was at her house that they were lodged and fed by Lord Castlemaine. The Duchess of York had used her services to no small extent. She was in fact a regular agent of the Catholic nobles in political intrigue, and in close connection with the Countess of Powis, whose husband, together with the Lords Petre, Arundel, Stafford, and Bellasis, was in the Tower on a charge of high treason, a woman of bold and active spirit and devoted to the Duke of York. The conduct of Mrs. Cellier was not such as to inspire confidence in the purity of her intentions. Armed with Mrs. White's information she repaired to one Gadbury, an astrologer, for Dangerfield's horoscope, pretending that she wished for a man to collect her husband's debts. To suppose that any sane person could use one of Dangerfield's stamp for the purpose would be absurd: it was certainly for other purposes that he was wanted. Their character soon became apparent. For there was in Newgate a prisoner named Stroud, a friend of Bedloe and thought capable of proving that the Earl of Shaftesbury was suborning witnesses against the lords in the Tower. Dangerfield was employed to make him drunk and learn what he could. So well did he perform his task that Mrs. Cellier paid his debts, whether to the amount of five pounds, as she, or of seven hundred, as he, said, and obtained his release. He was a handsome fellow enough, and found favour in her eyes. It was now the month of June. Dangerfield was maintained by his friend, and earned his wages by doing the work of messenger for the witnesses sent from beyond seas for the defence of the Five Jesuits, who stood their trial at this time.[367]

Clad in a decent suit, with money in his pocket, and the friend of Mrs. Cellier's bosom, Dangerfield began to go about the town. He was taken to Powis House and introduced to the Countess. He took notes at the trials of Wakeman and Langhorn and carried them to Lord Powis in the Tower. Indeed his appearance was so pleasing and his recommendation so high that he was allowed to take up his abode at Powis House, and even to sit with Lady Powis at table.[368] And now the serious business began. One Nevil, alias Payne, a writer of libellous pamphlets, was retained by Mrs. Cellier with others of his trade for the service of Lady Powis. Dangerfield's talents were added to the band, which carried on a lively production of ballads and pamphlets, such as "The Transforming of Traitors into Martyrs," "The Presbyterian Unmasked," "The Ballad of the Popish Plot," "The Danby Reflections," and an edition of the Five Jesuits' dying speeches, all launched against the Presbyterians. Dangerfield was an attorney's son and, having been bred a clerk, could write with some smartness. At the same time he was employed to go the round of coffee-houses frequented by old Presbyterians and new Whigs, to pick up what scraps of information against them he could.[369] The result was most satisfactory. Lists of names were obtained from the drawers. By means of Gadbury, Dangerfield was introduced to Sir Robert Peyton, the great Whig merchant whose apostasy was the first blow to the Whig cause. He thought of joining the King's Head Club himself, but was dissuaded on learning that he would be required to pay a subscription of one or two guineas. He began to find out the habits of Shaftesbury's partisans. Presently there appeared between Dangerfield and Mrs. Cellier those papers, the authorship of which each fastened upon the other, bearing witness to the existence of a Presbyterian plot. According to Mrs. Cellier's account Dangerfield brought the notes to her; they were written at the dictation of Lady Powis, was what he said. That point may be discussed later. It is at any rate certain that Lady Powis was acquainted with their contents and ready to act upon them. She took Dangerfield to her son-in-law, the Earl of Peterborough, Lord Peterborough to the Duke of York, the Duke of York to the king, and the papers, which contained an account of an extensive movement planned by Shaftesbury and Monmouth, were seen by all. The budget was headed "The State of the Three Kingdoms." The names of the leaders were noted down, commissions were stated to have already been granted, and a scheme for a revolutionary government was sketched. James gave the captain, as Dangerfield was styled by himself and Lord Peterborough, twenty guineas in reward for his zeal; the king added forty more and turned him over to Secretary Coventry. As earnest of his good faith, Dangerfield produced two letters addressed to Shaftesbury by Sir Richard Bulstrode, the minister at Brussels. They were on indifferent subjects; but how came they in Dangerfield's possession? Coventry was dissatisfied with the affair, and told the captain that if he were to be believed, something more material must be forthcoming. Dangerfield pressed for a general warrant to search, but on the advice of Chief-Justice North was refused. Evidently other means must be tried.[370]

On October 22 Dangerfield, having given notice of a parcel of Flanders lace smuggled into the country by one Colonel Mansell, obtained a warrant to search his lodgings, which were in the same house as his own. That is to say, Dangerfield had specially engaged rooms under Mansell's roof. The colonel was named in his list as quartermaster of the prospective

Presbyterian army. Under Dangerfield's guidance the customs' officers went through the rooms, but could find nothing. He begged them to look behind the bed and, when nothing came thence, himself darted behind, pulled out a packet of papers, and began to cry "Treason." The officers took their find to a justice of the peace, who, having regard to the suspicious circumstances, acted upon the maxim, He who hides can find, and issued a warrant for Dangerfield's apprehension. An investigation was immediately ordered by the council. On the next day, as Dangerfield was waiting to be examined, an officer of the Mint happened to pass and, recognising in him an old offender, had him arrested for coining false money. When Henry Coventry appeared in the council-room he was met by the somewhat surprising intelligence that his informer was in custody as a forger and coiner, and was known for a noted criminal. A thorough examination made the truth of the charges certain, besides bringing to light the fact, unfortunate for the captain, that he had stood twice in the pillory, had only escaped a third dose of the same punishment by breaking prison, and was in fine a mischievous and notorious rascal. It was proved beyond doubt that he had himself disposed the papers, containing a plain account of the so-called Presbyterian Plot, in Mansell's room and, since there were no contraband goods there at all, had only brought the customs' officials to perform what the refusal to grant a search warrant had prevented him from doing otherwise. As the result on October 27 Dangerfield was committed to Newgate. He had in the meantime sent a note to Mrs. Cellier, and by her assistance was let out for a couple of days on bail. Thus the authorities were enabled to follow Dangerfield's committal by a search at Mrs. Cellier's. Here on October 29 Sir William Waller found two bundles of papers, one behind the kitchen boiler, the other at the bottom of the meal tub, whence on this account the name of the plot was derived. One contained a copy of Dangerfield's letter to the king, offering to make yet greater disclosures; the other and larger proved to be a considerable amplification of the story he had told on his first introduction at court. Fearing that the captain would betray her, Mrs. Cellier had a message conveyed to him with the encouraging words, which she boasted as her motto, "I never change," and was immediately after carried to the Gatehouse. The Lady Errant, as she became known by her enemies, declared afterwards that her fear was lest Dangerfield should falsely use their connection to his own advantage. Whatever its nature, her fear was justified; for on October 31 he desired to be taken before Sir Robert Clayton, then Lord Mayor, and made confession that the Presbyterian Plot was, in a word invented by himself, a Sham destined to cover the intentions of the papists and to ruin their adversaries. The papers found in the meal tub, besides the treasonable letters he had put behind Colonel Mansell's bed, were dictated to him by the Countess of Powis, and approved by Lord Peterborough and Mrs. Cellier. He had resisted the bribe of £2000 offered him by Lord Arundel to murder the king, but had undertaken to the Earl of Powis to assassinate Lord Shaftesbury for a quarter of that sum. Divers attempts had actually been made on the Whig leader; twice he had been himself to the earl's residence, Thanet House in Aldersgate Street, and once Mrs. Cellier went in person, only to meet with failure. All this had been with the knowledge and at the direction of Roman Catholic priests. The next day Dangerfield was taken before the council and affirmed the truth of his statement.[371]

In the tangle of accusations and informations which followed and were laboriously examined at the council board, either side tried to throw the blame of the intrigue on the other. Protestants were jubilant at the detection of another Catholic plot, and swore by the whole truth of Dangerfield's confession. Catholics declared that the affair was designed by Lord Shaftesbury to injure the Duke of York, and that their leaders had been deceived by the captain, who had led them step by step to catastrophe and hid the treasonable packet at Colonel Mansell's with the sole intention that his own sketch of the Presbyterian designs might be discovered in Mrs. Cellier's meal tub.[372] The intricacy of these events will probably never be wholly developed. Every one concerned was ready to lie in his own interest. Every one of the principals did lie, it can hardly be doubted. Many committed perjury; and some were probably suborned to perjure. The tale of complex untruth and base endeavour is one that threatens to become dreary. Nevertheless there are indications of the truth on which a general opinion may be based. This is certain, that Dangerfield, perilous rogue as he was known to be, was taken from prison by Mrs. Cellier, the confidante of Lady Powis, supported in her house and at her cost. He was employed in maintaining the cause of their religion, his employment was known to Lord Peterborough, a friend of the Duke of York, and he was introduced to the duke by him as an active agent against their common enemies. By their account they took from him the tale of a Presbyterian plot; by his own he invented it at their direction. Were the Catholic statements accepted as true, they would convict the duke's party of most gross folly in trusting a man of character so depraved: more than that, for the man had been paid to play the spy and, it was admitted by his employers, had been given hints that it would be good to discover plots of the nature of that which he retailed to them; and to accept such a story without investigation, when it was known that the teller had orders beforehand to collect materials, argues at least some disingenuity. Nor is this all. There is reason to think that in some essentials Dangerfield's confession contained the truth. Supposing that, as Lord Peterborough and his friends declared, the captain had only hidden his parcel behind Mansell's bed in order to be detected, he would at least have taken the trouble to make discovery of evidence against Mrs. Cellier certain. The papers concocted between them were in his possession, and he had only to hide them without her knowledge where they could be easily found by an officer. On the supposition that he meant to turn informer against the Catholics their discovery at Mrs. Cellier's was necessary to his success. Without it there would be no more than his bare word to shew that they had employed him at all. As evidence the find of papers was invaluable to him. Yet he did not even attempt to supply that evidence. So far from concealing the incriminating notes himself, he gave them to Mrs. Cellier to dispose as she thought best. The natural thing for her to do was to burn them and, for all Dangerfield knew, she might have done so. For whatever reason she preferred the other course. She gave the papers to her servant to hide, and it was the servant who placed them in the regions of the kitchen where they were found by Sir William Waller.[373] Dangerfield could not possibly have known of their concealment or even of their preservation. The fact that Mrs. Cellier chose to conceal the evidence against her rather than deliver it to the council, which would have been her best course had she been wholly innocent, or burn it to destroy the traces of her guilt, if she were guilty, tells nothing; for on Dangerfield's arrest she hoped that he would still be faithful to her, and was not in any case so clean of hand as to court an inquiry into the nature of the services she had from him. She may well have hoped that their connection would escape notice. But beyond this it is plain that, even if she was not aware of Dangerfield's intention to fix the odium of a fictitious plot on the Protestant party, her relations with him were of so intimate a kind that only wilful ignorance could have saved her from knowledge of it. She knew of the treasonable papers in Colonel Mansell's room and, when a search warrant could not be procured, it was she who advised Dangerfield to have recourse to the customs house.[374] At least one who was closely acquainted with the Catholic leaders and could not be suspected of prejudice declared the whole affair to be a design of persons zealous for the Duke of York. Lord Peterborough and Lady Powis, wrote the French ambassador, thought to render a great service by bringing forward a man who would give evidence against the Earl of Shaftesbury. They had merely tried to use tools similar to those by which their enemies were thought to have achieved success.[375]

Though it was admitted that Dangerfield had tried to fit the Protestants with a forged plot and highly probable that the Catholics had a hand in the forgery, there is yet something to be said on the other side. The Presbyterian plot was a fiction; but there was a basis of Dangerfield's story that was not fictitious. An actual movement, the lines of which are partly known, was at the moment being concerted by the Whig leaders. The list of those concerned in the plot drawn up by Dangerfield contains the names of many undoubtedly implicated, and of many afterwards guilty of the treason of the Rye House Plot, which grew out of the designs at this time.[376] Another fact is of importance. To strengthen his story in the eyes of the secretary of state, Dangerfield produced two letters belonging to Lord Shaftesbury.[377] In his confession he declared he had stolen these on one of the occasions when he went to kill the earl. There is no need to linger over the tales of attempted assassination. Improbable as they were in themselves, they are set beyond the bounds of credibility by the informer's halting narrative and the ridiculous excuses he alleged for failure.[378] Nevertheless his production of the letters makes it evident that he had been with the Whig leader. There can be no doubt that he had some knowledge of the Whig designs. Most likely he was intriguing with both parties at the same time in order to see which he could with greater profit betray, and ended by betraying both, though the Catholics, since they had trusted him the more, were more severely affected by the results of his treachery. In the course of the next year Mrs. Cellier and the Earl of Castlemaine were tried for high treason. Lady Powis too had been committed to the Tower, but the bill against her was ignored by the grand jury. Both cases rested largely upon the evidence of Dangerfield, against whom records of crime were produced by the defence. As his pardon did not cover a felony of which he had been convicted, Mrs. Cellier was formally acquitted on the ground that he was no good witness and that only one other appeared against her; and when the pardon was afterwards corrected, the jury before whom Castlemaine was tried refused to believe the word of a man who bore the accumulated weight of sixteen convictions, guilty of "six great enormous crimes," and pronounced a verdict of not guilty after an absence of only a few minutes from the box.[379] Few will be found to quarrel with the judgment of the Lord Chancellor, who told Dangerfield: "You are a fine fellow, first to come to his Majesty and there tell him one story, then to my Lord Powis, and from thence to my Lord Shaftesbury's, discovering to one what discourse you held with the other; and thus to bring one story to the council, another to the Earl of Shaftesbury."[380]

The Duke of York's conduct in the Meal Tub Plot was characteristic of him. He had brought Dangerfield to the king and by his imprudence was the cause of much suspicion and distrust. No one felt certain how the affair would turn out. People thought that James would "never leave off tampering."[381] He was a man with the smallest aptitude for diplomacy. He was able neither to let events take their course without interference nor by fingering ever to improve them. He was always for action of a decided and generally a tactless kind. While he persistently endeavoured to make others change their views, his own were held with an obstinacy that nothing could uproot. His continual desire for activity was one of the difficulties which most hampered Charles II's policy. Apart from his itch for management and a preference shared with other politicians of the time for underhand dealing his very presence at court was as a trumpet call to his enemies. His severance from the Church of England was a severance from the English people likewise. The Church of Rome was traditionally held the enemy of the nation. It was responsible for many of the doubts and difficulties of the restored monarchy. Its action was coupled in the general mind with the aggression of foreign foes. For the heir to the throne at such a time to go over to it was an act of great hardiness. Nor could he do so without himself being proclaimed an enemy of the people and disloyal to his duty. The horror expressed at the notion that James should depart from the faith which his father had signed with blood was increased by contemplation of the results attending the step. The Roman Catholic religion, it was said, introduced an *imperium in imperio* and, were it settled in England, would at once destroy the liberties and drain the wealth of the country.[382] It seemed as if the duke must have some deep and sinister motive in his mind to leave the religion that had been won by so much blood. Many princes had changed their faith for reason of state, but the instance of one who departed from the church of the people against the clearest command of expedience and, as it seemed to them, the no less clear showing of reason was unparalleled. And the subtle influence of Jesuits who had wrought this in him was feared as well in the present as for the future. So long as the duke remained at the king's right hand there was the added terror that he would shape the royal policy in the direction whither he would direct it himself from the throne. Nothing could be devised to cure the distrust aroused by his attitude, except that he should return to the Protestant religion or withdraw from the king's presence. The latter was tried with success, the former without. By the advice of Danby, when it was certain that the elections for the parliament of 1679 were unfavourable to the court, James was unwillingly sent out of England and ordered to take up his abode in Brussels.[383] Episcopal powers of persuasion had already been tried on him in vain. Before he set out another attempt was made, with the like result. It is to the credit of his courage that no prospect of advantage could bring him to surrender his faith. The bishops brought forward every available argument, but were unable to boast any satisfaction. Rome was hopeful that he would withstand all similar proposals.[384] As the prosecution of the Popish Plot drove the storm higher against the court and the Catholics, the pressure put on James to recant his faith increased. A year later when the duke was in London during the prorogation a strong attempt was made by his friends. They knew that his conversion would mean the greatest embarrassment to the host of enemies who built high upon his opposition to the national temper. Should he consent they would be compelled to change all their plans and perhaps fail to find another weapon strong enough to serve the same purpose. At least he would be able to remain at court. Charles spoke forcibly on the subject. A more powerful advocate was found in the duchess, who despite James' gross and notorious profligacy exercised some influence on him and wished at any price to escape a third exile. Months went by and the agitation continued. James seemed to be weakening. As the day fixed for the meeting of Parliament drew near, the gossip of Whitehall had it that he would come over. Expectation was disappointed. On the day before the session opened the duke and duchess set sail for Edinburgh, as Catholic as ever.[385] There was nothing to be gained from him by argument. Nor was he to be driven. Even Charles' threat that unless he went to church the Exclusion bill should be passed failed to move him. Conscience and honour forbade him equally to deny and to dissemble his religion. Besides, if he were to consent, Shaftesbury would only put about that he had a dispensation from the pope and was still a Catholic at heart. His mind was fixed. By God's grace he was determined "never to do so damnable a thing."[386]

James' mind was fixed on other points as well. He could not understand that time had any value in the struggle between men or delay any merit. The king's policy of waiting was wholly unintelligible to him. Ultimate success seemed to him to depend upon immediate triumph, and for immediate triumph he was ready to stake everything. Each concession, each dilatory advance, each deceptive retreat appeared as sure tokens that he and the monarchy were on the verge of ruin, about to be hurled together into the abyss. There was little enough of sympathy between the brothers, who made a public show of friendship and in private kept secrets to themselves. When he afterwards compiled the memoirs of his life, James was able to exhibit some calmness in discussing their relations; for, as he said, the king was sensible that their interest was at bottom the same against common adversaries, since "his chief security lay in having a successor they liked worse than himself." "He resolved therefore," continued the writer, "to stick to the main chance, and suffer no diminution in the prerogative during his time; however, he thought it necessary to yield as far as he could to convince the world of his sincerity, and to put his enemies so much in the wrong (without parting with any essential thing) as that, if they forced him to break, he might have friends enough to assist him."[387] At the time this series of penetrating afterthoughts did not cross the duke's mind. He had so little conception of Charles' aim and point of view as to be in constant terror that he would be abandoned to the wrath of the opposing forces. He conceived himself, like his son-in-law the Prince of Orange, to be dealing with a volatile being of pleasure, and crying, as the captain of a ship to his helmsman in a storm: Steady, steady, steady.[388] Only positive commands and elaborate assurances, to which even then he attached little weight,[389] could induce him to leave the court at moments of crisis when his presence was likely to have the worst possible effects. He could never think that his absence would not serve only to embolden his enemies. Present, he was continually interfering and making unwise suggestions. Absent, he did not cease pressing for his recall.[390] Nor did he cease from

Belgium and Scotland to press on the king counsels of desperation. Anything tainted with moderation had to his nostrils the odour of surrender. He had not been two months at Brussels before he was urging Charles to steps which he knew must mean civil war. Ireland, Scotland, the fleet, the guards, the garrisons, were still in the king's hand. The Prince of Orange had given assurance that he would be on the side of royalty. Let Charles cease to countenance Monmouth and the party with him, let him think on the fate of Edward II, Richard II, and the king his father. "Now or never," wrote the duke, "is the time to save the monarchy."[391] This was of a piece with all his advice. All things, he thought, tended to a republic. Sir William Temple's council seemed to him to make the king little better than a Doge of Venice, and to leave him so little support that the Exclusion bill could hardly be resisted, a calamity by which the house of Stuart would be "absolutely ruined and given up." A short time after he expressed the opinion that if Charles would not submit to be less than a Doge of Venice a rebellion would be the necessary result. By June 1679 he was writing; "Things have been let go to that pass that the best I can expect is very great disorders, and unless something very vigorous is done within a very few days, the monarchy is gone."[392] Five months, six months, a year later the same counsel was being reiterated.[393] While Charles remained cool and undismayed in the midst of pressing danger, every fresh event abashed the mind of James.[394] He could not appraise facts at their true worth, since he was without insight; devoid of imagination, he was unable to attribute to others powers he lacked himself. His very friends spoke against his unenlightened zeal, and the pope favoured him and his wife each with a brief on the subject.[395] It was the beginning of that stream of protest which afterwards marked with increasing volume the course of his downfall.

Advice to others to act boldly is not uncommon. But James was ready on occasion to act on his own behalf. In May 1679 there appeared at Brussels one Colonel Fitzpatrick, a man of brave counsel and of great repute among his countrymen the Irish. He had come to arrange a rising in Ireland. The Catholics were groaning under an intolerable yoke and would follow him. By a small amount of assistance from foreign powers the coasts could be seized, arms and munitions landed, and success assured. Fitzpatrick was said to have for his project the consent of the Irish Catholic clergy and to have carried letters of recommendation into France before coming to Flanders. But French policy was opposed to assisting James in the formation of a strong party and the money was not to be obtained. Rather than run the risk of increasing hostility in England by the Colonel's presence near him, James dismissed him. With much murmuring Fitzpatrick left Brussels.[396] Though this proposal had to be refused, James kept the idea constantly before his mind. The more certain that the king's refusal to accept his violent advice became, the more his thoughts turned to the possibility of violence without the king's participation. With the approach of Parliament in the winter of 1680 the notion became further developed. James believed that open force alone could re-establish the royal authority, on the security of which he felt his own safety to rest. If he could compel his brother to act, a final rupture might be precipitated. His enemies would be forestalled, and out of the civil war that would ensue the power of the throne might issue triumphant. It was his policy to push matters to the point of extremity. When he was ordered from London to avoid the session he took northwards with him the intention to see to his own interest. Should the attack on him be pushed further, he thought to unite parties in Scotland in the royal cause and by exciting trouble there and in Ireland to bring the struggle to a head. Then he believed that a larger party than many imagined would be on his side in England.[397]

On the success of the Duke of York depended all the hopes of Roman Catholics for the future of their religion in the English realm. He was their secular head and the turning-point of their plans. His movements were watched with the keenest interest by the authorities of the church. Patience, prudence, and persistence was the policy they advocated. Exhortations to obedience, expressions of attachment and submission passed continually between him and his spiritual patrons. The papal nuncio at Brussels informed him of the deep concern that the Catholic religion had in his cause, and received the gratifying assurance that he would make it his first care to propagate the true faith by every means at his disposal.[398] How James fulfilled that promise is well known. However much devotion he expressed to the wishes of the Holy Father, his heart was more at one with the Society of Jesus than with the court of Rome. He chose Jesuits for his confessors, begged emoluments for them, took their policy for his guide. While his course drew from the Jesuits inexhaustible and still unexhausted praise, it was met by a series of remonstrances waxing in indignation from the pontiff. In the year 1687 fifty candidates for orders in the society were being prepared for work in the English province. King James, it is said, informed Father John Keynes, the provincial, that double or treble that number would be necessary to accomplish what he destined for Jesuit hands.[399] The result declared his wisdom. The mystery of the Revolution was that William of Orange, a Protestant invading the realm of a Catholic monarch, had the support of the Catholic emperor at the instigation of the pope. From the fierce battle of the Popish Plot Charles II tore a prize to deliver to the man by whose ill-judged efforts he had most nearly been robbed of it. At his death he left a kingdom compact, loyal, prosperous, ready to carry on the traditions that had been built up with labour and in the teeth of disaster. When that day came James behaved in perfect accord with his character. Within four years he had thrown away the fruits of a struggle that had lasted for a quarter of a century, and paid the penalty of folly and invincible obstinacy by the dragging existence of a pretender, an exile, a dependent, and a criminal.

CHAPTER III

SHAFTESBURY AND CHARLES

OF all men whose reputation was made or raised by the Popish Plot, none have since maintained their fame at so even a height as John Dryden. His person but not his name suffered from the changes of fortune, and at a distance of more than two centuries the sum of continuous investigation has little to add to the judgments passed on his times by the greatest of satirists. The flashes of Dryden's insight illumine more than the light shed by many records. In politics, no less than in society, his genius had ample room. The Plot gave him a subject worthy of a master:—

Some truth there was, but dashed and brewed with lies

To please the fools and puzzle all the wise:

Succeeding times did equal folly call

Believing nothing or believing all.

This plot, which failed for want of common sense,

Had yet a deep and dangerous consequence;

For as, when raging fevers boil the blood.

The standing lake soon floats into a flood,

And every hostile humour which before

Slept quiet in its channels bubbles o'er;

So several factions from this first ferment

Work up to foam and threat the government.[400]

The lines are a witness against the two great parties whose intrigues were woven to menace the security of the English state. Oates' false oaths ruined the hopes of the Roman Catholics: the designs of the English Whigs were grounded on them.

Anthony Ashley Cooper, Earl of Shaftesbury, was the first statesman to learn the art of organising support for policy from an entire nation. His course in life was determined by the belief that it is the business of a politician to succeed, and to that mass of mankind which is of the same opinion he should be at once apostle and martyr. No means which made for the end he had in view came amiss to his hand; by using good and bad alike, he won the power of drawing round him men who could make some show of virtuous conduct in company with scoundrels of the choicest villainy; and he used them with infinite address. From the age of twenty years he had lived in the glare of public life, ever rising on the tide, true to his own principles and false to all whom in their interest he could serviceably betray. In the Civil War he fought for the king and served him well. As a member of Barebones' Parliament he was for Cromwell against the Saints. When the Protector threw the lot for absolute rule, it was in him that parliamentary government found its keenest supporter. To this course Shaftesbury remained faithful. The throne on which "foolish Ishbosheth" sat became more rickety under his attacks. When that shadow of his father vanished from the scene, he strove with success against the despotism of the army. He was sent by the Convention Parliament as one of the two commissioners to invite Charles II to return to his kingdom. Under the restored monarchy Shaftesbury found a fair and a wider field for the exercise of talents which he devoted to the cause of religious and political freedom and commercial enterprise. At his request John Locke drew for the state of Carolina a constitution in which toleration was a prominent idea. In the office of Lord Chancellor he earned an abiding reputation for speed and purity of justice. He was an ardent foe of the Dutch republic, the threatening rival of English prosperity. He opposed the Stop of the Exchequer. As the last act in the service of government he counselled the Declaration of Indulgence, for when that was withdrawn there was nothing more to hope from the crown in the fight for liberty. At last he knew the Catholic tendency of the king and, learning perhaps the dupe that he had been made by the Treaty of Dover, flung himself into the bitterest opposition.

The foundation of the Whig party may be referred to the year 1675, when the French ambassador first contracted an alliance with a cabal consisting of four lords, Buckingham, Wharton, Ogle and, chief among them, Shaftesbury.[401] From that time onwards Shaftesbury enjoyed a growing ascendency over his partners. The fight over the bill of Non-Resistance brought them closely together; their victory, though it was by an artifice, gave them strength. But while the new party gained followers in Parliament and support in the country, it was some time before further success was achieved. The Cavalier, otherwise known by the nicknames of the Pensioned and the Pump, Parliament depended too much on the court to allow the possibility of complete triumph to the opposition.[402] Away from Westminster the terror of popery, with a Catholic successor to the crown in view, dominated the country, and on this basis the programme of the Whigs was constructed. Popery and slavery, to quote Shaftesbury's memorable phrase, went hand in hand. The Whigs aimed at securing the liberties of the nation and reducing the Catholic religion to impotence. The overthrow of Danby with his policy of Anglican supremacy, the dissolution of the House of Commons which lavish and ingenious corruption had bound to his side, the destruction of the Catholic strength in the House of Lords, the downfall of the Duke of York; these were the main ideas in their system. Yet so long as the Lord Treasurer led the Commons by his purse-strings they were unable to mark progress in the open, however much they might gain behind the scenes. So the next two years brought only failure. When Parliament met in February 1677 after a prorogation of fifteen months, the Whigs, resting their case on an obsolete statute of Edward III, elected to argue that after so long an interval it had no legal existence. The move resulted in immediate victory to the government, and Buckingham, Shaftesbury, Salisbury, and Wharton, the chief movers in the Lords, being ordered to ask pardon of the House for their offence, and refusing, were sent to the Tower. Thus, said Marvell, a prorogation without precedent was to be warranted by an imprisonment without example. Danby was strong enough to obtain an unconditional vote of £600,000. When however he introduced a bill for the better securing of the Protestant religion in case of a Catholic heir to the throne, though its drastic provisions passed the Lords easily enough, the mere fact that it seemed to legalise such a state of things roused against it the fury of the Commons, who threw it out, with the added indignity of noting in their journal, Because the body of the bill was contrary to the title.[403] After a few weeks three of the imprisoned peers made submission and were set at liberty; but Shaftesbury still lay in the Tower when in November the government reckoned another stroke to its credit in the marriage of William of Orange and Mary of York. It was not until February 1678 that he was released. To human reckoning it seemed as if the Whig cause was lost. Danby was firmer in power than ever, the royal marriage bade fair to conciliate the nation, the peace of Nymeguen was approaching its tardy conclusion. Well-informed persons believed that the leaders of the opposition were about to confess their defeat and bid farewell to politics.[404] Eight months later an auspicious wind blew Titus Oates on to the scene, and the aspect of affairs was completely changed.

There have not been wanting either among his contemporaries or in later times some to assert that Oates was procured and his story directed by the Earl of Shaftesbury. Once and again the case has broken down. Neither is there the slightest evidence for the notion, nor has it the least intrinsic probability. So clear a head as Shaftesbury's could never have been guilty of that monstrous stupidity. Clumsy forgery, feeble promises, lame excuses, bald melodrama characterised the informer's entry into public life. The tale he told was full of gross improbabilities. And with what truth it contained Shaftesbury could not have been acquainted. But what makes certainty still more certain is that on his first appearance Oates was so little sure of support from any quarter that he not only exonerated the Duke of York from complicity in the plot, but was so disobliging to the Whigs as to name him for a possible victim. The king at first thought he saw traces of Shaftesbury's hand, but was soon convinced that he erred. Before they had time to gauge the situation the Whigs laughed at the Plot as an artifice for keeping the army on foot.[405] Yet though he had no claim to be Oates' tutor, Shaftesbury welcomed him with alacrity. Fortune as if from heaven had fallen at his feet, and he prepared to make the most of it, and at the same time to vindicate the penetration of Colbert Croissy, who had called him "le plus fourbe, le plus injuste, le plus malhonnête d'Angleterre."

The wished occasion of the plot he takes,

Some circumstance he finds, but more he makes;

and, since the making of circumstance lies as well in the reception as in the invention of facts, justice must be admitted to the second line equally with the first. Circumstance was exactly what Shaftesbury could provide. He created the atmosphere for Oates to work in.

The miscreant who a few weeks before had been begging from the Jesuit fathers rose to an undreamed height of luxury and influence. Repeated addresses from the Commons obtained for him lodgings which he shared with Dr. Tonge in Whitehall.[406] The modest sum of £12 a week allotted him "for dyett and expenses" was eked out by occasional gifts of £50 "as of free gift and royal bounty" and the payment of long bills incurred for his witnesses at trials. Within twelve months the total amount made out to him reached the figure of £945 : 8 : 10. Yet Oates was but one of a host whom the popular fury enabled to batten on the royal resources; and during the same period the accounts of the secret service money, disbursed almost exclusively to informers, showed an expenditure of nearly £5000.[407] The Salamanca doctor made the most of his luck. Robed like a bishop and puffed with insolence he became the darling of the Whig party. He set up as "a solemn housekeeper" and kept a fine table. Each morning there waited at his lodgings to dress him two or three gentlemen who vied for the honour of holding his basin. He was received by the primate at Lambeth. The Bishop of Ely welcomed him as a frequent guest at dinner and was unable to set bounds to the brutality of his conversation, till Sir John Reresby administered a merited rebuke. He received the public thanks of the House of Lords. The House of Commons made the Duke of Monmouth responsible for his safety, the Lord Chamberlain for his lodging, the Lord High Treasurer for his nourishment. His sermons were public events, his person followed by admiring crowds. Popular odes were composed in his honour, popular dinners were given him in the city, designs represented him knocking the tiara from the head of "that infallible fop, the pope," or more exalted still, as an angel looking down from heaven. Among English merchants abroad his health was drunk next to that of the king. Everywhere he was courted, fêted, acknowledged. "Whig peers," writes Sir George Sitwell, "supported him by their subscriptions. Whig peers welcomed him to their houses in London and in the country. Whig peers rolled him down in their coaches to aid by his unblushing presence the election of Whig candidates, Whig peers defended him in council and flocked to support him at his trials, while their political followers were engaged in threatening and hustling the witnesses."[408] Oates had become for the moment the representative of the aspirations of the Whig party.

In this the influence of Shaftesbury is clearly visible. Though he did not procure Oates' appearance, it cannot be supposed that the informer's subsequent steps were without his knowledge and approval. At his first examination by the council Oates had declared that he knew no more than he had said against any person of what quality soever. Within two months he thought better of his memory in a way that points to refreshment from another source. The wife of one of the gentlemen of the bedchamber was entrusted with a message that, if the king would give way to it, Oates had somewhat to swear against no less a person than the queen. The royal leave was granted. On November 25 therefore Oates declared to the king in full council that if all other attempts upon his Majesty's life had failed the queen was to have been employed to murder her husband. Three days later he appeared at the bar of the House of Commons and raised his strident voice with the words, "I do accuse the queen for conspiring the death of the king and contriving how to compass it." It was a ludicrous invention of having heard the queen in conversation with certain Jesuits approve the plan for Charles' assassination and promise to assist it. Bedloe had a similar story, which the Lords also heard as well as that of Oates. When they asked what the two had meant by keeping back their information, Oates replied that by "no other person of quality" he had meant none other of the peers. Bedloe said he had forgotten. The House of Commons, stirred by their deep affection and care for the royal person, voted an immediate address for the removal of the consort and her household from Whitehall, and sent to beg the Lords' concurrence; but the Lords, dissatisfied with the depositions laid before them, refused, under protest of Shaftesbury and two of his followers, to join in the vote. Their consideration had been won by the queen's behaviour on the subject of Godfrey's murder, and they refused to allow her to be molested. In public she bore herself bravely, but her intimates knew how greatly she had been distressed by the attack. By an order from the king Oates was placed in strict confinement, his papers were seized, his servants dismissed, and free access to his rooms restrained. A strong remonstrance was prepared by the Commons, and Charles closed the incident by restoring the villain to his former liberty.[409]

The attack on the queen affords a clue to the ideas of both adversaries in the great battle that was being waged in the English state between authority and revolution. Mrs. Elliot, wife of Elliot of the bedchamber, had been the agent who took Oates' message to the king. She had also spoken to Tonge, and in a significant statement to the House of Lords confessed she had been sent to him by Lady Gerard of Bromley. The mention of this lady's name throws a ray of light on the doubtful intrigue, for she was in close connection with the Whig leaders; and were it in any case permissible to suppose that Oates had acted without assurance of support in bringing forward a charge of so delicate a nature, her appearance in the background would make it certain that this was not so. It may be taken that the move was directed from the headquarters of the Whig party. What then was the object? Catherine had never played any part whatever in politics. In obtaining favour for those of her religion she had held strictly to the terms of her marriage treaty. After the first shock at her husband's faithless impudence she had passed her time in gaiety, dancing, and frivolity. Only one end could be served by attempting to prove her a party to the Plot. It was to obtain her divorce and to marry the king to a wife who should bear him Protestant children. The knowledge of Catherine's childlessness had given rise before to talk of a similar project.[410] If it could actually be brought to completion and Charles beget a Protestant heir to the throne, there seemed a fair chance that the clouds which hung over the future of England would be dispelled. Desire for power alone did not then actuate Shaftesbury, but a purer hope for his country's prosperity. For had the scheme of divorce borne fruit and the Duke of York, with all the unrest and insecurity that his presence denoted, been removed from the succession by the appearance of a child who could hardly have been educated except as a Protestant, Shaftesbury could not have hoped himself to exercise a decisive influence on the king's policy. The storm gave Shaftesbury his power; when calm returned it would dissolve. This is his claim to real statesmanship. He was willing, it must be believed, to sacrifice power to principle, and to plan, though with odious implements, advantage to the nation, while he contemplated for himself a relapse into insignificance. What followed under Charles II's successor justified his position. Swift changes transformed his schemes and drove him to counsels of extremity, but the Revolution suspends judgment against him. The principle he embodied was that which William the deliverer came to England to save from utter ruin, the reasoned liberty of thought and action. For that he worked and made others work without sparing, bribed while his own hands were clean of gold, joined while his private life was pure with profligates of unrestrained license; for that he planned murder and brewed rebellion; for that he "fretted the pigmy body to decay";[411] for that he died. This particular proposal was not without recommendation. It was the simplest way out of the difficulty. It could cause no political commotion in the country. No principle would be overset by it nor any tradition overruled. It might be supposed to be not unpalatable to Charles. The English Reformation had followed one divorce; another might have rendered the English Revolution unnecessary. There was not however the smallest chance of success, for the king was unalterably opposed to anything of the sort. Badly as he had behaved to Catherine, he was not without gratitude and affection for her and was constant in his resolution not to add to his other faults the graver one of desertion.[412] Further, Charles was determined to let the royal power suffer injury in no respect. When the subject of the accusation prepared against the queen was first broached, he said privately that he was willing to give Oates line enough. It was the secret of the king's whole policy during the agitation of the Plot. He was playing the Whig party as a skilful angler plays his fish. Each length of line run out seemed to be the last of his reserve. Throughout his reign Charles had been striving to restore the power of the monarchy in England. Now it looked as if all his efforts had been in vain. His opponents appeared about to gain the final victory. The king's only chance was to let them exhaust themselves by the violence of their onslaught.

Having failed in one direction, Shaftesbury's attention was promptly turned to others. A difficulty confronting him in his hope of excluding the Duke of York from the succession was the choice of a substitute. The scheme of Charles' divorce and second marriage would have overcome this, but when that was dashed it became necessary to pursue the question further. At the time when Clarendon was chief minister, his opponents and among them the Duke of Buckingham proposed, in order to remove his son-in-law James, whose influence was thought to support him, that the Duke of Monmouth, the eldest of Charles' sons living in England, should be declared legitimate and heir to the crown.[413] The idea had created agitation at other times as well; and now Shaftesbury infused fresh life into it by adopting the bastard's cause and supporting him with a powerful following. It was this which rent the Whig party and destroyed its chance of success. Up to a certain point Shaftesbury could carry the other leaders. Halifax was at one with him on the treatment of the Plot, for he said that it must be handled as if it were true, whether it were so or no, and told Sir William Temple that, unless he would concur in points so necessary for the people's satisfaction, he would brand him everywhere as a papist. He demanded that Catholic priests should without receiving public warning be submitted to the rigours of a law unenforced since the reign of Elizabeth. He was willing to join with Shaftesbury in planning such steps as the French ambassador thought would tend to the entire annihilation of the royal authority and reduce England to a republic under kingly forms. But when it became apparent that Shaftesbury had adopted the cause of the graceful, popular, feather-headed Duke of Monmouth, Halifax drew away to the king's side and took with him "the party volant," which boasted with the proud title of Trimmers to hold the balance in the constitution. With them for the moment were also the more respectable of the old Presbyterian party under the lead of Lord Holles.[414] If the nation was divided by the Exclusion bill, those in favour of the project were divided among themselves by the problem in whose favour exclusion should be. Of the two claimants to consideration the Prince of Orange in virtue of his wife and his mother had obviously the better title. On the other hand it was thought that his father-in-law the Duke of York might have a dangerous influence over him; and there were fears that the republican party in Holland would in alarm cast itself into the hands of Louis XIV and thus ruin still more irretrievably the interests it was desired to preserve. The reasons against the Duke of Monmouth were evident. To alter the succession for the son of a prostitute, for the duke's mother was a woman of low character, could not but cause offence to many. Still more would resent the violation of the rights of an heir who had done nothing to forfeit them but adhere to the dictates of his conscience. Henry VIII had more than once altered the succession by act of Parliament, but though he declared his children bastards, they had yet been got in lawful wedlock. When it came to the point of a struggle, the Duke of York would have a good rallying cry. Monmouth was nevertheless secure of a strong party; all who were opposed to James for religion's sake, who were many, and all Scotland, which grew daily more exasperated under the unpopular government of Lauderdale. It may be believed that the weakness no less than the strength of Monmouth's position appealed to Shaftesbury. The Whig power lay not in support of the right, but in the constituencies, above all in London, where the sentiments by which Monmouth found favour had their strongest hold. Monmouth was moreover a man open to influence. Were the Duke of York successfully excluded, Shaftesbury was more likely to find room for the exercise of his talents under the rule of James' nephew than under that of his son-in-law, William of Orange. Of the two Monmouth gave far better promise to the earl that he would retain his power in the country and regain it in the government. Shaftesbury took his measures accordingly. Yet the Whig prospect looked by no means assured. Dissension in the party was widespread. "I must confess," wrote Algernon Sidney, summing up the arguments on the one side and on the other, "I do not know three men of a mind, and that a spirit of giddiness reigns amongst us, far beyond any I have ever observed in my life."[415]

The prorogation of Parliament in May 1679 filled the nation with ill humours. Members rode down to their country seats in high discontent.

Alarm was general and, wrote Sidney significantly, "they begin to look more than formerly unto the means of preserving themselves."[416] Scarcely were they clear of Westminster before news came that the Scottish Covenanters were up in arms and in possession of Glasgow. The outbreak was not unwelcome. Nor was it unexpected. As early as the beginning of the month Sidney had information that a rising might be expected at any moment. A few weeks before an inflammatory speech was delivered by Shaftesbury in the House of Lords; he charged the government with fomenting discord in Scotland by its evil rule, and declared that in England popery was to have brought in slavery, but in Scotland, while slavery went before, popery was to follow. By the next post, it was said, forty copies of his speech were carried up north to hearten the malcontents by the knowledge that they were favoured by a party in England. The subject was freely discussed by the Whigs in London. Even if they were not in direct communication with the rebels, there can be no doubt that they had let it be known on which side their sympathies lay,[417] The events of the ill-fated rebellion of Bothwell Brigg do not belong to this story. It did not fail for want of effort on the part of those who had encouraged its authors. Lauderdale had been attacked by an address of the Commons, and a deputation under the Duke of Hamilton now arrived to plead against him before the king. Charles remarked that "they had objected many damned things he had done against *them*, but there was nothing objected that was done against *his* service." When the revolt came up for discussion at the council, Lord Russell rose and expressed his wonder that war had not begun long ago rather than that it should have come at last, "since his Majesty thought fit to retain incendiaries near his person and in his very council." Lauderdale begged leave to retire, but the king turned to Russell with the words, "No, no. Sit down, my Lord. This is no place for addresses."[418] Charles, who boasted with some justice that he understood Scotch affairs better than any of his advisers, was for the immediate suppression of the rising by force. He was opposed by those who felt their interest advanced by its continuance. The Duke of Hamilton and his friends gave assurance that peace might be restored without bloodshed if only such men were employed as were acceptable to the nation. Shaftesbury did not conceal his desire that the rebels might at least be successful in obtaining a change of government. The Presbyterians and other sectaries were united in their hopes for their brethren in Scotland, and pamphlets were strewn about the town inciting the people to prevent the court from making preparations of war. By the suggestion of the Duke of Monmouth as commander-in-chief of the forces, the king gained his point. Shaftesbury had argued that English troops could not legally be sent to serve in Scotland. Glad to avail himself of the prestige his puppet would win from the campaign, he now consented to the arrangement, hoping that the duke would carry powers not only to beat but to treat with the rebels; more might perhaps be gained by negotiation than by arms. In this he was nearly successful. While the commission giving to Monmouth full powers was signed, Lauderdale sat silent. As the council rose he followed the king into his bedchamber and begged him, unless he wished to follow his father, to rescind that part of the commission which might be used to encourage rebellion in Scotland and raise another in England. "Why did you not argue this in council?" asked Charles. His gross but able administrator answered with emphasis, "Sire, were not your enemies in the room?" To the great disappointment of Monmouth and the Whigs as well as the Covenanters, peremptory orders were sent after him that he should not treat but fall on them at once. Shaftesbury's party discovered that they had been tricked. Lord Cavendish and Lord Gerard refused to serve under their commissions; Mr. Thynne declined to receive one; Lord Grey of Werke resigned his command of the horse. Even after Monmouth had started an attempt was made to obtain his recall and, had time allowed, a monster petition in favour of the rebels, to be signed by many peers and gentlemen and all the principal householders of London, was prepared for presentation to the king. Charles made use of the event, by an order which had the additional advantage of creating a difference between the Earls of Essex and Shaftesbury, to raise a troop of two hundred guards to be about his person.[419]

The copies of Shaftesbury's speech intended for such fatal use in Scotland were said to have been made in the Green Ribbon Club.[420] That famous society, founded in the year 1675, quickly acquired ascendency over the Whig party. To-day it has been almost forgotten; its influence was unknown to the classic historians of England, who were in politics mostly Whig; but during seven tumultuous years of English history it played a part that can only be compared to the work of the more notorious Jacobin organisation of a century later across the Channel. The club met at the King's Head Tavern at the corner of Chancery Lane and Fleet Street. Its character may be known at once from the fact that its members organised and paid for the imposing ceremonies of pope burning, by which the most fiendish lies of Oates were yearly sustained and the worst passions of the London mob, a word, it may be noted, itself derived from the club, systematically inflamed. Oates himself was a member, and Aaron Smith, his legal adviser; and under the leadership of Shaftesbury the club was filled with men of the same kidney, who crowded on to the balcony with pipes in their mouths and wigs laid aside to witness the papal holocaust with which each great procession ended opposite their windows. Here was the fountain of the inner counsels of the Whig party and the seat of its executive. Within the walls of the club the decision had been taken to agitate for the dissolution of Parliament after the long prorogation of 1677; here a few years later the Rye House conspiracy was schemed; here the actual assassination plot was hatched. Over the country the Green Ribbon Club enjoyed a profound influence. It was the centre of the party pamphleteers who devoted keen ability to incite the nation and defame the government, and their productions were scattered far and wide by means of a highly effective service of correspondents. While policy was debated and action resolved by the chiefs of the club, their agents at the coffee-houses in London and throughout the country obeyed orders from headquarters. At the elections their activity was unparalleled. Tracts poured into the constituencies. Industrious agents attacked the character of the court candidates and firmly organised the national opposition. It was the Green Ribbon Club which introduced the "Protestant flail" to London and clothed the town in silk armour as a defence against the expected daggers of papists. The club almost usurped the functions of Parliament. Many members of that body belonged to it, attended its consultations, took their cue from its decisions. Agents thronged the lobby of the House of Commons, posting members with arguments for debate, whipping in sluggards to a division, carrying the latest news back to the club. Men of all classes and various character belonged to the society, broken scoundrels and wealthy statesmen, pious enthusiasts and tired profligates, the remains of the Cromwellian party, the forerunners of the Revolution, poets, aldermen, country gentlemen, assassins, bound together in a common league of animosity against Charles II and his government, not a few traitors to that bond itself. Scarcely a name of note on the Whig side is absent from the list, which contained Shaftesbury and Monmouth, Buckingham, Ireton, Slingsby Bethel, Sir William Waller, the Spekes, the Trenchards, Howard of Escrick, Sir Robert Peyton, Russell, Holles, and Algernon Sidney. With the lapse of time the counsels of the club became more violent; and the most infamous of political tracts, "An Appeal from the Country to the City," which spread deliberate and abominable lies to incite the nation to rebellion, and urged the Duke of Monmouth to strike with force for the crown, not because he had a right to it, but because he had none, was written by Robert Ferguson, nicknamed the Plotter, himself a member, Shaftesbury's *âme damneé*.[421] More than a third of the whole number of members of the club were concerned in the Rye House Plot. Sixteen or eighteen took an active part in Monmouth's invasion. After the Revolution they obtained their reward. Shadwell, the poet of the club, was made laureate in place of Dryden. Aaron Smith became Chancellor of the Exchequer to King William. Lord Grey of Werke, basest of traitors, was given office and an earldom. Sir John Trenchard was made secretary of state. Dukedoms were conferred upon the Earls of Bedford and Devonshire and a marquisate upon Lord Mulgrave. Ireton became lieutenant-colonel of dragoons and gentleman of the horse to the king.

Oates was pilloried and pensioned. Speake, Ayloffe, Rouse, Nelthrop, and Bettiscomb were hanged.[422]

In August 1679 the chance of the Green Ribbon Club seemed to have arrived. After a hard game of tennis the king took a chill in walking by the river-side at Windsor. Fever ensued, and a horrible fear that Charles lay on his death-bed struck at men's hearts. The cry rose everywhere that he had been poisoned. The Duchess of Portsmouth was accused of having done the black deed. Amazement and horror were universal. People looked upon any ill that should happen to the king, said Sir William Temple, as though it were the end of the world. The privy council was obliged to take action to prevent an overwhelming rush of inquirers into the royal bedchamber. Algernon Sidney returning to town found the general apprehension such that, had the king died, there was no extremity of disorder that might not be expected. "Good God!" wrote Henry Savile from Paris, "what a change such an accident would make! the very thought of it frights me out of my wits. God bless you and deliver us all from that damnable curse,"[423] There were indeed good grounds for the fears so poignantly expressed. The Duke of York, who had been sent from the country in February, was still beyond seas. Monmouth had returned from Scotland, puffed with success in having pacified the Covenanters. Shaftesbury divided the court and seemed to have the nation at his back. If the king died, he was prepared to make a bold push for fortune. The second declaration of Monmouth, published in the following reign, made mention of a consult held at this time "for extraordinary remedies." No copy of the declaration can now be traced, but it was seen and the fact noted by David Hume. That consult decided upon notable measures. Early in the course of the next year Sir Robert Peyton was accused by Mrs. Cellier and Gadbury the astrologer of treasonable practices, and was examined before the privy council. Though he denied his guilt, he let it be understood that the charge was not baseless and confessed to the House of Commons that he had been intriguing with the Duke of York. His old associates turned against him, and Peyton was expelled the House; but his object was accomplished and he went over to the court side, to find a reward for his perfidy in the favour of James. No definite accusation was made against the heads of the popular party, but the extent of the Whig plans became vaguely known. On the news of the king's illness preparations had been quickly made for insurrection. Money was collected and old Cromwellian officers engaged. A large force would have been in the field at a few days' notice. Had Charles died at Windsor the leaders of the movement were ready to seize the Tower, Dover Castle, and Portsmouth, and to arrest the Lord Mayor and those privy councillors who should offer to proclaim the Duke of York king.[424]

The government was not idle in face of the danger. With the consent of the king Sunderland, Halifax, and Essex, most unstable of triumvirates, summoned the duke from Brussels. Leaving his wife and children, James set out in disguise and reached Windsor on September 2 without being recognised by more than two persons on the way. Charles received him with admirably feigned surprise. The danger was past; Jesuits' powder, the modern quinine, had already restored the king to the point of eating mutton and partridges, and within ten days he was again discussing important business with the French ambassador. Another issue of events had been expected. If the worst had taken place, the Lord Mayor and aldermen had concerted means to declare the duke their sovereign. Fortunately for the nation the Whigs were deprived of the chance to decide whether they or the government held the stronger hand. On the contrary the hopes raised by the king's illness brought on them a serious rebuff. Once in England James, who had continually pressed for his recall and thought his brother's behaviour was driving the country to ruin, shewed no desire to depart again. It was represented to him that his absence was for the king's advantage, and he consented to leave; but on conditions, for Sunderland suggested that Monmouth, whom his father's danger made yet more arrogant and his uncle's unexpected arrival sulky and furious, should quit the country too. James after a brief visit to Brussels took coach for Scotland, but Monmouth, to the delight of the court party deprived of his office of captain-general of the forces and his command of the horse guards, for Holland. There was some thought of his attempting to refuse, but milder counsels prevailed and he was persuaded that a willing submission would serve to invest him in the eyes of the people with the character of a martyr. The generalship was abolished and the business of the office handed over to Sunderland. Yet another slight was put upon the Whig party. Sir Thomas Armstrong, the intimate agent of Monmouth and a fierce opponent of the Duke of York, was banished from the king's presence and court for ever.[425]

As the year 1679 wore away the disturbance of the kingdom seemed to increase. A rising had been expected as the result of James' return to England, and alarms of the same nature were raised when the king paid a visit to London after his recovery. Guards were set in Covent Garden and Lincoln's Inn Fields; barges and an escort two hundred strong were in readiness to carry the royal party to the Tower in case of a tumult; but no stir was made and the day passed quietly. Fears of the vaguest character were abroad. "I am very confident," wrote Charles Hatton, "you will suddenly hear very surprising news, but what I am unable to inform you as yet." At the back of men's minds the feeling was growing that the Whigs could not attain their object except by plunging the country into civil war.[426] The agitation became greater than ever when at the end of

November the Duke of Monmouth returned without leave to England. He entered London at midnight to the sound of ringing bells and by the light of a thousand bonfires, crackling almost at the palace doors. His popularity seemed unbounded. Crowds followed him in the streets and stopped passers to drink his health. Nell Gwyn, cheered by the crowd as "the Protestant whore," entertained him at supper. He struck from his arms the bar sinister, which denoted the maimed descent: it was a fashion among the royal bastards, for the Duke of Richmond, Charles' son by Louise de Kéroualle, who was thought to have intentions on the queen's throne for herself, had done the same, and displayed the lions of England without diminution.[427] The king was incensed, refused to see the pretender, deprived him of all his offices, ordered him to quit London. Monmouth at length obeyed, but it was to make a royal progress through the west of England, captivating the people and laying the foundations of the support for his hapless attempt against his uncle's crown.[428]

Meanwhile the question arose when Parliament should meet. The elections had not much altered the complexion of the House of Commons, but it was noted that while the Whigs held their own in the counties and great corporations, the court began to gain in many small boroughs.[429] On the appointed day in October Charles first prorogued and then adjourned Parliament till the following January. Shaftesbury attempted to force the king's hand by appearing in company with sixteen other peers to present a petition that set forth the danger in which the monarch, the religion, and the government of England lay, and their prayer that his Majesty would make effectual use of the great council of the realm. Charles replied he would consider it, and heartily wished that all others were as solicitous as himself for the good and peace of the nation. Three days later he shewed the meaning of his answer by proroguing Parliament, without the advice of the council, to November 1680. He followed the stroke by summoning the Lord Mayor and aldermen to his presence to enforce on them their duty of preserving the peace and preventing ill-disposed persons from pursuing the ends of discord under cover of petitioning. The surprise of the Whigs was intense. Only one thing was left for them to do. They went on petitioning. Petitions, prepared in accordance with Shaftesbury's instructions, bombarded the king from all over the country. A proclamation issued to denounce merely had the effect of redoubling them. Charles' own answers were far more effective. The men of Wiltshire presented a petition as from their county, but lacking the sanction of the grand jury were rated as a company of loose and disaffected persons. The petitioners from London and Westminster were told by Charles that he was the head of the government and would do as he thought best; while to the Berkshire gentlemen he replied, "We will argue the matter over a cup of ale when we meet at Windsor, though I wonder my neighbours should meddle with my business." In one case alone Charles had the worst of a passage of arms. When a citizen of Taunton offered him a petition, the king asked how he dared do so? To which the man replied, "Sir, my name is Dare." The government was not behindhand in dealing with the situation. To shew that the petitioners did not represent the country, an immediate flood of counter addresses poured in, expressing confidence in the king's wisdom and abhorrence of the petitioners. Petitioners and abhorrers divided the nation, and it was by no other godfather than Titus Oates that the latter party, by a name famous in English history, was christened Tory.[430] In this clamorous contest the king gained an undeniable success. But success did not bring repose. Watchfulness was more severely needed than ever. To calm suspicion the penal laws were once more sharpened against the Catholics. Additional garrisons were thrown into the Tower and Tilbury Fort. Portsmouth and Sheerness were strengthened. London remained quiet, but the Christmas festivities were suspected of unfortunate possibilities. There was talk of threatening Shaftesbury with a prosecution.[431]

Instead of a prosecution Shaftesbury was drawn into a negotiation with the court. The French ambassador learned with agitation that the earl went secretly by night to Whitehall to discuss terms of settlement with the king. Shaftesbury offered to let drop the Exclusion bill and assure Charles an ample revenue for the rest of his life if he would consent to a divorce and to marry a Protestant. The king should make a show of resistance, to be overborne by apparently irresistible pressure, the country would be satisfied, and peace return to the land. Charles made believe that he viewed the notion with favour. Only Lord Holles and very few others were admitted to knowledge of what was passing. Soon Lauderdale, whose character and career were particularly displeasing to the Presbyterians, was added to their number. Holles drew back, then fell ill, and the scheme languished. Nevertheless Shaftesbury hoped for success. Suddenly his hopes were shattered. On January 29, 1680 Charles brought the matter to an end by declaring to the council that, since the Duke of York's absence had not produced the desired effect, he was about to recall him to England. A royal yacht left immediately for Edinburgh to convey him thence. On February 24 James arrived in London. The recorder of the city presented him with a complimentary address. A sumptuous banquet was given the royal brothers by the Lord Mayor. To crown the display a grand illumination was arranged to testify the extraordinary joy all good subjects were supposed to feel.[432] Shaftesbury might well harbour resentment at the artifice of which he had been a victim.

In the "Appeal from the Country to the City" the Duke of Monmouth was recommended by name to be the saviour of the people, since he who had the worst title was like to make the best king. Between that, the project of the queen's divorce, and the pretence that Monmouth was in fact the legitimate heir to the throne the minds of Whig politicians wavered. The last idea had already risen to such prominence that, when the Duke of York left the kingdom in March, a solemn declaration was drawn from Charles that he had never married or made any contract of marriage with any other woman than his wife, Queen Catherine, then living.[433] For greater security the king's signature was attested by his councillors and the deed enrolled in Chancery. Shaftesbury had no sooner emerged from his defeat of the midnight meetings at Whitehall than the fable sprang into renewed life. Mysterious tales were bruited abroad of a certain black box, which, if found, should contain the contract of marriage between the king and Lucy Walters, mother of the Duke of Monmouth. The box was said to be in the possession of Sir Gilbert Gerard. If it did not contain the actual contract, at any rate there lay in it a certificate from the hand of Dr. Cosens, late Bishop of Durham, who had solemnised the marriage. Others had it that one Dr. Clare, an eminent royalist parson, had read the service. At least the ceremony had been witnessed by a judge and three other persons of quality. The story attained such proportions that an extraordinary meeting of the council was held. Sir Gilbert Gerard was called to state what he knew. It appeared that he knew nothing. He had never seen either contract or box, and had no knowledge whatever of anything of the sort. The rumour was traced to a maternal aunt of the late Lucy Walters: who had set her on could only be conjectured. It cannot be doubted that the tale emanated from the office of the Whig party. The authors of it were men of versatility. Sir Gilbert Gerard's statement seemed to have dissolved the myth, but within a few weeks the appearance of a pamphlet entitled "A Letter to a Person of Honour concerning the Black Box" brought the facts again into question.[434] The whole account of the black box, affirmed the letter, was a mere romance, an ingenious device of the Duke of York to sham and ridicule the marriage, which indeed had no relation to it, for with the exposure of the box the true history would at the same time fall into discredit. It was notorious that assurance of Monmouth's legitimacy had been given to the Countess of Wemyss before she disposed her daughter in marriage to him. In a letter from the king to Mrs. Walters, intercepted by Cromwell's officers, he had addressed her as wife. And it was beyond doubt that she had actually received homage from many of the royalist party. Many copies of this pamphlet were scattered in the Exchange and dispersed throughout the kingdom. It had an instant effect. On June 7 another declaration was published by the king, condemning the libel, denouncing its falsehood, and forbidding all subjects on pain of the utmost rigour of the law to utter anything contrary to the royal pronouncement. The result was a second "Letter to a Person of Honour," in which Charles' word was contradicted and his motives traduced. All the former statements were repeated, some arguments added, and the pamphlet ended by the modest proposals, "That Parliament, being admitted to sit, may examine this affair, whereof they alone are competent judges; and that the Duke of York may be legally tried for his manifold treasons and conspiracies against the king and kingdom," which treasons were set out at length in thirty-four articles.[435] To carry the war still further into the enemies' camp, on June 26 Shaftesbury appeared in Westminster Hall in company with the Earl of Huntingdon, Lord Grey, Lord Gerard, Lord Russell, Lord Cavendish, and nine commoners to present the Duke of York to the grand jury as a popish recusant and to indict the Duchess of Portsmouth for a national nuisance. With them went Titus Oates, invested as it were with a representative authority on behalf of the Whig party. That both charges were true is certain; but the action of the Whigs was dictated by a purely partisan spirit, and Chief Justice Scroggs, judging the fact so, discharged the jury before they could find a bill. Four days later the attack was repeated in another court, and with the same result. The judges only followed their chief's example. James appeared downcast and knew well what danger he ran. His adversaries seemed to be throwing off the mask, strong in the support of which they were assumed to be conscious. When it was told to Shaftesbury that the king had railed at him and his party as seditious rebels, he replied aloud and in public, "The king has nothing to do but take the pains to punish rebels and seditious persons. We will keep with the bounds of the law, and we shall easily find means by the law to make him walk out of the kingdom." There were not many who could boast of having the last laugh in a game with Charles. Not many months after, when the law by which he held was put into operation against the Whig leader, Charles heard that Shaftesbury had accused him of suborning perjurers, and thereupon very pleasantly quoted a Scotch proverb. Veiled in the decency of a learned language it ran: "In die extremi judicii videbimus cui podex nigerrimus sit."[436]

Violent distempers were now feared on all sides. Partisans of the Prince of Orange were intriguing keenly on his behalf. In the spring of the year Charles was ill again, and the several parties hastily met to concert action. "God keep the nation," wrote Dorothy Sidney, "from the experiment what they could have done." The danger may be gauged by the fact that, had the king's illness continued, three hundred members of the Commons were determined to remain sitting despite the prorogation. A considerable movement was detected among the London prentices. The date of May 29 had been fixed for a large meeting to be held under pretence of burning the Rump; four or five thousand men had pledged themselves to attend, but information was laid, the leaders arrested, and the outbreak apprehended by the court did not take place.[437] Those of the opposite party were no less alarmed. Their chief enemy, James, was holding a brilliant court and still maintained himself against them. Shaftesbury left town for Easter, fearing a personal attack. Mr. William Harbord looked abroad to spy some safe retreat. Sir William Waller fled to Holland, thence to Italy, pursued by the watchful eye of the government. On the pretext of Catholic intrigues, the city guards were doubled.[438] A penetrating observer might have perceived a change drawing over the spirit of the times. While the Whig attack, far from having spent itself, grew only the more fierce, and a final struggle with authority seemed imminent, the nation had begun to reflect upon the turn of events. If passion was exasperated by the last bold step against the Duke of York, it shewed too the extremity to which his opponents were driving. Thereafter could be no thought of reconciliation: they must either ruin him or themselves end in ruin. It was not without some justice that Charles I called the English sober. As the future was dimly shaped to men in shadows of high misfortune, the fear of open strife and loss of all they had given so much to gain in recalling Charles II to the throne of his fathers weighed more heavily upon them. Innate reverence for authority, standing to the letter of its rights, returned in some of its ancient force. Though they were willing to see the royal prerogative curbed, there was no sympathy for those who would strike against its existence. And in the party which fostered terror and maddened the nation by the Popish Plot were not a few to whom this was the object, Independents and other sectaries, fierce republicans who had fought through the Civil War and might not be sorry at the chance of fighting through another. It was felt that the least accident might throw everything into confusion. People began at length to test the stories circulated for their consumption. Tales "that Holborn should be burnt down and the streets run with blood" were no longer accepted on the mere statement. The Irish Plot, loudly denounced about this time by Shaftesbury, found small credence except from the London mob, and even in London the busy merchants who feared disorder exercised an influence of restraint. At the end of July Sir Leoline Jenkins was able to write: "Letters from several parts beyond the seas do tell us that we are represented there as if we were already in a flame. God be praised! 'tis no such matter. All things are as still and peaceable as ever they were, only we are pelted at with impudent, horrid libels." Evidently the English nation was in no humour for a second civil war.[439]

The king met Parliament on October 21, 1680. James was again on his way to Edinburgh, induced to withdraw himself by a promise of full support, but inwardly persuaded that he was lost. Seven of the council had favoured the journey, eleven were against it. "Since he has so many friends for him," said Charles, "I see he must go." In spite of gay hearts the royal prospect was not bright. The king had tried a bout with the Whigs over the city elections, and was forced to accept their choice; and the Duchess of

Portsmouth, fearful of an attack on herself and with a heavy bribe in her purse, had gone over to the side of his enemies.[440] The session opened with turbulence almost unexampled even in the hot times that had passed. For discrediting the Plot in the last parliament, a member had been expelled by the Commons. He was now followed by two others. Petitioning was voted to be the right of the subject. Abhorrers were violently attacked. Charles had long expressed his willingness for any compromise that should leave his brother the title of king when he came to the throne, and offered Expedients, the effect of which would be to take all power from the hands of the sovereign. Similar proposals were made by others also. Halifax suggested that the duke should be banished for five years, Essex an association in defence of the Protestant religion, Shaftesbury would still be satisfied by a divorce. Otherwise he stood firm for Exclusion. James viewed the Expedients alike with horror, and the Commons rejected them with insult. Once let a popish king have the title, it was said, and he would take the power too. "Expedients in politics are like mountebanks' tricks in physic," cried Sir William Jones. The bill, the bill, and nothing but the bill, was the cry. Colonel Titus summed the matter up neatly. "You shall have the Protestant religion," he said, "you shall have what you will to protect you, but you must have a popish king who shall command your armies and your navies, make your bishops and judges. Suppose there were a lion in the lobby, one cries: Shut the door and keep him out. No, says another, open the door and let us chain him when he comes in." The metaphor became popular in verse:—

I hear a lion in the lobby roar;

Say, Mr. Speaker, shall we shut the door

And keep him out?—or shall we let him in

To try if we can turn him out again?[441]

On November 4 the Exclusion bill was introduced, heralded by denunciations of James. The violence of the debates beggars description. If swords were not drawn, their use was not forgotten. The prospect of civil war was freely mooted. "The case, in short, is this," exclaimed Mr. Henry Booth, "in plain English, whether we would fight for or against the law." Sir William Jones pursued, "The art of man cannot find out any remedy as long as there is a popish successor and the fears of a popish king." He was answered by Colonel Legge, a personal friend of the Duke of York: "There has been talk in the world of another successor than the duke, in a Black Box; but if Pandora's box must be opened, I would have it in my time, not in my children's, that I may draw my sword to defend the right heir." On November 11 the bill was passed, and four days later with a mighty shout was carried to the Lords by Russell, followed by a great body of the Commons. To signify the attitude of the city, he was accompanied by the Lord Mayor and aldermen. At the debate which followed Charles was present. He heard the passionate attacks of Shaftesbury, the grave force of Essex's oratory. He witnessed the treachery of Sunderland, who joined his enemies. He heard Monmouth urge Exclusion as the only safety for the king's life, and broke in with a loud whisper, "the kiss of Judas." He saw Halifax rise to champion the right, and heard him speak fifteen or sixteen times and carry the day by his inexhaustible powers of wit, sarcasm, and eloquence. At nine o'clock in the evening, after a debate of six hours, the bill was thrown out by sixty-three votes to thirty.[442] It was a memorable victory.

The fury of the Commons exceeded all bounds. Supplies were refused. Votes and addresses were passed against Halifax, against Jeffreys, Recorder of London, against Lord Chief Justice North, against placemen and pensioners, against the judges, against James. "No sooner does a man stand by the king but he is attacked," wrote the duke to William of Orange. To the attack against Halifax Charles answered suavely that "he doth not find the grounds in the address of this House to be sufficient to induce him to remove the Earl of Halifax." He told Reresby: "Let them do what they will, I will never part with any officer at the request of either House. My father lost his head by such compliance; but as for me, I intend to die another way." And Halifax took occasion to say to Sir John: "Well, if it comes to a war, you and I must go together." A bill for a Protestant association for the government of the country with Monmouth at its head was being prepared, when on January 10, 1681 the king suddenly prorogued and then dissolved Parliament, leaving twenty-two bills depending and eight more already ordered. The next parliament was summoned for March 21, and according to the old advice of Danby not in the capital, but at Oxford.[443]

Charles' wisdom in this course cannot be questioned. Before the last session Ferguson the Plotter had returned from concealment in Holland. An agent of Essex was busy in London concerning "the linen manufacture," for which he had enrolled three or four hundred men and spent as much as a thousand pounds. Hugh Speke sent down to the country to have his horse ready. "Get him in as good case as you can," he wrote, "for God knows what use I may have for him and how suddenly." There is reason to think that Shaftesbury had been planning to place Parliament under control of the city.[444] London had always armed the Whigs with the possibility of support other than parliamentary. The removal of Parliament to Oxford made it certain that the coming struggle would be fought on ground favourable to the king. No sooner was Charles' determination known than Shaftesbury, Monmouth, and Essex, together with thirteen other peers, presented a petition shewing that evil men, favourers of popery and enemies of the happiness of England, had made choice of Oxford as a place where the Houses would be daily menaced by the swords of papists who had crept into the ranks of the king's guards, and making their humble prayer and advice that the parliament should sit at Westminster as usual. "That, my lord, may be your opinion," returned the king to Essex; "it is not mine."[445] The Whigs promptly set to making the elections their own. Nothing was omitted to secure their success. Instructions from the Green Ribbon Club directed events in all parts of the country. Members bound themselves to prosecute the Plot, to demand restriction of the king's power to prorogue and dissolve Parliament, to support the Exclusion, the right of petitioning, the Association.[446] When the means of man were exhausted, supernatural powers were called to assist. On the one side and on the other were raised ghosts, who foretold doom to their opponents. The city of London elected its old representatives. They were begged to refuse supplies and assured that in pursuit of their ends they should have the support of the citizens' lives and fortunes. A host of scribblers, libellers, and caricaturists poured into Oxford. A rumour was spread that the city would be the scene of a massacre. The Whig chiefs rode down attended by bands of armed retainers. Guards of townsmen accompanied members from the boroughs. The Londoners appeared in a great company with bows of blue satin in their hats, on which were woven the inscription: "No Popery! No Slavery!" Tory crowds met them at the gates, red-ribboned, brandishing clubs and staves, and crying, "Make ready! Stand to it! Knock 'em down! Knock 'em down!" In the midst of his life-guards, among whom Essex had failed at Charles' polite request to point out the creeping papists, the king drove from Windsor. Information had come to hand of a plot to kidnap him at Oxford. Measures were taken accordingly. A regiment was moved up to the Mews in case of an attack on Whitehall. The constable of the Tower was advised to hold himself in readiness. Attention was given to Lambeth Palace and the forts on the Thames. The cannon at Windsor were looked to, and Lord Oxford's regiment was posted along the Windsor road, should Charles be compelled to retreat. "If the king would be advised," said Halifax, "it is in his power to make all his opponents tremble."[447] It was what he had come prepared to do.

Since the fall of Danby, Charles had lived in a state of poverty. Scarcely any supplies were furnished by Parliament. None came from France. His resources were at one moment so low that he even thought of recalling his ministers from the courts of foreign princes.[448] At the same time thousands of pounds were being absorbed by the informers against popish plotters, tens of thousands by the royal mistresses. The treasury was in the hands of Laurence Hyde, second son of Lord Chancellor Clarendon. That he was able to pay the way is a source of wonder and admiration. Such a state of affairs could not last for ever, and Charles had recourse to the mine whence he had drawn so much wealth before. Though Louis XIV had gained his immediate object by turning against his cousin, he felt as time went on that the tools he used might destroy his own work. His constant desire was to keep England in such a position that, if she would, she could not thwart his plans. For this he had joined the Whigs against Danby. From the same motive his ambassador supported Shaftesbury in his advertisement of Monmouth and bribed not only members of parliament, but city merchants and Presbyterian preachers. But there was a point beyond which he could not follow this line. It would be as little to his interest to see Charles' authority overthrown and English policy directed by a Protestant parliament as to contend with Charles adopting and leading the same policy. Therefore in the autumn of 1679 Barillon had tried to come to an agreement with Charles. He offered the sum of £200,000 for three years but, attempting to get more than the king was willing to give, found the proposal fall to the ground. Charles threw himself on to the side of the allies against France and in July of the following year concluded a treaty with Spain to resist the pretensions of Louis. Alarmed by the violence of the Commons and realising that their hostility to France could not be cured by gold, Barillon again broached the subject. The king hung back until just before the dissolution of the last parliament at Westminster and by skilful play obtained what he wanted. A verbal treaty was concluded in the queen's bedroom, between the bed and the wall. Charles agreed to disengage himself from the Spanish alliance and to prevent the interference of Parliament. In return he was to receive from Louis an amount equivalent to twelve and a half million francs in the course of the next three years. So close was the secret kept that besides the two kings only Barillon, Laurence Hyde, and the Duke of York had knowledge of the treaty.[449] Though he was tight bound by it for the matter of foreign policy, Charles had attained his object. Except for the advancement of his power at home and to quicken the growth of English commerce he did not care for foreign politics. So long as he could turn Louis' ambition to his own advantage he was satisfied. This the new treaty accomplished, and although Louis too gained handsomely by it, he was obliged to confess the victory not altogether his by the complete reversal of his policy of the last four years in England. Charles met Parliament strong in the consciousness of his independence.

The session that now opened gave little hope of a peaceful end. Meeting on March 21, the Houses listened to a speech of studious moderation from the throne. Charles promised consent to any means whereby under a Catholic successor the administration should remain in Protestant hands, but what he had already said with regard to the succession, by that he would abide—

there should be no tampering with that. There could be no mistake as to his attitude. "I, who will never use arbitrary government myself," he said with a proud lie, "am resolved never to suffer it in others." Charles could well offer a compromise, for he knew it would never be accepted. The two parties, it was said, were like hostile forces on opposite heights. The Commons refused the Expedients. They adopted the cause of a wretch named Fitzharris, whose obscure intrigue, by whomever directed, was certainly most base and most criminal, and tried to turn him into an engine of political aggression. It was evident that they meant to force the king to abandon James and recognise the Duke of Monmouth. Shaftesbury once more tried negotiation. In conversation with Charles in the House of Lords he pressed him in the public interest and for the peace of the nation to accept the position and give way. The king returned: "My Lord, let there be no self-delusion, I will never yield and will not let myself be intimidated. I have the law and reason on my side. Good men will be with me. There is the church," and he pointed to where the bishops sat, "which will remain united with me. Believe me, my Lord, we shall not be divided." It was an open declaration of war. On March 26 the Exclusion bill was voted. Monday, March 28, was fixed for the first reading. On Sunday the king busied himself with preparing the Sheldonian theatre for the Commons, who complained that Convocation House was too small; he viewed the plans, strolled among the workmen, congratulated himself on being able to arrange for the better comfort of his faithful subjects, and made all show of expecting a long session. That night his coach was privately sent a stage outside Oxford with a troop of horse. Next morning he was carried as usual to the House of Lords in a sedan chair, followed by another with drawn curtains, seeming to contain a friend. When the king stepped out his friend was found to be a change of clothes. He had come to make his enemies tremble. At the last moment an accident nearly wrecked the scheme. The wrong robes had been brought. Hastily the chair was sent back for the robes of state, while Charles held an unwilling peer in conversation that he might not give the alarm. Then, when all was ready, he swiftly took his seat on the throne and, without giving the Lords time to robe, summoned the Commons to attend. As Sir William Jones was in the act of appealing to Magna Carta as the safeguard of the subject's right, the Black Rod knocked at the door. The Commons thronged eagerly through the narrow passages to the king's presence, the Speaker leading with Russell and Cavendish at either hand. They thought they had come to receive Charles' surrender. When the tumult was calmed the king spoke; "My lords and gentlemen, that all the world may see to what a point we are come, that we are not like to have a good end, when the divisions at the beginning are such, therefore, my Lord Chancellor, do as I have commanded you." Finch thereupon declared Parliament, which had lived for exactly one week, to be dissolved, and Charles immediately left the throne. As he reached his dressing-room he turned to a friend, his eyes gleaming, with the remark that it was better to have one king than five hundred. He made a short dinner and, leaving by the back stairs, drove off in Sir Edward Seymour's coach to where his own was waiting. That night he was in Windsor.[450]

The dissolution scattered the opposition as a gust of wind the leaves of a tree in autumn. Shaftesbury in vain attempted to hold the Houses together. His followers in the Lords remained for an hour under pretence of signing a protest, while messengers were dispatched urging the Commons to fulfil their promises. But they were too much cowed by the stroke. They feared "if they did not disperse, the king would come and pull them out by the ears." Presently they fled. In a quarter of an hour the price of coaches in the town doubled. Oxford had the appearance of a surrendered city disgorging its garrison.[451] And with their flight the history of the Popish Plot comes to an end. On that the Whigs had staked all, and they had lost. The country was alienated by their violence and rapacity and fearful of the horrors of civil war. Once deprived of their means of action in Parliament they could do nothing but go whither the king drove them, to plot frank rebellion without the shadow of legality. Up to this point Shaftesbury had led a bold attack, not without good hope of success. Now he was left to sustain the defence, stubborn and keen, but in the end incapable of avoiding ruin. The tide had at last turned, and Charles, who since the first appearance of Oates had borne with unexampled equanimity a series of the most fierce assaults, found himself upon a pinnacle of triumph, his enemies lying crushed beneath his throne until he should goad them to complete disaster. Had he struck twelve months sooner the country would in all likelihood have been on their side; but he had gauged the temper of his people correctly and knew now that they would be with him. The history of these years is in brief the history of Charles II's reign, the history of a long struggle for the power of the crown. In the panic of the Popish Plot and the wild agitation of the Exclusion bill that struggle, exasperated by the Dover treaty and the Catholic intrigues, came to a head. Its consequence was the Rye House Plot, the perfection of Whig failure. In that struggle too the conflicting principles found their absolute exponents in the two wittiest and two of the most able statesmen in English history, each gifted with a supreme political genius, each exclusive of the other, each fighting for personal ascendency no less than for an idea, for principle no less than for power, Charles II and the Earl of Shaftesbury. Without a grasp of this the history of the times cannot be understood, and for this reason some historians have found in them, and more have left, a mere tangle of helpless chaos. Of the two Charles had the better fortune in his life, Shaftesbury after death. For Shaftesbury, ruined, disappointed, embittered at the loss of all his hopes, was yet the father of the Revolution: all that Charles had gained was thrown away by his less worthy brother. But the personal triumph of the king was unique. While to the world he seemed a genial debauchee, whose varied talents would have fitted him equally to be a chemist, shipwright, jockey, or dancing-master, the horseman, angler, walker, musician, whose energy tired while his company delighted the most brilliant of English courts, more admirable than Crichton had he not been more indolent, he laboured in an inner life at a great endeavour and, chiefly by letting himself be misunderstood, achieved it.[452] He restored the crown to its ancient place in the state, whence his father and his grandfather had let it fall. He gave Parliament just enough rope to hang itself.

TRIALS FOR TREASON

CHAPTER I

MAGISTRATES AND JUDGES

THE trials of the Popish Plot have remained the most celebrated in the annals of our judicial history. Their reports occupy three volumes of the State Trials and more than two thousand pages of crowded print. They contain twenty-two trials for treason, three for murder or attempt to murder, eleven for perjury, subornation of perjury, libel, and other misdemeanours. They gave rise to proceedings in Parliament against two Lord Chief Justices, and against two judges of the Court of King's Bench. They are a standing monument to the most astounding outburst of successful perjury which has occurred in modern times. It is due to their connection with these trials that posterity has branded the names of three[453] judges with lasting infamy, and that fourteen men executed as traitors have earned the reputation of martyrs. Not only are they filled and brimming with the romance of life and death, but there lies locked within them the kernel of that vast mass of treason, intrigue, crime, and falsehood which surrounds and is known as the Popish Plot. Strangely enough, therefore, they have been little studied and never understood.

The consequence of this has been unfortunate. Instead of going to the fountain-head for information, historians have for the most part contented themselves with relying on accounts supplied by writers on the one side or the other, sources which are always prejudiced and usually contradictory. To extract truth from the mutual opposition of two lies is an ingenious and useful task when evidence is not forthcoming at first hand; but it is a method less accurate than the examination of original authorities when these can be consulted. Nor is there only an obligation to devote attention to the trials themselves; they cannot be judged alone: and historians have not escaped error when, although they have studied the trials immediately within view from the actual reports, they have neglected to read them in the light of the preceding practice of the English courts of law, and to ground their opinions upon the whole judicial system which gave them their peculiar character, and of which they were an inseparable part. To appreciate properly the significance of the trials they must not be taken apart from their setting, and it is necessary before passing judgment upon the events recorded in them to review the past which lies behind them and the causes which influenced their nature.

The judicial system of England in the latter half of the seventeenth century was very different from its descendant in the twentieth. Its nature had been determined by the course of political events which moulded it into a form as unlike to that of two centuries after as the later Stuart constitution was to the Victorian.

Throughout the sixteenth and seventeenth centuries, from the time when Henry VIII broke the political power of Rome in England until the day when the last revolution destroyed the influence of the Jesuits in English politics, the English state lived and developed in an atmosphere charged with the thunderstorm and resonant with the note of war. War against foes within the land and without was the characteristic condition of its existence. Besides conflict with foreign powers, war and rebellion, constant in Scotland and almost chronic in Ireland, may be counted in eight reigns three completed revolutions, ten[454] armed rebellions, two great civil wars, and plots innumerable, all emanating from within the English nation alone. From beyond seas enemies schemed almost without ceasing to overturn religion or government or both as they were established at home. There is no need to wonder that the English government was a fighting machine. In this light it was regarded by all men. Where government is now looked on as a means of getting necessary business done, of ameliorating conditions of life, and directing the energy of the country to the highest pitch of efficiency, two centuries and a half ago it was anxiously watched as an engine of attack or defence of persons, property, and conscience. The first duty of government is to govern; to guard the tranquillity of the society over which it is set, to anticipate the efforts of malignants against the social security, and to punish crime, the commission of which it has been unable to prevent. This is at all times a heavy burden; but its weight is redoubled when private gives way to public crime, and the criminal turns his strength against the state itself. For acts directed against society in its corporate being are fraught with far more danger than those which touch it indirectly, however great their magnitude, not only because the consequences of the successful act in the former case are vital, but also because the restless class from which the actors are drawn commands a higher ability than that containing men to whom crime is a means to private gain, and is endowed with a reckless hardihood which springs from the certainty of detection and retribution in case of failure. In the seventeenth century this class was numerous, and the difficulties of guarding against it great. The state was always in danger, the government always battling for its own life and the safety of society, the morrow always gloomy for the success of their cause. To be for or against the government was the shibboleth which marked the peaceable man from the revolutionary. To be "counted to be a very pernicious man against the government"[455] was sufficient to weigh against the credibility of a witness before the highest tribunal of the kingdom. Therefore it was that far wider scope could then be allowed to acts of administration than ought to be allowed in peaceful times, and that the government might be sure of support for its bad as well as its good measures when they appeared to be directed towards the doing of rough justice on individuals whose presence was felt to be a common danger. It could be assumed that the means adopted for this purpose would not be too closely scrutinised.

Government was from necessity a fighting machine. But it was a machine so ill adapted for fighting that its action, far from attaining to mechanical precision and gravity, was coarse, spasmodic, questionable, and was driven to atone for want of ease and regularity by displaying an excess of often ill-directed energy. The means ready to the hand of the administration were scanty. Without an army, without police, without detectives, the order maintained in the country practically depended upon the goodwill of the upper and middle classes. The police of the kingdom consisted of watchmen in the cities and boroughs; in the country, of parish constables. Both were notoriously inefficient. The type of watchmen with which Londoners were familiar in the opening years of the seventeenth century is sufficiently known from the character of Dogberry. About the same time the parish constables were distinguished for being "often absent from their houses, being for the most part husbandmen, and so most of the day in the fields."[456] As late as 1796 the watchmen of London were recruited by the various authorities from "such aged and often superannuated men living in their respective districts as may offer their services," and were recognised to be feeble, half-starved, lacking the least hope of reward or stimulus to activity.[457] Without an excessive strain on the imagination it may be conjectured that in the intervening period the police system did not rise to a high pitch of perfection. In the capital the king's guards and the city trained bands were available forces, but in the provinces the only body on which reliance could be placed for the execution of justice was formed by the sheriff's officers or in the last resort the cumbrous militia. Even the militia could not be maintained under arms for more than twelve days in the year, for although the force of any county might be kept on foot for a longer period by the king's special direction, the Lord Lieutenant had no power to raise money with which to pay the men.[458] The only practicable instrument of government for the defence of the state was the judicial system of the country. As there was no method known for the prevention of crime by an organised force of police, and no deterrent exerted on would-be criminals by the existence of a standing body of soldiery, the only possible weapon to be used against them was to be found in the law courts. It followed that the judges and justices of the peace not only fulfilled the judicial and magisterial functions which are known to modern times, but constituted as well an active arm of the administration.

The justices of the peace combined in their persons the characters, which have since been distinguished, of prosecutor, magistrate, detective, and often policeman. They raised the hue and cry, chased malefactors, searched houses, took prisoners. A justice might issue a warrant for the arrest, conduct the search himself, effect the capture, examine the accused with and without witnesses, extract a confession by alternately cajoling him as a friend and bullying him as a magistrate, commit him, and finally give damning evidence against him at his trial. Such was the conduct of Alderman Sir Thomas Aleyn in the case of Colonel Turner, tried and convicted for burglary in 1664.[459] The alderman examined Turner in the first place, and charged him point-blank with the offence. He then searched his house. In this he was unsuccessful, but the next day, owing to information received, tracked the colonel to a shop in the Minories, where he was found in possession of money suspected to be part of the stolen property.[460] Aleyn carried him to the owner of the stolen goods, upon whose engagement not to prosecute Turner confessed that he knew where the plunder was concealed, and by a further series of artifices induced him to surrender, through the agency of his wife, part of the missing jewelry. On this he committed both Colonel and Mrs. Turner to Newgate, and finally appeared at their trial to tell the whole story of his manœuvres in considerable detail and with the greatest composure.[461] Twenty years later, as Sir John Reresby was going to bed one night, he was roused by the Duke of Monmouth's page to play a similar part. Mr. Thynne had been shot dead as he was driving in his coach along Pall Mall,[462] and Sir John was summoned to raise the hue and cry. He went at once to the house of the murdered man, issued warrants for the arrest of suspected persons, and proceeded to investigate the case. From a Swede who was brought before him he obtained the necessary information, and set out to pursue the culprits. After giving chase all night and searching several houses, he finally took the German officer who had been a principal in the murder in the house of a Swedish doctor in Leicester fields at six o'clock in the morning, and was able to boast in his diary that he had performed the somewhat perilous task of entering the room first and personally arresting the captain.[463] On another occasion Reresby deserved well of the government by his action in an episode connected with the Rye House Plot. Six Scotchmen had been arrested and examined in the North, and were being sent in custody to London by directions of one of the secretaries of state. Sir John however was led to suspect that the examination had not been thoroughly conducted and stopped the men at York. He examined them again and extorted confessions of considerable importance, which he was then able to forward to the secretary in company with the prisoners.[464]

Instances to illustrate the nature of these more than magisterial duties might easily be multiplied. The agitation caused by the Popish Plot was naturally a spur to the activity of justices throughout the country. Especially was this the case in the west of England, where the Roman Catholics had their greatest strength. In Staffordshire Mr. Chetwyn, in Derbyshire Mr. Gilbert, in Monmouthshire Captain Arnold were unflagging in their efforts to scent out conspiracy and popery. In consequence of information laid before the committee of the House of Lords Mr. Chetwyn, in company with the celebrated Justice Warcup,[465] searched Lord Stafford's house. Tart Hall, for a secret vault in which some priests were said to be concealed. The search was unsuccessful, but the vigorous manner in which it was conducted is testified by Chetwyn's furious exclamation "that if he were the king, he would have the house set fire to, and make the old rogues come forth."[466] The same magistrate also would have assisted in the work of obtaining Dugdale's confession, had he not been absent in London at the time.[467]

To Henry Gilbert, justice of the peace for Derbyshire, belonged the merit of tracking, arresting, and obtaining the conviction of George Busby, Jesuit, for being a Romish priest, at the Derby Assizes of 1681.[468] The evidence which Gilbert gave is very instructive as to the scope of a magistrate's duty.[469] As early as January 1679 William Waller had come to search Mr. Powtrel's house at West Hallam, where the Jesuit was said to be concealed, but was dissuaded on Gilbert's assurance that he had already been over the place several times in vain and believed Busby to have escaped from England. Since then however trustworthy information had come to hand that he was still in hiding. Gilbert first reconnoitred the house under the pretext of buying wood for his coal-pits. He then went away, returned with a constable and five or six other men and, fortified by the news that Busby had been seen in the garden only a few moments before, conducted a thorough search, which resulted in the discovery of various priestly vestments, an altar, "a box of wafers, mass-books, and divers other popish things."[470] This was on March 1, 1681. A fortnight later, in spite of some opposition from Mr. Justice Charlton, who was on circuit for the spring assizes, Gilbert sent the prize, which by law should have been burnt, back to West Hallam, in the hope of lulling the priest to a false security. On the same night he went to gather the fruits of his manœuvre. Posting men round the house, he made a noise and then waited to see "if they could spy any light, or hear any walking in the lofts or false floors."[471] A constable and further assistance was summoned, and about midnight Gilbert tapped at a window and demanded admittance. It was refused, and after a proper interval the constable broke in the door and the whole party entered the house. The priest's chamber was found in disorder; the fire had been lately extinguished, the bedclothes were lying about the room in heaps, and the mattress, which had been turned, was cold on the top, but warm underneath. This was the prelude to a thorough examination of the house.

The spies in the garden had heard the priest's footsteps near a corner under the roof as he retreated to his hiding-place. From one until ten in the morning of March 16 the search was carried on, Gilbert tapping on the plaster inside with his sword and the others meeting him by knocking on the tiles and walls from the other side. Hope was nearly abandoned when the searchers were spurred by the jeers of the people of the house to one last effort. At length they were rewarded. Sounding the roof inch by inch, they came upon a spot near some chimney stacks where the knocks from the two sides did not tally; breaking open the tiles, they discovered a priest's hole, and in it Busby, whom Mr. Gilbert forthwith bore off in triumph and committed to Derby gaol.

These exploits were no doubt typical of the range of activity common to busy justices of the peace throughout the kingdom. Important business passed through their hands, and they felt their position likewise to be important. They were an energetic body of men and spared not themselves, nor their neighbours, nor those against whom their action was directed in the execution of their duty as government officials. Each was sure to be in his way a local magnate, and thus the influence which the government exerted on the justices was through them spread widely over the country. Well known among provincial magistrates, and still more active than the two above mentioned, was Captain Arnold, whose name appeared in the commission of the peace for Monmouthshire. It was this Arnold who in 1679 assisted Dr. Croft, Bishop of Hereford, in his attack on the Jesuit college at Combe, near Monmouth. The college was dispersed and ten horse loads of books, seized in it, were removed to the library of Hereford Cathedral.[472] In December of the previous year he had been instrumental in the arrest of Father Pugh, formerly of the Society of Jesus, and in the seizure of papers and valuables belonging to Hall, another member of the society.[473] But Arnold exhibited something more than the zeal proper to an energetic and business-like justice. He was a keen adherent to the Whig and extreme Protestant party. In addition to the usual government reward of £50 for the apprehension of a Jesuit, he offered £200 from his own resources for each capture.[474] He made friends with the missioners and then procured their own dependents to give evidence against them. He armed bodies of servants to assist him in his expeditions, and brought the unfortunate priest whom Oates had named as prospective Bishop of Llandaff triumphantly into Monmouth at the head of a dozen horsemen.[475] Chief among his performances was the capture of two well-known Jesuits, David Henry Lewis and Philip Evans, popularly dubbed Captain. Lewis was taken by Arnold in person, Evans through his agency. Against both he produced the witnesses and managed the evidence.[476] Both were convicted of high treason under the statute of Elizabeth, for being priests in orders received from the see of Rome. Evans was executed at Cardiff on July 22,

Lewis at Usk on August 27, 1679.[477] In the summer of 1680 Arnold's name leaped into notoriety in London, when on July 16 John Giles was brought to the bar at the Old Bailey "for assaulting and intending to despatch and murder John Arnold, one of his Majesty's justices of the peace."[478] This incident however, which raised Arnold's importance so high with the Whig party that his popularity bade fair to rival even that of the murdered Sir Edmund Godfrey,[479] affords strong grounds for doubting the candour of motive in his official alertness; for there is reason to believe that no attempt whatever was made upon his life, and that the whole affair was trumped up in a most discreditable manner with a view to establishing more firmly the reputation of the Protestant party and the guilt of the Roman Catholics.[480] One more, and this again a characteristic instance, may suffice to illustrate the varied, almost intriguing, nature of a magistrate's position and the inquisitorial side which did not completely disappear from his duty until far into the nineteenth century.[481] At Lord Stafford's trial the three justices who had examined Dugdale immediately after his arrest in December 1678 were called by the prisoner to prove that the witness had then absolutely denied all knowledge of the Plot.[482] To rebut this evidence the managers of the prosecution called William Southall, coroner of the county of Stafford. This man, who was not even a magistrate and occupied the least judicial position known to the law, had taken the opportunity of some legal business which was to be transacted between a cousin of his and Dugdale to undertake a little private examination of the latter on his own behalf in the hopes of obtaining information about the Plot. According to his own account Southall acquitted himself with some skill and, by assuming a knowing air as if convinced of Dugdale's guilt and playing upon his hopes of pardon and reward, managed to extract from him a material confession. With this he repaired, not to the justices of the peace by whom Dugdale had originally been examined, but to three different magistrates, and in their company was present the next day at a detailed examination of Dugdale, who then swore to nearly the same evidence as he now gave at the trial of Lord Stafford.[483] Whether this story was true, or, as is suggested by the ease of Southall's success where others naturally better qualified had failed, the interview and its result was arranged beforehand between the two men, is at this point immaterial; for honest or fraudulent, the coroner's behaviour was accepted as a matter of course, and without the least hint that there was any irregularity in the action of an inferior official going behind the backs of his superiors, and finally transferring so delicate a matter out of their cognisance altogether into the hands of a third party.

Such were the functions of the justices of the peace in the seventeenth century, and so wide was the reach of the magisterial arm stretched out as a weapon in the service of the administration of government. And if the justices filled so important a position, still more important was that assumed by the king's judges. The justices were able administrators, dealers of small mercy to the evildoer, guardians of the peace in the name of which their commissions ran; but the judges took a place in the foremost rank as great officers of state. The character of their office had been determined by the famous conflict between James I and Lord Chief Justice Coke which came to a head in 1616 and ended in Coke's dismissal.[484] The Chief Justice's endeavour had been to erect the bench into an independent tribunal, founded on the ruins of broken agreement between king and Commons, and occupying the position of arbitrator and guardian of the constitution midway between the two. To the king and to Bacon, who advised him, this seemed intolerable; to James, because the ideal of absolutism which guided his mind could not admit in the state a constitutional oracle other than himself; to the Attorney-General, because his liberal instincts, wide statesmanship, and knowledge of political requirements made clear the impracticable nature of Coke's ideas, the bonds of crabbed technicality with which they sought to shackle the future, their essential conservatism. Coke's parchment knowledge, too good for James, was not good enough for Bacon. If Bacon inclined towards administrative absolutism, and Coke represented in the struggle the majesty of the law, assuredly the law for which the Chief Justice fought, for ever seeking guidance in the records of the past, was unfit to mould the future of a great nation. So when Coke fell, characteristically enough, over a sordid squabble into which a question of principle was inappropriately dragged, his fall demands our sympathy perhaps, but hardly our regret. Regret at a victory in the personal cause of the monarch and the check given to the forward march of constitutional progress is profitless. Between the ideas of Bacon and Coke there was no middle course open at the moment when a choice became necessary. It was impossible to avoid the conclusion that the judges must either become an independent power in the state, an irresponsible tribunal to which constitutional questions of the highest importance should be referred for decision in strict accordance with the rules of the Court of King's Bench, or be content to remain in subservience to the crown, supporters of the king's prerogative, and administrators of his policy. The expedient, which has since made the way plain, of the constitutional supremacy of the Commons of England was then unborn, and as yet in the light of practical affairs inconceivable. The Lord Chief Justice, "toughest of men," and too stubborn to yield, was broken; but his brethren on the bench gave way and offered assurances of their good conduct for the future and of their devotion to the royal will. James took the opportunity of the lecture which he read to the judges in the star chamber to compare their behaviour in meddling with the prerogative of the crown to the atheism and blasphemy committed by good Christians in disputing the word of God.

Thus the judges became, according to Bacon's wish, "lions, but yet lions under the throne," and carried themselves very circumspectly not to "check or oppose any points of sovereignty."[485] Of their regularity in this course there can be no doubt, for if any lapsed into forbidden ways, a judge he speedily ceased to be. His appointment was *durante beneplacito*[486] and revocable at the will of the king; and the king took full advantage of his power. The example offered by the case of Coke was not left long in isolation. The government was engaged in the hopeless attempt to uphold the constitution of the Tudor monarchy at a time when the nation had outgrown it, and had opened a war to the death with the progressive tendency of Parliament. In such a struggle the judges were the king's strongest weapon, and as a weapon that turns uselessly in the hand, the recalcitrant judge was discarded without scruple. When the better class of judges questioned the legality of acts of government they met with the same fate as their rugged predecessor. Under Charles I two Lord Chief Justices were dismissed and Chief Baron Walter was suspended from office. Judicial offices of consequence were filled with "men of confidence," men who enjoyed the confidence of the king and quickly lost that of every one else.[487]

In their support of the crown by technical legality and practical injustice the courts lost all repute as temples of the law. Even that high royalist, Lord Clarendon, recognised that reliance upon such means was a cause of weakness, not of strength, and that men ceased to respect judicial decisions when they were used to cloak the designs of government. "When they saw," he writes, "in a court of law (that law that gave them a title to the possession of all they had) reason of state urged as elements of law, judges as sharp-sighted as secretaries of state, and in the mysteries of state, ... they had no reason to hope that doctrine, or the promoter of it, would be contained within any bounds. And here the damage and mischief cannot be expressed that the crown and state sustained by the deserved reproach and infamy that attended the judges; there being no possibility to preserve the dignity, reverence, and estimation of the laws themselves but by the integrity and innocency of the judges."[488] To the thorough supporter of the administration the matter appeared in a different light. When the two dissenting judges gave way under pressure and adhered to the report of the majority in favour of ship-money, they were told by Lord Wentworth that it was the greatest service the legal profession had rendered to the crown during this period.[489]

For good or evil the work of reducing the bench to an arm of the administration had been done, and from this political degradation it did not recover for nearly three-quarters of a century, until William III was seated on the throne and the judges became independent of the crown.

The stirring events of the great rebellion, the Protectorate, and the Restoration, which so profoundly affected the life and institutions of the nation in other ways, touched the bench but slightly. In the early months of the Long Parliament a resolution was passed by both houses of Parliament to the effect that the judges' appointments should be for the future *quamdiu se bene gesserint*, and on January 15, 1641, the king gave effect to this by a declaration that they should no longer hold office at the pleasure of the crown but during good behaviour. For twenty-four years the improvement was maintained in theory; in practice the old system kept its hold unshaken. During the short remainder of Charles I's reign the judges were concerned on only two occasions in affairs of state. These were however enough to demonstrate that the change in the manner of their appointments had by no means the result of rehabilitating the character of the bench and restoring to it the quality, which it had long lacked, of independence. One of the first acts of the Long Parliament, after dealing with the vital question of ship-money, was to turn upon the judges who had lent the weight of their names to the decision which pronounced its legality. Finch was violently attacked as a traitor in the House of Commons, and his impeachment voted with scarcely a dissentient voice. The Lord Keeper preferred the path of safety to that of dignity and fled to Holland on board a royal vessel, leaving the impeachment to be formally concluded in his absence. At the same time proceedings were commenced against six other judges who had sat at Hampden's trial.[490] The effect of this was immediate. Only once again did the judges come into prominence before the outbreak of the Civil War. Scarcely five months after Finch's impeachment the House of Lords demanded their opinion whether or no the articles against Strafford amounted to making him guilty of treason. Without hesitation they replied unanimously that upon the articles which the Lords had voted to be proved it was their opinion that the Earl of Strafford did deserve to undergo the pains and penalties of high treason by law.[491] Not only was their conduct in delivering this extra-judicial opinion decidedly irregular,[492] but their decision was in flagrant opposition to the clearest dictates of justice and rules of law, for the accusations against Strafford cannot be regarded as tantamount, or even approaching, to a substantial charge of treason.[493] The fault lay not in their intelligence, but in the system which had made their honesty an asset in the treasury of government, and had robbed them of their ability to judge facts in the light of law and reason without reference to principles of statecraft or the struggle of parties. It was not upon the merits of the case that their decision was based now that it was unfavourable to the administration, any more than their favourable decisions had been based upon the merits of cases when the administration was in power: the only difference was that formerly they had feared dismissal from the service of an angry sovereign as the result of an independent opinion, whereas now they feared impeachment at the hands of the angrier Commons.

Under the Commonwealth and the Protectorate the bench fared no better. In October 1649 all judges and other officers of the law, down to the very clerks of the courts, who had shown themselves hostile to the Parliament and in sympathy with the monarchy, were summarily dismissed, and their posts filled by men in whom trust could be reposed. Even this was not sufficient. In affairs of state justice was at a still greater discount under the Protectorate than under the monarchy. The cause of right was pleaded in vain when it came into collision with the power and plans of the Protector. "For not observing his pleasure" judges were rebuked, suspended, dismissed. Special judicial commissions were appointed to do his work; obnoxious attorneys and critical counsel were imprisoned.[494] The jury which acquitted Lilburn after "the furious hurley-burleys" of his second trial were sharply examined on their conduct by the Council of State.[495] Moreover the new appointments to the bench in spite of all care were not entirely satisfactory to Cromwell's government. The judges still exhibited a bent which must have been far from pleasing to the republicans. Sir Matthew Hale withdrew as far as possible from all political trials and refused to sit on Penruddock's trial after the collapse of the rising at Salisbury.[496] Surely it is this rather than the respectability of their characters that should explain how it came about that at the Restoration nine out of the fifteen republican judges then in office were found acceptable to the new government.

The character of the bench was no more altered by the Restoration than by the rebellion. If the traditions of forty years had clung too closely to be shaken off by those who might perhaps wish to be rid of them, they were not likely to be removed ten years later by those whose interest it was to retain them. The only practical difference was that the judges, whose duty as partisans of the government had been sealed by time and recognised by all who were concerned in the government, could now return to their more natural sphere as servants of the crown as well. Thenceforward until the end of the Stuart monarchy they were indispensable as allies of the king, protectors of the administration, shining examples of loyalty well applied and labour serviceably directed. They possessed moreover the signal advantage of being able to enforce the example which they inculcated. Those who did not obtained an evil reputation at court; and Sir Matthew Hale was looked at askance as one who was suspected of not lending a whole-hearted support to the government.[497] Even the theoretical advantage which had been gained by the Long Parliament now disappeared. Charles II took advantage of the lengthy prorogation of 1665 quietly to reintroduce appointments "at the good pleasure" of the crown.[498]

There was however some change for the better. A large majority of the nation was for the first time for thirty years united in sympathy with the government. The universal desire was for peace and stability. The great constitutional questions which had rent the kingdom and distracted the bench lay for the moment at rest. Government was no longer divided against itself; what was now found in opposition was not a combination of popular feeling with constitutional principle, to crush which the law must be strained by a serviceable judiciary, but a discredited party of fanatics and dissenters, the dregs of a defeated rebellion, against whom the law could be directed legally and to the satisfaction of the vast majority of the king's subjects.

The demand therefore for that cast of mind which under Charles I had been the peculiarity of a successful judge no longer existed for Charles II. When definitions of law were no longer needed to support the crown in opposition to the other legitimate elements of the constitution, and when the government was in close accord with the people, there was no temptation to subject the law to such strains as it had formerly been made to bear in the effort to galvanise into life a system which had already died a natural death. Perhaps it was less that judges had become more scrupulous than that the objection to their scruples had disappeared. To whatever cause they were due, it is certain that the reign of Charles II was marked by the renewal of decisions which must have been obnoxious to the government. No doubt these are not to be found in particular cases which were regarded as of high consequence, but the tendency is perfectly visible, and in one instance at least proved to be of profound importance. This was the trial of Penn and Meade in 1670, for by the proceedings which arose from it was finally established the principle that a jury has an absolute right to give such a verdict as it thinks proper without being open to question therefore by any other person or authority whatsoever.[499] The Quakers had been indicted for an unlawful assembly, and the jury before whom they were tried, in spite of repeated direction and shameful abuse from the Lord Mayor and the Recorder, found a verdict of not guilty. For this the court sentenced the jurymen to a fine of forty marks apiece and imprisonment until the fine was paid. Bushell, the foreman, and his fellow-jurors obtained a writ of habeas corpus, and the point was argued at length on the return to the writ. Ten judges out of twelve affirmed the absolute discretion of the jury to believe or disbelieve the evidence given according to the dictates of conscience, and not only were the jurymen discharged from custody without paying the fine, but no attempt has ever been made since to contest the principle thus established.[500]

One further instance may be noted. In 1675 a consultation of all the judges but two was held to decide a case which was submitted to them by the

Attorney-General. A great riot had been made a month before by the weavers' apprentices in various parts and suburbs of London by way of protest against the increased introduction of looms into their trade; the looms had been broken, a large amount of property destroyed, and several persons injured. The Attorney-General now wished to indict the rioters for high treason; but the judges were divided, five for, five against the opinion that treason had been committed, and in spite of the evident anxiety of the government to proceed against the apprentices on the graver issue, the Attorney-General had to be content with laying the indictments for a riot and obtaining convictions for the lesser offence.[501] When it is remembered that the London apprentices perpetually drew upon themselves the watchful eye of the government by their obnoxious politics, and that a trade riot was always suspected of being the forerunner of a sectarian revolt, it is evident that the decision of the judges meant considerable annoyance, if not an actual rebuff, to the government.[502]

The general usefulness of the bench was not however impaired by such exceptions. The judges still formed one of the most important parts of the administrative machinery. They were consulted by the government, gave advice, and put into effect the results of their advice. They supplied the king during the long prorogation of 1675 with the pretext which he required for the suppression of the coffee-houses.[503] Before the trial of the regicides they had held a conference with the king's counsel, Attorney, and Solicitor-General to resolve debatable points which were likely to arise in the course of the trials.[504] When the Licensing Act expired in 1679, the judges were ordered by the king to make a report concerning the control of the press. Their unanimous decision was "that his Majesty may, by law, prohibit the printing and publishing of all newsbooks and pamphlets of news whatsoever, not licensed by his Majesty's authority, as manifestly tending to a breach of the peace and disturbance of the kingdom";[505] and their preaching was put into practice before many months had elapsed at the trials of Harris[506] and Carr,[507] the former of whom was sentenced to the pillory and a fine of £500, and the latter to the suppression of the newspaper which he owned.

Actions for libel had always afforded a wide field for the exercise of administrative authority. Under the Clarendon *régime* the sentence pronounced by Chief-Justice Hyde upon Twyn, the printer, had fully sustained the traditions of the trials of Prynne, Bastwick, and Lilburn.[508] With the multiplication of political pamphlets after 1678 trials and convictions for libel became frequent. Within two years six important prosecutions of authors, printers, or publishers were instituted, and not only resulted almost always in the infliction of heavy punishments, but offered at the same time opportunities for many caustic and edifying remarks from the bench. Some time after, the number of trials for political libels and seditious words held within the space of seven months actually mounted to the total of sixteen.[509]

The advantage of lectures thus delivered in court on general politics and the duties of a good subject was of considerable value to the government. In this part of their duties the judges rivalled even the courtly eloquence of divines whose chief occupation was the advocacy of the doctrine of non-resistance. On his elevation to the bench in October 1676 Sir William Scroggs "made so excellent a speech, that my Lord Montague, then present, told the king he had since his happy restoration caused many hundred sermons to be printed, all which together taught not half so much loyalty; therefore as a sermon desired his command to have it printed and published in all the market towns in England."[510] It was afterwards made a ground for proceedings in Parliament against Scroggs that he had publicly spoken "very much against petitioning, condemning it as resembling 41, as factious and tending to rebellion, or to that effect"[511] and it was said that Sir Robert Atkyns was dismissed from the bench for contradicting a dictum of the Chief Justice while on circuit, "that the presentation of a petition for the summoning of Parliament was high treason."[512] Similar behaviour was also made the subject of complaint against Mr. Justice Jones.[513] Even the courteous Lord Chancellor Finch, in delivering sentence upon Lord Stafford, undertook to prove by the way that Godfrey had been murdered, and London burnt, by the papists.[514] But most of all the influence and importance of the judges was shown in trials for treason. In those days state trials were not merely impartial inquiries into the question whether or no certain persons had committed certain acts, the nature of which was under examination: they were life-and-death struggles of the king and his government against the attacks of those who wished to subvert them. It was the business of those engaged in them to see that the king's cause took no hurt. In this light they were universally regarded, and to this end their conduct was undertaken. Judges and jurors alike were engaged in the recognised task of the defence of the state. To the hearers it was no quaint piece of antiquated phraseology when the clerk of the crown addressed the prisoner arraigned at the bar for high treason: "These good men that are now called, and here appear, are those which are to pass between you and our sovereign lord the king, upon your life and death"; it was a sober expression of vivid truth. The jury stood between the king's life and the intrigues of a defeated malefactor. Of his innocence they were indeed ready to be convinced, but it would require strong evidence to convince them. In his guilt their belief was already strong. They can scarcely have refrained from regarding themselves less as agents employed in the cause of truth to examine without prejudice the merits of the case before them than as executors of an already predetermined justice.

And here the weight of the judge's authority was preponderant. He directed those heavy advantages which weighed on the side of the king and against the prisoner. The stringent system of preliminary procedure, which rendered extreme the difficulty of properly preparing his case beforehand, his isolation when actually upon trial, and the unsympathetic atmosphere by which he was surrounded, and of which the counsel for the prosecution were ready to take advantage to press every point home, combined to render the accused almost helpless against the crown. Even when administered with mercy the system was severely favourable to the prosecution; and the adverse rules which hemmed in the prisoner were generally worked to the utmost. To understand these clearly, it will be necessary to pass shortly in review the history of criminal procedure in the English courts of law, and the developments which led to its state at the time of the trials for the Popish Plot.[515]

CHAPTER II

CRIMINAL PROCEDURE

THE Reformation, as in almost all other branches of modern history, constitutes the starting-point at which the study of public procedure must be begun. Rather it would be true to say that in this as in other subjects it should form the starting-point. Unfortunately the necessary materials are here wanting. The State Trials, which afford not only the greatest quantity but the finest quality of evidence on the judicial history of England, are printed from reports which do not begin before the reign of Queen Mary in 1554. From that date until our own day they are continuous, and form the greatest collection of historical documents in the English language. From that date too the history of criminal procedure in modern England may be said to begin. Throughout the seventeenth century the courts of law occupy for the student of history a position of singular importance. They were the scenes not only of profound constitutional struggles, but of brilliant and deadly political contests.

The study of criminal procedure is therefore indispensable to an understanding of the numerous historical problems which have been worked out in the courts of law; especially to an understanding of those, not few, which have been worked to a conclusion, but not to a solution.

The difference between the procedure in criminal cases as it exists to-day and as it existed two centuries and a half ago is but little known. It is the more difficult to understand because it is witnessed by few great landmarks in the history of the administration of justice, and owes its existence to no promulgation of new codes or rules to which a triumphant finger may be pointed. Rather the new system has emerged from the old by a procession of unconsidered changes, at different times, of varying importance, the results of which have come to be so universally known and approved, that to the backward glance they seem to be not the outcome of long experience, but inextricable parts of a system which has existed from all time. The essential change has been one of conduct less than of opinion, and is to be found rather in an altered point of view than in any variation of practical arrangements.

The evolution of the forms under which trials were conducted during the later Stuart period was slow and unpronounced. The all-pervading activity of the Tudor privy council in affairs of state had left a deep imprint upon the course of English justice, and one from which it did not soon free itself. It was then that the courts gained the inquisitorial character which they did not lose until after the restoration of the monarchy, and it was not until the Puritan Revolution that the judicial authority of the council, which had grown to such a height of severity in the preceding half century, was swept away. During that time the privy council played a part of high importance in political trials. When a suspected criminal was to be brought to justice a stringent preliminary inquiry was held. The accused was examined on oath and in secret by the council. His examination was taken down in writing and might afterwards be produced against him under the name of a "confession." The investigation here made had the greatest weight. "In point of fact," says Dr. Gardiner, "these preliminary investigations formed the real trial. If the accused could satisfy the privy council of his innocence, he would at once be set at liberty. If he failed in this, he would be brought before a court from which there was scarcely a hope of escape."[516] As a rule he did fail. The privy councillors were not apt to waste their time on persons who were not brought before them as suspect on good grounds, or objectionable for reason of state. Innocence moreover would be little protection to a prisoner in the latter case, for the political grounds against him would be unaffected by any scrutiny of evidence. If the accused was committed by the council, it was with no bright prospect before his eyes. Until the day of his trial he was kept close prisoner. He had no notice of the witnesses who were to be called against him or of the evidence which they would give. Nor was the evidence for the prosecution the only point in which the prisoner was at a disadvantage, for he was not allowed to call witnesses to set up a case for himself. This at least seems to have been the fact; but even had theory permitted the appearance in court of witnesses for the prisoner, in practice the difference made would have been trifling, for he certainly had no means of procuring their attendance or, supposing they came, of ascertaining what they would say. Even at the close of the seventeenth century, when witnesses for the defence were recognised and encouraged by the courts, great difficulty was experienced by prisoners in procuring the attendance of the right persons, and, when these came, they sometimes gave evidence on the wrong side.[517] The accused was brought into court in absolute ignorance of what would be produced against him, and was compelled to defend himself on the spur of the moment against skilled lawyers, who had been preparing their case for weeks or perhaps months beforehand. Neither before or at the trial was he allowed the aid of counsel or solicitor. On being brought to the bar, the prisoner was treated in such a way as to rob him almost of the possibility of escape. During his confinement examinations had been made of all other suspected persons, and their depositions had been taken. Not only could these now be produced in court against him, but the confessions of accomplices, when these could be found, were regarded as specially cogent evidence. No one, it was said, could have so great a knowledge of the crime as the accomplices of the criminal—a remark, it must be admitted, which, at a time when there existed no organised force of police, was not without some show of justice. No doubt such men were of bad character, but then it was not to be expected that one could raise the curtain on scenes of such ill-odour without coming into questionable company. The prisoner was not allowed to cross-examine the witnesses brought against him and had not even the right to confront them in court face to face.[518]

In a trial of any intricacy the case for the crown was usually divided between several counsel. Each worked out his part minutely before giving place to the next, partly by making direct statements, partly by a string of questions addressed to the prisoner. The trial was thus resolved into a series of excited altercations between the accused and the counsel for the crown. The success with which the defence was conducted depended entirely upon the skill and readiness displayed by the prisoner himself. At his trial for treason in 1554[519] Sir Nicolas Throckmorton maintained for close upon six hours a wordy conflict with Sergeant Stamford and the Attorney-General, and acquitted himself so well that the jury after deliberating for two hours returned a verdict of not guilty.[520] The Duke of Norfolk, convicted of high treason in 1571, was set an even harder task, for he was compelled to deal successively with no less than four eminent counsel who had undertaken different parts of the case against him.[521]

Apart from the opening speeches of the crown lawyers and the summing up of the evidence by the judge at the end of the trial, there was little room for any display of fine oratory, and practically none for the sentimental appeal to the jury which at a later date became so prominent a feature in the courts. Every point was argued by the opposing parties in a close and acrimonious conversation, which had at least the merit of throwing light from every possible point of view on the subject in hand. In this the judges presiding did not take much part, nor was the summing up regarded as of special importance; but explanatory remarks, and questions on points which seemed to the judges to have been overlooked, were occasionally interposed from the bench.[522]

But what weighed most heavily of all against the prisoner was the fact that rules of evidence, as they are understood at the present time, were practically unknown. The only distinction recognised was between the evidence of an eye-witness to the actual crime and everything else. If other than eye-witnesses were admitted, there seemed to be no reason why the most insignificant evidence upon hearsay of facts, however remotely connected with those alleged in the charge, should not be produced against the prisoner. Even the production of the originals of documents relied upon as evidence for the prosecution was not required.[523]

This was a fault in criminal procedure which persisted until at least the end of the seventeenth century and exercised a supreme influence upon the course of justice. Grave attention and decisive weight was given to evidence which in modern times would not be allowed to come into court at all. The most irrelevant detail was freely admitted against the prisoner. At Raleigh's trial in 1603 one Dyer, a pilot, swore that when he was at Lisbon he had accidentally met a man who said that Cobham and Raleigh would cut King James' throat before he could be crowned.[524] Evidence of a still more remarkable character was given at the trial of Benjamin Faulconer for perjury in 1653. After the charge had been proved, witnesses were called to testify to a variety of facts startlingly unconnected with the case. They swore that the prisoner had been guilty of using bad language, that he had drunk the devil's health in the streets of Petersfield, and that he had "a common name for a robber on the highway."[525] All this was allowed as good evidence to raise a presumption of his guilt. Instances of the lax rules of evidence in force might be multiplied. At Hulet's trial for having been executioner of Charles I witnesses were admitted for the defence to testify that they had heard Brandon, the hangman, say that he had himself cut off the king's head. On the other hand the evidence for the prosecution chiefly consisted of the testimony of persons who swore that they had heard Hulet admit the truth of the charge.[526] The trial of Hawkins for theft before Sir Matthew Hale in 1669 is still more notable. Not only was evidence allowed to prove for the prosecution that Hawkins had committed, and for the defence that he had not committed, two other thefts wholly unconnected with the case before the court,[527] but the prisoner, who was a country parson, was permitted to produce a certificate signed by over a hundred of his parishioners, to the effect that the prosecutor was "a notorious Anabaptist, an enemy to the Church of England, and a perfect hater of all ministers of the same, but in particular most inveterate and malicious against Robert Hawkins, clerk, late minister of the church of Chilton," and going on to express their belief in the innocence of Hawkins and the dishonesty of the prosecutor.[528]

The trials of Colonel Turner for burglary and of the Suffolk witches, who were condemned in the year 1665, afford perhaps the strongest instances of the slight extent to which the principles of evidence were understood. In the former the chief part of the evidence given by Sir Thomas Aleyn, the principal witness, was concerned with what other people had done and said, and would by modern methods have certainly been ruled out; in the latter the smallest apprehension of the value of testimony would have resulted in an abrupt termination of the case, for nothing which by courtesy could be called evidence was produced against the wretched old women who were being tried for their lives, and their conviction was obtained partly on the strength of a statement by Dr. Browne of Norwich, author of the *Religio Medici*, as to the nature of witches and their relations with the devil, no single word of which could have been spoken in a modern court of justice.[529] It was a state of things, due to lack of experience and of scientific vision, which prevailed until after the Revolution and exerted a powerful influence against the accused. In other points however criminal procedure in the English courts underwent changes of considerable importance. From the reign of Queen Mary until the Puritan Revolution it had remained almost unaltered, but during the Commonwealth and Protectorate several modifications were introduced. An apparently spontaneous change, inaugurated by no legislative enactment, bore witness to the fact that the view in which criminal trials were regarded was insensibly shifting from the ancient to the modern standpoint. The inquisitorial nature of the old trial was gradually disappearing. Chief among the differences which may be noted as having arisen is the fact that the prisoner was no longer systematically questioned in court. When he was questioned, it was now, if he were innocent, in his favour. His examination was no longer what it had been in the days of Elizabeth and James I, the very essence of the trial. Questions were still put to him, but now they were directed by the judges and not by the prosecution. The process was of no greater scope than was demanded by the necessities of the defence of a prisoner who has not the assistance of counsel. It was used as a natural means of arriving at the truth of statements made on one side or the other, and served to set in a clear light the strong and weak points of the defence. At the trial of the Turners, who were guilty, a lengthy examination of the prisoners by the court succeeded in shewing the great improbability of statements in their story, and tended directly to the conviction of the colonel.[530] On the other hand, in the case of Sir George Wakeman, who was innocent, the triangular series of questions between judge, witness, and prisoner had an effect which was by no means unfavourable to the accused.[531] The prisoner moreover could, if he wished, refuse to answer questions put to him.[532]

Two other results of the changing spirit of the times may be found in the criminal courts. Witnesses for the prosecution were now always brought face to face with the accused, unless reason such as would be valid to-day was given to the contrary; and the prisoner was not only allowed to cross-examine the witnesses against him, but to call evidence in his own behalf.[533] The value of cross-examination to the defence was doubtless an important advance in theory; practically it was greatly impaired by the natural difficulties, which to an untrained man are almost insuperable, of cross-examining witnesses without proper instruction. But the power of calling witnesses for the defence was in practice as well a gain of immense magnitude.

With these changes the procedure of Tudor times was handed on to the restored monarchy, and was retained without alteration until the end of the Stuart dynasty. The position of a person on trial, bettered as it was, was pitiable. The bench received the prisoner's witnesses with the utmost suspicion and treated them as if they were proved to be accomplices in his crime. It was pointed out to the jury that they were not upon oath. At the trial of one of the regicides in 1660 it was even hinted that their evidence might be disbelieved on this ground alone.[534] Later practice demanded that the jury should be directed to notice the fact and warned that witnesses not upon oath deserved no less credit for this reason; but opportunity was generally taken to slight their evidence in other ways. If the prisoner's witnesses were Roman Catholics, it was pointed out that their evidence might be tutored.[535] If not, the counsel for the prosecution could easily make an opening to call attention to the fact that mere words for the prisoner ought not to weigh as heavily as sound oaths for the king, and he would not be hastily checked by the court.[536] Theoretically, the court was "of counsel for the prisoner" in matters of law;[537] practically, as this conflicted with the judges' duty to the king and their watch over his life, the prisoner was allowed to shift for himself. To justify the denial of counsel to the accused, the argument was constantly used that, in order to convict him, the proof must be so plain that no counsel could contend against it.[538] Honestly enough, no doubt, this was the theory; but in practice the slightest complication of facts or the most awkward piece of perjury could not fail to render the prisoner in his eagerness and ignorance helpless to unravel the skein which was being wound round him.

In particular matters of law counsel might be assigned to argue such points as the court thought fit, but only when they had been proposed to the court by the prisoner himself.[539] When Colledge at his trial for high treason retorted that without the aid of counsel he could not tell what points to submit for argument, he was told by the Attorney-General that ignorance of the law was an excuse for no man.[540]

In countless ways the system worked, in accordance with the tradition of many years, in favour of the king and in glaring disfavour of the prisoner. Peculiar cruelty on the part of the judges has continually been assumed as an explanation of this. In reality recourse need be had to no such hypothesis. The judges handled the means which had come down to them as legitimate, without necessarily indulging the rare vice of spontaneous inhumanity which has been attributed to them by historians. They did their work and performed their duty as it came in their way; and the work of a judge in state trials in the seventeenth century was to modern eyes neither dignified nor pleasant. Nor, although their names are linked to no distinction in the annals of the law, were the judges, whose patents ran "during the good pleasure" of King Charles II, men devoid of talent. Lawyers were raised to the bench by influence at court, since all offices of state were to be obtained by favouritism; but their appointments were seldom devoid of some foundation of solid attainments. Some, like Scroggs, were by nature brilliant; others, like North and Pemberton, had grounded their fortunes on many years of laborious industry.[541] Such men, whose minds were not bent to reverence of the law by severe learning in it, were likely to be influenced by their position as lawyers less than by that as officers of state, and to regard their oaths as constraining them rather to the service of the crown than to an absolute pursuit of justice. Sometimes the rules under which they worked themselves prevented them from doing right to prisoners. They were unable, for instance, to summon or to protect witnesses for the defence, for their power ended with the confines of the court. When Colonel Turner on his trial in 1664 told the bench that his witnesses had sent him word that they did not dare to come without an order, the Chief Justice replied, "When witnesses come against the king, we cannot put them to their oaths, much less precept them to come."[542] At the trial of Langhorn, the Roman Catholic lawyer, for the Popish Plot, Lord Castlemaine complained to the court that the prisoner's witnesses were being threatened and assaulted by the mob outside and dared not "come to give their evidence for fear of being killed." The judges were indignant and declaimed loudly against the "very horrid thing," but they were powerless to do more than to threaten the offenders with severe punishment, if the earl could produce or point to them. As this was naturally impossible, nothing could be done.[543]

The inability of the court to allow real favour to the accused receives constant illustration from the trial of Lord Stafford. It might have been expected that a venerable peer, standing to be judged by his peers and surrounded by his relatives and old acquaintances, would receive an amount of respect and favour which was denied to meaner folk. But this was far from being the case. In spite of the evident desire of the Lord Chancellor, who presided in the capacity of Lord High Steward, to allow to the accused every advantage that was consistent with his duty, he found it impossible to contest against the managers of the prosecution in their demand that the rules should be exerted against him in all their usual harshness. Time after time the counsel pressed home points of procedure which lay in their favour. It roused the indignation of Jones and Maynard that the barristers retained by Lord Stafford to be his counsel on matters of law stood so near him that they might be suspected of wishing to prompt him in matters of fact, and they were forced to move to a greater distance from the prisoner.[544] When at the end of the second day of the trial Finch urged that before further proceedings a day's rest should be given to the prisoner to recover from his great physical fatigue, the managers withstood his proposal eagerly. The Lord High Steward asked what inconvenience would ensue. They could suggest none of consequence, but said that the delay would be highly unusual and that it was a most unreasonable thing to demand. Jones' zeal was such that he exposed himself to a well-deserved snub from the court.[545] Without being in the least abashed he pursued his speech and finally carried the point triumphantly.[546] A similar violation of the maxim *De vitâ hominis nulla est cunctatio longa*, which the Lord Chancellor quoted on this occasion, occurred during the trial of Lord Russell, when Chief Justice Pemberton would have granted a short respite to the prisoner but for the opposition of the prosecuting counsel. "Mr. Attorney, why may not this trial be respited till the afternoon?" To which the Attorney-General rudely replied, "Pray call the jury"; and Pemberton had nothing for it but to say to the prisoner, "My Lord, the king's counsel think it not reasonable to put off the trial longer, and we cannot put it off without their consent." On the last day of Lord Stafford's trial the court again displayed its weakness as a protector of the accused. Owing to the prisoner's excessive weakness and failure to make his voice heard, the Lord High Steward ordered a clerk to read the paper from which he was struggling to propose certain points of law to be argued. The managers immediately objected. It was contrary to custom and might be turned into a dangerous precedent. Finch was compelled to give way to their harsh insistence, and Stafford, tottering with fatigue, to make an effort which was almost beyond his strength.[547]

The old criminal trial of the English courts had been conducted strictly on the inquisitorial method of procedure, a system admirably contrived for the conviction of the guilty, but by no means so successful in ensuring the acquittal of the innocent. Of this character it was robbed by the Puritan Revolution, which rendered the administrative methods of continental nations odious to the English mind. But in its place nothing so complete or logical remained. The changes which were then introduced, beneficent as they were, did not institute an order capable, in the interest of justice and of the state, of guaranteeing the discovery of the truth or of safeguarding the rights of the individual. The rigorous system of preliminary procedure, the denial of counsel to assist the accused, the ignorance of the art of cross-examination and of the science of sifting evidence, combined to set judge, jury, and prisoner alike at the mercy of every man of villainy sufficient to swear away a man's life by a false oath, and of impudence sufficient to brazen out his perjury.[548] Not until greater knowledge of the principles of judicial administration was gained by a long and harsh experience, and until a more stable state of society produced the possibility of treating accused persons with the generosity which is characteristic of modern criminal procedure, were these evils remedied.

Society, as it was in the latter half of the seventeenth century, could neither afford nor pretend to be generous to the prisoner at the bar. In these latter days when a man comes to be tried, the jury are told that it is their first duty to believe him innocent until he is proved to be guilty. The burden of that proof lies heavily upon the shoulders of those who conduct the prosecution. Whatever doubt may exist is counted to the benefit of the accused. He is treated throughout with studied consideration. But when the fourteen men who died for the Popish Plot were brought to the bar, all this was unheard of. Then the prisoner came into court already in the minds of all men half proved an enemy to the king's majesty, and one to whom no more advantage than was his strict right could be allowed. To the satisfaction of one jury, indeed, he had been actually proved guilty, for the grand jurors "for our Lord the King" had presented upon their oaths that the prisoner "wilfully, feloniously, and of his malice aforethought" had committed the crime for which he was arraigned. Why should he be accounted innocent, to whose guilt at least twelve good men and true had positively sworn? The presumptive innocence of the accused is a modern fiction which has tacitly grown up in a society conscious that its strength is too firm to be shaken by the misdeeds of single offenders, and therefore willing that any individual suspected of offence against its laws shall retain all the advantages on his own side. Before this stage was reached, men thought otherwise. In the seventeenth century society and government were unstable and liable to sudden shocks. A comparatively trifling event might set the balance against the reign of law and order, and consequently the law meted out hard measure to those who came into contact with it. As soon as the accused was committed for trial he was sent to close confinement, from which he did not emerge until he was brought to the bar. Unless by extraordinary favour, he was allowed neither counsel nor solicitor to assist in the preparation of his defence. He was not allowed to see his witnesses before they came into court.[549] All the papers which he wrote in prison were taken from him.[550] The utmost he might claim was that one of his friends should visit him in order to summon the proper witnesses for his defence. Even these interviews, in any case of importance, could be held only in the presence of the jailor, that the prisoner might be cut off from all means of illicit intercourse with the outer world,[551] a precaution which was justified by the fact that, when all possible care had been taken, prisoners still found means underhand to receive communications which would have been prizes of considerable value to the government if they had been intercepted.[552] The age which knew the penal laws as active measures of administration, which was divided from the tragedy at Fotheringay by less than a hundred years and from the Gunpowder Plot by scarcely more than the span of a man's life, which had only recovered from the successive shocks of revolution and restoration to wait expectantly for the day when rebellion would have to be met once again, and on which within the ten ensuing years did burst another rebellion and a second revolution, could hardly be expected to rate the safety of society more lightly than the life of one who, at the best, was surrounded by incriminating circumstances. Even so late and well-ordered a man as Paley believed that it was better for the innocent to die than for the guilty to go free.[553]

CHAPTER III

TRIALS FOR THE PLOT

SUCH was the state of society and the procedure of the English courts when Edward Coleman was brought to the bar of the Court of King's Bench on November 27, 1678 to be tried on the charge of high treason. The trial was a test case. In point of importance it was chief among the series of trials for treason which arose from the Plot, for all the others which followed to some extent depended from this. If Coleman had been acquitted, there could have been no more to come. His letters formed, as they still form, the weightiest part of the evidence against the Roman Catholic intriguers,[554] and had they not secured his conviction, the Jesuits, Mr. Langhorn, Lord Stafford, and Archbishop Plunket would have gone unconvicted also. By his condemnation the way was opened by which they were sent to the scaffold, the innocent and the guilty alike, without favour or discrimination.

In the words of Sir George Jeffreys, Recorder of London, the indictment set forth "that the said Edward Coleman, endeavouring to subvert the Protestant religion and to change and alter the same, and likewise to stir up rebellion and sedition amongst the king's liege people and also to kill the king," did hold certain correspondence with "M. la Chaise, then servant and confessor to the French king."[555] In point of fact the indictment lays by far the greater stress on the former of these counts. The murder of the king is mentioned, but not insisted upon. The charges against Coleman are summed up in the accusation of a plot "to bring and put our said sovereign lord the king to final death and destruction, and to overthrow and change the government of the kingdom of England, and to alter the sincere and true religion of God in this kingdom as by law established; and wholly to subvert and destroy the state of the whole kingdom, being in the universal parts thereof well-established and ordained; and to levy war against our said sovereign lord the king within his realm of England"; and the letters in which he endeavoured to obtain aid and assistance for these objects are mentioned in particular.[556] Sergeant Maynard and Sir William Jones, Attorney-General, followed and opened the evidence for the crown. They too touched on the charge of killing the king and the evidence which Oates was prepared to give on the subject, but dwelt most heavily on Coleman's correspondence with Throckmorton, Cardinal Howard, and Père de la Chaize. "The prisoner at the bar," said Maynard, "stands indicted for no less than an intention and endeavour to murder the king; for an endeavour and attempt to change the government of the nation, so well settled and instituted, ... and for an endeavour to alter the Protestant religion and to introduce instead of it the Romish superstition and popery."[557] The matter could not be better or more briefly stated. The substantial charge against Coleman lay, not in the actual attempt of which he was accused to murder the king, but in the designs which he had formed to alter the established course of government and religion, as settled in the kingdom. By the recognised construction of the statute of Edward III such an attempt was held to include "imagining the king's death," and was as much high treason as an assassination plot of the most flagrant character.[558] All that was required was that the intention should be proved by an overt act, and the portion of Coleman's correspondence which had been seized afforded the plainest proof of his designs. This was the real offence which lay at his door, and for this he was legally and properly condemned to suffer the penalties of high treason. "Mr. Coleman," said the Chief Justice after the verdict had been delivered, "your own papers are enough to condemn you."[559]

The case for the prosecution was opened by the evidence of Titus Oates. After an admonition from the bench to speak nothing but the truth, permission was given him to tell his story in his own way. In the course of a long examination by the Chief Justice he reaffirmed the startling evidence which he had given before the two Houses of Parliament, and which had already become a powerful weapon in the Whig armoury. He deposed that he had carried treasonable letters from Coleman and various Jesuits in London to the Jesuit College at St. Omers; that he had carried to Père de la Chaize a letter written by Coleman in thanks for a promise from the confessor of £10,000 to be employed in procuring Charles II's death;[560] that Coleman had in his hearing expressed approval when he was told that the Jesuits had determined to kill the king;[561] and that Coleman had been engaged in distributing throughout the kingdom copies of certain instructions sent to the Jesuit Ashby concerning the assassination of the king, in order to give heart to those of their party who were not on the scene of affairs.[562] In the medley of wild accusations against the Jesuits and other Roman Catholics, which Oates mingled with this evidence against Coleman, the main point, as in his previous examinations, was the Jesuit consult held, he swore, at the White Horse Tavern in the Strand on April 24, 1678, to concert means for the death of the king. After the consult had broken up into smaller committees, it was at that which met at Wild House that Coleman had, according to Oates, given his formal approval to the project. Later, in a letter which Oates professed to have seen, he had expressed the desire "that the duke might be trepanned into this plot to murder the king."[563] Bedloe's evidence, which followed, was of the same nature, though not so wide in scope or so decisive in character.[564] He swore to treasonable correspondence between the Jesuits in London and Paris, to treasonable words which he had heard Coleman speak, to treasonable consults in Paris at which Coleman was not present, and on hearsay from Sir Henry Tichbourn bore out Oates' statement that Coleman had received a patent to be secretary of state under the new Jesuit *régime* in England.[565] This closed the oral evidence for the crown, and it was against this that Coleman directed the only part of his case which could be called a defence. He objected to Oates that his testimony was entirely untrustworthy. At the examination before the privy council, Oates had neither known nor accused him personally; yet now he pretended to be his intimate and conversant with all his plans.[566] Oates replied quickly that, when he was confronted with Coleman at the council board, the candles in the room gave so dim a light that he was unable to swear positively to his identity. "I then said," he declared, "I would not swear I had seen him before in my life, because my sight was bad by candle-light, and candle-light alters the sight much.... I cannot see a great way by candle-light." Here the monstrous ugliness of Oates' features came to his aid in a strange fashion. His eyes were set so deep in the sockets that they were universally noted as being out of the common. Contemporary descriptions of him all mark this feature as striking.[567] There must have been signs of something perhaps almost unnatural about them, which would lend colour to the idea that he needed a strong light to see clearly. His reply on the present occasion has been universally treated by historians with ridicule, but it is difficult to believe that it seemed so to spectators and even possible that there was some truth in what he said. The answer at all events was taken, and the court passed to what was in fact the more important point, Coleman's assertion that Oates had not charged him before the privy council with what he had since brought forward. "The stress of the objection," said the Chief Justice, "lieth not upon seeing so much, but how come you that you laid no more to Mr. Coleman's charge at that time?" To this the witness had no sufficient answer. His memory failed him completely. He declared with many turns and qualifications that he had not felt bound "to give in more than a general information against Mr. Coleman," and that he would have spoken in greater detail had he been urged. But he had been so wearied by two sleepless nights spent in tramping round the town to take prisoners that the king and council were willing to let him go as soon as possible. Unfortunately he let slip that he had accused Coleman in particular with writing treasonable newsletters to inflame the country.[568] Upon this the court seized. If he had been able to charge Coleman with this malodorous correspondence, why had he not been able to accuse him of any of the far graver acts of treason which he now laid to his charge Oates was thereupon subjected to a severe examination by the bench. The questions were constantly put to him: "Why did you not accuse Mr. Coleman by name? You were by when the council were ready to let Mr. Coleman go almost at large? Why did you not name Mr. Coleman at that time? How came you (Mr. Coleman being so desperate a man as he was, endeavouring the killing of the king) to omit your information of it to the council and to the king at both times?"[569] Oates' answers were the reverse of satisfactory. He became loud in protestation, swore that he had been so tired that he could scarcely stand, and appealed to the king to attest what had passed at his examination; but the Chief Justice kept close to the point and drove him from one position to another, until he seemed ready to take refuge in silence. The saviour of the nation was within an ace of a catastrophe which would have wrecked his whole future career when the prisoner restored the balance by a false move. Turning from the witness, Scroggs asked Coleman if he had any further question to put. With maladroitness singular in a man of his experience, Coleman reverted to the incident of the candles and Oates' inability to recognise him at the council. The question was threshed out minutely, for Coleman thought that he had found in Sir Thomas Dolman, clerk to the privy council, a witness who could prove that Oates had not only failed to recognise him, but had denied acquaintance altogether with the person of Mr. Coleman. This however Sir Thomas could not do, and the matter was left exactly where it was before: the evidence only shewed that Oates had not been able to identify as Coleman the man with whom he was confronted.[570] This Oates had already admitted and explained. But the examination of Dolman naturally led the court to call upon Sir Robert Southwell, another of the council clerks, to state his version of what had happened. From his evidence it appeared that at the examination before the council Oates had charged Coleman by name with having in person paid £5000 out of £15,000 to Sir George Wakeman as a fee for poisoning the king.[571] This was a fact which Oates had not mentioned in his evidence at the trial, when he only swore that Coleman considered £10,000 too small a sum for such a great work, and had advised that Sir George Wakeman should be paid half as much again.[572] He had moreover forgotten altogether that he had given any evidence of the sort before the council. On this no remark was made either by the court or by the prisoner. The omission however to point out his lapse of memory as of weight against the witness is patent of a genuine explanation. Clearly no possible amount of fatigue would have justified Oates in the eyes of the judges for having failed at his examination by the council to charge Coleman with treason of which he afterwards accused him; but it was a very different thing, and perfectly reasonable, to consider that the great exertions which he had undergone might fairly explain his forgetfulness of the charge which he had then actually made.[573] The question had been reduced to the issue whether or no Oates had then charged Coleman with the high crimes of which he was now giving evidence. This was now indisputably determined in favour of the witness and against the prisoner.

The first reflection upon this scene which occurs to the mind of one who comes to study it in the twentieth century is that in a modern court it could scarcely have taken place at all. It seems as if the elaborate care taken to discuss particular omissions and contradictions in Oates' evidence was only so much waste of time, for to the modern eye the whole bulk was of a character which would now be considered wholly inadmissible as good testimony. Writing of the evidence of the other informers as well as of Oates throughout the trials, Sir James Fitzjames Stephen says: "No one accustomed to weighing evidence can doubt that he and the subordinate witnesses were quite as bad and quite as false as they are usually supposed to have been. Their evidence has every mark of perjury about it. They never would tie themselves down to anything if they could possibly avoid it. As soon as they were challenged with a lie by being told that witnesses were coming to contradict them, they shuffled and drew back and began to forget."[574] The evidence which Oates gave against the accused consisted largely in his swearing that he had carried letters from one person to another, which upon a mental comparison with yet more letters, he recognised to be in the handwriting of a third person, being in this case that of Coleman.[575] Or that he had been told by Coleman of treasonable letters which he had written into the country to encourage the Catholic party. Or again, that he had been told by other persons that at a consult, from which he himself had been absent, various treasonable designs were formed and approved; or that it was generally understood among the conspirators that the accused had done this, that, or the other. Even definite facts sworn by the witness, as for instance when Oates swore that he had seen Coleman pay an extra guinea to the messenger who carried £80 to four Irishmen as payment for the king's death, and when Bedloe swore that he had heard Coleman say that "if there was an hundred heretical kings to be deposed, he would see them all destroyed,"[576] were statements which did not receive and were scarcely susceptible of corroboration. Nowadays it is an established principle that the uncorroborated evidence of an accomplice is not to be acted upon, and the direct evidence of witnesses in the Popish Plot, even when it was most definite and precise, would without exception have fallen under this rule. But in the seventeenth century the rule was unknown. Practically any statement made on oath in the witness box was accepted unconditionally, unless the witness was either contradicted by better evidence or else proved to be no "good witness." The competence of a witness was technically destroyed only by a record of perjury proved against him, but the credibility of evidence was a question for the judgment of the jury; and where the witness had been convicted of other crimes the jury sometimes disbelieved his word.[577] The evidence of accomplices was not only admitted but highly prized. That it should be uncorroborated excited no wonder, for it was regarded as a remarkable piece of fortune to obtain it at all. To our minds the dead weight of an oath seems to be of far less account in determining the trustworthiness of evidence than its intrinsic probability and the degree to which it is corroborated by other circumstances, but in the judgment of the seventeenth century an oath carried all before it. A remarkable illustration of this is received from the trial of the Five Jesuits in 1679. Fenwick objected that the evidence against him was wholly uncorroborated. "All the evidence that is given," he said, "comes but to this, there is but saying and swearing. I defy them all to give one probable reason to satisfy any reasonable uninterested man's judgment how this could be." "You say there is nothing but saying and swearing," answered the Chief Justice, "but you do not consider what you say in that matter. All the evidence and all the testimony in all trials is by swearing. A man comes and swears that he saw such a bond sealed, or heard such words spoken; this is saying and swearing; but it is that proof that we go by, and by which all men's lives and fortunes are determined.... Mr. Fenwick," he added in summing up to the jury, "says to all this: there is nothing against us but talking and swearing; but for that he hath been told (if it were possible for him to learn) that all testimony is but talking and swearing: for all things, all men's lives and fortunes are determined by an oath; and an oath is by talking, by kissing the book, and calling God to witness to the truth of what is said."[578] Fenwick's cosmopolitan education here gave him the advantage. By the light of experience he is seen to have been in advance of the times in England, but for the law and practice of the English courts his contention was vain. He was asking that the court should in his case lay down a rule which half a century later was new to the English mind.

The ignorance which was thus displayed of the proper nature of testimony has constantly been considered as a mark of atrocious ferocity and cowardly time-service in the judges of the period. Such a view is entirely erroneous. The evidence accepted at political trials did not differ in character from that acted upon at trials the causes of which were remote from politics. Fortunately there are means by which this can be proved exactly. It is fortunate, for it is improbable that the same type of perjured evidence should appear in any other than a political trial. Of perjured evidence there was no doubt plenty at every assize, as is witnessed by the case of the Rev. Mr. Hawkins,[579] where a considerable dose was nearly swallowed without being detected. But in this style of lie there was not the same boldness, the same play of fancy, the same overriding of the limits of likelihood which has rendered the acceptance of Oates' evidence unintelligible to historians except on the supposition of monstrous immorality in the judges and juries. "Witnesses," writes Fox, "of such a character as not to deserve credit in the most trifling cause, upon the most immaterial facts, gave evidence so incredible, or, to speak more properly, so impossible to be true, that it ought not to have been believed if it had come from the mouth of Cato; and upon such evidence, from such witnesses, were innocent men condemned to death and executed."[580] Such a state of things, thought Fox and many after him, is not to be explained on any supposition other than that of wilfully wicked blindness to the truth, and can hardly be paralleled in modern history. There is however, if not a parallel, at least a very great similarity between the evidence offered at the trials for the Popish Plot and that taken at another series of trials of almost the same date, to find which no one need go further than a different page in the same volume of reports. The same tangled farrago of wild nonsense with which Oates and his fellow-witnesses filled the courts is, on another plane, almost exactly reproduced in the witch trials of the seventeenth century.

In the first half of the century the numbers of women who had been condemned and hanged as witches may be counted almost by dozens,[581] and in the reign of Charles II at least five wretched creatures were put to death for practices in the black art. What is here noteworthy about their trials is that they exhibit just the same characteristics as the trials for the Popish Plot. The monstrous evidence offered by the witnesses and the credulity displayed by the court at the trials of the Suffolk witches in 1665 and of the Devon witches seventeen years later at least equalled, if they did not surpass, anything which is recorded of political cases of the same age. Two instances will suffice to demonstrate the truth of this. At the trial at Bury St. Edmunds, Margaret Arnold gave evidence as to the children who were said to have been bewitched: "At another time the younger child, being out of her fits, went out of doors to take a little fresh air, and presently a little thing like a bee flew upon her face and would have gone into her mouth, whereupon the child ran in all haste to the door to get into the house again, screeching out in a most terrible manner; whereupon this deponent made haste to come to her, but before she could get to her, the child fell into her swooning fit, and at last with much pain, straining herself, she vomited up a twopenny nail with a broad head; and after that the child had raised up the nail, she came to her understanding and, being demanded by this deponent how she came by this nail, she answered 'that the bee brought this nail and forced it into her mouth.'"[582] The information of Elizabeth Eastchurch against Temperance Lloyd, one of the three women condemned in 1682, is a fair specimen of the evidence which was, in the words of Fox, "impossible to be true," and which was nevertheless accepted and acted upon by the courts. "The said informant upon her oath saith. That upon the second day of this instant July, the said Grace Thomas,[583] then lodging in this informant's said husband's house, and hearing of her to complain of great pricking pains in one of her knees, she the said informant did see her said knee, and observed that she had nine places in her knee which had been pricked, and that every one of the said

- 203 -

pricks were as though it had been the prick of a thorn. Whereupon this informant afterwards, upon the same 2nd day of July, did demand of the said Temperance Lloyd whether she had any wax or clay in the form of a picture whereby she had pricked and tormented the said Grace Thomas? Unto which the said Temperance made answer that she had no wax or clay, but confessed that she had only a piece of leather which she had pricked nine times."[584]

When it is considered that the former of these trials was conducted by Lord Chief Justice Hale, the most famous and according to all testimony the most moderate judge of his time, it becomes brilliantly clear that it was not only by incompetent judges, as the nature of the cases makes it clear that it was not only in political trials, that unsound evidence was accepted as genuine, but that the common knowledge of the times did not discriminate in any appreciable manner between evidence which is, and that which ought not to be, sufficient to procure the conviction of prisoners. Without adornment the fact is that evidence which to modern ears is bad, to those of judges and juries of the seventeenth century seemed perfectly good.[585] One further point of similarity between the evidence given at witch trials and at trials for the Plot may be noted. Credence was given to flimsy tales of the devil and his practices, if not solely, at least all the more readily because such ideas were current in the popular mind, and scarcely more than a hint was needed for their embodiment as concrete facts. The same may be said of the revelations of the Popish Plot. For years men had expected nothing more certainly and had feared nothing more keenly than a great onslaught of Catholicism upon their own religion. What they now heard seemed only a just realisation of their prophecies. "They had," says Bishop Parker, "so familiarly accustomed themselves to these monstrous lies, that at the first opening of Oates' Plot they with a ready and easy credulity received all his fictions; for whatsoever he published, they had long before expected."[586]

It is necessary to lay stress upon this aspect of the evidence given by the witnesses at Coleman's trial, since at all those which followed it reappeared with little variation; but to Coleman himself it was not of the first importance. Sixteen letters selected from his correspondence with Roman Catholics abroad were read at length,[587] and formed the heaviest part of the case against him. From them the nature of his schemes was plainly visible. It was of little moment to him that they were taken as establishing the reality of the nightmare which Oates had sketched. Without anything in common with the blood and thunder tales which that miscreant poured forth, they contained more than enough of treasonable matter to cost the prisoner his head. It was impossible for him to deny the letters. All he could do was to say that he had meant no harm, and to express the hope that they would not be found to bear out the charge of high treason. "I deny the conclusion, but the premises," he admitted, "are too strong and artificial."[588] Chief among the correspondence read were three letters to and one from Père de la Chaize and the declaration which Coleman had drawn up to justify the prospective dissolution of Parliament.[589] On the subject of these an important discussion took place between Scroggs and the prisoner. Coleman insisted that there was nothing in his letters to justify the accusation that he had planned the death of the king; he might have used extravagant expressions; but if all the letters were considered together, surely it would be evident that, so far from designing any ill to the king and the Duke of York, his sole aim had been to exalt their power as high as possible. The Chief Justice pointed out that the letters openly declared, almost in so many words, an intention to overthrow the religion and government of the country by the help of foreign power; to say that he had attempted this for the benefit of the king was merely to offer a feeble excuse for his fault; with that the court had nothing to do. Coleman again began to explain his point of view in a rather muddled fashion. People said that he had made use of the duke's name without leave in his negotiations; was it likely that he had been so foolish as to imagine that his friends abroad would expend their money without the certainty that it was for the duke's service; still more, was it likely that the duke would use any sum thus obtained to the disservice of the king? "I take it for granted," he continued "(which sure none in the world will deny), that the law was ever made immediately subject to the king or duke; and consequently to the duke, I cannot think this will ever be expounded by the law of England or the jury to be treason." At this point the Chief Justice interrupted him impatiently. "These vain inconsequential discourses" served but to waste the time of the court. The plain truth was that the prisoner had formed a design "to bring popery into England, and to promote the interest of the French king in this place";[590] a fact which Coleman had not even attempted to deny. What Scroggs meant, and what, had he been a better judge, he would have made clear to the prisoner, was that such designs, according to the law which it was his duty to administer as it had been handed down to him, were technically evidence of high treason, whether or no they included an actual plot to kill the king; but he was so much irritated by Coleman's feeble efforts to say that this was not or ought not to have been so, that he neglected altogether to explain the matter, with the result that when Coleman came up for judgment on the following day he shewed that he was still in the dark about it.[591]

Concerning Coleman's letters a curious point arose at the trial. In opening the evidence for the crown Sergeant Maynard had remarked that the correspondence found at the prisoner's house extended only "to some part of the year 1675; from 1675 unto 1678 all lies in the dark; we have no certain proof of it, but we apprehend he had intelligence until 1678."[592] The Chief Justice took the subject up: "Mr. Coleman, I will tell you when you will be apt to gain credit in this matter.... Can mankind be persuaded that you, that had this negotiation in 1674 and 1675, left off just then, at that time when your letters were found according to their dates? Do you believe there was no negotiation after 1675 because we have not found them?" The prisoner replied, "After that time (as I said to the House of Commons) I did give over corresponding. I did offer to take all the oaths and tests in the world that I never had one letter for at least two years; yea (that I may keep myself within compass), I think it was for three or four."[593] After he had delivered sentence on the next day, Scroggs adjured the condemned man to confess that he had continued to correspond with agents abroad during the last three years. "I am sorry, Mr. Coleman," he said, "I have not charity enough to believe the words of a dying man; for I will tell you what sticks with me very much: I cannot be persuaded, and nobody can, but that your correspondence and negotiations did continue longer than the letters that we have found, that is, after 1675." "Upon the words of a dying man and the expectation I have of salvation," was Coleman's answer, "I tell your lordship that there is not a book or a paper in the world that I have laid aside voluntarily." Scroggs urged that he might have burnt them. "Not by the living God," returned the prisoner.[594] Coleman lied. The correspondence which he carried on with Paris and Rome, even in the fragmentary state in which it has been preserved, extended beyond the end of the year 1675. Between December in that year and December 1676 he received fifty letters from St. Germain at Paris, and a letter from the same quarter, dated October 5, 1678, was seized on delivery after Coleman's arrest. From January 1676 to January 1678 a correspondence was steadily maintained between Coleman and Cardinal Howard at Rome either personally or by his secretary Leybourn, and a letter from Leybourn seized on its arrival bore the date October 1, 1678. Shortly before, a "very dark, suspicious letter," dated September 28, 1678, had been seized on delivery. Coleman even received letters from Italy after his arrest by the help of his wife. The last doubts on the subject are resolved by the evidence of his secretary, Jerome Boatman, taken before the committee of the House of Lords: "I was employed to write home and foreign news. The correspondence was held on until my master was taken. There came letters by post since my master was taken. I delivered the letters to my mistress to carry to my master after he was under the messenger's hands."[595] Belief in the dying vows of the Jesuits and their friends is perhaps scarcely strengthened by Coleman's conduct in this matter. It is remarkable that the means taken for the preparation of the case were so haphazard that the crown lawyers had no knowledge of such valuable material as was in the hands of the committee of the upper house; and it is small testimony to the capacity of the noble lords who negotiated the business of the committee with the Attorney-General[596] that the latter should have been entirely ignorant of its existence.[597]

Throughout his trial Coleman was treated neither more nor less fairly than any other prisoner in any crown case of the period. The practice of the day weighed heavily against him. He did not receive nor could he expect any favour from it. Neither was he met by any special disfavour on political or any other grounds. One point of his defence however should undoubtedly have received more consideration than it did. Oates had charged him with paying a guinea as an extra fee for the king's murder, "about the 21st day of August."[598] Almost at the end of the trial, after the final speeches for the prosecution, Coleman announced that if his diary were fetched from his lodgings he could prove that he had been out of town from the 10th of August until the last day of the month.[599] His servant was called, but was unable to do more than say generally that he had been away from London during part of August. With the book, said the prisoner, he would be able to prove his statement exactly; but the Chief Justice would not allow it to be brought, on the ground that even if what he said were true, little would be gained to him.[600] This was no doubt true. Apart from the evidence of Oates, the testimony of Bedloe and his own letters were enough to hang the prisoner, and if Oates' word had been shaken in this point it would have been but little benefit to Coleman. But a great mistake was made by the court. To have proved a perjury against Oates so early in his career of witness would have inflicted a lasting injury on his character and redoubled the force of the catastrophe which befell him at the trial of Sir George Wakeman eight months later. This was not however apparent at the time, and the Chief Justice's determination, due to the lateness of the hour and the small extent to which the prisoner's interest was actually involved, is easy to understand. When he came up to receive judgment the next day Coleman produced the diary,[601] but it was then too late and the chance was gone.

Scroggs proceeded at once to recapitulate the evidence to the jury. What was important in his summing up was almost entirely concerned with the meaning and weight of Coleman's letters.[602] He pointed out acutely that the construction which the prisoner put upon them and the feeble explanation which he gave of his designs were repugnant to common sense and could not be entertained. "For the other part of the evidence," he terminated abruptly, "which is by the testimony of the present witnesses, you have heard them. I will not detain you longer now, for the day is going out."[603] The jury went from the bar and returned immediately with the verdict of Guilty. On the following day Coleman received sentence as usual in cases of high treason, and five days after was executed at Tyburn. As the cart was about to be drawn away he was heard to murmur, "There is no faith in man." A rumour spread throughout the town that until the end he had expected to receive a pardon promised by the Duke of York, and that, finding himself deceived, he had died cursing the master whom he had so diligently served.[604]

Coleman was not the first man to suffer for the Popish Plot. On November 26, the day Coleman was brought to trial, William Staley, a Roman Catholic goldsmith, had undergone a traitor's death at Tyburn. Staley was accused by two scoundrels of having in a public tavern uttered words which announced his intention of taking away the king's life. The chief witness was a wretch named Carstairs, who had eked out a precarious livelihood by acting as a government spy on conventicles in Scotland.[605] Two others of the same kidney corroborated his evidence. They swore that Staley had entered a cookshop in Covent Garden to dine with a French friend named Fromante, and had there burst into a rage against the king; the old man, Fromante, his friend, said "that the king of England was a tormentor of the people of God, and he answered again in a great fury, 'He is a great heretic and the greatest rogue in the world; here is the heart and here is the hand that will kill him.'... In French the words were spoken, he making a demonstration stamping with his foot: 'I would kill him myself.'"[606] By an act passed early in Charles II's reign, "malicious and advised speaking" had been made an overt act of high treason, and on this Staley was indicted. Over his sentence historians have gone into ecstasies of horror, on the ground that it is impossible to believe that "a great Roman Catholic banker" in the position of Staley should have spoken such words.[607] Staley however was not the banker, but the banker's son, and was not therefore of the same highly responsible age and position as has been supposed. "Young Staley," as he is called in a letter of the time,[608] is identified by Von Schwerin, ambassador of the Great Elector to the court of Charles II. On November 19 he writes: "Auch ist der Sohn eines sehr reichen Goldschmieds gefänglich eingezogen worden, weil er bei einem Gelage— wiewohl in trunkenem Zustande—Reden geführt hat: die Conspiration sei noch nicht ganz entdeckt, so habe er noch Hände den König zu ermorden."[609] But the decisive evidence on the point is the fact that William Staley's father, the banker, was alive some three weeks after he should, according to the received account, have been hanged and quartered. On December 18 his clerk and cashier were examined before the committee of the House of Lords on the subject of a reported connection between their master and Sir George Wakeman. The cashier had been in his service for seven years. The next day Mr. Staley, as ordered, himself attended the committee, bringing with him "the books wherein he has kept his accounts the last two years."[610] Obviously this man had been head of the firm for more than the previous month, and the account given by the Brandenburg envoy is correct.[611]

To hold that the words attributed to Staley by the witnesses at the trial were spoken "advisedly and maliciously" was undoubtedly to drive the act as far as it would go against the prisoner; but that they were spoken seems almost certain. He hardly denied that he had called the king a rogue and a heretic.[612] His only explanation of the words to which Carstairs swore was that instead of saying "I would kill him myself," he had said "I would kill myself." The difference between the words *Je le tuerais moi-même* and *Je me tuerais moi-même* is small enough to account for an easy mistake made by a hearer, but it was unfortunate for Staley that, as was pertinently remarked by the Attorney-General, the latter would not make sense in the context. Still more damning was the prisoner's omission to call as a witness for his defence Fromante, who had taken part in the conversation, and could, if Staley had been innocent, have cleared the point in his favour; but although every facility was given him for doing so, he refused either to call his friend or to make use of the copy of his previous examination, which the Attorney-General offered to lend him.[613] The case was not terminated even by Staley's sentence and death. In consideration of his exemplary conduct in prison, where he "behaved himself very penitently, from the time of his conviction until the time of his execution, which was attested by the several ministers which visited him during that time," leave was given by the king that his body should be delivered to his friends after execution for private burial. With great want of tact, and "to the great indignity and affront of his Majesty's mercy and favour, the friends of the said Staley caused several masses to be said over his quarters, ... and appointed a time for his interment, viz. Friday, the 29th of November 1678, in the evening, from his father's house in Covent Garden, at which time there was made a pompous and great funeral, many people following the corpse to the church of St. Paul's, Covent Garden, where he was buried": in consequence of which an order was given for the disinterment of the body, and to vindicate the majesty of justice his quarters were affixed to the city gates and his head set up to rot on London Bridge.[614]

A fortnight after Coleman's execution, Whitebread, Fenwick, Ireland, Pickering, and Grove were brought to the bar of the Old Bailey. Thomas White or Whitebread, alias Harcourt, was a man sixty years of age. He had been educated at St. Omers, became a professed father in the Society of Jesus in 1652, and was chosen provincial of the English province at the beginning of the year 1678.[615] It was by his means that Oates had entered the Jesuit College at St. Omers after expulsion from Valladolid, and it was he who Oates swore had boxed his ears on learning that the plot was betrayed.[616] Fenwick, less well known by his real name Caldwell, was ten years his junior. He had joined the English mission from Flanders in 1675, and was now the London agent for the college at St. Omers. Both were noted in the society for their success in the missionary field.[617] Ireland, alias Ironmonger, had come into England in 1677 as procurator of the province.[618] All five were accused by Oates of being principals in the plot and privy to the king's death. Pickering, a Benedictine, and Grove, a Jesuit lay-brother, were named as the actual agents in one of the schemes for his assassination. Oates' evidence was long and highly coloured. He had been sent over by the Jesuits to murder Doctor Tonge. He had seen instructions for the murder of the Bishop of Hereford and Dr. Stillingfleet. He had been in the thick of a scheme of Fenwick's contrivance to raise rebellion in Scotland and Ireland. Whitebread had sealed commissions for the popish army under the seal of Johannes Paulus de Oliva, general of his order. Fenwick had been present when Coleman paid the famous guinea to quicken the message which was to be fatal to the king. All the prisoners had been present at the consult on April 24, 1678, when a resolution to kill the king was signed by at least forty persons, Pickering was to have thirty thousand masses and Grove £1500 for the deed. They had dogged the king in St. James' Park, and had twisted the silver bullets of their carbines that the wound made might be incurable. Charles would infallibly have been shot had not the flint of Pickering's pistol been loose, and Pickering had undergone penance of thirty lashes for his carelessness. To use their own words, "they did intend to dispose of the duke too, in case he did not appear vigorous in promoting the Catholic religion."[619] To all this there was little to be said. The prisoners put some questions to Oates, and were in turn slightly questioned by the court. All that appeared was that Grove had known Oates more intimately than he wished to represent, and that the witness had borrowed from both Grove and Fenwick money which had naturally never been repaid.[620] Fenwick however offered to bring a document from St. Omers, under the seal of the college and attested by unimpeachable witnesses, that Oates had been at the seminary at the time when he swore that he was present in London at the consult at the White Horse Tavern. This was refused by the court without hesitation. Fenwick exclaimed bitterly that the judges seemed to think there was no justice out of England.[621] But in supposing that a special piece of unfairness was directed against himself and his friends he was mistaken. It was a regular and unbroken rule of the court that no evidence could be brought, if such an expression may be used, from outside the trial. Such evidence as reports of other trials, the journals of the Houses of Parliament, the minutes of the privy council was allowed to be used on neither side. It was one of the points in which the practice of the day pressed hardly on the accused, but the judges could not, as Scroggs truly said, "depart from the law or the way of trial." The theory of the law was that the evidence at a trial might be disproved by the defence, or its value might be destroyed if the witness were proved not to be competent; but neither could it be shaken by such a document as Fenwick proposed to produce,[622] nor could evidence afterwards be called against it to shake the credit of a witness at a previous trial. To effect this the witness must be indicted and convicted for perjury and the record of his conviction proved. Every trial stood by itself, and everything alleged at it had to be proved or disproved on the spot, either by direct evidence or by judicial records sworn at the trial to be correct.[623]

Bedloe was then called. He began by giving evidence of the Plot in general, in pursuit of which he had been employed, he swore, for the last five years to carry letters between Jesuits and monks in England, Ireland, and France, and Sir William Godolphin and Lord Bellasis.[624] But of the prisoners in particular he could only speak to Ireland, Pickering, and Grove. Whitebread and Fenwick he knew by sight alone. At the trial of Reading he confessed that this was a lie.[625] There he explained that he would have borne witness before against the two Jesuits had not Reading been intriguing with him at the time, and that he kept back his evidence in order to lead the attorney deeper into the business.[626] Not only was this admitted by the court as sufficient justification of his conduct, but at their later trial, when Bedloe gave decisive evidence against them, Whitebread and Fenwick hardly made any objection to his credibility upon this ground.[627]

One witness having failed, the prosecution attempted to supply his place by reading a letter written to summon a father of the society to the Jesuit congregation which the provincial had fixed for April 24. But this the Chief Justice would not permit. The letter was from Edward Petre, afterwards confessor to James II, to William Tunstall. It had been found with Harcourt's papers and did not mention Whitebread's name at all. The contents might substantiate Oates' evidence as to the date of the congregation, but they could not conceivably be construed, as the crown lawyers suggested, into evidence touching the prisoners. Scroggs' opposition prevented the manœuvre, and after a strong warning to the jury he allowed the letter to be read, "to fortify the testimony of Mr. Oates, that there is a general plot: it is not applied to any particular person."[628]

It was now apparent that the crown had only one witness against the two chief of the accused, which in a case of high treason was not sufficient to procure a conviction. Thereupon Scroggs, with the approval of the other judges, discharged the jury of Whitebread and Fenwick and recommitted them to prison.[629] Six months later they were again tried and executed for the same treason. Whitebread then urged that he had been given in charge once, that on the insufficient evidence he should have been acquitted, and that he ought not to be tried again; but the whole court held without hesitation that the objection was baseless.[630] Afterwards this decision was held up to scorn, and has since often been condemned;[631] but it was grounded upon good authority and supported by the general practice of the courts.[632]

The three remaining prisoners proceeded to make their defence. Beyond repeated assertions of their innocence this amounted, as far as Pickering and Grove were concerned, to little. Ireland made a better effort. Oates had sworn that he was in London in August of the year 1678 and present at a treasonable meeting in Harcourt's rooms.[633] The prisoner now called evidence to contradict this. His mother and his sister testified that he had left town on August 3 and did not return until the middle of September. Sir John Southcot's coachman swore that he had been at various places in Staffordshire and on the way thither, in company with his master, from August 5 until the third week in that month, and another witness gave evidence that he had seen Ireland at Wolverhampton shortly after St. Bartholomew's day, and again on the 7th and the 9th of September.[634] To rebut this the prosecution called a woman who belonged to the household of Lord Arlington. She had once been in the service of Grove, the prisoner, and had at that time seen Ireland constantly and waited upon him with letters from her master. She now swore positively that she had seen him in London at the time when the king went to Windsor in August. By the evidence of Sir Thomas Dolman this was calculated to be the 13th of the month.[635] Oates again took the opportunity to swear that Ireland was in town on the 1st or 2nd of September. It was an unfortunate interruption, for it formed the perjury assigned in the indictment upon which he was convicted at his second trial six years afterwards.[636] Only one more witness was produced. Sir Denny Ashburnham, member of Parliament for the borough of Hastings, was called by Ireland to testify to Oates' character. Instead however of damaging the informer's credit, he came forward to say that, although he might have had little respect for Oates' veracity in the days of his youth, the manifold circumstances by which his testimony was now supported had entirely convinced him of the truth of his statements; "and," said he, "I do think truly that nothing can be said against Mr. Oates to take off his credibility";[637] which was of small value from the point of view of the defence.

The prisoners complained bitterly that they had been allowed neither time nor facility to produce their witnesses. At Oates' second trial for perjury on May 9, 1685 there were called for the prosecution no less than forty-five witnesses, who proved conclusively where Ireland had been on every day but one between August 3 and September 14, 1678, the dates when he left and when he returned to London.[638] Five months after Ireland's execution, Whitebread, Fenwick, and Harcourt called at their trial, to prove the same points, ten witnesses, whose evidence covered a considerable part of the time in debate,[639] Had he been able himself to call even those ten, not to say the whole number afterwards collected, it can scarcely be doubted that their evidence must have procured his acquittal and have given birth to the reaction against Oates which every additional conviction postponed. As it was, there were for the defence only four witnesses, two of whom were intensely interested in the prisoner's acquittal, against the hitherto unshaken credit of Oates himself and the testimony of a disinterested person called to support him. Scroggs put the point quite fairly to the jury,[640] and the jury chose to disbelieve the prisoner's witnesses. The real hardship lay, not in the prejudice of the court or the violent speech which the Chief Justice appended to his summing up of the evidence,[641] but in the fact that the accused were kept wholly in the dark as to the evidence which was to be produced against them. The practice of the law, as it is still the theory,[642] made it impossible for the accused to defend himself with certainty against the evidence which might be brought against him. The preparation of his defence had to be undertaken in the dark and conducted at random.

On the same day Ireland, Pickering, and Grove received sentence of death from Jeffreys, as Recorder of London, in a speech which wavered between pure abuse and a sermon which would have done credit to the most strenuous divine.[643] More than a month later Ireland and Grove were executed at Tyburn. Had Ireland's execution been postponed, an insurrection was feared. Pickering was respited by the king for so long that the indignant Commons on April 27, 1679 petitioned urgently that the law might take its course on the man who "did remain as yet unexecuted, to the great emboldening of such offenders, in case they should escape without due punishment;" and on May 25 Charles sent a message to the House by Lord Russell to say that the sentence should have effect.[644] All three died protesting their innocence to the last.

Round the dying vows of the fourteen men who were executed for the Plot controversy raged hotly. To Roman Catholics their solemn denials seemed so conclusive that they fancied the effect must be the same on others too.[645] When it became apparent that such earnest assertion was met with frank unbelief, they attributed the fact to the black malice and the wicked prejudice of heretical hearts. To Protestants, on the other hand, the protestations of the Jesuits were clearly the logical result of their immoral doctrines. If anything, they afforded a further confirmation of guilt. Able pamphleteers undertook to prove that according to the principles of their order "they not only might, but also ought to die after that manner, with solemn protestations of their innocency."[646] Protestant pulpits reverberated with demonstrations that the Jesuits would not "stick at any sort of falsehood in order to their own defence." Good Bishop Burnet was shocked at the violence of his brother divines and "looked always on this as an opening of their graves, and the putting them to a second death."[647] Few however were of his mind, and Algernon Sidney expressed the common opinion when he wrote to his cousin: "Those who use to extol all that relates to Rome admire the constancy of the five priests executed the last week; but we simple people find no more in it than that the papists, by arts formerly unknown to mankind, have found ways of reconciling falsehood in the utmost degree with the hopes of salvation, and at the best have no more to brag of than that they have made men die with lies in their mouths."[648] Party spirit could not fail to be aroused in its most virulent form by the speeches of the condemned men, and to seize upon them as evidence on either side. They were, in point of fact, evidence for neither one party nor the other. Oaths sworn in such a manner were wholly worthless.

As Bedloe lay on his death-bed in the autumn of 1680 he reaffirmed with every protestation of truth, and as he hoped for salvation, the ghastly mass of perjured evidence by which he had sworn away the lives of men. His conscience was clear, he said, and "he should appear cheerfully before the Lord of Hosts, which he did verily believe he must do in a short time."[649] Three years later the man who has been held up to posterity as the most truthful of his age died, calling God to witness his innocence of the treason for which he was condemned.[650] Yet Lord Russell was a member of the Council of Six and had engaged actively in the preparation of an extensive rebellion. He was an intimate friend of the men who hatched the actual Rye House Plot. If he was unaware that the king's life was aimed at directly and indirectly, it was because he had deliberately shut his eyes to the tendency of his own schemes and those of his associates.[651] This must be the test of the value of such declarations. The unbounded immorality with which the politics of the reign of Charles II were stamped so clouded the minds of men that truth became for them almost indistinguishable from falsehood. They had only not reached the point of view of the native of Madras, who said of the value of death-bed confessions: "Such evidence ought never to be admitted in any case. What motive for telling the truth can a man possibly have when he is at the point of death?"[652]

Mention has already been made of the trial of Reading.[653] This was the first of a series of important cases which were conducted in the course of the ensuing year. Briefly, they were trials of Roman Catholics for fraudulent endeavours, in the words of the time, to stifle the Plot. Not to speak of the notorious Meal Tub Plot, the most determined and unscrupulous effort of the Roman Catholic party to remove the accusation of treason from themselves to their opponents,[654] there may be noticed four distinct attempts to impair by fraudulent and criminal means the evidence offered for the crown. As early as February 1679 information was laid before a committee of the privy council that an Englishman named Russell, who belonged to the household of the French ambassador, had endeavoured to suborn witnesses to invalidate the credit of Oates and Bedloe, and had offered the sum of £500 for the purpose. The council addressed to the ambassador a request for the delivery of the accused to stand his trial; but the case did not come into court, probably because Russell had either absconded or been shipped abroad.[655] The incident was kept secret and produced no consequences. But within twelve months three other attempts of the same nature were proved against Roman Catholic agents and exercised a considerable influence against their party. The trials of Reading for a trespass and misdemeanour, of Knox and Lane for a misdemeanour, and of Tasborough and Price for subornation of perjury must not be overlooked in forming a judgment on the events of which the courts of justice were the chief scene.

Nathaniel Reading was a Protestant attorney of some standing in his profession. Thirty years before he had been secretary to Massaniello in the insurrection at Naples, and was now living in London and enjoying a fair practice. He had been the friend and legal adviser of Lord Stafford for several years, numbered other gentlemen of title and repute among his acquaintance, and was of a position to receive an invitation to dinner from the Lieutenant of the Tower when he went to visit his client in prison.[656] During the Hilary term of 1679 he had been engaged in procuring the discharge on bail of several prisoners for the Plot, and had gone by leave of the secret committee of the House of Lords to advise the lords imprisoned in the Tower on the like subjects. In the course of his negotiations for them he had become acquainted with Oates and Bedloe, and acted as counsel for the latter in obtaining his pardon from the king. Bedloe was constantly in his company, and the two talked frequently of the nature of the Plot and the witness' charges against the prisoners.[657] In public Reading exhorted Bedloe to reveal all his knowledge and bring the guilty to justice, but in private conversation suggested that it might be profitable to reduce his evidence against certain of those incriminated. The plot was blown to the winds, the king's life out of danger, Bedloe would be able to feather his own nest, and no harm would be done. Bedloe promised to consider the matter and, as earnest of his good intentions, withdrew his evidence against Whitebread and Fenwick.[658] At the same time he carried the news of the intrigue to the committee of secrecy. Prince Rupert, the Earl of Essex, and Mr. Speke[659] were informed of the business, and Bedloe was advised to continue his negotiation in the hope of extracting something of importance. Reading had in the meantime gone to the lords in the Tower and brought from them promises of ample reward if Bedloe would consent to save them. A meeting was appointed for March 29, to make the final arrangements.[660] Before Reading appeared, Speke and another witness were hidden in the room in such a position that they could overhear every word which passed between the two men. They heard Bedloe ask, "What say my lords in the Tower now?" Reading replied that Lord Stafford had promised to settle an estate in Gloucestershire on the informer, and that he had orders to draw up a deed to that effect and sign it ten days after Lord Stafford's discharge from prison. The Earl of Powis, Lord Petre, and Sir Henry Tichbourne also promised rewards if Bedloe would procure their acquittal. Bedloe then drew up an abstract of his evidence against the lords, and Speke saw Reading take the paper to deliver to them in the Tower. Two days later the attorney met Bedloe by appointment in the Painted Chamber at Westminster and gave him in answer to this a corrected version of the evidence which the accused had drawn up for his actual use at their trials. Bedloe without looking at the paper handed it at once to Mr. Speke, who carried it to a committee room in the House of Lords for examination.[661] This paper was read in court, and proved to contain an amended version of Bedloe's testimony so vague and slight that it could not have possibly been of any use to the prosecution.[662]

Reading's defence was sufficiently feeble. He was treated by the bench with the greatest indulgence and allowed to make a lengthy and unsupported discourse on Bedloe's character. It is noteworthy that he objected to the witness not on the ground that he had perjured himself in holding back evidence at the trial of Whitebread, Fenwick, and Ireland, but on account of treasonable practices, which were covered by his pardon. He protested that the first proposal of the intrigue came from Bedloe, and that he only joined in it to prevent the shedding of innocent blood. The estate in Gloucestershire spoken of had been promised by Lord Stafford to himself, if he obtained his acquittal, and not to Bedloe, though hardly it seemed without the understanding that the informer was to have some share in it. He would have thought it a crime not to engage in the business; it was a duty which he owed to God and his country. By saying this he practically confessed to the whole indictment, and after a concise summing up the jury immediately returned a verdict of guilty. Reading was sentenced to be pilloried, to pay a fine of £1000, and to imprisonment for one year.[663]

The case of Knox and Lane was a still more disreputable affair. Thomas Knox was in the service of Lord Dumblane, the Earl of Danby's son. John Lane and one William Osborne were servants to Titus Oates. These two were discharged by Oates in April 1679, Lane, who had some acquaintance with Dangerfield, was lodged by him and Mrs. Cellier under an assumed name at the house of the Countess of Powis.[664] At Dangerfield's suggestion they approached Knox on the subject of the charges which Oates had made against the Lord Treasurer.[665] Knox agreed to their suggestion, and together they arranged the details of the scheme. Osborne and Knox lodged information that Oates had conspired with Bedloe to bring false accusations against Lord Danby, while Lane charged his master with using obscene language concerning the king and with the commission of an unnatural crime. But under examination Knox and Lane broke down, and all three were driven to confess that there was not a word of truth in the story which they had concocted. Osborne fled the country, and his two accomplices were clapped into gaol. News however was brought to Lane as he lay in prison that Knox was prepared to stand by his original story. He forthwith retracted his confession, and on November 19, 1679 indictment was brought against Oates "for an attempt to commit upon him the horrid and abominable sin of sodomy." The grand jury ignored the bill, and a week later the two miscreants were brought to the king's bench bar on the charge of "a conspiracy to defame and scandalise Dr. Oates and Mr. Bedloe; thereby to discredit their evidence about the horrid Popish Plot." After a long trial, in which the defendants were treated with all fairness and in which each attempted to throw the blame on the other, the jury returned a verdict of guilty without leaving the bar. The prisoners were sentenced to fine and imprisonment, and Lane in addition to stand for an hour in the pillory. The verdict was received with a shout of applause, "many noblemen, gentlemen, and eminent citizens," adds the account which was drawn up under Oates' direction, "coming with great expectations of the issue of this trial, which was managed with that justice, impartiality, and indifference between the king and the defendants, that some have been heard to say they could never believe a plot before, but now they were abundantly satisfied."[666]

The labyrinthine nature of the intrigues connected with the Popish Plot is amply illustrated by these two trials. The third case presents less intricacy, but no less dishonesty. In January 1680 John Tasborough and Anne Price were tried for subornation of perjury in having offered a bribe to the informer Dugdale to retract the evidence which he had given at the trial of Whitebread, Harcourt, and Fenwick. Mrs. Price had been a fellow-servant with Dugdale in the household of the Roman Catholic peer, Lord Aston. On the night before the trial of the five Jesuits[667] she came to him and begged him not to give evidence against Father Harcourt, who was her confessor. When the trial was over she renewed her solicitations, offering him the reward of £1000 and the Duke of York's protection if he would recant what he had then sworn. Dugdale was introduced to Tasborough, a gentleman belonging to the duke's household.[668] Meetings were held at the Green Lettice Tavern in Brownlow Street and at the Pheasant Inn in Fullers-rents. Tasborough confirmed the promises made by Mrs. Price. The informer was to sign a declaration that all his evidence had been false, to receive £1000 in cash, and to be maintained abroad by the Duke of York. The name of the Spanish ambassador was also mentioned. But Dugdale, as

Bedloe before him, had secreted witnesses at these interviews. The intriguers were arrested, and the whole story was proved beyond the possibility of doubt at their trial.[669] Tasborough was sentenced to the fine of £100, Price to the fine of twice that sum. All parties at the trial were at considerable pains to exonerate the Duke of York. There was in fact no direct evidence against him; but it is improbable that the culprits had been using his name entirely without authority. They must have known that Dugdale would not put his name to the recantation without substantial guarantee for the reward, and certainly neither was in a position to pay any sufficient part of the sum mentioned from his own resources.

The evidence which Dugdale should have retracted was considerable. His reputation was still undamaged. He had been steward of Lord Aston's estate at Tixhall, in Staffordshire, was thought to have enjoyed a fair reputation in the county, and to have been imprisoned in the first instance for refusing to take the oaths of allegiance and supremacy.[670] Although he had laid information before the privy council as early as December 1678, it was not until the trial of the Five Jesuits[671] on June 13 of the year following that he appeared in court. The case for the prosecution was opened, as usual, with the evidence of Oates, He reaffirmed the story which he had told at the trial of Whitebread, Fenwick, and Ireland, and gave similar evidence against Harcourt, Gavan, and Turner. Dugdale was then called. He swore to treasonable consults held at Tixhall in September 1678, where Gavan and Turner were present, to treasonable letters between Whitebread, Harcourt, and others, and to a letter dispatched from London by Harcourt on October 20, 1678, addressed to Evers, another Jesuit, and containing the words "This night Sir Edmond Bury Godfrey is dispatched."[672] The death of the king was to be laid at the door of the Presbyterian party. A general massacre of Protestants was to follow, "and if any did escape that they could not be sure of were papists, they were to have an army to cut them off."[673] Bedloe followed with the evidence which he had before suppressed against Whitebread and Fenwick, and swore similarly to the treason of Harcourt. Some trifling evidence from Prance closed the first part of the case for the crown.[674] But almost more important than the oral testimony were two letters which were read in court. The one was a note from Edward Petre, containing a summons to the congregation fixed for April 24, 1678; the other a letter from Christopher Anderton, dated from Rome, February 5, 1679, in which occurred the following sentences: "We are all here very glad of the promotion of Mr. Thomas Harcourt; when I writ that the patents were sent, although I guess for whom they were, yet I know not for certain, because our patrons do not use to discover things or resolutions till they know they have effect. And therefore in these kind of matters I dare not be too hasty, lest some might say, a fool's bolt is soon shot." Both had been found among Harcourt's papers several days after Oates was examined by the privy council.[675] They seemed to confirm his evidence in a remarkable manner. He had constantly spoken of the Jesuit design; the former of the letters contained the same word and enjoined secrecy on the subject. The latter seemed to refer to the patents which Oates had declared were sent to the commanders of the popish army. The prisoners explained that the "design" of the congregation was but to settle the business of their order and to choose a procurator to undertake its management at Rome. As for the patents, Anderton had meant to say *Literae Patentes*, and referred only to Harcourt's patent as new provincial. *Literae Patentes*, contended the court, when used in reference to one person, meant a patent; but when the phrase was translated patents, it necessarily pointed at more than one. Oates, said the Chief Justice, interpreted the matter more plainly than the accused.[676]

The Jesuits proceeded to make their defence. Sixteen witnesses were called to prove that Oates had been at St. Omers from December 1677 to June 1678, and had not left the college at the time when he swore that he was present at the consult in London. This was the perjury upon which he was convicted at his first trial in 1685. Five witnesses were called to testify that Gavan had not been in town in April 1678; ten, that Ireland had been in the country in August and September of the same year. Very similar evidence to that now given was accepted six years later by the court to substantiate the charge against Oates, but at the trial of Whitebread, Harcourt, and Fenwick it was disbelieved. The witnesses were examined in detail and gave an elaborate account of the life at the seminary. But the story which they told was not altogether satisfactory. Under examination they shuffled and prevaricated. Sometimes they contradicted one another on points of time. They came prepared to speak to the date of the consult and the time immediately before and after it. When questions were put about dates less closely concerned, they seemed unwilling to answer. One, who declared that he had left Oates at St. Omers on taking leave for England to go to the congregation, was confounded when Oates reminded him that he had lost his money at Calais and had been compelled to borrow from a friend. Another confused the old and new styles. A third stated that whenever a scholar left the college the fact could not but be known to all his fellows. He was immediately contradicted by Gavan, who said that care was taken that the comings and goings of the seminarists should be unnoticed.[677] A rumour was spread abroad that witnesses had been tutored, and was repeated by Algernon Sidney in a letter to Paris.[678] For once rumour was not at variance with truth. Sidney's information was perfectly correct. Three of the lads from St. Omers were arrested on their arrival in London by Sir William Waller, and their examinations were forwarded by him to the secret committee of the House of Commons. One of these was Christopher Townley, alias Madgworth, alias Sands, who had been a student in the seminary for six years. He admitted that "his instructions from the superior was to come over and swear that Mr. Oates was but once from the college at St. Omers, from December 1677 to June following." Of his own knowledge he could say no more than that he had been in the seminary all the time during which Oates was there; "the said Mr. Oates might be absent from St. Omers in that time for several days and at several times, but not absent above one week at a time, this examinant being lodged in the college where Mr. Oates was, but did not see him daily."[679] At the trial he did not scruple to say that he had seen and talked with Oates on every day throughout April and May and that, if Oates had ever been absent, he must certainly have known it.[680] Nor was this all. At his examination he deposed that Parry, Palmer, and Gifford were all absent from St. Omers while Oates was an inmate of the college. At the trial Gifford, Palmer, and Parry were produced to give evidence of their personal knowledge that Oates had been there the whole of the time.[681] No credence whatever can be given to such witnesses. It is worthy of remark that they were housed and entertained by no other than Mrs. Cellier, who was afterwards deeply concerned both in the Meal Tub Plot and in the case of Knox and Lane, and was pilloried for an atrocious libel in connection with the murder of Sir Edmund Berry Godfrey.[682] No doubt can exist on the subject of Oates' repeated and astounding perjuries. It is as little open to doubt that the witnesses who were opposed to him at this trial were almost equally untrustworthy. They were in fact very cleverly parroted. If his infamy remains undisturbed, the unctuous indignation with which it was denounced by the Jesuits, at the very moment when they were employing means as unhallowed as his own to controvert his statements, at least entitles them to a place by his side in the pillory of history.

Even at this point the false evidence given at this terrible trial was not ended. The crown produced seven witnesses to prove that Oates had been in London at the end of April and the beginning of May 1678. Of these the only two who gave evidence of any weight were Smith, who had been Oates' master at Merchant Tailors' School, and Clay, a disreputable Dominican friar, whom Oates had taken out of prison. Both were afterwards proved to have been suborned by Oates and to have perjured themselves.[683]

The Jesuits concluded their defence with speeches of real eloquence. Scroggs summed up the evidence in an elaborate speech and strongly in favour of the crown; and after a quarter of an hour's absence the jury returned to court with a verdict of guilty against all the prisoners.[684]

On the next day Richard Langhorn was indicted at the Old Bailey for practically the same treason as that for which the Five Jesuits were convicted. Langhorn was a Roman Catholic barrister of considerable eminence.[685] He was the legal adviser of the Jesuits, and conducted for them much business which would now more naturally pass through the hands of a solicitor. Oates consequently named him as an active agent in the Plot and prospective advocate-general under the new government.[686] His trial was a continuation of the trial of Whitebread, Harcourt, and Fenwick, and exhibited all the same characteristics, of perjury on the one side, on the other of prevarication and falsehood. The same evidence was developed at length, and with the same result. Two fresh points of importance alone occurred. To Oates' great alarm the hostess of the White Horse Tavern in the Strand was called by the defence. Oates had sworn that as many as eighteen or twenty Jesuits had met together there in one room at the congregation of April 24. The woman now declared that no room in her house would hold more than a dozen persons at the same time, and that when a parish jury had once met there the jurors had been compelled for want of space to separate into three rooms. This would undoubtedly have produced an effect, had not three of the spectators in court immediately risen to swear that there were two rooms in the inn which were large enough to hold from twenty to thirty people without crowding them unduly. An unfavourable impression concerning the evidence for the defence was created, and the king's counsel was able to score an effective point.[687]

Of greater weight than this was a portion of Bedloe's evidence. He swore that he went one day with Coleman to Langhorn's chambers in the Temple, and from the outer room saw the lawyer transcribing various treasonable letters brought by Coleman into a register at a desk in his study within.[688] The nature of cross-examination was so imperfectly understood at the time that Langhorn did not attempt to question the witness on the shape of his rooms or to shake his credit by calling evidence to the point. In his memoirs, which were published in the course of the same year, he wrote the following comment on Bedloe's statement: "Every person who knows my said chamber and the situation of my study cannot but know that it is impossible to look out of my chamber into my study so as to see any one writing there, and that I never had at any time any desk in my study."[689] This was supported by other evidence. When Oates and Bedloe exhibited in 1680 "articles of high misdemeanours" against Scroggs before the privy council, they charged him in one that at the previous Monmouth assizes he "did say to Mr. William Bedloe that he did believe in his conscience that Richard Langhorn, whom he condemned, died wrongfully." To which the Chief Justice answered "that at Monmouth assizes he did tell Mr. Bedloe that he was more unsatisfied about Mr. Langhorn's trial than all the rest; and the rather, that he was credibly informed, since the trial, that Mr. Langhorn's study was so situated that he that walked in his chamber could not see Mr. Langhorn write in his study; which was Mr. Bedloe's evidence."[690]

This was not the first incident which shook the credit of the witnesses in the Chief Justice's mind. He had in the meantime received a still more striking proof of their worthlessness. On July 18, four days after the execution of Langhorn and nearly a month after that of the Five Jesuits, Sir George Wakeman, in company with three Benedictines, was brought to trial at the Old Bailey. Wakeman was accused of having bargained with the Jesuits for £15,000 to poison the king. The other three were charged with being concerned in the Plot in various degrees. Feeling had run so high after the last two trials that the case was postponed from the end of June for nearly three weeks, that it might have time to cool.[691] Interests were at stake which had not been present in the previous trials. In November of the year before, Oates and Bedloe had accused the queen of high treason, and Oates had sworn that Sir George Wakeman, who was her physician, had received from her a letter consenting to the king's death.[692] The queen was now implicated with Wakeman, and the trial was regarded as the prelude to an attack on herself.[693]

Before the crown lawyers opened the direct attack, witnesses were, as usual, produced to testify to the reality of the plot. Prance and Dugdale reaffirmed their previous evidence, and Jennison, himself the brother of a Jesuit, swore that he had met Ireland in London on August 19, 1678, thus proving to the satisfaction of the court that Ireland had died with a lie in his mouth.[694] The prosecution then came to the prisoners. Oates told again the story how he had heard the queen at a meeting at Somerset House consent formally to the plot for murdering the king, and swore that he had seen a letter from Wakeman to the Jesuit Ashby, which was occupied chiefly with a prescription for the latter during his stay at Bath, but mentioned incidentally that the queen had given her approval to the scheme. He had also seen an entry in Langhorn's register of the payment of £5000 made by Coleman as a third part of Wakeman's fee and a receipt for it signed by Wakeman himself.[695] Bedloe gave evidence which would prove equally the guilt of the queen and her physician, and both swore to the treasonable practices of the other prisoners.[696] To rebut this, Wakeman produced evidence to prove that he had not written the letter for Ashby himself, but had dictated it to his servant Hunt. The letter was addressed to Chapman, an apothecary at Bath, who read it and then tore off and kept the part containing the prescription. Hunt proved that the letter was in his handwriting and was corroborated by another servant in Wakeman's household. Chapman proved that the body of the letter was in the same handwriting as the prescription, that it contained nothing about the queen or any plan for the king's murder, and that Oates had given an entirely inaccurate account of the prescription, which was so far from ordering a milk diet, as Oates had sworn that milk would have been not far removed from poison for a patient who was drinking the waters at Bath. Scroggs was afterwards accused of having grossly favoured the prisoner in order to curry favour at court; but the manner in which this evidence was received is an absolute proof to the contrary. The bench held, in a way that now excites surprise, but at the time did not, that Oates had meant that the milk diet was prescribed for Ashby before he went to Bath, and was therefore not at all inconsistent with drinking the waters while he was there; and that Wakeman might easily have written two letters on the same subject. No doubt, said the judges, the witnesses for the defence spoke the truth. What had happened was that Sir George had dictated one letter, which consisted of nothing but medical directions, and of which the apothecary and the other witnesses spoke; but he must certainly have written another, containing the treasonable words to which Oates swore. The court treated the matter as if this were beyond a doubt. To the prisoner's objection that he was unlikely to have written two letters to convey the same instructions, Mr. Justice Pemberton replied, "This might be writ to serve a turn very well"; and Scroggs closed the discussion by remarking, "This your witnesses say, and you urge, is true, but not pertinent."[697] Shortly before Wakeman turned to his fellow-prisoners and said, "There is my business done." He knew that in all human probability he would be condemned. Suddenly, without any warning, there occurred the most unexpected event, which, in a dramatic moment unsurpassed by the most famous in history, shattered the credit of Oates and produced the first acquittal in the trials for the Popish Plot.[698] Sir Philip Lloyd, clerk to the privy council, was asked to state with what Oates had charged the prisoner at his examination before the council. The evidence deserves to be given in Sir Philip's own words: "It was upon the 31st of September," he stated; "Mr. Oates did then say he had seen a letter, to the best of his remembrance, from Mr. White to Mr. Fenwick at St. Omers, in which letter he writ word that Sir George Wakeman had undertaken the poisoning of the king, and was to have £15,000 for it; of which £5000 had been paid him by the hands of Coleman. Sir George Wakeman, upon this, was called in and told of this accusation; he utterly denied all, and did indeed carry himself as if he were not concerned at the accusation, but did tell the king and council he hoped he should have reparation and satisfaction for the injury done to his honour. His carriage was not well liked of by the king and council, and being a matter of such consequence as this was, they were willing to know further of it; and because they thought this evidence was not proof enough to give them occasion to commit him, being only out of a letter of a third person, thereupon they called in Mr. Oates again, and my Lord Chancellor desired Mr. Oates to tell him if he knew nothing personally of Sir George

Wakeman, because they were in a matter of moment, and desired sufficient proof whereupon to ground an indictment; Mr. Oates, when he did come in again and was asked the question, did lift up his hands (for I must tell the truth, let it be what it will) and said, 'No, God forbid that I should say anything against Sir George Wakeman, for I know nothing more against him.' And I refer myself to the whole council whether it is not so."

Great Birnam wood to high Dunsinane Hill, marching against Macbeth, or the duke uncloaking to Angelo could not create a greater sensation. "My lord," cried Sir George Wakeman, "this is a Protestant witness too." Oates began to bluster. He remembered nothing of all this. He did not believe that any such question was asked him at the council board. If there had been, he was in such a state of exhaustion after being deprived of his rest for two nights in succession that he was not in a condition to answer anything. "What," returned Scroggs, "must we be amused with I know not what for being up but two nights?... What, was Mr. Oates just so spent that he could not say, I have seen a letter under Sir George Wakeman's own hand?" The informer swore that to his best belief he had spoken of the letter; or if he had not, he believed Sir Philip Lloyd was mistaken; or if not that, he was so weak that he was unable to say or do anything. Then he completely lost control of himself and broke out recklessly: "To speak the truth, they were such a council as would commit nobody." "That was not well said," put in Jeffreys quickly. "He reflects on the king and all the council," cried Wakeman. At this the wrath of the Chief Justice burst out on the perjured miscreant. "You have taken a great confidence," he thundered, "I know not by what authority, to say anything of anybody"; and becoming more grave, pointed out the decisive importance of what had been proved against him, Oates did not open his mouth again during the rest of the trial.[699]

The case still dragged on its weary length. Numerous other witnesses were called to prove and disprove points of varying importance and connection with the matter at issue. All the prisoners against whom Oates and Bedloe had sworn made long speeches and discoursed on a hundred irrelevant topics. Marshal, the Benedictine, lectured the court and delivered an impassioned harangue on the injustice of the English nation and on the future state. He was stopped and, beginning again, drew down on himself from Scroggs a violent rebuke in which he declared his belief that it was possible for an atheist to be a papist, but hardly for a knowing Christian to be a Christian and a papist. When the heated wrangle which followed was ended, the Chief Justice summed up, setting the evidence on both sides in a clear light and pointing out where its strength lay against the prisoners, but plainly intimating his opinion that the revelation made by Sir Philip Lloyd went far to invalidate Oates' testimony. As the jury were leaving the box

Bedloe broke in: "My lord, my evidence is not right summed up." "I know not by what authority this man speaks," said Scroggs sternly. After the absence of about an hour the jury returned. Might they, they asked, find the prisoners guilty of misprision of treason? "No," replied Jeffreys, the Recorder, "you must either convict them of high treason or acquit them." "Then take a verdict," said the foreman; and returned a verdict of not guilty for all the prisoners.

Scarcely was the trial over when a storm broke upon the head of the Lord Chief Justice. He had already earned the hatred of the ferocious London mob by accepting bail for Mr. Pepys and Sir Anthony Deane, who were in prison on account of the Plot.[700] Now the feeling against him amounted to positive fury. Sir George Wakeman, after visiting the queen at Windsor, fled the country to escape the effects of the popular rage.[701] Scroggs stood his ground. The London presses teemed with pamphlets against him. *Some observations upon the late trials of Sir George Wakeman*, etc., by Tom Ticklefoot; *The Tickler Tickled*; *A New Year's Gift for the Lord Chief in Justice* are among those which deserve to be remembered for their especial virulence. The Portuguese ambassador had the egregious folly to call publicly upon Scroggs the day after the trial and to thank him for his conduct of the case.[702] It was immediately said that the Chief Justice had been bribed. A barrel packed with gold had been sent to him. "Great store of money" had been scattered about. The jury had been bribed. A good jury had been impanelled, but was never summoned, and a set of rascals was chosen in its place.[703] When Scroggs went on circuit for the autumn assizes he was met in the provinces with cries of—A Wakeman, a Wakeman; and at one place a half-dead dog was thrown into his coach.[704] Early in the year following Oates and Bedloe exhibited thirteen articles against the Chief Justice before the privy council, and Oates declared that "he believed he should be able to prove that my Lord Chief Justice danced naked." On January 21 Scroggs justified himself in a set reply of great skill and wit, and the informers met with a severe rebuff.[705] His other traducers were treated with no greater courtesy. At the opening of the courts for the Michaelmas term of 1679 Scroggs made an able speech of eloquence, distinction, and almost sobriety, in which he grounded his belief in the Plot on the correspondence of Coleman and Harcourt and vindicated the integrity of the judicial honour; and on May 20, 1680 one Richard Radley was fined £200 for saying that the Chief Justice had "received money enough from Dr. Wakeman for his acquittal."[706] In September 1679 he was received with great favour at the court at Windsor and in December caused horrid embarrassment to Lord Shaftesbury and several other Whig noblemen, whom he met at dinner with the Lord Mayor, by proposing the health of the Duke of York and justifying his own conduct on the bench.[707] In January 1681 he was impeached by the Commons. When the articles of his impeachment were brought up to the House of Lords he was treated, to the indignation of the Whig party, with great consideration and favour; but although the lords refused even to put the question "whether there shall now be an address to the king to suspend Sir William Scroggs from the execution of his place until his trial be over?" he was absent from court at the beginning of the Hilary term, and did not take his place upon the bench during the rest of the term.[708] Three days after the opening of the Oxford parliament Scroggs put in his answer to the impeachment. He denied the truth of the articles exhibited against him severally, and insisted that the nature of the facts alleged in them was not such as could legally be made the ground for a charge of high treason. He prayed the king for a speedy trial.[709] Copies of his answer and petition were sent to the House of Commons, but before further proceedings could be taken Parliament was dissolved on March 28, and the impeachment was blown to the winds in company with other Whig measures of greater importance and still less good repute. The Chief Justice was not left long in the enjoyment of his triumph. In April 1681 Charles removed him from the bench and appointed Sir Francis Pemberton to be Chief Justice in his place. The move was no doubt directed by the approaching trial of Fitzharris. For this was undertaken in the teeth of the bitter opposition of the Whig party, and it was expedient that a man who was already odious to Shaftesbury's adherents should not endanger the success of the crown by his presence on the bench on so important an occasion. The late Chief Justice was compensated by an annual pension of £1500 and the appointment of his son to be one of "his Majesty's counsel learned in the law."[710]

Sir William Scroggs, Chief Justice of the court of king's bench, was a man of a type not uncommon in the seventeenth century. He was vulgar and profligate, a great winebibber, stained by coarse habits and the ignorant prejudices common to all of his day but the most temperate and learned, but a man of wit, shrewdness, strong character, and master of the talents which were necessary to secure success in the legal profession as it then was.[711] The prominent position into which he was brought by the trials for the Popish Plot has earned for him a reputation for evil second in the history of the English law courts only to that of Jeffreys. He has been accused of cowardice, cruelty, time-service, of allowing his actions on the bench to be swayed by party spirit, and of using his position with gross injustice to secure the conviction of men who were obnoxious to the popular sentiment. These charges cannot be substantiated. When the evidence of interested partisans by whom he was lauded or abused is stripped away, they rest on two grounds: the fact that he presided at trials where men were condemned for the Popish Plot, and at one where men were acquitted of similar charges; and the nature of his speeches in court at those trials. It was said that he obtained the acquittal of Sir George

Wakeman because he realised that the king "had an ill opinion" of the Plot, and because he had been told that the popular leaders had no support at court; and that he had taken an opposite course at the previous trials because he believed the contrary to be true.[712] These statements have passed for truth ever since they were made, and have been repeated by one writer after another. They were in fact feeble attempts to explain what their authors did not understand. They are contradicted not only by the statements of other contemporaries, which are of small weight, but by the whole course of the Lord Chief Justice's action and the circumstances by which he was surrounded. From the very outbreak of the Popish Plot it was notorious in official circles that the king discredited the evidence offered by the informers.[713] It is absurd to suppose that Scroggs was ignorant of the fact. If anything, Charles was rather more inclined to believe in the Plot in the spring of 1679 than on Oates' first revelations.[714] No judge could possibly have expected to gain favour at court by an exhibition on the bench of zeal which was directed against the court. Still more absurd is it to suppose that a man in the position of the Lord Chief Justice should have imagined that the Earl of Shaftesbury exercised a favoured influence over the king's mind. Nor does Scroggs' conduct on the bench afford good ground for these accusations. His behaviour in the test case, the trial of Sir George Wakeman, was exactly the same as it had been in all the previous trials, and exactly the same as it was at the later trials over which he presided, whether they were of priests charged with treason on account of their orders, of persons charged with treason in the Plot, or for offences of a less high character.[715] It is scarcely surprising to hear that after the attack made on him by Oates and Bedloe, "whensoever either of them have appeared before him, he has frowned upon them, spoke very frowardly to them and reflected much upon them."[716] Nevertheless he treated their evidence quite fairly. The rule was that only a conviction of perjury could disqualify a witness, and Scroggs enforced it without prejudice.[717] Throughout he had the entire support of the other judges, and not least that of Chief Justice North.[718] His mind was filled, equally with theirs, with the fear and horror of popery, and as the chief part of the speaking fell to his lot he expressed this more often and more emphatically than his brethren. But he made up his mind on the merits of each case in accordance with the evidence which was then given and with the stringent and unjust rules of procedure which had been handed down to him. Scroggs was neither a judge of remarkable merit nor a lawyer of learning, but on the evidence which was brought before him, and which was not then, as it would be now, rendered incredible by its own character, he did in a rough manner sound justice.

For the violence and brutality of his speeches there can be no more excuse than for the coarseness and violence of all speech and action in the age in which he lived. But his words must not be judged alone, nor must his manner of speech be considered peculiar. Language in the latter half of the seventeenth century was harsh and exaggerated to a degree hardly comprehended to-day. Scroggs constantly launched forth into tirades against the Roman Catholic religion, full of heated abuse. Sometimes he attributed to the Jesuits, at others to all papists, the bloody, inhuman, abominable doctrine that murder, regicide, and massacre were lawful in the cause of religion. "Such courses as these," he declared, "we have not known in England till it was brought out of their Catholic countries; what belongs to secret stranglings and poisonings are strange to us, though common in Italy."[719] He told Coleman, "No man of understanding, but for by-ends, would have left his religion to be a papist.... Such are the wicked solecisms in their religion, that they seem to have left them neither natural sense nor natural conscience: not natural sense, by their absurdity in so unreasonable a belief as of the wine turned into blood; not conscience, by their cruelty, who make the Protestants' blood as wine, and these priests thirst after it; Tantum religio potuit suadere malorum?"[720] The onslaught on Ireland, Pickering, and Grove was still more virulent: "I would not asperse a profession of men, as priests are, with hard words, if they were not very true, and if at this time it were not very necessary. If they had not murdered kings, I would not say they would have done ours. But when it hath been their practice so to do; when they have debauched men's understandings, overturned all morals, and destroyed all divinity, what shall I say of them? When their humility is such that they tread upon the necks of emperors; their charity such as to kill princes, and their vow of poverty such as to covet kingdoms, what shall I say to them?... This is a religion that quite unhinges all piety, all morality, and all conversation, and to be abominated by all mankind."[721] Yet Scroggs' language was no stronger than that of his brothers on the bench. Jeffreys in sentencing Ireland, Wild in sentencing Green, Jones in sentencing Tasborough attained an exactly similar style. At the trial of Penn and Mead in 1670 the court was at least equally ill-mouthed, and nothing ever heard in a court of justice surpassed the torrents of venomous abuse which Coke, as Attorney-General, poured upon the head of Raleigh at his trial in 1603. One fact in judicial procedure exercised an immense influence on the nature of speeches from the bench. The judges took no notes.[722] In summing up the evidence they relied solely upon memories developed for this purpose to an extent which seems almost marvellous. But another result besides this remarkable mental training was that in his summing up the judge had no set form by which to direct himself. There was not the constraint which comes from the necessity of following a definite guide on prosaic slips of paper. It followed that the whole of this part of his work was far more loose and undefined than it has come to be since the additional burden of taking notes has been imposed. Not only could he, but it was natural that he should, break off from the course of the evidence to interpose comments more or less connected with it; and in the days of little learning and violent religious prejudice, the judge's comment was likely to take the form of abuse of the creed which he did not profess.

Men of the seventeenth century habitually expressed their thoughts with a coarseness which is disgusting to the modern mind. A man named Keach, who had taught that infants ought not to be baptized, was indicted for "maliciously writing and publishing a seditious and venomous book, wherein are contained damnable positions contrary to the book of common prayer."[723] At his speech at the opening of Parliament in 1679 Lord Chancellor Finch likened the Roman Catholic priests and their pupils to "the Sons of Darkness," and declared that "the very shame and reproach which attends such abominable practices hath covered so many faces with new and strange confusions, that it hath proved a powerful argument for their conversion; nor is it to be wondered at that they could no longer believe all that to be Gospel which their priests taught them, when they saw the way and means of introducing it was so far from being Evangelical."[724] Other parties were equally violent; and on two separate occasions Shaftesbury swore that he would have the lives of the men who had advised the king to measures obnoxious to his party. The most notorious of all Scroggs' utterances, an acrid sneer at the doctrine of transubstantiation: "They eat their God, they kill their king, and saint the murderer," is paralleled almost exactly by Dryden's couplet:

Such savoury deities must needs be good.

As served at once for worship and for food;[725]

and Dryden, who at this time belonged to the court and high church party, became within five years himself a Roman Catholic. The whole literature of the time bears witness to the fact that such language was scarcely beyond the ordinary. It was a convention of the age and must be accepted as such. There would be no greater mistake than to attribute to words of the sort too great an influence on action. The results which attended them were unimportant. Of all Chief Justice Scroggs' harangues the most consistently brutal and offensive was that directed at Marshal, at the trial of Sir George Wakeman.[726] Yet it was followed immediately by a fair summing up and the acquittal of the prisoners.

Only one other case demands attention in this review of the trials for the Popish Plot. The trial of Elizabeth Cellier for high treason belongs rather to the history of the Meal Tub Plot; those of Sir Thomas Gascoigne, Sir Miles Stapleton, Thwing, and Pressicks to the provincial history of the Plot; that of Archbishop Plunket to its history in Ireland. The acquittal of Lord Castlemaine is chiefly important as an episode in the infamous career of Dangerfield, the informer. The proceedings against Fitzharris belong rather to the history of Whig conspiracy against the crown, the transition to which they mark.[727] But the trial of Lord Stafford calls for more lengthy notice. It was the last of the treason trials for the main Popish Plot, and ranks in importance with the weightiest of those which went before. More than two years had now elapsed since the beginning of the ferment caused by the Plot. During that time it had exercised a magic over men's minds. This influence was now suffering a decline. The acquittals of Wakeman, Lord Castlemaine, and Sir Thomas Gascoigne had wrought the mob to fury against the court and the Roman Catholics, but they had also sown doubts in the judgment of intelligent persons as to the credit of the informers and the truth of the facts to which they swore. At the end of the year 1680 it was doubtful, said Sir John Reresby, "whether there were more who believed there was any plot by the papists against the king's life than not."[728] The situation of the Whig party was critical. Their violent espousal of the Plot and the concentration of all their efforts upon the propagation of ultra-Protestant designs had brought about the result that, should the Plot be discredited before they had gained their object in excluding the Duke of York from the succession to the throne, their power would vanish into thin air. To stave off a day of such evil and to re-establish on its former firm footing the general belief in "the bloody designs of papists," the trial of Giles for the bogus attempt on Captain Arnold's life had been undertaken.[729] With the same object Lord Stafford was brought to trial. His imprisonment had already lasted for two years and two months.[730] He was now brought to the bar in preference to any of the other four noblemen who had been imprisoned with him because, as was believed at court, his advanced age and bodily infirmity rendered him a more easy prey to the rancour of the House of Commons.[731] On all sides the case was regarded as of the utmost importance. If the prisoner were condemned the Whigs would gain a great advantage. If he were acquitted, the prosecution of the Plot, which was their sole weapon, would suffer a disastrous check.[732]

Stafford's trial was conducted upon a scale befitting its consequence. Seven days were occupied in its process, a length which was at the time unprecedented. As many as sixty-one witnesses were called on the one side and on the other. For those who appeared for the prosecution the cost of summons and entertainment amounted to a hundred pounds.[733] The court of the Lord High Steward was held in Westminster Hall. Round the hall were arranged galleries, from which privileged persons watched the proceedings with the keenest interest. From her seat in a private box the Duchess of Portsmouth exerted her charms upon the members of the House of Commons stationed near her, distributing "sweetmeats and gracious looks." Another box was reserved for the queen. In a third sat the king, a constant attendant during every day of the trial.[734] Opposite the bar was the seat of the Lord High Steward, and near by were placed the managers of the prosecution, Sir William Jones, Sergeant Maynard, Winnington, Treby, Trevor, Powle, the most distinguished lawyers of the House of Commons.

On November 30, 1680, his sixty-ninth birthday, Thomas Howard, Lord Viscount Stafford, was brought to the bar. That nothing might be omitted against the prisoner, the managers called witnesses to prove the reality and general designs of the Popish Plot. The whole story was gone into at immense length. Oates, Dugdale, Jennison, a secular priest named John Smith, and Bernard Dennis, a Dominican friar, gave a volume of evidence to the point. The records of the conviction of nineteen persons for treason and other charges connected with the Plot, beginning with Coleman and ending with Giles, were proved and the record of Coleman's attainder was read. Thus the whole of one day was occupied.[735] On the following morning the managers proceeded to call witnesses to the treason of Lord Stafford. The mass of evidence which they gave may be reduced to three points. Dugdale swore that at a certain meeting held at Tixhall, in Staffordshire, about the end of August or the beginning of September 1678, the accused had given his full assent to the plot for taking away the king's life, and in September had offered him the sum of £500 to be the actual murderer.[736] Oates swore that he had seen letters to various Jesuits, signed Stafford, containing assurances of his zeal and fidelity to the design; that the prisoner had in his presence received from Fenwick a commission constituting him paymaster-general of the forces; and that, in conversation with Fenwick, Lord Stafford had said he did not doubt that "Grove should do the business," adding with reference to the king, "he hath deceived us a great while, and we can bear no longer."[737] Lastly Turbervile, a new witness, swore that after a fortnight's acquaintance with the prisoner in Paris, in the year 1675, he had directly proposed to him to kill the king of England, who was a heretic and a rebel against Almighty God.[738] Round these charges the contest was waged hotly. Lord Stafford and his witnesses doing battle against the managers and theirs. On the third day the attack was directed on Dugdale. A servant of Lord Aston proved that the informer had lived in bad repute at Tixhall, that he was discharged from his post of steward, that he ran away to escape his creditors, was caught and imprisoned for debt, and that he had sworn by God that he knew nothing of any plot.[739] The last was confirmed by the magistrates who had arrested Dugdale for debt. He had then been examined about the Plot and denied all knowledge of it. Only two days later he made a full confession.[740] Two servants of the accused were called to prove the nature of the interview in which Dugdale swore that Lord Stafford offered him £500 to kill the king. Every circumstance of it was fully explained. The witnesses had been in the room the whole time, and deposed that the conversation had turned upon nothing more serious than the chances of a horse-race in the neighbourhood.[741] Other Staffordshire men testified to Dugdale's evil reputation, and two artisans of Tixhall stated that Dugdale had offered them separately money to swear against Lord Stafford.[742]

Of Oates' evidence little could be made for the defence, but Stafford was able to point out that after having solemnly declared to the House of Lords that he could accuse no other persons "of whatsoever quality they be," he had proceeded to charge the queen herself with high treason.[743]

Again Dugdale was called and cross-examined on his deposition of December 24, 1678, which was read from the journal of the House of Lords. In that he had said "that presently after one Howard, almoner to the queen, went beyond seas, he was told by George Hobson (servant to the said Lord Aston) that there was a design then intended for the reformation of the government of the Romish religion." He now swore that he did not know Hobson before the latter came into Lord Aston's service in 1678. Stafford seized upon this as evidence either that Dugdale was lying, or that his information, sworn two years before, was false. Dugdale contended that the meaning of the clause "was that Hobson told me that presently after almoner Howard went over, there was such a design carrying on." It is a testimony to the obscurity of the style of ordinary English prose at the end of the seventeenth century that the court held, in apparent opposition to common sense and common justice, that the construction which Dugdale gave to the sentence was not only possible, but the more probable.[744]

Turbervile, the third of the informers, was met in his evidence by numerous contradictions. It was proved that in his original deposition he had altered two dates the day after having sworn to their accuracy. Both in his deposition of November 9, 1680 and at the trial in the course of examination he had sworn that he had constantly seen Lord Stafford in Paris during a fortnight in 1675 when Stafford was ill with gout, and that the prisoner then pressed him to undertake the murder of the king. Two of Lord Stafford's servants who had been with him in Paris now proved that they had never once seen Turbervile during that time, and that their master had not been ill or lame with gout for at least seven years.[745] Material evidence was brought against the witness on other points. He had sworn that at the end of 1675 Lord Stafford had returned to England by Calais, sending him by Dieppe. The contrary was now proved by an independent witness. It was also proved by a French servant belonging to the household of Lord Powis that Turbervile had lodged with him in Lord Powis' house in Paris at a time when he professed to be in fear for his life of the earl himself, and by his brother, John Turbervile, that whereas he had sworn that Lord Powis threatened to have him disinherited, he had not at any time had even a remote chance of any inheritance whatsoever.[746]

On the fourth day of this ponderous trial Lord Stafford closed his main defence. He pointed to the turpitude of Oates' character, and spoke with emotion of his abhorrence that a man guilty of such immorality as to profess a change of religion which he did not experience should be allowed to give evidence against a peer among his peers. "I appeal to your lordships," he cried, "whether such ... is not a perjured fellow, and no competent witness? No Christian, but a devil, and a witness for the devil." Even Oates himself was flustered and had to be restrained by the managers from breaking into excesses.[747]

The prosecuting Commons however were undismayed. They called a swarm of witnesses to set up the character of the informers and to destroy that of witnesses for the defence. It was proved by word of mouth and the production of letters that servants of Lord Aston, Lord Bellasis, and Mr. Heveningham had attempted to suborn persons to give false evidence against Dugdale.[748] The new witnesses were in turn contradicted by the defence, and this wonderful series of contradictions was carried still one step further when fresh evidence was called to corroborate them.[749]

On the fifth day Lord Stafford summed up his defence. He laid special stress on the infamous character of his accusers and his own clean record, the points in which the witnesses had been contradicted, and the general improbability of the charge. His speech was badly received. The opportunity of a slight pause was seized by Lord Lovelace to spring to his feet and denounce with indignation the presence in court of a well-known Roman Catholic.[750] Moreover the prisoner made a grave tactical mistake in proposing for argument a number of points of law, of which some were frivolous and others had already been authoritatively determined. Of these the only one which could be considered material was the question whether or no in a case of high treason two witnesses were necessary to prove each overt act alleged, since the witnesses against Lord Stafford had sworn separately, and never together, to the commission of several acts. This had in fact been determined in the case of Sir Harry Vane,[751] but now with remarkable consideration for the prisoner the opinion of the assembled judges was taken: it was unanimous to the effect that the evidence of two separate witnesses to two distinct acts constituted a proof of high treason. The other points were easily disposed of by Jones and Winnington.[752]

In a speech of great ability Sir William Jones answered the accused. Here especially the professional training of the managers had weight. With the ease and decision of a practised lawyer the leader ran over the trial, setting the strong points of the prosecution in a clear light and minimising the value of the defence. His zeal was evident, but hardly unfair. If here and there a statement overshot the mark of strict accuracy, the effect of his speech was only enhanced by the patience with which he submitted to correction from the prisoner. Concluding with a short but powerful address, he demanded that the court should do "that justice to your king and country as to give judgment against these offenders, which will not only be a security to us against them, but a terror to all others against committing the like offences."[753] On the night of Saturday, December 4, Stafford petitioned to be heard again in his defence. His request was granted, but the rambling speech to which the court listened on the Monday following was calculated to produce any effect rather than that of advancing his cause. The managers only found it necessary to reply very briefly before the court adjourned to consider its verdict.[754]

At eleven o'clock on the next morning the votes were taken. Thirty-one peers pronounced Lord Stafford innocent, fifty-five guilty. The verdict was not unexpected. Stafford had conducted his defence so feebly as to make his acquittal improbable.[755] Physical weakness accounted largely for this; but he had made the mistake of speaking as much as possible, and his remarks were halting, nebulous, indecisive. On the night before the verdict was delivered Barillon wrote that there was every appearance that it would be adverse to the accused.[756] Sir John Reresby was staggered by the evidence for the prosecution, and only maintained his belief in Stafford's innocence by fixing his mind firmly on the depravity of the witnesses.[757] Anglesey, Lord Privy Seal, afterwards pressed hard for Lord Stafford's pardon, but at the trial he felt constrained to vote against him, "secundum allegata et probata."[758] Even Charles, although he knew that Oates and his crew were liars and publicly called them rascals, thought that the evidence against the accused was strong, and that he might well be guilty;[759] and the Countess of Manchester, who was present at the whole trial, wrote to Lady Hatton before the verdict was known, that the charge "was so well proved that I believe not many was unsatisfied, except those that were out of favour with the party might wish it other ways."[760] Charles was present in Westminster Hall while the peers delivered their verdict, and took notes of the sides on which they voted. When it became evident that the majority were for condemnation, his face to those who were near him shewed profound disappointment.[761] Whether or no he believed in Stafford's innocence, the conviction was a blow to the king's cause. But the votes were not directed by political considerations alone. These would probably have ensured an acquittal. If Charles had exerted his personal influence on the court, an acquittal would have been certain.[762] The peers gave judgment on what seemed to them the merits of the case. Three eminent members of Lord Stafford's family voted for the death.[763] The same verdict was delivered by the Lord Chancellor, the Lord Privy Seal, the Earl of Oxford,

Lord Maynard, and the Duke of Lauderdale. Among the thirty-one who found for the accused were such staunch Whigs as Lord Holles, Lord Lucas, and the Earl of Clarendon. All these, had party spirit directed the votes, must have determined to the contrary. The fact must be faced that so late as December of the year 1680, more than two years after Oates' first revelations, and after the disclosure at Wakeman's trial had rendered certain the fact of his perjury, many of the most honourable and intelligent men in the kingdom sincerely accepted as credible the evidence offered against Lord Stafford, and as earnest of their belief sent to the scaffold one of their own number, a man bowed down with years and infirmity, the victim of miscreants supported by the enemies of the king, for the false plot against whose life he was now to die. It was a memorial to all time of the ignorance of the principles of evidence and the nature of true justice which characterised their age.

Sentence as usual in cases of high treason was pronounced on the condemned man, but at the request of the peers the king commuted the penalty to beheading alone. Efforts were made to obtain a pardon, but without avail. Charles was determined to let the law take its course that he might not be said to balk the ends of justice.[764]

The sheriffs disputed the validity of the warrant for Stafford's decapitation and requested the advice of the House of Commons on the following questions: "Can the king, being neither party nor judge, order the execution? Can the lords award the execution? Can the king dispense with any part of the execution? If he can dispense with a part, why not with all?" To the ingenuity of Sir William Jones was due the studied insult offered to Charles in the answer of the House: "The house is content that the sheriffs should execute William, late Viscount Stafford, by severing his head from his body."[765] The excitement which prevailed in London was intense. Throughout the trial Stafford had been hooted in the streets on his way to and from the Tower. Angry brawls arose between the witnesses and the crowd at the doors of Westminster Hall. When Dugdale swore that the prisoner had offered him £500 to kill the king, a savage hum arose in the precincts of the court itself and drew a severe rebuke from the Lord High Steward.[766] On December 29, 1680 Stafford was led to the scaffold. From the place of execution he read a lengthy speech, which was published in print on the same afternoon, asserting his innocence and vindicating his religion.[767] His words fell on deaf ears. A vast crowd was assembled to witness his death. Almost all historians have repeated the assertion that the spectators were touched and answered with cries of, "We believe you, my Lord; God bless you, my Lord."[768] The story is a mere fable. Lord Stafford died with howls of execration of the bigoted London mob ringing in his ears. The cries with which he was met testify relentlessly that the belief in his guilt was firmly fixed in the mind of the nation.[769] The Popish Plot was not yet a thing of the past. But the result of Lord Stafford's trial was not altogether what was expected. Shaftesbury and his party indeed gained a temporary victory, but the ultimate triumph was to the king. His steadiness, restraint, and readiness for compromise contrasted favourably with the intolerance and unconciliating attitude of the Whigs. Their game was played for the crown and, when their rejection of all offers short of that made their motive plain to the nation, Charles had the nation at his back. The violence with which they attempted to force the king's hand alienated public feeling. He was able to dissolve the Oxford Parliament in safety, and the Whigs were driven to plan open rebellion and the treason of the Rye House Plot.

APPENDICES

APPENDIX A

LONGLEAT MSS. COVENTRY PAPERS xi. 393

April 29, 1679. Dover. Francis Bastwick to Henry Coventry.

THIS day I received advice of one Col. Scott coming from Folkestone to take horse here for London, and on his arrival I seized him and sent for the Comm. of the passage. His examination I send you enclosed, upon which we found cause to commit him (which was accordingly done by the deputy mayor) into safe custody until we had further orders from one of his Majesty's principal secretaries what to do with him. He owns himself to be the same person we have had orders for several months past to seize at his landing. Col. Strode, deputy formerly, had an order to seize Col. Scott as I remember from Mr. Secretary Coventry, but I am not certain but Col. Strode or his deputy are at present in the place.

I am your most humble servant Fran. Bastwick. I desire your speedy answer when you have acquainted my L^d. Sunderland. Col. Scott has been found in many contrary tales, and went at his landing by the name of John Johnson.

COVENTRY PAPERS xi. 396

From the examination of Colonel Scott at Dover, April 29, 1679. That he is a pensioner to the prince of Condi, and hath formerly commanded the prince of Condi's regiment of horse in the French service. And that the said prince of Condi sent him over in September last in order for the surveying of several parcels of lands and woods in Burgandie and Picardie was the occasion of his going over.

That the occasion of his return is to see his native country, and his profession is a soldier. The said Colonel offered to take the oaths of allegiance and supremacy and the test.

COVENTRY PAPERS xi. 397

Undated. Paper headed: An account of what the Earl of Barkeshire desired Colonel John Scot to communicate to His Ma^ty. with what passed before the discourse. (Endorsed by Coventry in the same words.)

The Earl of Barkeshire, that had lain long of a languishing sickness in Paris, was pleased to let me know he desired to advise with me about a physician. This was in March last. I told his lordship I was acquainted with an able man of our own nation, and one of the college of physicians in London, but I was of opinion his Lordship's Roman Catholic friends would not approve of him because he was not only a strict protestant, but one that did publicly defend the doctrine of the church of England, and as publicly declare the English Roman Catholics were prosecuted on just grounds. His Lordship said that mattered not, he should not dispute that point with him, nor did he value any man the worse for differing from him in judgment, and that he was not so strait-laced as others of his opinion, and did commit himself to the charge of the said Doctor Budgeon; but it did prove too late, for this gentleman soon told his Lordship what condition he was in, and he came to my lodgings and signified to me his Lordship's great desire to speak with me, telling me his Lordship in all human probability could not live long; and I waited upon his Lordship the morning following, and he having commanded his servants out of the chamber, and to suffer nobody to come in till he called, spake to me as I remember these very words:—

Colonel Scot, you are my friend; I must commit a secret to you; there has been a foolish and an ill design carried on in England: I don't tell you the Roman Catholic religion is a foolish business, for it is the faith I will die in, but 'tis the giddy madness of some of that religion I blame. I knew nothing on't till my Lord Arundel, Mr. Coleman, and others told me the business could not miscarry, and that I should be looked upon as an ill man if I came not in in time, and truly I believed them. I was none of the contrivers, I was not consulted with till towards the latter end of the day, nor did I ever hear anything mentioned about killing the king; if I had, I would have discovered it, and so indeed I ought to have done what I did know, as well for the personal obligations I had to his Majesty as that which my allegiance obliges me to, and every man too; for my Lord Bellasis is an ill man; he and others were accustomed to speak ill of the king, indeed very irreverently.

Then I asked his Lordship who those others were; but he answered, prithee, good Colonel, ask me no questions; if I had known of approaching dangers to the king, I should have told him. He then fetched a great sigh and wept, but presently said, Friend, I see things will go as you will; for God's sake promise me you will find some way to tell the king every word I say, and that though some passages in letters of mine may look a little oddly, I would have run any hazard rather than have suffered any injury to have been done to his Majesty's person: 'tis true I would have been glad to have seen all England Catholic, but not by the way of some ill men. My Lord Stafford was all along a moving agent, and was here in France about the business; the man of himself is not very malicious. My Lord Powis his covetousness drew him in further than he would have gone. I believe and hope there will hardly be found matter against them to take away their lives, but pray the king from a poor dying man not to have to do with any of those four Lords I have named, for they love not his person.

My Lord Peeter has always had a great love and reverence for the king's person; 'tis true this last wife of his is foolishly governed by priests and influences him; but he was ever averse to all things of intrigue in this matter. I need not desire you to be secret, your own safety will oblige you. My Lord Cardigan and others being at the door and calling to this Lord, the servants were ordered to let them in, and before them he said, pray don't forget the hundredth we spake of, nor the business at Rohan. I was there once more with the Doctor, but he grew exceeding deaf; he said only then to me: Colonel, don't forget what I said to you for God's sake. This is the very manner he spake it.

JOHN SCOT.

COVENTRY PAPERS xi. 171

December 23, 1676. Hague. A letter, unsigned. Note by Coventry at head—To one Johnson: at foot—shewed his Maj. 23rd of Dec. 76.

In my last I made some observations to you of the working of the old spirit in the Popish party: at this time will now only add that the same seemeth not to be restrained to England.... The popish humour beginneth to spread itself over the English regiments, especially the regiment lately Col. Tanwicke. One Wisely is made Col., being Lieut. Col. before. Archer the major is made Lieut. Col., both Irish Papists, and the rest of the officers are generally papists and mad Irish, and for aught we know for the most part recommended by the Duke of York. Now albeit this be true that this congregating of Papists together in a body be in the dominion of another state, yet it is true they are subjects of England and in regard to the ... circumstances of England in my poor opinion worthy the public notice.

COVENTRY PAPERS xi. 506

Undated. Letter without address or signature; deciphered from numbers written in very light ink in place of all important words, so that all those in the decipher stand between the lines.

Col. Scot doth send his letters by way of Mons. Gourville, in whose chamber he writes them, so that I see little hopes of doing what you know, though the undertaker doth still insist for the contrary. I am ready for the journey, hoping Mr. Secretary will be so just as to spare naming me till that service is done, for I should be sorry to trust any other who I do know to have contrived my being disliked in this court. A lady of quality, my good friend, returned yesterday from Bretagne and assures a great arming upon those coasts and an army of forty thousand men ready to ship at Nantes, Brest, etc., whenever commanded to sea, to save (as they report) the K. of England from destruction. The lady, if there were no disguise in the outward state of things in England (which many do think there is), might I think be brought to use her knowledge for his Majesty's service, but my hands are tied, and you know how things stand with you.

COVENTRY PAPERS xi. 313

May 21 1678. St. Malo. Thomas Kelly to Mr. William Talbot in Corn Market, Dublin.

I pray you to pay to Mr. John Plunket the sum of 89 pounds sterling by the review of this letter; in doing so you will satisfy your creditor. Made the 21st of May at St. Malo, 1678.

THOMAS KELLY.

[The above is in plain dark ink. What follows is light and indistinct; the characters were evidently written in milk or lemon-juice, and made visible by being held to the fire.]

When I came from Paris to St. Germaine where I stayed some time and among other speeches I heard in dophin Chamber from some which were there that if the English should make war against them they should easily excite a rebellion both in Scotland and Ireland, and sending by some Marshal of France 10 men of war with all things necessary for to make up 2000 soldiers in Ireland and that, by the help of some skillful Irishmen, and under their conduct all the Irish should be, they may easily overcome all Ireland. This was the discourse of those gentlemen in Dorphin Chamber, but whether it comes to effect or not I cannot tell.... [Goes on to give particulars of the numbers and strength of the French navy on the north coast.]

COVENTRY PAPERS xi, 310

July 6, 1678. Kimper. David Neal to John Plunket at sign of the Ship in the Corn Market in Dublin.

[Of the same character as the last. The letter, in black ink, is frivolous. Interlined in light writing as follows.]

I have been over all places where I was bound, but the fairest places is Brest, and afterwards Havre and St. Malos for merchants. The names of them that are capable to serve I did send long since. All other places are nothing after these places neither is there any man of war in them other places unless they should stay for a day or two expecting to convoy others.... [Gives other particulars of ships and a list of names of captains of French men of war. Concludes—]

If you please I intend to go home since the time is past whenever I was engaged, neither will my friends have me to apply myself to it. Your resolution hereupon I will willingly see as soon as possible, for I have not much money to stay long in ... country as dear as this is.

COVENTRY PAPERS xi. 317

June 17, 1678. Rochford. Walter B—— à Monsieur Patric Roch à la place au blé à Dublin. (Endorsed in Coventry's hand): Mr. Burke.

[Of the same nature as the last two, and in the same handwriting.] There is nothing here worthy of relation only that all the people of this country is very desirous to have war against you, and specially all the seamen desire no other thing but it.... [Further particulars of French ships, mostly merchant vessels. One passage in the black ink deserves to be noted.] This is the fourth letter which I did write to your honour without receiving any answer.

COVENTRY PAPERS xi. 204

April 14, 1678. St. Omers. Sam Morgan to his father. (Copy of same 205.)

(Endorsed in Coventry's hand.) Send to Doc^t. Lloyd to learn where Morgan the father liveth, and how I may write to him.—Mr. Morgan the father lives at Kilkin in Flintshire near the Bp. of Bangor.

Honoured Father! These are next to my humble duty unto yourself and my mother to acquaint you with my present condition. I am here entered in a College called Flamstead amongst good gentlemen, and am well beloved of them all. The place is very good for meat and drink and other necessaries, but my fear is and am in good measure satisfied that my uncle intends me for a priest. He spoke nothing unto me as yet, but I partly understand that he is of that opinion, which when I considered on is clean against my conscience. I daily see and know what they are, and am utterly dissatisfied with and condemn the principles and practices of their diabolical opinions, for I dare not call it religion. If you would be pleased to call for me home I think I should be very well; for now (I thank God) I got more learning here since I came than I should have gotten anywhere in Wales in 7 or 8 years. I have competent skill in Greek and Latin, and can write a little of both: if you would be pleased to take me home, I should thank my uncle for my learning, and let him take whom he thinks fit for his priest.

I must stay here 18 years yet, and God knows who would be alive then; and for all that, if I were like to be a comfort to my friends, I would stay with all my heart, though I utterly abhor their ways. If you intend to take me home it must be done within this two years at furthest; otherwise it will be too late; and if you be of that resolution put two strokes in the bottom of your letter; be sure you mention it not publicly in my letter, for then the Reader, which is the master of the house, will come to know it; for there is not a letter that comes in or goes out of the house but he has the perusal of it, but now I write this and deliver it privately to an honest man that set out this day hence; so that the master knows nothing of it. No more but that you would use some means to redeem me from this great captivity, who am in extraordinary haste.

Your dutiful son,
SAM MORGAN.

JOSEPH LANE.

P.R.O. ROMAN TRANSCRIPTS. VAT. ARCH. NUNT. DI FRANCIA 332

December 2, 1678. L'Abbᵉ G. B. Lauri à S. EMᶻᵃ.

Ancor che lo stato presente d'Inghilterra, e la risposta datami la settimania passata dal Sigʳ di Pomponne non mi facessero sperare cos' alcuna di buono intorno all' assistenza richiesta a favore del Sigʳ Duca di Yorch; nondimeno a proporzione della premura di N.S. e dell' importanza dell' affare, ne rimovai le instanze al suddetto ministro Martedì passato, nel qual giorno per questi e per altri negozii pendenti mi portai à Varsaglia; egli soggiunsi che il credito talvolta e l'assistenza del Re di Francia avrebbe potuto ristabilire il partito del Sigʳ Duca di Yorch e de' Catholici di quel regno, quando S. Mᵗᵃ si fosse dichiarata per loro. Rispose tuttevia il Sigʳ di Pomponne che tutti i Catholici d'Inghilterra ò erano imprigionati ò erano stati discacciati di Londra. Il medᵐᵒ Sigʳ Duca di Yorch restava escluso dall' essercizio delle sue cariche, e tutti indifferentemente venivano osservati in maniera che il dichiararsi nello stato presente per loro altre non sarebbe stato che un accrescergli le persecuzioni, e finir di ruinare il partito Catholico di quel regno; per queste ragioni avere stimato S. Mᵗᵃ che non sia tempo di prestar l'assistenza richiesta, mentre il cambiamento delle cose faceva ogni conoscere che tal consiglio non era pin utile, come ragionevolmente avra per altro potuto stimarsi prima che succedessero le mutazioni accennati. Io dunque essendo cosi cambiate di faccia le cose d'Inghilterra, ed incontrando que le scritte difficoltà, tralascierò di fare altre istanza per quest' affare finche da V.S., informata che sia delle cose che passano, mi vengano nuovi comandamenti.

APPENDIX B

LONGLEAT MSS. COVENTRY PAPERS xi. 237

October 28, 1678. Copy of the letter sent to Mr. Sec. Coventry subscribed T. G. Concerning the murder of Sir Edmond Bury Godfrey.

This is to certify you that upon his Majesty's Declaration I have been both at Whitehall and at your own house these three days together, and never can be admitted to come to the speech of your worship. Whereupon I thought fit to give you an account what it is I can declare, which is as follows:—Being on Tuesday the 15th, of this instant October, in a victualling house in White Friars I chanced to hear two persons a discoursing, the one saying to the other that if he would go down to Billingsgate he would treat him there with wine and oysters, whereupon the other replied and said: "What you are uppish then are you?" Upon which words he swore, God dampe him (*sic*), he had money enough, and draws a bag out of his pocket and says. There were fifty pounds. Whereupon the other party was very inquisitive to know how he came by it, and did importune him very much, and at the last he told him that if he would swear to be true to him and never discover, he would tell him. Whereupon he did make all the imprecations and vows that could possibly be that he would never discover, whereupon he told him that the last night he with three men did murder Sir Edward Bury Godfrey and he had that £50 for his pains, and said that he believed he could help him to some money if he would go along with him on the morrow night following. Upon these words the other asked him where it was done and who the other three was that was with him, and he told him that he murdered him at Wild House, and the other three that was concerned with him was gentlemen. Two belonged to my Lord Bellasis, and the other to my Lord Petres, but of the Monday before, there was a court held at Wildhouse and there they tried him, and there was a man like a priest who passed sentence of death upon him; and likewise he asked him how he came to be concerned in it, and he told him that there was a broker that lodged in Eagle Court in the Strand that spoke to him of it: so this is all I can testify of, but only that I can give some account in what a barbarous manner they murdered him. This man's name is Hogshead, he liveth (?) at the Temple and Whitefriars very much. So, Sir, if you please to give orders to your servant, and let me come to the speech of you, I will come and make oath of it, and with this proviso that I may have the liberty to make a fuller discovery of it, I not being anything out of pocket myself; I desire your answer to-morrow morning to be left at the place mentioned in my former letter, and withal desire it may be more private than the last.

Your humble servant to command,
T. G.

From the Temple this
28th instant 1678.

COVENTRY PAPERS xi. p. 235. Coventry's answer to this.

October 28, 1678. To his very loving friend T. G. these.

(Note added by Coventry below the address): This letter was sent to the Rainbow Coffee House, but never called for, and was brought back by Col. Vernon.

I have yours, and am abundantly satisfied with it, but know not how to answer it at large. Will you tell me by what name I shall subscribe it to you; whether your own or another it matters not so you are sure to receive it. If you enquire for one Mr. Evans at my house to-morrow or any morning he shall bring you to me, when I will give you my best advice and assistance in what you desire.

I am,
Your humble servant,
HENRY COVENTRY.

BRIT. MUS. ADD. MSS. 11058: 244

Nov. 7, 1678. Mr. Bedloe's confession before his Majesty of the murder of Sir Edmund Berry Godfrey.

He saith that the Saturday Sir Edmund Berry Godfrey was missing, about two in the afternoon as he (Godfrey) was going home, two or three gentlemen met him and said they could discover some persons near the Strand Bridge that were agitators in the Plot, upon which Sir E. Godfrey showed great readiness, but they desired him to walk into a houseyard till a constable was got ready; but Sir E. Godfrey had scarce made two or three turns but several people rushed out upon him and stopped his mouth; two friars and some of Lord Bellasis' servants executing the same, and having carried him into an inner chamber demanded of him Mr. Oates his deposition, promising they would save his life if he would render it to them; yet their design was to have taken away his life though he had given them that satisfaction. Sir Edmund Berry told them that the king and council had them, and therefore he could not possibly do what they desired. Upon which expression they began to use him inhumanly and barbarously, kneeling upon his breast till they thought he was dead; but they opened his bosom and found his heart panted; then they took a cravat and tied it hard about his neck, and so ended his life. He says further that he came too late to be assistant in the murder, for he found him strangled and lying dead on the floor, but presently received an account from the actors in what manner it was performed. His corpse was laid at the high altar of the Queen's chapel, and continued there till they had consulted a way for removing the same secretly from thence.

He further saith that two guineas were the reward promised among the undertakers, and on Wednesday following the corpse was conveyed in a sedan to Lord Bellasis' house, and from thence carried in a coach to the place where it was found. He also acquainted the Lords that he had several things to communicate to them which related to the Plot, and that he was able to confirm several passages which Mr. Oates had discovered concerning the plot, but he desired leave to give his testimony in writing, that so he might make no other discovery than what he could be able to testify.

Actors: Mr. Eveley, Mr. Leferry, Jesuits; Penchard and Atkins, laymen; the keeper of the Queen's chapel and a vally de chambre to the Lord Bellasis.

P.R.O. S.P. DOM. CHARLES II 407: ii. 29. LONGLEAT MSS. COVENTRY PAPERS xi. 272–274.

7th Nov. 1678. Before his Majesty.

Mr. Bedloe informs,

A contrivance between Charles Wintour and the governour of Chepstow Castle, and Mr. Charles Milbourn and Mr. Vaughan of Cont ... and his son, to be in arms when my Lord Powis would in Cardiganshire, to give up the castle to Mr. Charles Wintour and army of 20^m men.

Mr. Thimbleby in Lincoln: under Lord Bellasis was to have 20^m men. 20^m religious men were to meet at St Jago to come over into Wales from the Groin, and meet Lord Powis and the aforesaid gentlemen in arms.

20^m out of Flanders to meet Lord Bellasis and Mr. Thimbleby: to land at Burlington Bay. Has known this by being four years among them.

Qu. What proofs.

Resp. Has lived among the Jesuits four years, and had all he had from them, etc.

Has been in Spain. Employed from five Jesuits to Sir W. Godolphin, Stapleton, Latham, Le Fere, Cave and Sheldon.

Cave and Le Fere sent him to Doway last summer 12 months. 20 months since, and thence by Paris, etc., to Madrid.

Le Fere told him of this design.

Lodges where Captain Atkins lodges, where Walsh the priest lodges, near Wild House.

Mr. Selvyns at the back door of the Palgrave's Head will show where Captain Atkins lodges, and consequently where Le Fere.

Le Fere is an Englishman, calls himself a Frenchman. The passage of the 20^m men from Flanders was to be from Newport.

As to Sir Edmond Godfrey; was promised 2000 guineas to be in it by Le Fere, my Lord Bellasis' gentleman, and the youngest of the waiters in the Queene's chapel, in a purple gown and to make the people orderly. They did not tell him at first who was to be killed nor till he was killed.

They murdered him in Somerset House in the corner room, the left hand as you come in, near Madame Macdonnel's lodgings, and near the room where the duke of Albemarle lay in state.

Stifled him with a pillow, then he struggling they tied a cravat about his neck and so strangled him.

Le Fere told him so, having sent for him by a footman in a blue livery to Somerset House in the walk under the dial. 'Twas done in hopes the examinations he had taken would never come to light.

Obj. The King. The parties were still alive to give the informations.

Resp. In hopes the second informations taken from the parties would not have agreed with the first, and so the thing would have been disproved and made it not be believed. For this reason the Lord Bellasis advised it. Coleman and my Lord Bellasis advised to destroy him.

The informant was born at Chepstow, bred up an indifferent scholar. His friends all protestant since the world began. Went into the Prince of Orange's army, where finding the religious houses kind and obliging, he hearkened to their arguments, etc., and so was persuaded.

Was never an officer in the Prince of Orange's army. Was designed to be lieutenant to Vaudepert, a captain. Employed some time to make levies in England from Holland, etc.

My Lord Bellasis' gentleman is he that waits on him in his chamber, and none other dresses him but he. Middle stature. Little whiskers like a Frenchman.

The Trappan. They persuaded Godfrey that if he would go a little way into the Strand they would make out a great discovery to him. He called a constable and appointed him to meet him at Strand bridge with power, in the interim of which they persuaded him, Godfrey, to walk into Somerset House, where walking with two of them, the Lord Bellasis' gentleman and a certain Jesuit whom he knows not, others came and with gloves stopped his mouth and hurried him into the room.

The Informant escaped yesterday fortnight by the coach from the Talbot in the Strand to Bristol. Coming to Bristol sent for his mother, and upon her blessing she charged him to discover whatever he knew. Will take his oath and the Sacrament of all this. Has had racks of all this for a year in his conscience. Would have gotten from them three months ago when the king was at Windsor, they about the time whispering something, but not so as to let him know it.

Conyers is a Jesuit, and Pridgeot, and Lewis. Sir John Warner was in the Plot. Le Fere, Keimes, Welsh, Lewis, Pridgeot.

Keimes is in the north of Scotland or beyond the sea. Went two months ago into the north; was with Le Fere the night before. He went to Ernham to Mr. Thimbleby and so northwards.

Mr. Welsh, the chapel-keeper, Le Fere, my Lord Bellasis' servant, strangled him.

The Chapel keeper carried him off. They carried him off in a chair about Piccadilly and so on to the fields.

He did not see him after he was dead.

Le Fere sent to him by a foot-boy immediately afterwards to tell him of it.

Wintour told him two years ago that if he would keep private so great a design, he should be governour to Chepstow Castle, etc. My Lord of Worcester has kept a very ingenious gunsmith, one David Winkett, in his house for many years to make arms. Mr. Charles Price, steward to my Lord of Worcester, took them off from time to time and disposed of them to my Lord Powis. Mr. Christall, my Lord Powis' servant, told him my lord had the finest arms of that man's making, etc. Mr. Jones, a sugar baker on College Hill, can tell where his the informant's brother is. His brother was with him in Spain, and wondered how he could live as he did.

Le Fere.
Lord Bellasis' gentleman.
The usher of the Queen's chapel, etc.

LORDS JOURNALS xiii. 343

Bedloe's statement at the bar of the House of Lords. Die Veneris 8 die Novembris.

The Lord Treasurer reported by his Majesty's directions, "That yesterday one William Bedlowe was examined at Whitehall concerning the discovery of the murder of Sir Edmond Bury Godfrey, and that his Majesty had given order he should be brought to give this house an account thereof."

Who being brought to the Bar and had his oath given him, made a large narrative to this effect.

"That he was born in Monmouthshire and was of the Church of England till within these two years, that by Persuasion and Promises from the Jesuits he was drawn over to them: that he is not in orders. He knows that Sir E. B. Godfrey was murdered in Somerset House, on the Saturday, by Charles Walsh and—Le Fere Jesuits, and two laymen, one a gentleman that waits on the Lord Bellasis, the other an underwaiter in the Queen's Chapel. That he saw the body of Sir E. B. Godfrey, after he was murdered, before he was carried out, and Le Fere told him 'He was stifled between two pillows,' and he was offered 2000 guineas to be one of the three to carry out the body, which was kept either in the room or the next where the D. of Albemarle lay in state: That the Chairmen who carried out the body on Monday night at nine of the clock are retainers to Somerset House; but he knows them not."

He saith "That Walsh and Le Fere and Pritchard told him 'that the Lord Bellasis employed them in this business.'"

He said further "That Walsh and Le Fere informed him 'That the Lord Bellasis had a commission to command Forces in the North, the Earl of Powis in S. Wales, and the Lord Arundell of Warder had a commission from the Pope to grant commissions to whom he pleased': That Coleman had been a great agitator in the design against the King; And that he, asking the Jesuits 'Why they had not formerly told him what they had designed concerning the king's death?' they answered him 'That none but whom the Lord Bellasis gave directions for were to know of it.' He desired he might have time to put the whole narrative into writing (which he had begun).

"And being asked if he knew Titus Oates, he denied it."

P.R.O. S.P. DOM. CHARLES II 408: ii. 47

Prance's examination before the Council. The notes are in Sir Joseph Williamson's handwriting. Dec. 24, 78. Prance called in, etc.

On a certain Monday—with a twisted handkerchief—in the corner near the stables. Carried him into a house in the dark entry, leading up out of the lower court into the upper. Left at that house where Hill lived then, two days, in the dark entry—by the water-gate. There Hill and Gerald and the cushion-man (Green) carried him away. About ten Hill told this informant to go to the other side of the house. Green told him that he thought he had broke his neck before he was carried into Hill's house. After that, 4 days after. Hill carried him and shewed him the place where he lay with a dark lanthorn about 9 o'clock—and Hill brought him back to his house. Green and Gerald were there—and not having conveniency for keeping him in his own house, conveyed him into another house on the other side.—Hill procured a sedan, and had him carried in a sedan from Hill's out at the end gate of the upper court. This was Wednesday night.—Was carried as far as the Greyhound in the Soho. He was one that carried him. Green and Gerald and Irishman who lay over the stables in certain lodgings that Green has there.—From Hill's house first he was carried somewhere to the other side of the house, towards the garden, and Hill met them about the new church with a horse, and he was set upon that horse and carried away, and the sedan was left in one of the new houses when they came back. He came back to his house, and Hill went with the body. Green, Gerald, and the Irishman went also with the body.—Gerald said to him that my Lord Bellasis engaged them to the thing, and said there would be a reward, not yet. Does not know my Lord Bellasis.—Killed him because he loved not the Queen or her servants, therefore Green and Hill, etc.—One Owen in Bloomsbury was in the shop where he changed £100.—Two or three went to his house to ask after him, the maid answered he was not within, etc. They found him out and dogged him, till he came over against the water-gate, came from St. Clement's, about 9 o'clock, etc. Hill, etc., dogged him. He was not there.—Two feigned a quarrel in the gate, and he was called in to appease the quarrel.—He knew Gerald a year and a half. Hill upon five years. Green about a year, etc.—Hill was without and prayed Godfrey to walk in to quiet the quarrel. He walks within the gate (?) and the upper Court.—Knows not if any guard at the gate. Knows not if any company. About 9 at night—He was strangled in the upper court on the stable side in a corner that is railed (?). He struggled. Carried in at the water-gate.—He had the £100 in gold from Owens in Bloomsbury. Being to go out of town as a papist he got this informant to get it for him. It was nothing to this ... [a line very indistinct]. He stood at the water-gate while he was strangled. Bury the porter stood the other way, he watched also there.—Hill dwells in Stanhope Street, keeps a victualling house.

As to the Plot. Was in Ireland's chamber. Groves, Fenwick were there. Ireland said there would be 50ᵐ men in arms. So Fenwick. Two or three days after Groves came to his house to buy two swords.—Said my Lords Powis, Bellasis, Peters, Arundell should become councillors.—That Bellasis, Powis, Arundell were to govern the army.... [Some words indistinct].

One Le Fere came to his shop to ask for a silver sword hilt. Knows not who he is more than that he is.—Knows not Walsh, Pritchard, nor Le Fere not by the names.—50^m men.—They hoped Cath. Rel. would be established in a little time, etc.—Heard nothing of the killing of the King, etc.—Godfrey was kept from the time of his being killed in a sitting posture, etc.—One Mr. Moore, servant to the D. of Norfolk, being on a great horse, etc., would we had 10^m of them, etc.—His ill-will to Godfrey (that the Queen could not protect her servants)—Knows nothing of the plot nor of any person in it.—That one—a Messenger belonging to Lord Arundell said—He hoped the R. C. Rel. would before long flourish in England.

Has declared everything he knows, everything, etc.—Green, Hill, etc., said Godfrey had used some Irishman ill—Owen knows nothing of all this that he learns (?).—Saw Ireland last at Will's coffee house in Covent Garden and Dr. Southwell were drinking with him in his own house the night before Pickering was taken, etc.

APPENDIX C

LONGLEAT MSS. COVENTRY PAPERS xi. 148

Lord Windsor to Henry Coventry. July 8, 1676.

I was yesterday at the trial of Studesbury of Broadly at Worcester assizes, where Judge Atkyns sat upon the bench. The treason was fully proved against him according to that information I did send you. The judge took occasion by advice of those justices which were upon the bench to make the trial long, the better to discover whether he were distracted or not: upon the whole examination and by the answers he made to the many questions that were asked him, it was the opinion of all that sat upon the bench (which were many) that he was very sensible and in no way mad, but in justifying Venner's action and holding the worst of the fanatic opinions, and often using their ranting way of talking; he said he held a halberd at the trial of the late King, and repeated some of his words with Bradshaw's answers to them, and said the putting of Venner and his associates to death was murder. The chief witness against him (besides his own confession) was one Harrington, an anabaptist mentioned in the first examination, which Harrington being asked if he did judge Studesbury mad upon the first discourse he had with him (which held near an hour) when he would have advised him to take arms against the King, he declared he found nothing of that mind in him, but thought he designed to ensnare him; yet notwithstanding all this the jury found him a madman. Upon that the judge told them that he and all that sat with him were of a contrary opinion and desired them to withdraw and consider better of't, which they did do and came in again of the same opinion, one of them saying that if he were not mad he would not have said what he did.

BRIT. MUS. ADD. MSS. 28042: 19

Memorandum by the Marquis of Danby. (Endorsed) Mem^d (7–8/9.)

To put forth a declaration. To examine the present state of the revenue: to consider about stop of payment and when: what is yet to come in upon the accounts and at what times: To know what is due to the ships abroad: at what times those ships are expected: in what state the victualling is. In what hands the militia; the justices of the peace: the judges. When the dissolution ought to be: what preparation for a new Parliament and when: About the sheriffs: the next Lord Mayor: the Cinque Ports: the Port towns by the commissioners of the customs, of treasury, of Navy: who have a particular interest in Borrows. To consider what grateful things may be done in this interval of Parliament: what should be said in the declaration upon the dissolution: for these qᵉ Sir R. W. (Weston) and let the journals of the Commons be searched for their proceedings in this last session: To consider wherein they have exceeded all the due limits of their own power as in imprisonment of men who are not their members, etc., and meddling with the King's prerogatives and private accounts, etc.: To keep Lord Roberts by some encouragement: About another Attorney-General, viz.: Sir R. W. (Weston) (which is of main importance): what change of Councillors. In what condition all the garrisons are as to their fortifications: what number of forces and where placed after the disbanding: to inquire into the riots at the last elections. How conventicles should be inquired after, and what penal laws should be put in execution: who to be in the Treasury and in the treasury of the Navy: what can be done for the suppressing of seditious prints and papers: About directing somebody to write both about the present state of things to give the world a better impression of them than they are now possessed with and to give constant weekly accounts of what is done at any time which may be for the satisfaction of men's minds. Q. Whether the Plot not triable out of Parliament. Q. About securing the arms of all who have been officers in the late Rebellion. To take their names and abodes in all counties. Q; how for to take notice of them and dissenters from the Church how busy they have appeared of late and what reasonable cause of danger to the government from them. Parliament to be called to some other place: the King to reside out of London: Tower to be well secured: Lᵈ Ossory sent to the Navy: that to be officered so as to have influence upon their men: To have a control to know justly when the army is all disbanded and whether there be any remains. About the Tower in case of insurrection: To take some course about the reasons of the Commons which are printed, (?) to suppress them and to have something writ to satisfy the people.

BRIT. MUS. ADD. MSS. 32095; 196

(Paper endorsed) Popish Plot. This paper was presented to the King by the D. of York, Oct. 20ᵗʰ 1679.

That in or about May or June last Col. Fitzpatrick delivered to the Pope's internuncio at Brussels a letter or paper subscribed by four R. C. bishops, two of which were Plunket archbp. of Armagh, and Tyrel bp. of Clogher, recommending the said Fitzpatrick for the only person fit to be entrusted general of an army for establishing the R. C. religion in Ireland under the French sovereignty, which paper after coming to the internuncio's hands was seen by several clergy and laymen, known to Father Daly, procurator, F. O'Neill, commissary. F. Macshone, guardian of the Irish Franciscans, and F. Macmahone alias Matthews, Prior of the Dominicans in Lovain, among whom 'tis also said that Fitzpatrick carried such another instrument into France, where he first arrived from Ireland and whence he went into Flanders, where he resolved to settle at Brussels. But he was forced to remove thence by his R.H. commands, which he obeyed not without much regret and murmuring.

P.R.O. ROMAN TRANSCRIPTS. VAT. ARCH. NUNT. DI FIANDRA 66

Di Brusselles dal Sig.^r Internuncio, May 24/June 3, 1679.

In Ibernia, dove il numero de' Cattolici è molto maggiore che quello de' Protestanti, ha gran seguito e autorità il Colonello Fitzpatrice, onde il Duca d'Jorch a mostrato haverlo veduto malvolontieri venire à Brusselles, per dubbio che il Parlamento pigliando gelosia del ricorso di lui à S. A. Reale prenda motivo di maggiormente inasprirsi contro la medesima, contro di essa, e contro il Duca d'Ormond. N'è perciò egli partito per Olanda à titolo di veder quel paese, ma precedentemente ha tenuta una segreta conferenza col Sig.^r Duca d'Jorch, dopo la quale mi ha lasciato intendere soffrirsi troppo patientemente da S. A. Reale l'audacia de' Parlamentarii, e doversi di gia pensare almeno à modi di respingerla quando la temerità loro e la debolezza del Rè d'Inghilterra passasse à porre in esecutione il projetto della sua diseredatione. Toccante l'Ibernia ha detto chiaramente essere insofferibile il giogo sotto l'oppressione del quale gemono quei Cattolici, e ha aggiunto che apprendendosi per massima naturale il difendersi in qualsivoglia maniera, non dubita egli che non fussero per commoversi tutti concordemente, non solo se il Sig.^r Duca d'Jorch ma se qualunque barbaro Principe con qualque denaro, e con assistenza di pochi vascelli si accostasse alle spiaggie dell' Isola, e portasse armi e munitioni da guerra à quelli habitanti.

APPENDIX D

"THE trial of John Giles at the Old Bailey, for assaulting and attempting to murder John Arnold, Esq.," is a case which presents some difficulty.[770]

Arnold's character for activity against the Roman Catholics has already been mentioned. The way in which this trial is regarded materially affects the answer to the question whether or no he exceeded the legitimate bounds of his magisterial duty. If Giles was rightly convicted, the excess was not great; if wrongly and the attempt on Arnold's life was a sham, not only did Arnold lend himself to a criminal and most disreputable intrigue, but all his other actions must be more severely judged. The case was as follows. Arnold had accused Mr. Herbert, a Roman Catholic gentleman of Staffordshire, of speaking seditious words against the king and government.[771] They were both ordered to appear before the privy council on April 16, 1680.[772] On the day before that date it was alleged that Giles, who was a friend of Herbert,[773] attempted to murder Captain Arnold. For this Giles was tried on July 7, before Jeffreys, the Recorder of London, and convicted after what seemed to be a singularly fair trial. The case for the prosecution was that, as Arnold was going between ten and eleven o'clock on the night of April 15 to see his solicitor, he was assaulted in Bell-yard, Fleet Street, by the accused and one or two other persons, and but for the appearance of the neighbours would have been murdered. Giles had spoken disrespectfully of the Plot and the Protestant religion, had been seen to dip handkerchiefs in the blood of the Jesuit Lewis who was executed the year before at Usk,[774] and was supposed to have attacked Arnold in revenge for the part he had played in the capture of Evans. Arnold himself gave evidence of the fact. He swore that he had been dogged by two or three men into Bell-yard. One of these went by him and then stood still while the magistrate passed. By the light of a candle which a woman was holding at the door of a neighbouring house Arnold saw the man whom he afterwards recognised to be the prisoner. As he crossed a lane which ran into the yard, a cloak was thrown over his head and he was knocked down into the gutter, though not before he had time to draw his sword. As he lay on the ground the men stabbed at him with their swords. He was cut in the face, the arm, and the stomach, but the men were unable to pierce the bodice of whalebone which he wore under his coat. One of them cried, "Damme, he has armour on; cut his throat." A light in Sir Timothy Baldwin's house, hard by, and a boy coming into the yard with a link disturbed the murderers and they made off. As the cloak was pulled from his head, Arnold again recognised the prisoner by the light of the link.

The men swaggered away and one turned back to call, "Now, you dog, pray for, or pray again for the soul of Captain Evans."[775]

The evidence called to support and to oppose this was very contradictory. It was sworn that, talking about the affray at a tavern next day, Giles said, "God damn him, God rot him, he had armour on"; but the witness admitted that he might have said, "God rot him, he had armour on, they say."[776] The prisoner declared that he merely told it as a common piece of news that Arnold would have been killed had he not worn armour, and called a witness who affirmed that this was so, that Giles had called the attempt "a cruel assassination" of which he was sorry to hear, and had made use of no oaths at all.[777] Evidence was given for the crown that Giles had hurried through Usk on May 5, saying that he was afraid of being arrested for the assault on Arnold, and at a cutler's shop where he went to have a sword mended said he had been fighting "with damned Arnold."[778] This was contradicted by the Mayor of Monmouth, who proved that Giles had not hurried through Usk, but stayed there several hours; and by the cutler's apprentice, who proved that when the prisoner was asked, "How came your sword broke? Have you been fighting with the devil?" so far from speaking the words alleged, he had answered, "No, for I never met with Arnold."[779] A great deal of evidence was given concerning the prisoner's movements on the night of April 15. He had passed the evening in company at various taverns, and had finally gone to sleep at the King's Arms in St. Martin's Lane; but as the witnesses arrived at the times o'clock to which they deposed by guess-work alone, their evidence was naturally contradictory; and it seems now quite impossible to know certainly whether Giles was, as the prosecution contended, seen last at ten o'clock and did not go to bed till one in the morning, or, as the witnesses for the defence stated, had been in company till the hour of eleven or twelve.[780] According to the evidence therefore, which Jeffreys summed up at length and with moderation,[781] it was open to the jury to find either for or against the prisoner, and after deliberating for half an hour they returned a verdict of guilty. Giles was sentenced to the fine of £500 and to be pilloried three times. On July 26 he was pilloried in Lincoln's Inn Fields and was pelted so severely that his life was in danger; and when the remainder of the sentence was carried out in Holborn and the Strand, he had to be protected from the mob by a guard of constables and watchmen.[782]

The real case against Arnold and in favour of the prisoner did not come into court. Sir Leoline Jenkins, secretary of state, employed an agent to draw up a report on the subject. The report was confined entirely to the assault itself and did not discuss the movements of either Arnold or Giles before or afterwards. It is notable that Arnold himself was the only witness as to the manner of the attack and the incidents connected with it, and that the important part of his evidence was wholly uncorroborated. Although he wished to deny the fact, he was well acquainted with Giles, who had been his chief constable, and probably knew enough of his movements to lay a false charge against him without running too great a risk of detection.[783] Jenkins' information throws a curious light upon his evidence. It does not afford proof that Arnold lent himself to a bogus attempt on his life, but it raises strong suspicion that this was the case. There was no motive for the reporter not to tell the truth in points of fact. His deductions are lucid and apparently sound. The government probably refrained from bringing forward the new material owing to the intense opposition which the effort to obtain Giles' acquittal would have raised. I quote the most important portion of the minute at length from the S.P. Dom. Charles II 414: 245. The paper is undated, but from internal evidence is seen to have been composed before the trial. It is without title, but is endorsed by Jenkins: "Mr. Arnold and about his being assassinated."[784]

"1. Mr. Arnold was found near two at night April 15th, 1680 sitting in the dirt, wounded, leaning his head against the wall, some four yards within Jackanapes Lane, and immediately upon crying out, Murther.

"2. Quaere:—the manner of the assault. When and where he received his wounds; whether before his crying out or just at the time: what words passed on the one side and on the other, and concerning their going away laughing and triumphing.

"3. He was struck down, muffled in a cloak, and they stamped upon his breast; and yet he was found with a white hat on his head, no dirt upon it, and his clothes only dirty where he sat; though the land was fouler at that time than ordinary.

"4. Two pricks in his arm, the one so just against the other, that it seemed to be one wound; and yet hard to imagine how it should pass, for the bone.

"5. Upon his crying out, a woman held a candle from a window just over him, and two of the neighbours' servants went immediately to him; but neither could see nor hear of anybody near him.

"6. If wounded before he cried out, 'tis a wonder that one of these boys should not hear either the blows or the scuffle; especially standing within 6 or 7 yards of him in the street, and having a duskish view of his body so long before he cried out, till upon his knocking at the door of the Sugar-loaf for drink, a servant of the house came downstairs, took his errand, went down for drink and came up again, in the meantime.

"7. Or if before this boy knocked, 'tis a wonder that upon that knocking he did not immediately cry out for succour, hearing people within distance of relieving him.

"8. If he was stunded when they left him, how could he take notice of what they said, and that they went laughing and triumphing away? Beside the danger of being heard into Sir Timothy Baldwin's house, on the one side, and Mrs. Camden's on the other, that looked just on to the place.

"9. If he could not be heard to cry out because he was muffled, how should he hear what the ruffians said? For they durst not speak so loud as he might cry; neither with a cloak over him could they well come at his throat.

"10. If they meant to kill him, they might have stabbed the knife into his throat; as well as have cut him; or having him down they might well have thrust him into his belly when they found the sword would not enter his bodice.

"11. There was no blood seen upon the ground neither where he lay, or thereabouts."

The balance of probability seems to be undoubtedly that no attempt whatever was made on Arnold's life, and that he deliberately engaged in a worse than dishonest scheme to inflame popular prejudice against the Catholics.

This result supports the evidence received from other quarters. The opinion at court and of the king himself was that the attack on Arnold was a part of the Whig political machinery. Barillon, writing on April 26/May 6, 1680, says:—"Ce prince (Charles II) n'est sans inquiétude, il voit bien par ce qu'il s'est fait sur le prétendu assassinat de Arnold que ses ennemis ne se rebuttent pas et qu'ils veulent de temps à temps faire renaître quelque occasion d'animer le peuple contre les Catholiques."

In his manuscript history of the Plot (118) Warner gives the following account of the affair: "Supra dictum nihil magis commovisse plebem quam Godefridae eirenarchae caedes. Tentandam alterius caedem visum, eundem ad finem et aptus visus Arnoldus personam in ista tragicomica fabula sustineret, et Londini ... qui tum versabatur. Omnibus ad eam exhibendam paratis, designata hora ix vespertina, nocte illumi. Cum ergo biberet cum sociis in taberna publica, monitus a famulo instare tempus, quod ad causidicum condixerat, se statim inde proripit et conjicit in obscurissimam angiportum, destinatam scenam. Illic magnis clamoribus civium opem implorat; a papistis sibi structas insidias, sicarios ibi expectasse, jugulum haurire voluisse, sed errante ictu mentum vulnerasse; eos fuga elapsos, ubi cives convenire vidissent; eorum neminem sibi notum sed unum in tibia laesum; hunc ex vulnere, reliquos ejus indicio comprehendi posse. Hoc xix Aprilis contigit. Hinc tragice debacchant in Catholicos factiosi, Oate praeeunte: legum beneficio juste privari qui leges susque deque haberent; gladio utendum in publicos sicarios, internecione delendos, ut ne catulus quidem reliquatur; averruncandam semel pestem omnium vitae imminentem. Inventae una nocte omnes Catholicorum domus cruce cretacea signatae, percussoribus indiciae, ubi hospitarentur. Nihil deesse visum quam qui signum daret: hoc saluti fuit Catholicis sub cruce militantibus, cruce signatis. Brevi motus ipsi subsiderunt, dum constitit leniter tantum perstrictam cutem; nec constare a se, an ab alio id factum; nemo vero Catholicus erat, in quem facinoris invidia derivaretur. Testati chirurgi neminem in tota civitate vulnus in tibia habere. Unus tandem inventus in familia Powisii qui attritam lapsu tibiam oleo lenibat. Hic tentatae caedis arcessitur coram consilio regio inde ad Arnoldum deducitur. Sed cum hic eum non accusaret, et ipse probaret se navem conscendisse Brillae xix Aprilis (id est, eodem die quo tentatum facinus) et tantum tertio post die Londinum appulisse, et ipse demissus est, et Arnoldi fictae querimoniae cum risu transmissae."

Strangely enough, Warner seems to have known nothing about the arrest and trial of Giles. Sir James Fitzjames Stephen, judging from the report of the trial, regards the attempt to murder Arnold as an act of revenge for the magistrate's energy against the Roman Catholics, and quotes it in support of Macaulay's suggestion that Sir Edmund Godfrey was murdered by some Catholic zealot for a similar motive.[785] In the face of the probability that no real attack was made on Arnold, this support falls to the ground. It is far more likely that the rumours at court that Oates had murdered Godfrey to gain credit for the plot suggested to Arnold or his wire-pullers the method of continuing the credit of the Whig party by the shameful means of a bogus attempt on his own life.

APPENDIX E

1#1. *Eliz. cap.* 1 (Act of Supremacy), 1559.

No foreign potentate shall exercise ecclesiastical power in the Queen's dominions.

All the Queen's servants, all temporal and eccles. officers, all with degrees in the universities shall take the oath of supremacy.

None shall maintain the jurisdiction of any foreign potentate in the Queen's dominions under penalty of fine and imprisonment for the first offence, for the second of Præmunire (*i.e.* to be put out of the King's protection and forfeit all goods and chattels to the crown), for the third of high treason.

5#2. *Eliz. cap.* 1, 1562.

None shall maintain the jurisdiction of the Bishop of Rome within the Queen's dominions under penalty of Præmunire.

Two judges of assize or justices of the peace in sessions have power to hear and determine this offence.

All members of Parliament, schoolmasters, attorneys, officers of the courts, etc., shall take the oath of supremacy on penalty of Præmunire for the first and high treason for the second offence of refusal.

13#3. *Eliz. cap.* 1, 1571.

All obtaining or putting in use any Bull of absolution or reconciliation from the church of Rome shall be guilty of high treason, their concealers of misprision of treason, their comforters of Præmunire. All bringing into the Queen's dominions crosses, beads, etc., shall be guilty of Præmunire.

23#4. *Eliz. cap.* 1, 1581.

All persons pretending to have power to absolve the Queen's subjects from their natural obedience and converting them to the church of Rome shall be guilty of high treason, and their aiders and maintainers of misprision of treason. None shall say mass under penalty of two hundred marks' fine and a year's imprisonment, or hear mass under penalty of one hundred marks' fine and a year's imprisonment.

Every person above sixteen years of age who forbears to attend church regularly (according to the Act of Uniformity 1 Eliz. c. 2 § 3) shall forfeit to the Queen the sum of £20 monthly.

27#5. *Eliz. cap.* 2, 1584.

All Jesuits, seminary priests, or priests in orders from the see of Rome, being born within the Queen's dominions and returning into or remaining in them, shall be guilty of high treason.

All others educated in Roman Catholic seminaries and not yet having received orders shall be guilty of high treason, unless they return within six months after proclamation made in London and take the oath of supremacy. Penalty for concealing a priest or Jesuit for more than twelve days, fine and imprisonment during pleasure.

29#6. *Eliz. cap.* 9, 1587.

All Popish recusants shall, on conviction, pay into the exchequer twenty pounds a month: in default, two-thirds of their goods and two-thirds of their lands shall be forfeited to the Queen.

35#7. *Eliz. cap.* 2, 1592.

All Popish recusants above sixteen years of age shall, on conviction, repair to their usual dwellings and not remove thence more than five miles, on pain of forfeiting all goods, lands, and annuities.

A Popish recusant, not having land worth twenty marks and goods worth forty pounds yearly, and not complying with this, shall abjure the kingdom, or not abjuring the kingdom, shall be adjudged a felon.

A Jesuit or priest refusing to answer shall be committed to prison until he do answer.

All married women shall be bound by this act, save only in the case of abjuration.

1#8. *Jac. I, cap.* 4, 1603.

All statutes of Queen Elizabeth confirmed and appointed to be put in execution. The heir of a Popish ancestor, not conforming before the age of sixteen years, shall suffer the penalties of the above statutes and forfeit two-thirds of his land to the King to answer the arrears of twenty pounds a month, according to the act of 23 Eliz. cap. 1.

None shall send a child beyond seas to be instructed in the Roman Catholic religion, on pain of the fine of one hundred pounds.

3#9. *Jac. I, cap.* 4, 1606.

The recusant that conforms shall receive the sacrament within one year of his conforming and once in every year, on pain to forfeit for the first offence twenty pounds, for the second forty, and so on. In forementioned cases the King may at will refuse the twenty pounds a month from a Popish recusant and take the two-thirds of his lands, saving only the recusant's mansion-house.

The Bishop of the diocese or the justices of the peace may tender the oath of allegiance to any persons (except noblemen), being eighteen years of age and being convicted or indicted for recusancy.

Penalty for refusal to take the oath, Præmunire.

To withdraw the King's subjects from their natural obedience, to reconcile them to the church of Rome, or to move them to promise it, is high treason.

None shall be punished for his wife's offence.

3#10. *Jac. I, cap.* 5, 1606.

Informers discovering any harbouring Popish priests or hearing mass shall have a third of the forfeiture due for the said offences, or if the whole exceeds £150, then £50.

No Popish recusant shall come to court on pain of the fine of a hundred pounds, or to London or within ten miles of it, unless a tradesman, on pain of the same fine, half to the King, half to the informer.

No Popish recusant shall practise law, medicine, or hold office in any court, ship, castle, or fort on pain of the same fine.

None whose wife is such shall hold any office in the commonwealth unless he educates his children as Protestants and takes them to church.

A married woman, being a Popish recusant, must conform a year before her husband's death, or forfeit two-thirds of her jointure and be incapable of administering her husband's estate.

Popish recusants must be married in open church by an Anglican minister, and must cause their children to be similarly baptised on pain of the fine of one hundred pounds, to be divided between the King, the prosecutor, and in the latter case the poor of the parish.

Popish recusants must be buried in the Anglican churchyard, on pain of a fine of twenty pounds from the executors.

Popish recusants are disabled from presenting to benefices, and from being executors, administrators, or guardians.

Two justices of the peace have power to search the houses of all Popish recusants, and of all whose wives are such, for Roman Catholic books and relics, to burn and deface them.

By warrant from four justices all arms, gunpowder, and ammunition belonging to Popish recusants may be seized.

7#11. *Jac. I, cap.* 6, 1609.

Popish recusants may be required by justices of the peace (or if barons and baronesses by three privy councillors) to take the oath of allegiance. Penalty for refusing, Præmunire and imprisonment until the oath is taken. Those refusing shall be incapable of holding any office and of practising law, medicine, surgery, or any liberal science for gain.

A married woman, being a Popish recusant, and not conforming within three months after conviction, may be imprisoned by warrant of two justices of the peace (or if a baroness, of a privy councillor or bishop) until she conform, unless the husband pay £10 monthly, or forfeit a third of all his lands.

3#12. *Car. I, cap.* 2, 1627.

None of the King's subjects shall go, or send, or cause to be sent any one to be trained beyond seas in the Roman Catholic religion, or pay any money for the maintenance of others for that purpose, on pain of forfeiting all his goods, lands, and chattels, and being disabled from prosecuting any suit at law.

16#13. *Car. II, cap.* 4, 1664. (The Conventicle Act, directed against all Nonconformists.)

All meetings, other than those of the family, of more than five persons declared to be unlawful and seditious conventicles.

Penalty for first offence, a fine of £5 or imprisonment for 3 months; for second, a fine of £10 or imprisonment for 6 months; for third, transportation for 7 years, or a fine of £100.

17#14. *Car. II, cap.* 2, 1665. (The Five Mile Act, directed against all Nonconformists.)

No person preaching in an unlawful conventicle or meeting to approach within 5 miles of any corporation sending members to

Parliament, without having taken an oath "that it is not lawful upon any pretence whatsoever to take arms against the King."

No such person shall teach in any public or private school.

Penalty for not complying, a fine of £40.

25#15. *Car. II, cap.* 2, 1673.

All persons holding office, civil or military, or having command, or receiving pay in whatever capacity in the service or household of the King or the Duke of York, shall before a specified date appear in the court of Chancery or King's Bench or of their respective counties openly to take the oaths of allegiance and supremacy.

And the said officers shall receive the sacrament of the Lord's Supper according to the usage of the church of England on or before August 1, 1673 in some parish church upon some Lord's Day.

Penalty for refusing to take the oaths, incapacity to hold any office or position of trust either civil or military, and for executing office after refusal, incapacity to prosecute any suit at law and fine of £500.

30#16. *Car. II, cap.* 1, 1678.

No peer or member of the House of Commons shall sit or vote until he has taken the oaths of allegiance and supremacy and subscribed to a declaration that the worship of the church of Rome is idolatrous.

Penalty for peers and members offending, disability to hold office and a fine of £500.

Provided that this does not extend to the Duke of York.

MATERIALS FOR THE HISTORY OF THE POPISH PLOT

1. *Manuscripts.*

Public Record Office.

> State Papers Domestic, Charles II 407–416. The state papers of the period have not been calendared and are preserved in loose bundles, some of which are ill arranged. Thus in referring to the S.P. Dom. Charles II 407, I have been compelled to add *e.g.* i. 285, ii. 23, as there are two sets of papers in the bundle bearing the same numbers.
>
> State Papers, Ireland 339.
>
> Transcripts from Paris: dispatches of the French ambassadors.
>
> Transcripts from the Vatican archives in Rome.

British Museum.

> Additional MSS.: 11,058, 17,018, 24,136, 28,042, 28,053, 28,054, 28,093, 34,195.
>
> Harl. MSS.: 3790, 4888, 6284.
>
> Land. MSS.: 1235.
>
> Stowe MSS.: 144, 180, 186, 302.

Longleat.

> MSS. belonging to the Marquis of Bath. Coventry Papers xi. xx. lx. By the generous permission of the Marquis of Bath and the courtesy of the authorities at the British Museum I have been enabled to use these important papers (of which an unsatisfactory account will be found in the appendix to the 4th report of the Hist. MSS. Com.) in the Manuscript department of the Museum. I am greatly indebted to Mr. S. Arthur Strong, librarian of the House of Lords, for his kind offices in obtaining access to the papers for me.

> I have also to express my thanks to Mr. Warner and Mr. Bickley of the British Museum, and to Mr. Hubert Hall and Mr. Salisbury of the Record Office for much kind help and courtesy shewn to me during my work in their departments. The manuscripts in the Vatican archives of which I have made use were copied for me by Mr. Bliss,

who most generously interrupted his other work to make the transcripts.

Cambridge University Library: "Persecutionis Anglicanae et Conjurationis Presbiterianae Historia." Autore P. Warner, S.J., Regi Jacobo II^do a sacris. 181 pp. fol. Letter-book of John Warner, S.J.

> These manuscripts, of which the former is the more important, have, I believe, never been used before. They were seen by Henry Foley, compiler of the Records of the English Province, S.J., but do not appear to have been used by him. A notice of them is so deeply buried in his laborious and unordered work (v. 289) that it has escaped the notice of the author of Warner's life in the *Dictionary of National Biography*. Foley left inside the cover of Warner's *History* a note, which I quote below. Few are likely to agree with him that it is "probably the best, the fullest, and the most truthful ever recorded." The account of the Jesuit father is naturally prejudiced in favour of his society and partakes of the nature of a martyrology. There are nevertheless points of considerable interest contained in it. The euphuistic style of Warner's writing marks him as a man of learning and culture.

Note by Henry Foley. 13 Nov. 1876.

> "The original draft of this valuable MS. in the hand of the Rev. Father John Warner, S.J., is in the British Museum, Harlean MSS. 880.
>
> "It is closely written, divided into 8 chapters—f.c. 4to . The writing is so bad that it is difficult to make it out.
>
> "Father Warner succeeded Father Thomas Whitbread, who suffered at Tyburn 30 June 1679, as Provincial of the English Province, S.J., and remained in that office for three years.
>
> "In 1686 he was appointed confessor to King James II. He died at the court of St. Germains the 2nd of Nov. 1692, aet. 64. He was a very learned man and wrote several controversial works.
>
> "HENRY FOLEY.
>
>
> "The history of these terrible times is probably the best, fullest, and most truthful ever recorded. The learned author was upon the spot and had his own personal share in the sufferings.
>
> "The facts recorded are fully borne out by the *Litterae Annuae, Prov. Angl. S.J.* of the time, and likewise by contemporary writers. *Vide* Echard, *Hist. Engl.*, etc.

"One new fact is ascertained—that the meeting of the Fathers in London (upon the affairs of their body) was not held, as sworn by Oates and his associates, at the White Horse Tavern, Strand, but at St. James' Palace, the residence of the Duke of York. The Fathers who were tried and suffered death could have proved this upon the trial, but were silent, preferring death to the danger of compromising the Duke."

2. *Printed Documents and Sources.*

Historical Manuscripts Commission: appendices to 1st Report (Lefroy MSS.); 4th Report (Bath MSS.); 7th Report, Part II. (Verney MSS.); 11th Report, Part II. (House of Lords MSS. 1678–1688); 11th Report, Part V. (Dartmouth MSS.); 12th Report, Part VII. (Le Fleming MSS.); 12th Report, Part IX. (Beaufort MSS.); 14th Report, Part VI. (Fitzherbert MSS.); 14th Report, Part IX. (Lindsey MSS.); 15th Report, Part II. (Elliot Hodgkin MSS.); 15th Report, Part V. (Savile Foljambe MSS.).

Ailesbury (Thomas, Earl of): Memoirs. Written by himself. Ed. W. E. Buckley. Roxburgh Club. 1890.

Arnauld (Antoine): Œuvres, 42 tomes. T. xiv. Apologie pour les Catholiques. Paris et Lausanne. 1775–1783.

Avrigny (Hyacinthe Robillard d'), de la campagnie de Jésus: Mémoires pour servir à l'histoire universelle de l'Europe. Paris. 1757.

Anglesey (Earl of): Memoirs. London. 1693.

Bedloe (William): Narrative and Impartial Discovery of the horrid Popish Plot. London. 1679.

Calamy (Edmund): An Historical Account of my own Life. Ed. J. T. Rutt, London. 1829.

Campana de Cavelli (Marquise de): Les Derniers Stuarts à St. Germain en Laye. Paris. 1871.

Clarke (Rev. J. S.): Life of King James the Second. London. 1816.

Dalrymple (Sir John): Memoirs of Great Britain and Ireland. Edinburgh. 1771.

Danby (Earl of): Impartial State of the Case of the Earl of Danby. London. 1679.

—— Copies and extracts of some letters written to and from the Earl of Danby (now Duke of Leeds) in the years 1676, 1677, and 1678, with some particular remarks upon them. Published by his Grace's direction. London. 1710.

—— Memoirs relating to the Impeachment of Thomas, Earl of Danby (now Duke of Leeds) in the year 1678. London. 1710.

Evelyn (John): Memoirs. London. 1827.

Grey (Hon. A.): Debates of the House of Commons. London. 1769.

Florus Anglo-Bavaricus. Liège. 1685.

Groen van Prinsterer: Archives de la Maison d'Orange Nasau. 2nd série. T. v. Utrecht. 1861.

Hale (Sir Matthew): Historia Placitorum Coronae. London. 1736.

Halstead (Robert): Succintes Genealogies. London. 1685.

Hatton Correspondence. Camden Society. Ed. M. Thompson. 1878.

Journals of the House of Lords.

Journals of the House of Commons.

Jurieu (Pierre): La Politique du Clergé de France. 1681.

L'Estrange (Roger): Brief History of the Times. London. 1687, 1688.

Luttrell (Narcissus): Brief Historical Relation of State Affairs. Oxford. 1857.

Kirkby (Christopher): A Complete and True Narrative of the Manner of the Discovery of the Popish Plot to his Majesty. London. 1679.

North (Roger): Examen, London. 1740.

—— Lives of the Norths. Ed. Jessopp. London. 1890.

Oates (Titus): True Narrative of the Horrid Plot and Conspiracy. London. 1679.

Orléans (Pierre Joseph d'): History of the Revolutions in England under the family of the Stuarts. London. 1722.

Palmer (Roger), Earl of Castlemaine [ascribed to; see Wheatley's note to Pepys' Diary, Dec. 1, 1666]: The Catholique Apology, with a reply to the answer.... By a person of honour. 3rd Edition, much augmented. 1674.

Parliamentary History iv. London. 1808.

Pomponne (Marquis de): Memoires. Ed. Mavidal. Paris. 1860, 1861.

Prance (Miles): True Narrative and Discovery. London. 1679.

Reresby (Sir John): Memoirs. Ed. Cartwright. London. 1875.

Sidney (Algernon): Letters to the Honourable Henry Savile, ambassador in Paris in the year 1679. London. 1742.

Sidney's Charles II. Ed. Blencowe. London. 1843.

Smith (William): Intrigues of the Popish Plot. London. 1685.

Schwerin (O. von): Briefe aus England über die Zeit von 1674 bis 1678. Berlin. 1837.

Secret Service Expenses of Charles II and James II. Camden Society. Ed. J. Y. Akerman. 1851.

Somers Tracts vii. viii. London. 1812.

State Trials 6, 7, 8, 10. Cobbett's Collection. London. 1809.

Treby (Sir George): A collection of letters. London. 1681.

—— The second part of the collection of letters. London. 1681.

Temple (Sir William): Works. Edinburgh. 1754.

Welwood (James): Memoirs. London. 1718.

Wood (Anthony à): Life and Times. Oxford. 1892.

3. *Histories and Biographies, etc.*

Acton (Lord): The Secret History of Charles II. Home and Foreign Review i. 146.

Airy (Osmund): The English Restoration and Louis XIV. London. 1888.

—— Charles II. London. 1901.

Boero (Giuseppe): Istoria della Conversione alla Chiesa Catholica di Carlo II, Rè d'Inghilterra. Roma. 1863.

Brosch (Moritz): Geschichte von England. Gotha. 1892.

Burnet (Gilbert): History of My Own Time. Ed. Airy. Part I. Oxford. 1897, 1900.

Campbell (Lord): Lives of the Lord Chancellors of England. London. 1856–1857.

—— Lives of the Chief Justices of England. London. 1849–1857.

Carte (Thomas): An History of the Life or James, Duke of Ormond. London. 1736.

Chantelauze (Régis de): Le Père de la Chaize. Paris. 1859.

Christie (W. D.): Life of Anthony Ashley Cooper, Earl of Shaftesbury. London. 1871.

Cooke (G. W.): History of Party. London. 1836.

Courtenay (T. P.): Life of Sir William Temple. London. 1836.

Cretineau Joly (J.): Histoire politique, religieuse, et literaire de la compagnie de Jésus. Paris. 1844.

Douglas (R. K.); Article on Titus Oates in Blackwood's Magazine. February. 1889.

Echard (Laurence): History of England. London. 1707.

Foley (Henry): Records of the English Province of the Society of Jesus. London. 1879.

Forneron (H.): Louise de Kéroualle, Duchesse de Portsmouth. Paris. 1886.

Fox (Charles James): History of the Early Part of the Reign of James II. London. 1808.

Foxcroft (H. C.): Life and Letters of Halifax. London. 1898.

Gentleman's Magazine: January 1866. Article on the conversion of Charles II.

—— July 1848. Notes on Sir E. B. Godfrey.

—— September 1849. Notes on the Popish Plot.

Gneist (Rudolf): History of the English Constitution. Trans. Ashworth. London. 1891.

Hallam (Henry): Constitutional History of England. London. 1884.

Hargrave (Francis): Opinion and Argument in support of Lady A. S. Howard's right to the new Barony of Stafford. 1807.

Harris (Dr. William): Historical and Critical Account of the Life of Charles II. London. 1814.

Irving (H. B.): Life of Judge Jeffreys. London. 1898.

Jesse (J. H.): The Court of England under the Stuarts. London. 1855.

Kennet (Dr. White): A Complete History of England. London. 1706.

Klopp (Onno): Der Fall des Hauses Stuart. Wien. 1875–1888.

Lingard (John): History of England. London. 1831.

Macpherson (James): History of Great Britain. London. 1775.

Macaulay (Lord): History of England. London. 1849.

Madden (R. R.): History of the Penal Laws enacted against Roman Catholics. London. 1847.

Oldmixon (John): History of England during the Reigns of the House of Stuart. London. 1730.

Parker (Samuel): History of his Own Time. London. 1727.

Parkinson (Father): The Yorkshire Branch of the Popish Plot. The Month xviii. 393.

Ralph (James): History of England. London. 1736.

Rapin Thoyras (Paul de): Histoire d'Angleterre. La Haye. 1724–1736.

Ranke (L. von): Englische Geschichte. Leipzig. 1877.

Russell (Lord John): Life of William Lord Russell. London. 1853.

Shaw (W. A.): The Beginnings of the National Debt. Owens College, Manchester, Historical Essays. Ed. J. F. Tout and J. Tait. London. 1902.

Sitwell (Sir George Reresby): The First Whig. Privately printed. 1894.

Seccombe (T.): Titus Oates in *Twelve Bad Men*. London. 1894.

Spillmann (Joseph) S. J.: Die Blutzeugen aus den Tagen der Titus Oates-Verschwörung. Freiburg i. B. 1901.

Stephen (Sir J. F.): History of the Criminal Law in England. London. 1883.

Traill (H. D.): Shaftesbury. London. 1888.

Wilson (Walter): Life and Times of Defoe. London. 1830.

FOOTNOTES

1 7 State Trials 128. Evidence of Sir Denny Ashburnham, *ibid.* 1097.

2 Anthony à Wood, *Life and Times* ii. 417. 7 State Trials 1094.

3 Burnet ii. 157.

4 Smith, *Intrigues of the Popish Plot* 4. Oates, *Narrative* 35, 36. It was at this house that Baxter was insulted in 1677 by a Catholic gentleman, who accused him of having been tried at Worcester for the murder of a tinker. Baxter's *Relation* iii. 179.

5 Burnet ii. 157. 7 State Trials 1320.

6 7 State Trials 1320.

7 *Ibid.* 1096, 1320, 1321. Burnet ii. 157. Foley, *Records* v. 12.

8 *Absalom and Achitophel* 646–649. Father John Warner describes Oates in similar terms: "Mentis in eo summa stupiditas, lingua balbutiens, sermo e trivio, vox stridula et cautillans, plorantis quam loquentis similior. Memoria fallax, prius dicta nunquam fideliter reddens, frons contracta, oculi parvi et in occiput retracti, facies plana, in medio, lancis sive disci instar, compressa, prominentibus hic inde genis rubicundis nasus, os in ipso vultus centro, mentum reliquam faciem prope totam aequans, caput vix corporis trunco extans, in pectus declive, reliqua corporis hisce respondentia, monstro quam homini similiora." MS. history 104.

9 *Lettre écrite de Mons à un ami à Paris*, 1679. 7 State Trials 1322.

10 *Absalom and Achitophel* 657–659.

11 Sir William Godolphin to Henry Coventry, on information obtained in Spain, November 6/16, 1678, Longleat MSS. Coventry Papers lx. 264.

12 7 State Trials 358, 1322. Burnet ii. 158. *Florus Anglo-Bavaricus* 93.

13 See below in Trials for Treason.

14 *The Grounds and Occasions of the Contempt of the Clergy and Religion enquired into.* By John Eachard, D.D., Master of Catherine Hall, Cambridge, 1670.

15 7 State Trials 360–375. 10 State Trials 1097–1132.

16 *Florus Anglo-Bavaricus* 93, 94, 95.

17 7 State Trials 324, 1325, *Lettre écrite de Mons à un ami à Paris. Florus Anglo-Bavaricus* 95.

18 Simpson Tonge's Journal, S.P. Dom. Charles II 409: 39. Simpson Tonge to L'Estrange, *Brief Hist.* i. 38. Simpson Tonge's Case, House of Lords MSS. 246–249.

19 S.P. Dom. Charles II 414: 185. Sydney Godolphin to Sir Leoline Jenkins, September 25, 1680.

20 S.P. Dom. Charles II 409: 36.

21 Evelyn, *Diary* January 25, 1665.

22 Simpson Tonge's Journal S.P. Dom. Charles II 409: 39. Simpson Tonge to the King, *ibid.* 414: 139. Simpson Tonge to L'Estrange, *Brief Hist.* i. 38. Kirkby, *Compleat and True Narrative* 1. *Impartial State of the Case of the Earl of Danby* 14. *Brief Hist.* ii. 100–125. Burnet ii. 158. North, *Examen* 170. Ralph i. 382, 542. In this account of Oates and the revelation of the Plot I have made considerable use of Mr. Seccombe's monograph on Titus Oates in *Twelve Bad Men*, and of Sir George Sitwell's study of *The First Whig*. I am unable however to follow these writers, and especially Sir George Sitwell, to whom I am much indebted for a loan of his book, in placing much reliance upon witnesses on the Catholic and Tory side. These labour under as great a bias as their opponents, and on some points are convicted of falsehood. This applies in particular to the evidence of L'Estrange and Simpson Tonge, upon whose authority the story of the deliberate concoction of the Plot by Oates and Dr. Tonge rests. That Tonge was a fanatic and Oates a villain is unquestioned; and it is probably as just to call Tonge villain and Oates fanatic. But that their rascality took this form is not proved. Simpson Tonge was also a rascal, and his repeated contradictions, in the hope of gain from both parties, make it impossible to discover the truth from him. In the winter of 1680 L'Estrange challenged Oates (*Observator* i. 138) to prosecute young Tonge for defamation of character. The challenge passed unnoticed; but the fact proves nothing, for however many lies Tonge had told, Oates was not then in a position to risk a rebuff or to court an inquiry into his own conduct. And L'Estrange's bare assertion is no proof of the truth of the fact asserted. The way I have treated this, as all other doubtful evidence in the course of this inquiry, is always to disbelieve it, unless it is corroborated from other sources, or unless the facts alleged are intrinsically probable, and the witness had no motive for their falsification. When the test is applied to the present case, I believe that no other result than that stated above can be obtained.

23 See, for instance, *La Politique du Clergé de France*, by Pierre Jurieu. Arnauld, *Apologie pour les Catholiques, Le Jesuite sécularisé*, and *La Critique du Jesuite sécularisé*, Cologne, 1683.

24 Barillon, January 16/26, 1680. See below in Trials for Treason.

25 He was wrongly said to be the Duchess's confessor. Sarotti, October 26/November 4, 1678. Ven. Arch. Inghil. 65.

26 *Parl. Hist.* iv. 780, 781, 782. C.J., November 8, 1675.

27 *Ibid.* Reresby, *Memoirs* 98, 99. Ralph i. 292. Verney MSS. 466. Foley i. 276 *seq.* Lingard xii. 278–282. Antoine Arnauld, *Œuvres* xiv. 532, 533. Foley i. 276, 277. Wood, *Fasti Oxon.* (ed. Bliss 1815–20) ii. 350.

28 Ralph i. 292. Verney MSS. 466. Burnet ii. 104.

29 Ruvigny, November 7/17, 8/18, 1675.

30 Fitzherbert MSS. 112, 76; St. Germain to Coleman, December 3/13, 1675; January 5/15, 1676.

31 Sarotti, who might have been expected to have heard of the case favourably to St. Germain, writes of him simply as "un Padre Jesuita che fu capellano della medesima Signora Duchessa e già tre anni in circa fuggì, ritrandosi a Parigi per le differenze ch' hebbe con un ministro Calvinista della casa del Signor di Rouvigny," October 26/November 4, 1678, as above.

32 See Appendix E.

33 L.J. xi. 276, 286, 299, 310. Kennet, *Register and Chronicle* 469, 476, 484, 495. Orleans, *History of the Revolutions in England* 236. *Letter from a Person of Quality to a Peer of the Realm*, 1661. *Collection of Treatises on the Penal Laws*, 1675. Continuation of Clarendon's *Life*, by himself, 140, 143.

34 December 6, 1662. Kennet, *Register and Chronicle* 848–891. Baxter's *Life* ii. 429.

35 February 27, 1663.

36 July 25, 1663. C.J. Feb. 27, 28, April 27, May 30. L.J. xi. 478, 482, 486, 491, 558, 578. Clarendon 245–249. James i. 428.

37 For a general statement of the Catholic case see *The Catholique Apology*, attributed to the Earl of Castlemain, and on the other side *An Account of the Growth of Popery and Arbitrary Government in England*, by Andrew Marvell.

38 Ranke iv. 323. W. A. Shaw, "The Beginnings of the National Debt," *Owens College, Manchester, Historical Essays*. Mr. Shaw's remarkable essay throws a flood of light on the financial difficulties of the early part of the reign. He considers the year 1667, when the Commons attacked the administration and voted a commission to examine public accounts, to be the point beyond which patriotic action could be expected on the part neither of the Commons nor of the king.

39 Ruvigny, January 17/27, 1675: "Que les finances du roi ne pouvaient pas mieux être employées qu'à la destruction d'un puissant ennemi, qui soutenait tous les autres."

40 As to the date of Charles' conversion see Ranke iv. 383, 384.

41 Ranke iv. 384–386. *Gentleman's Magazine*, January 1866. Lord Acton, "Secret History of Charles II," *Home and Foreign Review* i. 146. Hallam ii. 387.

42 Acton, *op. cit. Gentleman's Mag.* January 1866. Boero, *Istoria della Conversione alla Chiesa Cattolica de Carlo II.* Welwood, *Memoirs* 146.

43 Brosch 420, n. Ranke v. 88.

44 *Lectures on Modern History.*

45 April 1675.

46 Clarke, *Life of King James II* i. 440, 629. In referring to this work I adopt Lingard's plan of mentioning it simply as "James," except where the passage referred to is based, as here, upon James' original memoirs, when I refer to it as "James (Or. Mem.)." Klopp i. 235. Foley i. 272 *seq.*

47 Cardinal Howard to Coleman, April 18, 1676. Treby i. 85. Courtin, April 2, 1676.

48 Ruvigny, August 19/29, 1675. Courtin, October 9/19, 1676, January 11/21, 15/25, 1677. Barillon, December 17/27, 1677. Giacomo Ronchi, October 3/13, 1678, in Campana de Cavelli i. 233. Longleat MSS. Strange to Warner, December 28, 1676; Bedingfield to Warner, December 28, 1676; Coleman to Whitehall, January 1, 1677; Mrs. Coleman to Coleman, January 1, 1677, January 4, 1677; Coventry Papers xi. 245, 246, 247. MS. diary of Lord Keeper Guildford, Dalrymple ii. 199, 200. *Parl. Hist.* iv. 1035. Hist. MSS. Com. Rep. i. Ap. 56. *Floras Anglo-Bavaricus* 136. Forneron, *Louise de Kerouaile* 136, 161, 179. Ralph i. 272. Burnet ii. 51, 99.

Coleman is described by Warner, MS. history 41: "Hunc proxime secutus est Edwardus Colemannus, serenissimae Ducissae Eboracensi a secretis, in haeresi educatus, quam detectis erroribus ejuravit, et totus in Catholicorum partes transiit, quas exinde promovit pro virili, magno zelo sed impari prudentia. Magnum a natura sortitus est et festivum ingenium, cui dum nimium indulgeret, et liberrimis censuris quae parum a satyris abessent curules perstringeret, divûm nulli parcens, multorum, praecipue, Danbaei, offensam incurrit, a quibus tandem oppressus est."

The imputation that he diverted the Frenchmen's gold to his own use was put upon Coleman by Whig historians. Of this his character has been cleared by Sir George Sitwell (*First Whig* 25, note). The Whig Committee of the House of Commons appointed to examine Coleman reported his confession "that he had prepared guineas to distribute among members of Parliament, but that he gave none and applied them to his own use" (C.J. November 7, 1678). The committee was composed of men who themselves received money from the French ambassador, and therefore had the strongest motive to conceal the facts. But the truth slipped out two years later in a speech made in the House by Mr. Harbord (December 14, 1680). Coleman, he said, did confess "that he had twenty-five hundred pounds from the French ambassador to distribute amongst members of Parliament, and your committee prudently did not take any names from him, it being in his power to asperse whom he pleased, possibly some gentlemen against the French and Popish interest." The prudence of the committee in attributing to Coleman statements which he never made is also indubitable.

49 Coleman to Ferrier, June 29, 1674. Ferrier to Coleman, September 25, 1674. Coleman to Ferrier in answer to above. Coleman to La Chaize, September 29, 1675. Treby i. 1, 3, 6, 109. Chantelauze, *Le Père de la Chaize* 4.

50 Berkshire to Coleman, March 24, 1675. Treby i. 103.

51 Throckmorton to Coleman, April 27, May 1, 1675. Fitzherbert MSS. 70. Burnet ii. 103.

52 Chantelauze, *Le Père de la Chaize* 4. See below in Trials for Treason.

53 In 1672 Howard was appointed bishop-elect of England with a see "in partibus" but not consecrated. In 1675 he was created cardinal by Clement X, and in 1679 nominated by Innocent XI Cardinal Protector of England and Scotland.

54 Some of the letters could not be deciphered; see for instance Albani to Coleman, January 12, 1675. Treby i. 121.

55 Treby i. 109–116.

56 Colbert, November 10/20, 1673, on the information of St. Évremonde. Mignet, *Negotiations* iv. 236.

57 Treby i. 110. Ferrier to Coleman, September 25, 1674; and Coleman's answer to Ferrier, Treby i. 3, 6. The Duke of York to Ferrier, Treby i. 119. This last letter Coleman declared at his examination in Newgate to have been written by himself in the duke's name and without his knowledge. 7 State Trials 54. There is however no reason to accept his statement as true. Answering Ferrier's letter Coleman writes, "His royal highness has received the letter that you sent him by Sir William Throckmorton, which he has answered to you himself." Treby i. 3. Supposing Coleman to have told the truth to his examiners, he must have forged the letter, a work of

considerable difficulty, since James' writing would certainly have been well known at the French court. Throckmorton and Coleman must also in this case have conspired to divert Ferrier's letter to James and never deliver it; for there could be no reason for the duke to meet with a marked rebuff a letter so flattering to him and written in his interest, and unless he refused to send an answer, Coleman would have no motive to forge one. Nor can it be supposed that Coleman carried on his correspondence without the duke's knowledge. Beyond the certainty that Coleman was in James' confidence, this is plain from the fact that on several occasions either Coleman's correspondent desires him particularly to show his letter to the duke or he mentions that he has done so. And Coleman had the strongest motive to shield his master by taking on himself the authorship of the letter. That he was believed is probably due to Oates' careful exoneration of the duke from concern in the Plot at a time when he was not certain of a favourable reception for his story. Another misunderstanding would be welcomed by Coleman. This letter was said at the time to have been addressed to La Chaize, and the belief would suit Coleman, since the letter would be less likely to be connected with his own written to Ferrier at the same time. The confessor to whom it was sent was certainly Ferrier and not La Chaize, for Throckmorton, who is mentioned in it, was dead some months before the latter came to court. The erroneous idea was probably owing to the manner in which Ferrier is spoken of in the letter in the third person, an use common with the writers in this correspondence.

58 Treby i. 110, 111, 112.

59 Treby i. 112. Coleman to Throckmorton, February 1, 1675. Treby ii. 1. Throckmorton to Coleman, November 28, December 1, 1674. Fitzherbert MSS. 50, 51. Same to same, February 13, 1675. Treby i. 73.

60 Sheldon to Coleman, July 13, 1675. Treby i. 49.

61 Treby i. 112. Throckmorton to Coleman, December 8, December 22, 1674, January 19, 1675. Fitzherbert MSS. 51, 62, Treby i. 66. Coleman to Throckmorton, February 1, 1675. Treby ii. 1. Sheldon to Coleman, July 13, 1675. Treby i. 45.

62 Albani to Coleman, August 4, 1674. Coleman to Albani, August 21, 1674. Treby i. 21: 7.

63 Albani to Coleman, October 19, 1674. Treby i. 23.

64 Coleman to Albani, October 23, 1674. Albani to Coleman, January 12, 1675. Treby i. 12, 25.

65 Fitzherbert MSS. 113. *Parl. Hist.* iv. 1024, 1025. Burnet ii. 104.

66 Coleman to Throckmorton, February 1, 1675.—"The duke having the king wholly to himself, he would no longer balance between the different motives of his honour and the weak apprehensions of his enemies' power; but then the duke would be able to govern him without trouble, and mark out to him what he ought to do for the establishment of his grandeur and repose. For you well know that when the duke comes to be master of our affairs the King of France will have reason to promise himself all things that he can desire. How shall we get this parliament dissolved? ... by the King of France and the help of three hundred thousand pounds. This parliament is revengeful to the last degree, and no man that offends them must think to escape. But as for a new parliament that will be better natured and will doubtless accord to his Majesty all that he shall need for his occasions. And this for very good reason, since they will more depend upon his Majesty upon other accounts than his Majesty upon them for money. And to conclude where we began, the duke by the dissolution will be all-powerful" (Treby ii. 1, 2, 3).

Coleman to Albani, August 21, 1674.—"So that if the duke can happily disengage himself of those difficulties wherewith he is now encumbered, all the world will esteem him an able man, and all people will entrust him in their affairs more willingly than they have done formerly. And the king himself, who hath more influence on the East India Company (Parliament) than all the rest, will not only re-establish him in the employment he had before, but will put the management of all the trade into his hands. We have in agitation great designs, worthy the consideration of your friends, and to be supported with all their power, wherein we have no doubt but to succeed, and it may be to the utter ruin of the Protestant party" (Treby i. 78).

Coleman to Albani, October 2, 1674.—"If the duke can shew to the king the true cause of all these misfortunes and persuade him to change the method of their trade, which he may easily do with the help of money, he will without difficulty drive away the Parliament and the Protestants who have ruined all their affairs for so great a time, and settle in their employments the Catholics, who understand perfectly well the nature of this sort of trade" (Treby ii. 6).

67 Treby ii. 21–25.

68 Coleman to Albani, October 2, 1674. Treby ii. 6.

69 Coleman to Albani, February 12, 1675. Treby ii. 8. John Leybourn, president of the English College at Douay, to Cardinal Albani, June 17, 1675. Vat. Arch. Misc. 168. *Parl. Hist.* iv. 673, 674. Brosch 431, 432.

70 Ranke v. 184, 185, 186. Airy, *The English Restoration* 235, 236, 237. Brosch 432. *Parl. Hist.* iv. 715 *seq.* Schwerin, *Briefe aus England* 24. Andrew Marvell, *Growth of Popery.* Treby i. 114.

71 This is awkwardly expressed. What they were about before was to have the duke put again over the fleet, but not to have this done at the request of Parliament; for it was then the object to have Parliament dissolved.

72 Treby i. 116. Sec also Coleman to Albani, February 12, 1675. Treby ii. 8.

73 Treby i. 117.

74 Treby i. 117, 118.

75 Halifax, *Maxims of State:*—

XXIII.—The Dissenters of England plead only for conscience, but their struggle is for power; yet when they had it, have always denied to others that liberty of conscience which they now make such a noise for.

XXVI.—They that separate themselves from the Religion of the State and are not contented with a free Toleration, aim at the Subversion of it. For a conscience that once exceeds its bounds knows no limits, because it pretends to be above all other Rules.

The dangerous nature of Coleman's correspondence was recognised at the time by sensible people, as well Catholics as Protestants. Barillon, October 3/13: "On trouve dans les papiers de ceux qui ont été arrêtés beaucoup de commerces qui paraissent criminels en Angleterre, parce qu'il s'agit de la religion." October 10/20, 1678: "On continue toujours ici la visite des papiers du Sieur Coleman.... Tous les gens raisonnables croyent que la conjuration contre la personne du Roi de la Grande Bretagne n'a aucun véritable fondement. Les commissaires du conseil qui instruisent l'affaire parlent de la même manière sur cela, mais en même temps ils disent qu'il paraît un commerce fort dangereux pour l'État avec les étrangers. Qu'il s'emploie de grandes sommes pour soutenir les cabales et pour augmenter la religion catholique, et que par les lois d'Angleterre la plupart de ceux qui sont arrêtés sont criminels. Ils parlent bien plus affirmativement du Sieur Coleman. On a trouvé dans ses papiers des minutes de toutes les lettres qu'il écrivait à Rome, en France, et ailleurs. On prétend qu'il y a quantités de projets qui tendent à la ruine de la religion protestante en Angleterre et à l'établissement d'une autorité souveraine en Angleterre et d'un changement de gouvernement par le papisme."

Il Nuntio di Vienna al Nuntio in Francia, Nimega, October 18/28, 1678: "Al Colman oltre l' insufficienti imputationi di complicità s'adossa hoggi corrispondenza per altri capi criminali, che lo mettono in gran pericolo della vita." Vat. Arch. Nunt. di Francia 329.

J. Brisbane to Henry Coventry, October 14/24, 1678.—M. de Pomponne and M. Courtin treat the whole matter of the plot *en ridicule* and say that "le pauvre Coleman est mort seulement pour être Catholique." February 11, 1679.—Finds that those who did not long ago canonise Mr. Coleman, do now acknowledge his execution to have been a just punishment. Bath MSS. 242, 243.

76 25 Edward III St. 5, c. 1.

77 Third Institute 6, 12, 14.

78 Hale, *P.C.* i. 109, 110.

79 *History of the Criminal Law* i. 268. See on the whole subject Stephen i. 241–281 and Hale, *P.C.* i. 87–170.

80 S.P. Dom. Charles II 407: i. 128.

81 12 State Trials 646.

82 *Parl. Hist.* iv. 519.

83 See above.

84 7 State Trials 60, 67.

85 Hale, *P.C.* i. 110.

86 Evidence of Jerome Boatman, his secretary, House of Lords MSS. 8.

87 St. Germain to Coleman, March 28, April 8, April 15, September 6, 1676. Treby i. 32, 40. Fitzherbert MSS. 81. Treby i. 42, ii. 18. Courtin, March 23, April 1, July 16, August 11, August 13, 1676. Pomponne to Ruvigny, April 1, 1676. Both Ruvigny and Courtin were in London at this time.

88 St. Germain to Coleman, January 15, 29, February 1, 5, 8, March 18, April 13, November 18, 1676. Fitzherbert MSS. 76, 78, 79, 96, 107. Treby i. 30, 32, 35.

89 Leybourn, Howard's secretary, to Coleman, May 16, June 20, September 5, September 21, 1676, June 25, July 10, July 16, August 6, 1677, January 1, 1678. Fitzherbert MSS. 102, 103, 104, 105. Treby i. 94, 95, 96. Howard to Coleman, March 1, April 18, 1676. Treby i. 81, 85. Courtin, March 13/23, March 22/April 1, April 3/13, April 10/20, July 6/16, November 9/19, November 22/December 2, November 30/December 10, 1676. Correspondence later on the same subject March 29, April 8, 1679; the Duke of York to the Pope; the Duchess to the Pope. Vat. Arch. Epist. Princ. 106. The internuncio at Brussels to the Pope. Nunt. di Fiandra, 66.

90 See below in Trials for Treason.

91 Above, 43.

92 St. Germain to Coleman, January 29, April 15, July 25, 1676. Treby i. 30, 43. Fitzherbert MSS. 80.

93 *Mémoires du Marquis de Pomponne* i. 538.

94 This distinction was widely recognised, see 7 State Trials 475. Ralph i. 91, note. *Parl. Hist.* iv. 274. It corresponded in the ideas of the time to the difference between a simple Roman Catholic and "a Jesuited Papist."

95 Stafford's statement; House of Lords MSS. 43. Burnet i. 346. Foley v. 19.

96 Foley v. 80. John Leybourn, April 19/29, 1674; same to Cardinal Albani, June 7/17, 1675. Vat. Arch. Nunt. di Inghilterra and Misc. 168.

Pietro Talbot (the Jesuit Archbishop of Dublin), Primate de Irlanda al Nuntio F. Spada, Nuntio in Parigi, April 3/13, 1675. Nunt. di Francia, 431. "V. S. Illma si compiaccia de aggiungere le inchiuse propositioni del Sig^n Giovanni Sargentio alle altre sue; tutte (come V. S. Illma vede) sono heretiche o almeno inferiscono l'heresia."

Continual references to the same subject are found in the Papal despatches of the time.

97 *Maxims of State* lxv.

98 See D'Avrigny, *Mémoires pour servir à l'histoire de l'Europe* 47, 48. Arnauld, *Œuvres* xiv. 410.

99 Leybourn to Coleman, May 2, 1676. Fitzherbert MSS. 102. John Verney to Sir Ralph Verney, March 30, 1676, "The Duke of York did declare that he would never more come under the roof of Whitehall chapel, which makes every one say he is a perfect papist.... 'Tis said he publicly goes to mass. God bless him and preserve the King." Verney MSS. 467. Courtin, March 23, April 2, October 2/12, 1676. Le ministre des affaires étrangères à Courtin, April 1/11, 1676. *Mémoires du Marquis de Pomponne* i. 491. Marchese Cattaneo al Duca di Modena, April 20/30, 1676: "In alcune parti d'Inghilterra si e cominciata l'esecuzione delle legge contro i Cattolici, imprigionandoli e confiscandogli i beni.... Delle rincrudite persecuzioni verso i Cattolici e accagionato il Duca d'York perche non ha voluto nella Pasqua recarsi alla capella Regia (Protestante)," in Campana de Cavelli i. 171. Longleat MSS. Proclamation of October 3, 1676. Coventry Papers xi. 154.

100 The interpretation of the following letter seems doubtful, but it is worth quoting. It is a curious fact that Lord Castlemaine should have either taken, or intended to take, orders in the Church of Rome.

January 1, 1677. To the Lord Castlemaine at Liège: "118 and 109, as I am privately told, are now perfectly reconciled to the Duke of York, and fully resolved to serve him and his interest, so that if the Lords and Commons when they meet do nothing, the King will dissolve them and once more publish a toleration. Consider if Mr. Skinner can make a seasonable check of mettlesome stuff for the conjuncture. By a letter from Mr. Warner at Paris I find D. of Cleveland persuaded that Ld. Castlemain is already made a priest by the Jesuits' underhand contrivances, and that she obstructed it what she could at Rome. I should think it expedient that she should continue in that belief, that she may think it now too late to go about to hinder it." Unsigned Longleat MSS. Coventry Papers xi. 347.

101 Throckmorton to Coleman, January 9, February 20, 1675. Fitzherbert MSS. 60, 66. Berkshire to Coleman, n.d. Treby i. 102.

102 Journal of Sir Joseph Williamson, March 12, 30, 1672, in Cal. S.P. Dom. 1671–1672, 608. Longleat MSS. Francis Bastwick to Henry Coventry, April 29, 1679. Examination of Col. Scott at Dover of same date. Coventry Papers xi. 393, 396. Two letters in the same collection seem to show that Scott was a regular spy of the English Government, but they are so vague that much reliance cannot be placed on them. Coventry Papers xi. 171, 506. See Appendix A.

103 Longleat MSS. "An account of what the Earl of Berkshire desired Colonel John Scott to communicate to his Majesty." Coventry Papers xi. 397. See Appendix A. See too Collins' *Peerage*, 1812, iii. 163.

104 Scott afterward gave evidence before the House of Commons against Pepys, whom he charged on report with having given information of the state of the navy to the French court; but the affair was never thoroughly investigated. Grey, *Debates in Parliament* vii. 303–309.

105 House of Lords MSS. 43, 44. Burnet i. 345, 346; ii. 276, 277. Airy, *The English Restoration* 240.

106 Longleat MSS. Coventry Papers xi. 310, 313, 317. See Appendix A.

107 J. P. Oliva Generale dei Gesuiti al Cardinale Altieri, September 23/October 3, 1674. Vat. Arch. Archivio di Propaganda Fide. Ranke v. 91.

108 Dal Sig^r Internuncio, May 24/June 3, 1679. Vat. Arch. Nunt. di Fiandra 66. Add. MSS. 32095: 196. See below in Politics of the Plot.

109 L.J. November 21, 1678. Foley v. 221, 222. Longleat MSS. Coventry Papers xi. 483, a version of Du Fiquet's information in French.

110 7 State Trials 1007.

111 Brusselles Dal. Sig^r Internuncio, April 19/29, 1679. Vat. Arch. Nunt. di Fiandra 66.

112 Longleat MSS. St. Omers, August 14, 1678. Sam Morgan to his father, Coventry Papers xi. 204. See Appendix A.

113 Pepys, *Memoires relating to the State of the Royal Navy in England* 4, 5, 8.

114 Longleat MSS. Letter of December 23, 1676. Coventry Papers xi. 171. See Appendix A.

115 Treby i. 19. September 18/28, 1678.

116 L'Abbate G. B. Lauri a S. Em^{za}, November 22/December 2, 1678. Vat. Arch. Nunt. di Francia 332. See Appendix A.

117 Barillon, October 21/31, 1680. "Il (le Duc d'York) me fit entendre. ...qu'il ne comprenait pas que le Roi son frère voulût mettre tous les Catholiques en désespoir et les persécuter sans aucunes mesures. Il ajouta à cela en termes pleines de colère et ressentiment que si on le poursuit à bout, et qu'il se voit en état d'être entièrement ruiné par ses ennemis, il trouvera le moyen de les en faire repentir et se vangera d'eux.... M. le Duc de Bouquinham m'a dit plusieurs fois qu'il avait bu fort souvent avec le Roi de la Grande Bretagne, mais qu'il n'avait jamais vu ce Prince dans une débauche un peu libre qu'il ne temoignât beaucoup d'aigreur et de la haine même contre son frère."

118 Examinations of Saunders, Coulster, and Towneley, April 28, 1679. House of Lord MSS. 149–152.

119 Macaulay iv. 649–652. Lord Acton, *Lectures on Modern History*. If Charles' word when he was sober can be trusted, he believed there was no ground to suspect the duke of any intention against his life. Barillon, November 22/December 2, 1680. "Le Roi de la Grande Bretagne dit encore en jurant avant hier au conseil: Mon frère ne m'a point voulu faire tuer, ny pas un de vous ne le croît." It was however Charles' constant policy to uphold the Duke of York. See too Reresby, *Memoirs* 146.

120 Ralph i. 382.

121 It is a tribute to the liveliness of Oates' imagination that Pickering, said to be an agent in the Jesuit plot, was a Benedictine lay-brother.

122 Kirkby, *Compleat and True Narrative* i. Simpson Tonge's Journal 38; S.P. Dom. Charles II 409.

123 Simpson Tonge's Journal 39.

124 Kirkby, *Compleat and True Narrative* 2. Simpson Tonge's Journal 40, 41. *Impartial State of the Case of the Earl of Danby* 13, 14.

125 *Impartial State of the Case* 14, 15.

126 *Florus Anglo-Bavaricus* 95.

127 *Impartial State of the Case* 15. Kirkby, *Compleat and True Narrative* 2. 7 State Trials 96, 328, 345. Simpson Tonge's Journal 39, 59.

128 *Impartial State of the Case* 15.

129 *Impartial State of the Case* 15, 16. Kirkby, *Compleat and True Narrative* 2, 3. Simpson Tonge's Journal 64, 65, 124. L'Estrange, *Brief Hist.* ii. 4–15. *Observator* ii. 150–153, October 1684. James (Or. Mem.) i. 518, 519. Ralph i. 383, 384. Burnet ii. 158.

130 Simpson Tonge's Journal 135. Kirkby, *Compleat and True Narrative* 3. *Impartial State of the Case* 16. James (Or. Mem.) i. 518. Temple, *Works* i. 398. Reresby, *Memoirs* 147. Burnet ii. 158.

131 Simpson Tonge's Journal 152. 7 State Trials 29, James (Or. Mem.) i. 518–521. Warner MS. history 26. *Florus Anglo-Bavaricus* 98. Foley v. 16. Burnet ii. 160. North, *Examen* 58.

132 Barillon, September 30/October 10, 1678. 7 State Trials 656. Foley v. 17, 18, 20, 21. Schwerin, *Briefe aus England* 330, 334, 342.

133 Barillon, October 3/13, 10/20, 1678. 7 State Trials 29, 30, 33. *Impartial State of the Case* 17. Add. MSS. 28,042: 32. Notes by Danby for a letter to be sent to a member of the House of Commons. Danby to Lord Hatton, March 29, 1678. *Hatton Correspondence* i. 184.

134 Il Nuntio di Vienna al Nuntio in Francia. Nimega, October 18/28, 1678. Vat. Arch. Nunt. di Francia, 329.

135 Barillon, October 3/13, 7/17, 10/20, 17/27, 1678. Paolo Sarotti, Ven. arch. October 11/21, 1678. Schwerin, *Briefe aus England* October 4/14, 1678. Luttrell, *Brief Relation* i. 1. Halstead, *Succinct Genealogies* 433. Reresby, *Memoirs* 145. North, *Examen* 177. Evelyn, *Diary* October 1, 1678. *Caveat against the Whigs* ii. 42. Foley v. 18. Burnet ii. 161, 162.

136 Calamy, *Own Life* i. 83, 84. Christie, *Life of Shaftesbury* ii. 309. Burnet ii. 165. North, *Examen* 206. Luttrell, *Brief Relation* i. 12, 21. Schwerin, *Briefe aus England* 336, 351, November 18, 1678.

137 See the prologue to Dryden's tragi-comedy, *The Spanish Friar*, produced early in 1681:—

A fair attempt has twice or thrice been made

To hire night murderers and make death a trade.

When murder's out, what vice can we advance,

Unless the new-found poisoning trick of France?

And when their art of rats-bane we have got,

By way of thanks, we'll send them o'er our Plot.

Scott suggests that the allusion is to the murder of Mr. Thynne, but this did not occur till some months after the production of the play. Christie refers it to the assault made upon Dryden himself in Rose Alley in December 1679; but the reference to the plot makes it far more probable that Dryden had in his mind the murder of Godfrey and the sham attempt on Arnold eighteen months later. He would certainly class the two together, for he attributed Godfrey's death to Oates:—

And Corah might for Agag's murder call

In terms as coarse as Samuel used to Saul.

Absalom and Achitophel, 676, 677.

138 Sir George Sitwell gives a most instructive and entertaining description of these, *The First Whig*, chap. vi.

139 *What Gunpowder Plot was* 13.

140 Tuke, *Memoirs of Godfrey* 1–15. Sidney Lee, Article on Godfrey in *Dict. of Nat. Biog. Gentleman's Magazine*, January 1848. Godfrey's Christian names are variously spelt. I give the most correct form in writing, but in quoting retain that used by the writer or reporter.

141 Tuke, *Memoirs* 39–51.

142 Sidney Lee, *op. cit. Gazette* No. 88. Ralph i. 139.

143 Pepys, *Diary* May 26, 1699. Tuke, *Memoirs* 36–39. Tuke is mistaken in saying that Godfrey was knighted on this occasion, in recompense for the injury done him. The knighthood was conferred in September 1666.

144 An engraving by F. H. van Hove is inserted in Tuke's *Memoirs*.

145 Tuke, *Memoirs* 19, 20. North, *Examen* 199.

146 Tuke, *Memoirs* 52, 53.

147 Kirkby, *Compleat and True Narrative* 2, 3.

148 Kirkby, *Compleat and True Narrative* 3. Simpson Tonge's Journal 126, 135.

149 Tuke, *Memoirs* 22, 23, 29, Burnet ii. 163. North, *Examen* 199, 200.

The author of the Annual Letters of the English Province S.J. is probably inaccurate in stating, "He was especially kind to the Roman Catholics, and was moreover a great confidant of the Duke of York" (quoted Foley Records v. 15); but the statement is only an exaggeration of the truth. Warner MS. history 26, "Nec alius in eo magistratu aut Carolo fidelior aut Catholicis, etiam Jesuitis, quorum multos familiarissime noverat, amicior."

150 Burnet ii. 164. Depositions of Henry Moor, Godfrey's clerk. L'Estrange, *Brief History* iii. 203, 204, 208. The depositions collected by L'Estrange in this work must be regarded with suspicion. The statements in many are obviously untrue, and L'Estrange was not above falsifying evidence to suit his purpose. Among other reasons for the use of great caution is the fact that most of the depositions were not taken until eight or nine years after the event. Their exact dates cannot be ascertained, as they are seldom quoted by L'Estrange, and the original documents are missing. They are supposed to have been stolen from the State Paper Office immediately after the Revolution (Sitwell, *First Whig* ix.). Only after careful scrutiny can these papers be used as evidence. Moor's evidence was taken for the coroner. He afterwards went to live at Littleport, in Cambridgeshire, and died apparently in 1685 or 1686. *Brief Hist.* iii., Preface vii. 171.

151 *Brief Hist.* iii. 204, 205.

152 *Brief Hist.* iii. 205, 206. Depositions of Pengry and Fall.

153 *Brief Hist.* ii. chap. vi, 199, iii. 195–201. The evidence that the news of Godfrey's absence was known before Tuesday, October 15, is not to be relied on. It consists wholly of depositions taken by L'Estrange several years after. Some contain such ridiculous statements as that before 3 P.M. on Saturday, October 12, it was a common report that Godfrey was murdered by the Papists. (Dep. of Wynell, Burdet, Paulden, 195, 196, 200.) At this time even his household could not possibly have known that he would not return. Another declares that on the morning of Sunday "it was in all the people's mouths in that quarter that he was murdered by the Papists at Somerset House." (Dep. of Collinson, 200.) At this time it was not known in Hartshorn Lane that Godfrey had not spent the night at his mother's. In another a false statement can fortunately be detected. Thomas Burdet deposed (196, 197) that Godfrey and Mr. Wynell had an appointment to dine on the Saturday with Colonel Welden, that Godfrey did not keep his appointment, and that the surprise which was caused by this was increased by the immediate report of his murder. As a matter of fact Godfrey had no appointment to dine with Welden, and so could not have caused surprise by not appearing. He had been invited, but could not

promise to come. Welden gave evidence before the Lords' Committee: "He came on Friday night with officers of St. Martin's, and at going away I asked him to dine with me on Saturday. He said he could not tell whether he should." (House of Lords MSS. 48.) North's assertions to the same effect (*Examen* 201) are equally worthless. Burnet is positive that the news of Godfrey's absence was not published before Tuesday, October 15. Burnet's character has been sufficiently rehabilitated by Ranke and Mr. Airy; but I may remark that, as he was opposed to the court, did not believe in Oates' revelations, and had access to excellent sources of information, his evidence upon the Popish Plot is of remarkable value.

154 Burnet places this tale at a time before the news was public, and says that the suggestion was credited by Godfrey's brothers. Very likely they may have believed it, but a comparison with Moor's evidence (see above) makes it probable that this explanation was the first given after his absence was known.

155 Burnet ii. 164. North, *Examen* 202. *Diary of Lord Keeper Guildford,* Dalrymple ii. 321.

156 John Verney to Sir Ralph Verney, Verney MSS. 471.

157 Lloyd to L'Estrange, *Brief Hist.* iii. 87. Burnet ii. 164. North says the body was found upon Wednesday, October 16 (*Examen* 202), but this is a mistake.

158 "7 guineas, 4 broad pieces, £4 in silver." The coroner's evidence.

159 Evidence of the coroner and Rawson before the Lords' Committee. House of Lords' MSS. 46, 47. Evidence of Brown, the constable, at the inquest. *Brief Hist.* iii. 212–215, 222.

160 Deposition of White, coroner of Westminster. *Brief Hist.* iii. 224.

161 Quoted from the printed copy published by Janeway in 1682. *Brief Hist.* iii. 232.

162 "The jury's reasons for the verdict they gave." *Brief Hist.* iii. chap. xii.

163 Evidence of Collins, Mason, and Radcliffe. *Brief Hist.* iii. 252, 300. Some not very good evidence was collected several years afterwards as to Godfrey's movements later in the day. It cannot be considered trustworthy. 8 State Trials 1387, 1392, 1393. *Brief Hist.* iii. 174, 175.

164 The coroner's evidence before the Lords' committee; "There was nothing in the field on Tuesday." House of Lords MSS. 47. Evidence of Mrs. Blith and her man at the inquest. *Brief Hist.* iii. 244.

165 Deposition of Robert Forset. 8 State Trials 1394, 1395.

166 Sir George Sitwell says: "The bruises or discolourations upon his chest might well have been produced by those who knelt upon it in stripping off the clothes" (*First Whig* 41). Bruises however cannot be made to appear upon a corpse beyond the time of three and a half hours after death (Professor H. A. Husband in the *Student's Handbook of Forensic Medicine*), nor is there any evidence that the body was so treated. Marks which look like bruises may be caused after death by the process of hypostasis or suggillation, the gravitation of the blood to the lowest point in the dead body. But if the marks on Godfrey's body had been thus caused, the face and neck would have shown pronounced signs of discolouration, since the head was lower than any other point in the body. It had moreover been in that position for at most only twenty-four hours, so that the blood would not have gravitated to the chest immediately after death at all.

167 L'Estrange afterwards persuaded the surgeon Lazinby to say that the mark was caused by the pressure of the collar. *Brief Hist.* iii. 259. But his evidence in court was, on the contrary, that it was caused "by the strangling with a cord or cloth." 8 State Trials 1384.

168 The evidence as to the exact condition of the neck, varies slightly, but the doctors, and indeed all who saw the body, were agreed that it was broken.

169 Evidence of the surgeons Cambridge and Skillard at the trial of Green, Berry, and Hill. 7 State Trials 185, 186. Evidence of the coroner before the Lords' committee. House of Lords MSS. 46. Evidence of Hobbs and Lazinby, surgeons, and the two Chaces, apothecaries, at the trial of Thompson, Pain, and Farwell. 8 State Trials 1381–1384.

170 Evidence of Brown, Skillard, and Cambridge at the trial of Green and others. 7 State Trials 184, 185, 186. Evidence of Hazard, Batson, Fisher, Rawson, Mrs. Rawson, Hobbs, Lazinby, the Chaces, at the trial of Thompson and others. 8 State Trials 1379–1384. Depositions of Skillard, Rawson, and others. *Brief Hist.* iii. 265–271. Some of the witnesses in their depositions before L'Estrange spoke of the presence of a greater quantity of blood than they had previously remembered. Obviously their earlier impressions are the more trustworthy. Even at the later date the quantity to which they swore was not considerable.

171 *Brief Hist.* iii. 271. He does not attempt however to give any evidence for his statement.

172 *Brief Hist.* iii. 230.

173 Mr. W. M. Fletcher, M.B., Fellow of Trinity College, Cambridge, has kindly furnished me with his opinion on this point. He says: "A sword transfixing the living body and at the same time driven through the cavity

of the heart would cause violent hæmorrhage from one or other of the external wounds, except only under a set of circumstances which could be present only by the rarest chance; the hæmorrhage, that is to say, could be restrained only by an accidental block produced not only at one but at two points on either side of the heart cavity, where the torn tissues might happen so to fit outwards upon and closely against the undisturbed sword as to form a kind of valve. Such an accidental valve formation, occurring at two separate points on each side of the pent-up blood, is improbable enough, but could not be imagined as a prevention of hæmorrhage if the sword were bent, twisted, or withdrawn after the infliction of the wound."

174 7 State Trials 295. Information of Mrs. Warrier. *Brief Hist.* iii. 142. Burnet ii. 164. Evidence of the coroner before the Lords' committee. House of Lords MSS. 46. L'Estrange produces two depositions to the effect that the ground was quite dry and not muddy, and in doing so contradicts the argument upon which he lays stress in arguing against Prance's story (see below) that if the body had been brought to Primrose Hill upon a horse, the feet and legs must have been covered with mud. *Brief Hist.* iii. 261, and see 8 State Trials 1370 for the same point in Thompson's libel.

175 8 State Trials 1359–1389.

176 Barillon, October 21/31, 1678. "Ce Godefroy s'est trouvé mort à trois milles d'ici sans qu'on sache qui l'a tué. Le Roi d'Angleterre et M. le Duc d'York m'ont dit que c'était une espèce de fanatique et qu'ils croyent qu'il s'était tué lui-même."

177 Burnet ii. 165. Blencowe's *Sidney* lxii. Lady Sunderland to John Evelyn, December 25, 1678.

178 See the letter subscribed T. G. to Secretary Coventry and Coventry's reply. Longleat MSS. See Appendix B.

179 John Verney to Sir Ralph Verney, Verney MSS. 471. This did not take place till November, but it may be noted at this point.

180 Barillon, January 16/26, 1679. Despatches of Giacomo Ronchi, secret agent of the Duke of Modena in London, January 20, 1679. Campana de Cavelli i. 239. *Memoirs of Thomas, Earl of Ailesbury* i. 29.

181 Lansd. MSS. 1235: 76. North, *Examen* 202, 204, 205. North alone relates the incident of the pulpit. As Ranke observes, he has never been contradicted, so that the story may be accepted. Burnet ii. 165. Ralph i. 392. Echard 950. Oldmixon 620.

182 *Parl. Hist.* iv. 1022. L.J. xiii. 299. House of Lords MSS. i.

183 Longleat MSS. Coventry Papers xi. 232. The information of October 27 is practically the same as that given below from the Lords' Journals.

184 Examination of Charles Atkins, Esq. 6 State Trials 1479. L.J. November 12, 1678.

185 Evidence of C. Atkins before the Lords' Committee. 6 State Trials 1474.

186 6 State Trials 1473–1492.

187 6 State Trials 1484, 1491.

188 There is unfortunately a gap from October 28 to December 11 in the minutes of the committee of inquiry of the House of Lords, so that it is impossible to check Atkins' statements exactly.

189 See 6 State Trials 1476, 1481.

190 *Ibid.* 1474.

191 *Ibid.* 1481.

192 See the conversations between Charles and Samuel Atkins on the stairs of the committee room, November 6, and in Newgate, November 8. *Ibid.* 1480, 1484. North, *Examen* 243–247.

193 S.P. Dom. Charles II 407; i. 285. Bedloe to Williamson, October 31, 1678; ii. 23. Williamson to Bedloe, November 5. *Brief Hist.* iii. 7. Coventry to Bedloe, November 2.

194 See Appendix B.

195 Whence Lingard derives the words I cannot discover, xiii. 98. *Brief Hist.* iii. 16. Ralph i. 393. Burnet ii. 168. Burnet, who relates that Charles told him the same thing of Bedloe, must have misunderstood the king's words, unless, which is quite possible, Charles deceived him intentionally.

196 Add. MSS. 11,058: 244. See Appendix B.

197 S.P. Dom. Charles II 407: ii. 29. See Appendix B.

198 Deposition of November 8 before the Lords' committee. 6 State Trials 1487.

199 *Ibid.* 1489.

200 *Ibid.* 1484.

201 7 State Trials 347, 349. Exam. of November 7. S.P. Dom. Charles II 407. See Appendix B. Care, *History of the Plot* 127.

202 Warner MS. history 36. Exam, of Mary Bedloe (see below). Burnet ii. 168. *Florus Anglo-Bavaricus* 127, *Lettre écrite de Mons à un ami à Paris*, 1679. L.J. xiii. 392. Reresby, *Memoirs* 149.

203 L.J. xiii. 343, November 12.

204 Deposition of Alice Tainton, alias Bedloe, taken this 14th day of November 1678, before the Rt. Rev. father in God William Lord Bishop of Landaffe, one of his Majesty's justices of the peace in the county of Monmouth. Deposition of Mary Bedloe of Chepstow of same date before the Bishop of Landaffe. Deposition of Gregory Appleby, December 2, 1678 before the Bishop of Landaffe. Longleat MSS. Coventry Papers xi. 287, 307.

205 L.J. November 24, 28; xiii. 389, 391.

206 6 State Trials 1489, 1490. Sitwell, *First Whig* 51. North, *Examen* 248.

207 6 State Trials 1490, 1491. For Staley's case see below in Trials for Treason. North, *Examen* 249.

208 Evidence of Captain Vittells and his men before the Lords' committee. House of Lords MSS. 49, 50, 51. Evidence of Vittells and Tribbett at Atkins' trial. 7 State Trials 248.

209 6 State Trials 1491, 1492.

210 7 State Trials 238–240.

211 Bedloe's evidence. *Ibid.* 242, 243.

212 *Ibid.* 241, 245.

213 *Ibid.* 246–249.

214 *Ibid.* 249. North, *Examen* 250, 251. North's account is as usual highly coloured, and contains at least one untrue statement.

215 Bedloe's deposition before the Lords' committee. L.J. November 12, xiii. 350, 351.

216 7 State Trials 237.

217 See below in *Trials for Treason.*

218 Burnet ii. 191. 7 State Trials 183. *True Narrative and Discovery* 20. *Brief Hist.* iii. 52, 53, 65. L'Estrange alone gives the words. The fact that Prance was questioned about the periwig makes it probable that they are more or less correct. L'Estrange also says that the meeting was prearranged by Bedloe and Sir William Waller. Reasons for disbelieving this will appear later.

219 House of Lords MSS. 51.

220 L.J. xiii. 431. Blencowe's *Sidney* lxii. Lady Sunderland to John Evelyn, December 25, 1678.

221 C.J. ix. 563. L'Estrange comments on this: "It makes a man tremble to think what a jail delivery of discoverers this temptation might have produced" (*Brief Hist.* iii. 55). Surely it is more natural to suppose that the information was directed not to the common malefactors, but to those already imprisoned in Newgate on account of the plot. If an examination of Prance was taken by the Commons' committee, it was never reported to the House. On December 30, 1678 Parliament was prorogued, and on January 24, 1679 dissolved. The new parliament did not meet till March 6, when the trial for Godfrey's murder had already taken place, and Green, Berry, and Hill had been hanged.

222 L.J. xiii. 436.

223 The deposition begins, "That it was either at the latter end or the beginning of the week that Sir E. Godfrey," and so on. The rest of the examination is only intelligible on the ground that Saturday was the day of the murder. Prance's reasons for prevaricating in this statement will be the subject of discussion below.

224 L.J. xiii. 437, 438. 7 State Trials 191, 192. Evidence of Sir Robert Southwell, clerk to the privy council. There exists among the state papers the notes taken by Sir Joseph Williamson, secretary of state, of Prance's first examination before the council. They only differ from the account in the Lords' Journals in that they begin "On a certain Monday." The paper is worth studying for the wonderful vividness in which Williamson's disjointed sentences bring the scene to the mind. See Appendix B.

225 L.J. xiii. 439.

226 House of Lords MSS. 52.

227 Warner MS. history 37. S.P. Dom. Charles II 407: ii. 17. Note of the proceedings at the council on December 30. 7 State Trials 177, 210. Evidence of Richardson and Chiffinch. James (Or. Mem.) i. 535. Burnet ii. 193. *Brief Hist.* iii. 61, 62, 65. L'Estrange says that the king saw Prance alone on the evening of December 29, and called in Richardson and Chiffinch afterwards. This is contradicted by Richardson and Burnet. It would moreover have been a piece of imprudence unlike Charles' caution; and as none of the Whig writers, who would have given much to obtain such a handle against the king, mention a private interview, the story is probably without truth. The events which passed between Prance's first confession and his final adherence to it will be discussed below.

228 7 State Trials 167, 168, 169.

229 *Ibid.* 179–183.

230 L.J. xiii. 437.

231 7 State Trials 169–173.

232 *Ibid.* 186, 187.

233 *True Narrative and Discovery* 12.

234 7 State Trials 169, 188, 189.

235 7 State Trials 174. *True Narrative* 18.

236 7 State Trials 190.

237 7 State Trials 195–200.

238 *Ibid.* 201, 202.

239 *Ibid.* 204, 205, 206.

240 *Ibid.* 207, 208, 209.

241 7 State Trials 213–221.

242 *Ibid.* 223–230. Burnet ii. 194, 195.

243 Luttrell, *Brief Relation* i. 9.

244 7 State Trials 228.

245 *Brief Hist.* iii. 26, 27.

246 *Brief Hist.* iii. 66, 67.

247 *Ibid.* 67, 68. Cooper's information of January 9 and January 11.

248 *Ibid.* 69, 75. Informations of Boyce.

249 Lloyd's report to the Council. *Brief Hist.* iii. 69. Lloyd to L'Estrange. *Ibid.* 82.

250 Lloyd's report to the Council. Fitzherbert MSS. 154. *Brief Hist.* iii. 69, 71. Lloyd to L'Estrange. *Ibid.* 85.

251 Burnet ii. 193, 194.

252 Burnet ii. 194. *Brief Hist.* iii. 85, 86.

253 State Trials 1183–1188. This was also a Jesuit story. Warner MS. history 37, "fidiculis tortus et se reum asseruit, et complius [sic. qu. complures] se accusaturum."

254 7 State Trials 1199, 1200, 1210–1212.

255 Evidence of Fowler. *Ibid.* 1194–1197, 1204–1209.

256 The improbability does not lie in the unlikelihood of the application of torture to witnesses at this date so much as in the nature of the particular facts alleged, which cannot be believed. *Brief Hist.* iii. 76, 77, 78, 80. L'Estrange procured Corral to contradict his evidence at the trial. *Ibid.* 102, 106. It is important to insist upon the falsehood of the charge in this case, because it has been adopted without question by Foley v. 29, n., and see Echard, 503 *seq.*

257 *Brief Hist.* iii. 84.

258 *True Narrative* 11.

259 7 State Trials 180.

260 *True Narrative* 13, 14.

261 7 State Trials 172. *True Narrative* 15.

262 7 State Trials 173. *True Narrative* 16, 17.

263 6 State Trials 1487. 7 State Trials 182.

264 6 State Trials 1488.

265 *Ibid.* 1487.

266 Prance to L'Estrange, January 17, 1688. *Brief Hist.* iii. 127.

267 *Brief Hist.* ii. 52, 53.

268 It is worthy of remark that Sir James Fitzjames Stephen, judging only from the evidence which Prance gave at the trial, has come to the same conclusion. *Hist. Crim. Law* i. 393.

269 It was ordered that an examination should be held on the subject, but Coleman was never questioned on Godfrey's death. House of Lords MSS. 48. L.J. xiii. 303, 307, 308.

270 Warner MS. history 27: "Rem totam Eboracensi detulit," *Florus Anglo-Bavaricus* 97. James (Or. Mem.) i. 534. North, *Examen* 174. Lingard xiii. 69. Sitwell, *First Whig* 40.

271 *Brief Hist.* iii. 181–186.

272 See above, 89.

273 James (Or. Mem.) i. 517–519. *Impartial State of the Case of the Earl of Danby.* Lingard xiii. 68.

274 North, *Examen* 174. *Florus Anglo-Bavaricus* 97, 98. Godfrey "rem totam Edwardo Coleman ... per literas aperuit: quod non neminem usque adeo offendit, ut Godefredus haud ita multo post violenta morte suam in Catholicos benevolentiam luerit." Warner MS. history 26, 31, to the same effect. Warner names Danby as the probable author of the murder.

275 7 State Trials 168. House of Lords MSS. 47. *Brief Hist.* iii. 187. Burnet ii. 163.

276 Burnet, *ibid.*

277 7 State Trials 29.

278 Welden's evidence before the Lords' committee. House of Lords MSS. 48.

279 Reresby, *Memoirs* 325. Warner MS. history 27. "Ad congregationem provincialem ubi ventum est, cui se interfuisse mentitus predicat Oates, Carolus ab eo petiit, ubinam convenissent Jesuitae? Respondit alter, magna cum fiducia, convenisse Londini, in plataea quae Strand dicitur, in oenopolio cui insigne Equi Albi. Hoc falsum esse sciebat Carolus, cui notum ipsos in ipsa Eboracensis Aula convenisse; cujus tamen rei nec Carolus nec ullus alius Catholicorum apologista mentionem fecit donec persecutio plane desaevisset, ne augeretur inde in Eboracensem invidia."

280 At Lord Stafford's trial in 1680 Dugdale, the informer, declared that Godfrey had been murdered by the Duke of York's orders because Coleman had made disclosures to him. He did not however suggest what the nature of those disclosures was. A theory not unlike that set out in the text was therefore in the air at the time. As almost every conceivable hypothesis to account for the murder was being discussed, this is not surprising; but there was this difference, that then Dugdale had no good reason to offer in favour of the truth of what he said. He was at the time of the murder in communication with various Jesuits in Staffordshire: but it is most unlikely that, even if they knew anything about it, they would have told him. If he had known anything, it would probably have been that the Jesuit congregation was held at St. James'; and he was certainly ignorant of this. Burnet tells, on the authority of the Earl of Essex, that the king prevailed on Dugdale to stifle this part of his information because it pressed on the Duke of York; but, as Essex, or Burnet, taking the tale from him, was mistaken as to the date when Dugdale first told the story, and as Dugdale could beyond doubt have had a better price for his information from Shaftesbury than from Charles for the suppression of it, this cannot be believed without corroboration, which is not forthcoming. Burnet ii. 190, 191. 7 State Trials, 1316, 1319. And see below in Trials for Treason.

281 See below (in materials for the history of the Popish Plot), Foley's note on Warner's MS. history.

282 Slip appended to examination of November 7. Longleat MSS. Coventry Papers xi. 276.

283 7 State Trials 168. Burnet ii. 163.

284 James (Or. Mem.) i. 527, 528. Burnet ii. 174. House of Lords MSS. 52. 7 State Trials 154. L.J. xiii. 353.

285 7 State Trials 172, 192.

286 Burnet ii. 164, 165. L'Estrange produced some bad evidence, which he does not even seem to have believed himself, to the effect that these stains were of mud, and not wax. *Brief Hist.* iii. 326, 336. Sir George Sitwell says: "The drops of wax ... may have been spilt the evening before, when Sir Edmund, for some mysterious reason, was engaged in burning a quantity of his private papers" (*First Whig* 41). But the evidence for this is wholly valueless, being told on hearsay from a bad witness by a worse. *Brief Hist.* iii. 179.

287 Evidence of the coroner before the Lords' committee, House of Lords MSS. 46.

288 Examination of Charles Atkins, October 27, 1678. Slip appended to the examination in Coventry's hand. "Mr. Charles Atkins lodgeth at the Golden Key in High Holborn, over against the Fountain Tavern." Longleat MSS. Coventry Papers xi. 234. Examination of Bedloe of November 7. "Lodges where Captain Atkins lodges, where Walsh the priest lodges, near Wild House." S.P. Dom. Charles II 407: ii. 29. Longleat MSS. *ibid.* 272–274; *ibid.* 278, on a slip appended to the examination, "Le Fevre: about fifty years of age, with a flaxen periwig, a handsome man. He lodges where Captain Atkins lodges, near Wild House."

289 L.J. xiii. 353. Evidence of Diana Salvin, Elizabeth Salvin, John Saunders, Alexander Oldis.

290 6 State Trials 1475–1477.

291 *Parl. Hist.* iv. 1113. *Secret Services of Charles II and James II*, payment to Prance 22.

292 L.J. November 15, 1678. Ralph i. 398.

293 For example the libel, "A copy of a letter dropped in the exchange," 1679.

294 See above and Appendix B.

295 See above, 122.

296 James (Or. Mem.) i. 528. Schwerin, November 22, 1678. "Bedloo hat in Somerset House das Gemach gewiesen in welchem ihm der todte Körper gezeigt worden ist; allein weil er in derselben Kammer eine Thüre angab, die sich nicht daselbst vorfand,—überdem die Königin damal in diesem Gemache wohnte,—und der Ort, an welchem ihm der todte Körper gezeigt worden sein soll, ein steter Durchgang und Aufenthalt aller Domesticken der Königin ist, so wird die Angabe von vielen für verdächtig gehalten." *Briefe von England* 352.

297 James, Duke of York, to the Prince of Orange, December 24, 1678, "... some are not well pleased with what this man says, because it contradicts Bedloe." Foljambe MSS. 127.

298 House of Lords MSS. 52.

299 7 State Trials 343.

300 *Ibid.* 425, 612, 613.

301 *Ibid.* 1320.

302 Lloyd to the council, January 11, 1679. Examinations of Prance of December 26, 1678, January 13, March 19, March 22, 1679. Fitzherbert MSS. 154–158. 7 State Trials 1226, 1231. Warner MS. history 37. *True Narrative* 2–8, 26–40.

303 Lloyd to L'Estrange, April 16, 1686. *Brief Hist.* iii. 83.

304 Burnet ii. 195.

305 Warner MS. history 37: "librum edidit in quo pauca de Jesuitis, eaque leviora retulit ... et in sacerdotes saeculares fanda infanda conjecit, tanquam e plaustro probra jaceret (qu, tanquam e plaustro = histrionis more. v. Hor. *A.P.* 275 ap. Facc.), ipsa maledicentiae magnitudine fidem sibi detrahens: quam apud paucissimos invenit."

306 *Florus Anglo-Bavaricus* 103, 128.

307 7 State Trials 228. House of Lords MSS. 1689–1690, 61.

308 House of Lords MSS. 1689–1690, 61. Foley v. 285, 286.

309 S. A. Tanari, Internuncio at Brussels, to the papal secretary of state, June 17, 1679: "Nella salute della sua persona consistevano tutte le speranze di veder ristabilita la vera religione in Inghilterra." Vat. Arch. Nunt. di Fiandra 66.

310 Luttrell, *Brief Relation* i. 8.

311 Memorandum by Danby. "Q. Whether the Plot be not triable out of Parliament?" Add. MSS. 28042: 19. Henry Coventry to the king, October 7, 1678.... "It will be worth your serious consideration when you return on which side the greater inconveniency will be, either in the suppressing them [Coleman's letters] or publishing them, or whether any middle way can be taken." Add. MSS. 32095: 119.

312 A narrative of proceedings in the House of Commons. Harl. MSS. 6284: 35, 36.

313 *Parl. Hist.* iv. 1021–1026.

314 House of Lords MSS. 16, 17. Lady Sunderland to John Evelyn, October 28, 1678. Correspondence of John Evelyn, 1852, 251.

315 W. Harrington to George Treby, February 1679. Fitzherbert MSS. 14. John Verney to Sir Ralph Verney, November 11, 1678. Same to same, May 12, 1679. Verney MSS. 471. Sarotti, November 15/25, 1678. Ven. Arch. Inghilterra 65. Lives of the Norths i. 70. Le Gros to Sir Charles Lyttleton, November 26, 1678. Longleat MSS. Coventry Papers xi. 301.

316 Sir W. Godolphin to Henry Thynne, August 14/24, 1679. Longleat MSS. Coventry Papers lx. 275. S.P. Dom. Charles II 408: i. 119, 120; ii. 70, 79.

317 Earl of Conway to Sir L. Jenkins, September 26, 1681. S.P. Dom. Charles II 416: 30.

318 Longleat MSS. Coventry Papers xi. 17–54. *Narrative of Edmund Everard* 1679.

319 Longleat MSS. Coventry Papers xi. 67, 92, 98, 100, 114, 138, 140. *Ibid.* 148, Lord Windsor to Henry Coventry, July 8, 1676. See Appendix C. Verney MSS. 465. Earl of Danby to the Lord Chancellor, April 4, 1676. Leeds MSS. 13. Particulars of Conventicles. Leeds MSS. 15. John Smith to Henry Coventry, January 24, 1676. Longleat MSS. Coventry Papers xi. 172. A paper endorsed by the Earl of Danby; "Fifth monarch meetings in London and Southwark. This was given me by the Bishop of London in October 1677." Add. MSS. 28093: 212. And see Gooch, *English Democratic Ideas in the Seventeenth Century* 326.

320 Longleat MSS. Coventry Papers xi. 117, 120, 122, 124, 126, 132.

321 "Memd. of his Majesty's directions for interrupting Coleman's letters." December 10, 1676. Henry Coventry to Col. Whitely, December 11, 1676. Longleat MSS. Coventry Papers xi. 168, 170. And the letters intercepted, *ibid.* 224, 245, 246, 247, 248. And see above, Designs of the Catholics 32, n.

322 Spillmann. Pater Spillmann's work is in general of little value. Bishop Morley to the Earl of Danby, June 10, 1676. Leeds MSS. 14. Courtin, August 6, 1676.

323 Leeds MSS. 17.

324 Foley v. 11, 12, 13. Diary of Lord Keeper Guildford, Dalrymple, ii. 200, 320. Articles of *Impeachment against the Earl of Danby* iv. *Parl. Hist.* iv. 1068.

325 See above 78.

326 Memorandum by Danby, undated, but probably in 1677. "State and present condition of the crown, which cannot be amended but by force or by compliance.

"[Compliance to the old parliament would mean war with France and the enforcement of all laws against papists and dissenters; with a new parliament, war with France and general toleration except for the papists.] From all this it seems as if compliance must necessarily conclude in a resolution to give satisfaction in point of France. [Force could hardly be exerted without foreign aid, which would certainly mean a total conquest.]" Add. MSS. 28042: 17.

327 Earl of Danby to Sir W. Temple, November 19, 1678. Add. MSS. 28054: 196. Burnet ii. 97, note, 151, 152. See also Lindsay MSS. 399. Forneron, *Louise de Kéroualle* 153. Harris, *Life of Charles II* 226 *seq.*

328 Memoranda by Danby. Add. MSS. 28042: 53.

"The three points to be considered by the committee of trade every Thursday:—

"(1) A treaty marine with France.

"(2) What should be proposed to the king to be done by his example in not permitting French commodities to be worn in the court.

"(3) A treaty of commerce with France."

Add. MSS. 28042: 60.

"For the 30 ships# #

In 1677		£90,000 0 0
In 1679	[?8]	339,735 0 0
In 1679	before the 25th March	47,957 0 0

£584,978

477,692

£107,286 remaining in the Exchequer, Lady Day, '79."

See too Campana de Cavelli i. 290–294. Barillon, March 3/13, 1679.

329 Webster MSS. Hist. MSS. Com. Rep. iii. 421. Article by Mr. Sidney Lee on Osborne (Thomas) in the *Dict. of Nat. Biog.* Danby obtained his knowledge of Montagu's connection with the nuncio from Olivencranz, the Swedish ambassador. Sir Leoline Jenkins to the Earl of Danby, January 13, 1679. Lindsey MSS. 398. Grey, *Debates* vi. 388. The authorities for the story of Danby's fall are well known and too numerous for citation.

330 *Parl. Hist.* iv. 1039–1045, 1052. Burnet ii. 176, 178. Barillon, November 25/December 5, 1678. Ferguson, *Growth of Popery*, Part II. 219.

331 *Parl. Hist.* iv. 1034. Sitwell, *First Whig* 63.

332 Reresby, *Memoirs* 149. *Parl. Hist.* iv. 1035. Barillon, October 17/27, 1678. Ranke v. 236.

333 Barillon, February 17/27, February 24/March 6, 1679. Edm. Verney to Sir R. Verney, February 24, 1679. Verney MSS. 471, Fitzherbert MSS. 12, 13. Foljambe MSS. 127. *Caveat against the Whigs* i. 47. Ranke v. 244, 245. Sir Thomas Browne, *Works*, 1836, 240. Sitwell, *The First Whig* 54, 55.

334 Barillon, December 30, 1678/January 9, 1679, January 30/February 9, May 12/22, June 2/12, 1679. John Verney to Sir R. Verney, May 22, 1679. Verney MSS. 472. *Parl. Hist.* iv. 1086, 1121.

335 *Parl. Hist.* iv. 1092–1111. Burnet ii. 205 and note 2. And see Temple i. 412. Seymour had formerly been on the court side, and after Danby's imprisonment made up the quarrel. A memorandum in the Leeds papers contains the following note on Seymour; "This man, the most odious to the House, till he disturbed your Majesty's affairs." Add. MSS. 28042: 21.

336 See Reresby, *Memoirs* 170, 171. Temple i. 396–414.

337 *Parl. Hist.* iv. 1122. Algernon Sidney wrote that Halifax was the author of the scheme. *Letters* 34. James had news that the Duchess of Portsmouth bragged that she had helped to make it. James to the Prince of Orange, May 8, 1679. Foljambe MSS. 129.

338 Temple i. 414–419, 473–477. Barillon, April 7/17, April 21/May 1, April 24/May 4, April 28/May 8, 1679. Dalrymple ii. 216, 217. Reresby,

Memoirs 168. North, *Examen* 76, 77. Ferguson, *Growth of Popery*, Part II. 238; and see Foxcroft, *Life of Halifax* i. chap. vi.

339 Burnet ii. 209.

340 Barillon, February 5/15, 1680. Luttrell, *Brief Relation* i. 19, 33. Burnet ii. 246, 248, 249. Temple i. 419, 420, 441–444. Ailesbury, *Memoirs* i. 35. Foxcroft, *Life of Halifax* i. 173–178, 192. Christie, *Life of Shaftesbury* ii. 357. Airy, *Charles II* 240.

341 Barillon, May 26/June 5, 1675. *Parl. Hist.* iv. 1125–1149. Temple i. 424, 429–432. Burnet ii. 210–215. Reresby, *Memoirs* 173. North, *Examen* 506. Ralph i. 453, 454, 455.

342 Burnet ii. 263, 264. House of Lords MSS. 136. And see Ferguson, *Growth of Popery*, Part II. 246.

343 See Lord Keeper Guildford MS. diary. Dalrymple ii. 91, 321. "It is certain the Church of England men joined in this cry as heartily as any else, for they were always most eager against Popery, although they had friendship with the Cavalier papists, and many considering men seeing an army kept up against an act of Parliament were zealous that fetters might be put on the King, and therefore would join in showing any discontent." The Whig party on Temple's council tried to purge the commission of the peace of justices on the other side, but Charles prevented this by a very droll device. North, *Examen* 78. Nevertheless the weight of the commission was against the court. See below in Trials for Treason.

344 W. Harrington to Sir G. Treby, February 20, 1679. Fitzherbert MSS. 14. Thomas Ward to Sir J. Williamson, November 15. Sir Francis Chaplin to same, November 30. Henry Layton to same, December 9, 1678. S.P. Dom. Charles II 407; i. 108, 167; ii. 117. George Beckett, vicar of Castham, to Sir Peter Pindar at Chester, October 28. Examination of same, November 4, 1678. Longleat MSS. Coventry Papers xi. 229. Dr. Henry Corneil to Sir J. Williamson, December 23, 1678, January 20, 1679. S.P. Dom. Charles II 408: ii. 59; 411: 69.

345 Add. MSS. 32095: 160. S.P. Dom. Charles II 408: i. 36.

346 Longleat MSS. Coventry Papers xx. 120–130. S.P. Ireland 339. Carte, *Life of Ormonde* 477–481.

347 S.P. Dom. Charles II 407: i. 268. *Parl. Hist.* iv. 1034. John Verney to Sir R. Verney, June 12, 1679. Verney MSS. 472. Barillon, April 19/May 1, June 12/22, 1679. And see Klopp ii. 193.

348 Burnet ii. 179. Add. MSS. 28042: 19. See Appendix C.

349 Klopp i. 26.

350 Foley v. 95, 96.

351 Ranke v. 233. Das papistische Complot erscheint als ein Symptom der zwischen den Bekenntnissen wieder angeregten heftigen Antipathien.

Schwerin, *Briefe* 330. Es sei nun an dieser Conspiration viel oder wenig, so ist es doch gewiss, dass diese Nation sowohl gegen die Papisten als gegen Frankreich—dem es besonders beigemessen wird—von neuem erbittert wird.

352 L.J. xiii. 408. Airy, *Charles II* 70.

353 Warner MS. hist. 29 from *Gazette de Hollande*, November 22, 1678. Schwerin, *Briefe* 340, 348. Duchess of York to Duke of Modena, November 3, November 24, December 16, 1678. Ronchi, January 20, February 23, November 21, 1679. Campana de Cavelli i. 229, 236, 239, 240, 242. Warner MS. Letter book, December 3, December 30, 1678. Fitzherbert MSS. 12. House of Lords MSS. 39, 126. Foljambe MSS. 123. L.J. xiii. 482, 485, 502, 512. Foley v. 21, 23, 80, 482–488, 915, 965, 966. 8 State Trials 532, 533.

The internuncio at Brussels acutely noted as the three causes of the feeling aroused—"l'odio de' Protestanti, gli amatori di novità, e li nemici della casa Reale." October 30/November 9, 1678. Vat. Arch. Nunt. di Fiandra 66.

354 7 State Trials 995.

355 7 State Trials 959–1043, 1162–1183. C.J. December 16, 1680. *Narrative of Lawrence Mowbray* 1680. *Narrative of Robert Bolron* 1680. Depositions from York Castle, Surtees Society xl. 1861. Foley v. 759–767. *The Month* xviii. 393.

356 Foley v. 19, 21. Warner MS. history 29. Misera Catholicorum omnium conditio, maxime vero Jesuitarum, quos et communia mala et omnium insuper invidia gravabat, etiam apud simul patientes. *Ibid.* 36.

Maxime odiosum Jesuitarum nomen, sacerdotibus etiam et saecularibus et regularibus et ipsis Catholicis laicis, quod ab iis orta feratur ista saevissima tempestas quae totam religionem Catholicam evertet.

357 Brosch 432.

358 S.P. Dom. Charles II 411: 87, a paper endorsed by Sir Joseph Williamson, "25 January, 78/9. Gavan the priest. Information, etc." *Ibid.* 92. "It was Sir William Waller who, by a warrant from the council, seized Gavan in Count Wallenstein the Imperial ambassador's stables in bed." Foley v. 454. Le Fleming MSS. 155.

359 See above 53.

-360 Di Brusselles dal Sig^r Internuncio, March 20/30, 1680. Vat. Arch.
Nunt. di Fiandra 66. S.P. Dom. Charles II 413: 252. Order in Council for a
passport for Henry, Duke of Norfolk, May 26, 1680.

361 7 State Trials 496. Foley v. 460.

362 Sidney's diary in Sidney's *Charles II* i. 82, 163, 165, 166, 174–176.
Sidney, *Letters* 154. *Domestic Intelligence*, September 26, 1679. C.J. March 26,
1681. Foley v. 80, 81, 460–467. Burnet ii. 228.

It has been supposed that John Sergeant who bore witness against Gavan
was a different person from the eminent controversialist of the same name
(see his life in *Dict. of Nat. Biog.* by Mr. Cooper). His identity is however
placed beyond question by the advertisement in the *Domestic Intelligence*
above cited, by despatches of Roman ecclesiastics which refer to "il
Dottore Sargentio" without hinting at any change of person, and by the
indignant exclamation of Warner (MS. hist. 132), "et, proh dolor! Johannes
Sergeantius et David Mauritius" in speaking of the witnesses for the Plot.
So too Luttrell (*Brief Relation* i. 21): "One Sergeant, a secular (who hath writ
against Dr. Stillingfleet), is expected from Holland, and 'tis said he will
discover several matters about the plot." The letter of the internuncio from
Brussels of March 20/30, 1680 contains the following passage: Ho pregato
S. A. di discorrere opportunamente col Sig^r Duca d'Jorch, excitandolo ad
opporsi ad ogni tentativo che potesse tentarsi dal Frate Valesio, e delli
Dottori Sergeant e Mauritio accioche non si propongà a Catt^{ci} il giuramento
di Fedeltà, gia censurato dalla S. Sede, ò non se ne inventi nuova formula
che non sia precedentemente approvata da S. B^{ne} quale ho assicurato esser
per mostrarsi sempre propenso verso le convenienze di S. A. Reale. Vat.
Arch. Nunt. di Fiandra 66.

363 Di Brusselles del Sig^r Internuncio, April 28/June 8, 1680. Circa il
giuramento di fedeltà condannato altre volte dalla S. Sede, e pur troppo
vero che il Sig^r Duca di Jorch lo presto anni sono, sedotto dall' esempio di
molti allevati nella Religion Catt^{ca} e non informato che lo stesso fosse stato
prescritto da Sommi Pontifici. Vat. Arch. Nunt. di Fiandra 66.

364 Di Brusselles dal Sig^r Internuncio, August 16/26, August
22/September 2, 1679. Vat. Arch. Nunt. di Fiandra 66.

365 See below in Trials for Treason. 7 State Trials 617. Burnet ii. 196–198.

Thomas Jennison, S.J., died in Newgate on September 27, 1679.

366 See below in Trials for Treason.

367 7 State Trials 1049. Dangerfield's *Particular Narrative* 1–7. *Malice
Defeated: or a Brief Relation of the Accusation and Deliverance of Elizabeth Cellier*
12, 13, 28. Col. Mansell's *Exact and True Narrative* 7, 60.

368 Dangerfield's *Narrative* 8. *Malice Defeated* 13, 39. Mansell's *Narrative* 39, 47, 60, 69.

369 Mansell's *Narrative* 43, 53, 54, 69. *Malice Defeated* 13, 14. Dangerfield's *Case* 2. North, *Examen* 268.

370 Dangerfield's *Narrative* 30–36. *Malice Defeated* 14. Mansell's *Narrative* 57, 58, 62. North, *Examen* 267.

371 Dangerfield's *Narrative* 37–49. Dangerfield's *Information* 1680. *Malice Defeated* 14–18. Mansell's *Narrative* 18–40.

372 Ferguson, *Growth of Popery* ii. 265. Sidney, *Letters* 152, 153. Halstead, *Succinct Genealogies* 434–437. North, *Examen* 261, 262. And see Burnet ii. 244, 245. Hatton Correspondence v. 201, 202.

373 *Malice Defeated* 15. Examination of Anne Blake, Mansell's *Narrative* 41.

374 *Malice Defeated* 15.

375 Barillon, November 27/December 7, 1679.

376 See below in Shaftesbury and Charles. Dangerfield's *Narrative* 30.

377 Dangerfield's *Narrative* 39.

378 Traill shews the absurdity neatly, though he makes the mistake of joining Mrs. Cellier with Dangerfield. *Shaftesbury* 154.

379 7 State Trials 1043–1111.

380 Mansell's *Narrative* 40.

381 Barillon, November 27/December 7, 1679. Sidney's *Diary*, October 7, October 14, in Sidney's *Charles II* i. 181, 185.

382 *Parl. Hist.* iv. 1029, 1030.

383 Dartmouth MSS. 36.

384 Sir W. Temple to the Earl of Essex, October 25, 1673. Essex Papers. Burnet ii. 31. James (Or. Mem.) i. 530, 536, 537. *Clarendon Cor.* ii. 467–471. Brusselles Dal. Sig[r] Internuncio, March 8/18, 1679. Vat. Arch. Nunt. di Fiandra 66.

385 Barillon, July 19/29, October 4/14, 14/24, 21/31, 1680.

386 James to Col. Legge, December 11, 1679, January 25, December 14, 1680. Dartmouth MSS. 40, 47, 55. James i. 657.

387 James i. 550, 551.

388 Temple i. 382.

389 Barillon, October 21/31, 1680.

390 James i. 554, 556, 574, 659, 660. Dartmouth MSS. 35, 36, 39, 41, 45, 47, 58. Savile Foljambe MSS. 134, 135.

391 James to Col. Legge, May 28, 1679, Dartmouth MSS. 33, 34.

392 James to the Prince of Orange, May 14, May 29, June 1, 1679. Savile Foljambe MSS. 129–131. To Col. Legge, July 22, Dartmouth MSS. 36. And see James (Or. Mem.) i. 551.

393 *E.g.* Dartmouth MSS. 38, 42, 46, 54.

394 Barillon, July 1/11, July 24/August 3, October 21/31, 1680.

395 Campana de Cavelli i. 302, 304.

396 Vat. Arch. L'Abb^c G. B. Lauri a S. Em.3^a October 23/December 2, 1678. Nunt. di Francia 332. Di Brusselles dal Sig^r Internuncio. May 24/June 3, 1679. Nunt. di Fiandra 66. Add. MSS. 32095: 196. See Appendix C.

397 Barillon, August 9/19, September 20/30, October 21/31, 1680.

398 Vat. Arch. Di Brussells dal Sig^r Internuncio, June 7/17, September 6/16, October 18/28, November 15/25, 1679. Nunt. di Fiandra 66.

Ibid. July 30/September 9. La sera però di detto giorno fattomi introdurre nel suo gabinetto (del Duca d'Yorch), m'incarico di dar parte del successo a S. B^{ne}, e di confermargli nuovamente che in ogni luogo e stato havrebbe sempre vissuto figlio obedientissimo della S. Sede, e che nell' animo suo a qualsivoglia altra consideratione o interesse havrebbe prevaluto il riguardo di conservare la fede, e di propagarla per quanto sarà in suo potere.

399 Foley v. 152, 157.

400 *Absalom and Achitophel* 114–117, 134–141.

401 Ranke v. 186.

402 John Verney to Sir R. Verney, May 19, 1677. "The people about town call this the Pump Parliament, alluding, as a little water put into a pump fetches up a great deal, so, etc." Verney MSS. 469, and see *The Pump Parliament* by Sir Charles Sedley.

403 Ranke v. 201, 220. *Parl. Hist.* iv. 861–863. C.J. April 4, 1677. Ralph i. 310–314, 318. Andrew Marvell, *Growth of Popery*, Part I. 149.

404 Burnet ii. 155.

405 Burnet ii. 179. Barillon, September 30/October 10, 1678.

406 Sir Edward Carteret provided his rooms at the rent of £60 a year.

407 *Secret Services of Charles II and James II* 3–15. I do not know if the very comic accounts said to have been presented by Oates and Bedloe are authentic (L'Estrange, *Brief Hist.* iii. 121–124. Lingard xii. 363). They are not inconsistent with the men's character, but L'Estrange was quite capable of having invented them. In any case they were not paid.

408 State Trials vii. 796, ix. 489, 490, x. 134, 136, 137, 1275, 1299. Reresby, *Memoirs* 196. Evelyn, *Diary* October 1, November 15, 1678. Smith, *Intrigues of the Popish Plot.* Luttrell, *Brief Relation* i. 112. North, *Examen* 223. *Lives of the Norths* ii. 180. Hatton Correspondence i. 198. Sitwell, *First Whig* 43, 44. I am indebted to Sir George Sitwell for some of these references, and have ventured to quote a portion of his admirable description, some strokes of which however are drawn from sources not beyond doubt. The epithet applied to the Pope is from "Rawleigh Redivivus."

409 Grey, *Debates* vi. 296. Barillon, November 25/December 5, 1678. L.J. xiii. 389–392. C.J. November 28, 29, December 6, 7. Danby's notes of Oates' examination, November 25. Add. MSS. 23043: 5. James to the Prince of Orange, November 26, 1678. Foljambe MSS. 125. See too House of Lords MSS. 66. Lord Ossory to the Duchess of Ormonde. Hist. MSS. Com. Rep. vi. App. 723. James (Or. Mem.) i. 529. Burnet ii. 173, 174. Even Oldmixon did not believe the accusation. *History of the House of Stuart* 618.

410 Burnet i. 470–474. In 1671 Burnet propounded the questions; "Is a woman's barrenness a just ground for divorce or polygamy; and is polygamy in any case lawful under the Gospel?" The answer to both was in the affirmative.

411 Sarotti describes him as "un cadavere spirante." December 12/22, 1679.

412 Burnet i. 474, ii. 180. North, *Examen* 186. Airy, *Charles II* 137, 138, 230. The relations between the king and queen became much better about this time in consequence, one may imagine, of these intrigues. Countess of Sunderland to Henry Sidney, August 15, 1679: "The Queen, who is now a mistress, the passion her spouse has for her is so great...." Sidney's *Charles II* i. 86.

413 Pepys, *Diary* December 24, 31, 1662. Burnet i. 469, 470.

414 Barillon, April 28/May 8, May 5/15, 1679. Temple i. 421, 423, 426, 429. MS. diary of Lord Keeper Guildford, Dalrymple ii. 322. Burnet ii. 233. Foxcroft, *Life of Halifax* i. 173–178. Hatton Correspondence v. 192.

415 Sidney, *Letters* 52, 53.

416 *Ibid.*

417 Ralph i. 434. North, *Examen* 86. Sidney, *Letters* 52, 90.

418 Burnet ii. 235. *Parl. Hist.* iv. 1130. North, *Examen* 79. This story may be accepted, since North probably had it from his brother the Chief Justice. And see Sidney's *Charles II* i. 5, where Henry Sidney states that Charles supported Lauderdale at the council.

419 Barillon, June 12/22, 1679. Sidney, *Letters* 95–97, 104–107, 112–113. Temple i. 420, 427, 428. North, *Examen* 81, 82. Burnet ii. 234, 235, 239. S.P. Dom. Charles II 412: 26. Sunderland to Essex, July 1679, 262. Essex to the King, July 21, 1679.

420 Sitwell, *First Whig* 70.

421 MS. diary of Lord Keeper Guildford, Dalrymple ii. 322, 323. North, *Examen* 571–575. *Parl. Hist.* iv. App. ix. Ralph i. 476, 477, 483. Sitwell, *First Whig* 83–89. And see the trial of Benjamin Harris, the publisher of the Appeal, 7 State Trials 925. Wilson, *Life of Defoe*, chap. i. Defoe, *Review* ix. 152. "As to handing treasonable papers about in coffee-houses, everybody knows it was the original of the very thing called a coffee-house and that it is the very profession of a coffee-man to do so, and it seems hard to punish any of them for it."

422 Sitwell, *First Whig*, 87, 88.

423 Barillon, September 4/14, 1679. Temple i. 433. Countess of Sunderland to Henry Sidney, September 2. Henry Savile to Henry Sidney, September 11, 1679. Sidney's *Charles II* i. 122, 140. Sidney, *Letters* 143. Ralph i. 477.

424 Barillon, July 3/13, 1679, January 12/22, 1680. Dangerfield's *Particular Narrative* 30, 60. *The Case of Thomas Dangerfield* 5. Mansell's *Exact and True Narrative* 62. Grey, *Debates* vii. 358, 359, viii. 136–149. *Gazette*, No. 1476. Ralph i. 496, 497. *Parl. Hist.* iv. 1233. Le Fleming MSS. 174.

425 Burnet ii. 242. Carte, *Life of Ormonde* ii. 493. Barillon, September 4/14, 11/21, 15/25, 1679. Temple i. 433–438. Foljambe MSS. 137, 138. Foxcroft, *Life of Halifax* i. 189–191. *Gazette* 1449. S.P. Dom. Charles II 412: 24. Conway Papers, September 11, 1679. Airy, *Charles II* 245. James (Or. Mem.) i. 566, 570–580.

426 James (Or. Mem.) i. 563. James to the Prince of Orange, Foljambe MSS. 137. Burnet ii. 243. Hatton Correspondence i. 194. Barillon, September 15/25. December 1/11, 1679.

427 Dal. Sigr. Internuncio Brusselles, June 8, 1679. Arch. Nunt. di Fiandra 66. Ferguson, *Growth of Popery*, Part II. 276.

428 Barillon, December 1/11, 8/18, 1679. Sidney, *Letters* 165. Charles Hatton to Lord Hatton, November 29, 1679. Hatton Correspondence i. 203. Ralph i. 484, 497.

429 Sidney, *Letters* 143, 144.

430 Temple i. 441. Ralph i. 490–494. Le Fleming MSS. 165. North, *Examen* 541–548. Defoe, *Review* vii. 296.

431 Barillon, December 11/21, 15/25, 18/28, 1679. James i. 581.

432 Barillon, January 8/18, 12/22, 15/25, 19/29, January 29/February 8, March 11/21, 1680. James (Or. Mem.) i. 587. Ralph i. 494.

433 The declaration was made twice, on January 6 and March 3, 1679.

434 The author was probably Ferguson. Sec Sprat's *History of the Ryehouse Plot*, where a printer's bill made out to him is printed in the appendix, one item of the bill being for the Letter. The pamphlet was published on May 15, 1680.

435 S.P. Dom. Charles II 413: 103, 105, 107, 118, 120, 131, 132, 229, 231. Informations and examinations concerning the Black Box. *Gazette*, Nos. 1507, 1520. Somers Tracts viii. 187–208. James I 589.

436 Barillon, June 28/July 8, July 1/11, 8/18, 1680. 8 State Trials 179. Burnet ii. 300.

437 S.P. Dom. Charles II 413: 75, Lord Massareen to Lord Conway. 76, Francis Gwyn to same, March 23, 1680. Barillon, March 25/April 4, May 17/27, 20/30, July 1/11. Countess of Sunderland to H. Sidney, May 18, 1680. Sidney's *Charles II* ii. 60. Luttrell, *Brief Relation* i. 38.

438 William Harbord to H. Sidney, April 1680. Sidney's *Charles II* ii. 23. Countess of Sunderland to same, April 16. Sir L. Jenkins to same, *circa* May 20. Sir W. Temple to same, April 27. Sidney's *Diary*, May 25. *Ibid.* 52, 53, 64, 66. Barillon, October 7/17, 1680.

439 Barillon, December 1/11, 11/21, 1679, January 5/15, April 5/15, July 1/11, 1680. S.P. Dom. Charles II 413: 82. Sir James Butler to Lord Craven, March 25, 1680. Temple i. 450. Sir L. Jenkins to Henry Sidney, July 24, 1680. Sidney's *Charles II* ii. 86. A concise account of the extreme difficulties of the time may be found in a letter from Henry Sidney to the Prince of Orange, October 7, 1680. Groen van Prinsterer v. 422.

440 Ralph i. 502, 503. Groen van Prinsterer v. 428. Burnet ii. 253. Barillon, October 21/31, 1680. James (Or. Mem.) i. 591–600. And see Somers Tracts viii. 137. *Articles of Impeachment against the Duchess of Portsmouth.*

441 *Parl. Hist.* iv. 1118, 1160–1175, 1291. Beaufort MSS. 112. Burnet ii. 212, 256. Temple i. 421. Foxcroft, *Life of Halifax* i. 154, 208, 224, 236. Ralph i. 444. Groen van Prinsterer v. 435, 437.

442 *Parl. Hist.* iv. 1175–1215. L.J. xiii. 666. Barillon, November 18/28, 1680. James (Or. Mem.) i. 617, 618. Temple i. 453. Halstead, *Succinct Genealogies* i. 204. Reresby, *Memoirs* 192, 197. Burnet ii, 259. Foxcroft, *Life of Halifax* i. 246–249. James to the Prince of Orange, November 23, 1680, Groen van Prinsterer v. 440.

443 *Parl. Hist.* iv. 1215–1295. Reresby, *Memoirs* 191, Groen van Prinsterer v. 444.

444 Sitwell, *First Whig* 142. S.P. Dom. Charles II 414: 101, Robert Ferguson to his wife, August 14, 1680. 243, Hugh Speke "for Mr. Charles Speke at Whitelackington." 275, James Holloway to the Earl of Essex, December 14, 1680.

445 Charles' actual words are in doubt, but it is certain that he received the deputation coldly and sent it away unsatisfied.

446 "Instructions for members of Parliament summoned for March 21, 1681, and to be held at Oxford."

447 North, *Examen* 100–102. Reresby, *Memoirs* 204. S.P. Dom. Charles II 415: 37. Answer of the Earl of Essex, January 27, 1681. 66, The Earl of Craven's proposition, February 14, 1681. "About the disposing of the king's forces." 126, Information of Mr. John Wendham of Thetford against Wm. Harbord, M.P. 156, Quarters of his Majesty's forces, March 22, 1681. Luttrell, *Brief Relation* i. 70. Ralph i. 562, 563. Sitwell, *First Whig* 144, 145. Klopp II. 308. And see the trial of Stephen Colledge 8 State Trials 549–724.

448 Barillon, January 13/23, 1679.

449 Barillon, *passim*. There was however talk of the negotiations in diplomatic circles. Brosch 452.

450 North, *Examen* 104, 105. Barillon March 28/April 7, 1681. Beaufort MSS. 83. Reresby, *Memoirs* 207–211. Ralph i. 570–580. *Parl. Hist.* iv. 1298–1339. Airy, *Charles II* 257. Ailesbury, *Memoirs* i. 57. Luttrell, *Brief Relation* i. 72. "Some are pleased to call it the Jewish Parliament, it being dissolved on the eighth day, alluding to that people's manner of circumcision on the eighth day."

451 Lord Grey's confession 12, 13, 14. North, *Examen* 105.

452 It is remarkable that every one thought he understood Charles and that most who opposed him paid in the end the penalty of their mistake by

failure. Only the most acute indeed were able to realise the strength of the character which they began by thinking weak. Thus Courtin believed that Charles could do nothing but what his subjects wanted. Jusserand, *A French Ambassador* 150. Barillon, with the possible exception of Gremonville, the ablest of Louis XIV's diplomatists, whom Ranke compares to the Spanish ambassador Mendoza of the time of the League, thought when he first came to England that he could in every instance measure Charles' weight in the balance. Before the Popish Plot had ceased its course, he perceived that he could not. He writes on January 15/25, 1680: Il est fort difficile de pénétrer quel est dans le fonds son véritable dessein. Again on September 9/19 of the same year; Le Roi de la Grande Bretagne a une conduite si cachée et si difficile à pénétrer que les plus habiles y sont trompés. And again on January 13/23, 1681: Je ne puis encore expliquer aver certitude à V.M. l'état des affaires de ce pays-ci. Ceux qui approchent de plus près du Roi d'Angleterre ne pénètrent point le fonds de ses intentions. See too Burnet II 409 n. 3, 467 n.

453 If Pemberton is counted.

454 Pilgrimage of Grace; Insurrection in West; Kent; Wyatt; Rising in North; Essex; Penruddock; Booth, 1659; Venner; Monmouth.

455 See the evidence of Lord Ferrers against Southall at the trial of Lord Stafford. 7 State Trials 1485.

456 Dalton, *Justice*, quoted Stephen, *History of the Criminal Law*, i. 195. Temp. James I.

457 Colquhoun, *Treatise on the Police of the Metropolis*, quoted Stephen i. 195.

458 Ralph i. 399. See also the Statutes: 13 C. II c. 6, 14 C. II c. 3, 15 C. II c. 4.

459 6 State Trials 566–630.

460 £1000 was stolen in cash, and over £2000 in jewelry.

461 6 State Trials 572–575.

462 By two Germans and a Pole, acting, it was said, under orders from Count Königsmark, who had been courting Mr. Thynne's bride.

463 Reresby, *Memoirs* 235, 236.

464 Reresby, *Memoirs* 281, 282.

465 This was the recognised appellation of a J.P. in the seventeenth century.

466 House of Lords MSS. 39, under date May 29, 1679.

467 7 State Trials 1471.

468 8 State Trials 525–550.

469 Gilbert's evidence, *ibid.* 531–534.

470 8 State Trials 531.

471 *Ibid.* 532.

472 Foley v. 891. House of Lords MSS. 89. See also Fitzherbert MSS. 18, 19.

473 Foley v. 34. House of Lords MSS. 89.

474 Foley v. 883.

475 "A true narrative of the imprisonment and trial of Mr. Lewis," written by himself. Foley v. 917–928. His account of the trial is inserted in 7 State Trials 249–260.

476 Foley v. 885. 7 State Trials 249, 252.

477 Foley v. 96. Catalogue of those who suffered in Oates' Plot and on account of their priesthood, taken from Dodd and Challoner.

478 7 State Trials 1131.

479 Ralph i. 570.

480 See Appendix D, where Giles' trial is discussed. Lawrence Hyde to the Prince of Orange, April 16, 1680. "This I say is a very unfortunate accident to revive men's fears and apprehensions of the Plot, which were pretty well asleep, but there is no care or watchfulness can prevent the folly and wickedness of men that are so given to it." Groen van Prinsterer v. 395.

481 See Stephen i. 228.

482 7 State Trials 1397–1399.

483 Southall's evidence. 7 State Trials 1467–1471.

484 For the following paragraph I have used Gardiner's *History of England* iii. 1–27.

485 Essay of Judicature.

486 This rule was not without exception. Baron Flowerdue, raised to the bench in 1684, held office *quamdiu se bene gesserit.* (Prothero, *Statutes and Constitutional Documents* 143). And we learn from Coke (Inst. iv. 117) that the Chief Baron always held office on a permanent tenure (Prothero cviii.). Of course it made no difference, for good behaviour in the eyes of the

king, with whom the decision rested, was likely to have much in common with his good pleasure.

487 Gneist, *Constitutional History of England* (trans. Ashworth) 550.

488 Clarendon, *Hist. Reb.* (Oxford, 1826) i. 123, 124.

489 Gneist 552 n. See *Gardiner* viii. 208.

490 Gardiner ix. 246, 247. Gneist 555.

491 L.J. May 6, 1641. *Parl. Hist.* ii. 757.

492 In a somewhat similar case the judges under Charles II refused to give an opinion until the matter had been argued before them by counsel. The Attorney-General, among other questions put to the judges at the outbreak of the agitation of the Popish Plot, asked "Whether there be any evidence against these particular persons besides the single testimony of Mr. Oates?" To which it was answered that it was a question of fact, and could only be determined in court. S.P. Dom. Charles II 407: i. 128.

493 Gardiner ix. 306, 307. Gneist 555 n. Hallam (ii. 107) attempts to uphold the judges' decision, but Stephen's argument (i. 362, 363) must be held to settle the question.

494 Gneist 570 n. (2).

495 4 State Trials 445–450.

496 Foss, *Judges of England* vii, 109, 110. Burnet, *Life and Death of Sir Matthew Hale.* Mr. J. M. Rigg in his article on Hale in the *Dictionary of National Biography* doubts the truth of this on the ground that Penruddock was tried at Exeter, and Hale belonged to the Midland circuit. Hale however changed his circuit on at least one occasion. See Foss vii. 112, and the *Gentleman's Mag.*, July 1851, p. 13, where an anecdote is told which shows that Hale had belonged at one time to the Western circuit.

497 North, *Life of Lord Keeper Guildford* 119. Dryden, *Prose Works* (ed. Malone) iv. 156.

498 Gneist 600 n. (2).

499 6 State Trials 951–1013.

500 See also Hallam iii. 8. Stephen i. 373–375.

501 Hale, P.C. i. 143–146.

502 Compare the attempt to create a riot among the apprentices in July 1679, immediately after the trial of the Five Jesuits.

503 *Parl. Hist.* iv. 803. Ralph i. 297. North, *Examen* 139.

504 Amos, *The English Constitution in the Reign of Charles II* 302.

505 *Gazette*, May 5, 1680.

506 7 State Trials 926–931.

507 *Ibid.* 1111–1130.

508 Twyn and two other printers were sentenced to the pillory, imprisonment, and heavy fines. Amos 249. 6 State Trials 513–539. See also the trials of Dover, Brewster, and Brooks, which followed on Twyn's case, *ibid.* 539–564.

509 April 30 to November 28, 1684. Luttrell, *Diary*, printed 10 State Trials 125–129.

510 *Clarendon Correspondence* i. 2.

511 8 State Trials 193, *i.e.* as resembling the opinions of 1641.

512 Gneist 600 n.

513 8 State Trials 194.

514 7 State Trials 1556–1567.

515 In this I have constantly used, as will be seen, Sir J. F. Stephen's *History of the Criminal Law in England* (vol. i., especially chapters viii. and xi.), a work to which I am under the deepest obligations.

516 *History of England* i. 125.

517 See the trial of Ireland, Pickering, and Grove. 7 State Trials 126–129, and 10 State Trials 1087.

518 See Raleigh's Trial, 2 State Trials 18. Jardine, *Crim. Trials* 421, where the court decided unanimously against Raleigh's repeated demand for the production of Lord Cobham, not, according to Sir James Fitzjames Stephen's opinion, without fair colour of law. *Hist. Crim. Law* i. 335, 336.

519 1 State Trials 869.

520 Not indeed without grievous consequences to themselves. Being brought to question for their verdict, four of them submitted and apologised at once. The remainder were imprisoned by order of the Star Chamber and fined heavily. Stephen i. 329.

521 1 State Trials 957–1042.

522 Stephen i. 326.

523 *Ibid.* 336, 350.

524 2 State Trials 25.

525 4 State Trials 354–356.

526 5 State Trials 1185–1195.

527 6 State Trials 932–936.

528 *Ibid.* 938.

529 6 State Trials 697.

530 6 State Trials 605–610.

531 7 State Trials 591–688. And see below 93 *seq.*

532 See Lilburn's Trial. 4 State Trials 1342.

533 Stephen i. 358.

534 Trial of Hulet, who was said to have been the actual executioner of Charles I. 5 State Trials 1185–1195. In summing up, Sir Orlando Bridgeman, L.C.S., said to the jury:—"Gentlemen, you hear what has been proved on behalf of the prisoner, that is, if you believe the witnesses that are not upon oath." Hulet was convicted, but the evidence was thought so unsatisfactory that the judges afterwards procured a reprieve.

535 See the Lord Chief Justice's remarks on the witnesses for the Five Jesuits. 7 State Trials 41. As to the amount of truth in the allegation see below.

536 At the trial of Colledge:—Sergeant Maynard: "It is Mr. Oates' saying; it is Mr. Turbervile's oath." 8 State Trials 638.

537 See *e.g.* the statement of Hyde, L.C.J., at Twyn's trial in 1663. L.C.J.: "If I did not mistake, you desired to have counsel; was that your request?" Twyn; "Yes." L.C.J.: "Then I will tell you, we are bound to be of counsel with you in point of law; that is, the court, my brethren and myself, are to see that you suffer nothing for your want of knowledge in matter of law; I say we are to be of counsel with you.... To the matter of fact, whether it be so or no; in this case the law does not allow you counsel to plead for you, but in matter of law we are of counsel for you, and it shall be our care to see that you have no wrong done you." 6 State Trials 516, 517. See also the 5th Resolution in the case of Sir Harry Vane. 6 State Trials 131.

538 See *e.g.* Coleman's trial. 7 State Trials 14. L.C.J.: "The labour lies upon their hands, ... therefore you need not have counsel, because the proof must be plain upon you." See also Don Pantaleon Sa's case. 4 State Trials 466.

539 See Colledge's trial. L.C.J. North: "Counsel you cannot have, unless matter of law arises, and that must be propounded by you; and then if it be a matter debatable, the court will assign you counsel; but it must be upon a matter fit to be argued." 8 State Trials 570. Similarly Jones, J., *ibid.* 571.

At Sidney's trial Jeffreys, L.C.J.: "If you assign any particular point of law, then, if the court think it such a point as may be worth the debating, you shall have counsel."

540 8 State Trials 579.

541 See Burnet ii. 196, 291. Pepys, *Diary* January 21, 1667. North, *Life of Guildford* 195, 196, 291.

542 6 State Trials 570.

543 7 State Trials 463.

544 7 State Trials 1339. That the barristers withdrew is evident from Winnington's subsequent remark: "We did perceive his counsel come up towards the bar and very near him, and therefore we thought it our duty to speak before any inconvenience happened." *Ibid.* 1340.

545 Sir W. Jones: "My Lords, we do not presume at all to offer our consent to what time the court shall be adjourned." L.H.S.; "No, we do not ask your consent."

546 7 State Trials 1371–1373.

547 7 State Trials 1544.

548 The trial of Hawkins for theft in 1669 is of great interest in this connection. It was evidently considered to be an extreme piece of good fortune that the accused was able to prove the conspiracy against him, and it was only owing to the folly and clumsiness of the prosecutor that he could clearly prove the perjury. 6 State Trials 922–952.

549 Sometimes this gave rise to great hardship, as in Oates' second trial for perjury, where a witness named Sarah Paine was summoned, but the wrong Sarah coming, the mistake was not detected until she was put in the witness-box. 10 State Trials 1287.

550 This however was considered rather unfair at the time. See the case of Atkins. 6 State Trials 1491. The action of the government and the judges in Colledge's case (8 State Trials 570–587) in depriving the prisoner of papers which leave had been given him to write, that the crown case might be managed accordingly, strained this practice still further, and is justly termed by Sir J. F. Stephen "one of the most wholly inexcusable transactions that ever occurred in an English court." *Hist. Crim. Law* i. 406.

551 This was certainly so in Newgate and the other London prisons, but Reading's intrigue with the Five Popish Lords seems to shew that the rule was relaxed for the Tower. 7 State Trials 301.

552 See the cases of Coleman and Fitzharris. Mrs. Coleman managed to convey letters to her husband in prison after his arrest. House of Lords MSS. 8. Mrs. Fitzharris also was used, according to the information received by the government, to convey messages to her husband from the leaders of his party. She used, while talking to him in the presence of a warder, to lower her voice so that he alone could hear, and then repeat the message in the middle of their ordinary conversation. Information of Lewis the spy. May 30, 1681. S.P. Dom. Charles II 415: 334.

553 *Principles of Moral and Political Philosophy* ii. 310.

554 That this was recognised at the time is evident from the attention which they received in the debates in the Commons on the Duke of York. That on the Lords' Provision in the Popery bill exempting the duke was carried on amid cries of "Coleman's letters! Coleman's letters!" 4 *Parl. Hist.* 1044. And see the whole of the Debate on a Motion for Removing the Duke of York, where they had the greatest weight. *Ibid.* 1026–1034.

555 7 State Trials 6.

556 *Ibid.* 3, 4.

557 *Ibid.* 7–13.

558 See above 45–48.

559 7 State Trials 70.

560 *Ibid.* 16, 17.

561 *Ibid.* 18.

562 *Ibid.* 22.

563 7 State Trials 18, 19.

564 *Ibid.* 30–33.

565 *Ibid.* 23, 31.

566 *Ibid.* 25.

567 Dryden, *Absalom and Achitophel* 646: "Sunk were his eyes." Warner MS. history 104. "Oculi parvi et in occiput retracti." L'Estrange, *Hue and Cry after Dr. O.* "His eyes are very small and sunk."

568 7 State Trials 25.

569 *Ibid.* 25–27.

570 7 State Trials 27–29. L.C.J.: "What did he (Oates) say?" Dolman: "That he did not well know him." L.C.J.: "Mr. Oates, you say you were with him (Coleman) at the Savoy and Wild-House; pray, Sir Thomas, did he say he did not know him, or had seen Mr. Coleman there?" Dolman: "He did not know him as he stood there." Dolben, J.: "Did he say he did not know Mr. Coleman, or that he did not know that man?" Dolman: "He said he had no acquaintance with that man (to the best of my remembrance)."

571 7 State Trials 29, 30.

572 7 State Trials 21.

573 Oates' work had certainly been remarkably hard, and his fatigue was no invention of his own. See the evidence of Sir Thomas Dolman at Sir George Wakeman's trial. 7 State Trials 656. Oates was confronted with Coleman, and charged him with high treason on the night of Monday, September 30. Dolman: "My Lord, Mr. Oates did appear before the king and council, I think on the Saturday before which was Michaelmas eve. The council sat long that morning, the council sat again in the afternoon, and Mr. Oates was employed that night I think to search after some Jesuits, who were then taken, and that was the work of that night. The council I think sat again Sunday in the afternoon. Mr. Oates was then examined; the council sat long, and at night he was sent abroad again to search the lodgings of several priests and to find out their papers, which he did seize upon, and one of the nights in that season was a very wet night; he went either with a messenger or with a guard upon him. On Monday morning the council sat again, and he was further examined, and went abroad; and Monday night Mr. Oates was in as feeble and weak a condition as ever I saw man in my life, and was very willing to have been dismissed for that time, for he seemed to be in very great weakness and disorder, so that I believe he was scarce able to give a good answer."

The whole incident is very similar to that which occurred at Wakeman's trial, with the exception that then the evidence went against the witness, whereas now it was against the prisoner. The conduct of the court on the two occasions was perfectly consistent. *Ibid.* 651–653. See below.

574 *Hist. Crim. Law* i. 385.

575 Compare the trial of Whitebread, Harcourt, Fenwick, etc. When Oates had finished his evidence, Fenwick said: "Pray, my Lord, be pleased to take notice that this man's evidence all along is that he saw such and such letters from such and such persons. They have no evidence but just that, they saw such and such letters." 7 State Trials 358.

576 7 State Trials 21, 32.

577 As in the case of Dangerfield. 7 State Trials 1110.

578 7 State Trials 359, 411.

579 See above 293.

580 Fox, *History of the Early Part of the Reign of James II* 34.

581 Gardiner, *History of England* vii. 323–326.

582 6 State Trials 693.

583 One of the women supposed to be bewitched.

584 8 State Trials 1021. *Lives of the Norths* i. 167.

585 An extraordinary instance of the nature of the ideas of the time on the subject of evidence appears in an examination before the Lords' committee of inquiry. Oates complained that the Bishop of Chichester and Justice Bickley had reviled his evidence. A witness named Nicholas Covert was examined: "says he was at the public meeting at Chichester, but he remembers not that anything was said reflecting on Dr. Oates. The discourse was concerning the Narratives, and somebody there said that he had contradicted himself twenty-two times." House of Lords MSS. 146. If a score of self-contradictions were not generally taken as an objection to a witness, it is hard to imagine what would have been.

586 *History of his own Time.* London, 1727, 386.

587 Ralph i. 412.

588 7 State Trials 13.

589 *Ibid.* 35–53.

590 7 State Trials 59, 60.

591 Being asked what he had to say he returned again to the subject: "As for my papers I humbly hope ... that I should not have been found guilty of any crime in them but what the act of grace could have pardoned."... *Ibid.* 71.

592 7 State Trials 8.

593 *Ibid.* 15.

594 *Ibid.* 76.

595 House of Lords MSS. 8, November 6, 1678.

596 House of Lords MSS. 14.

597 This misunderstanding is so extraordinary that I was tempted at one time to adopt the theory that the prosecution was aware of the existence of the later letters, and suppressed the knowledge from motives of expedience. Certainly the managers of the prosecutions for the plot were guilty of conduct which not only would now be thought unprofessional, but was on any consideration highly suspicious, as for instance in the suppression of the forged letters sent by Oates and Tonge to Father Bedingfield (see Ralph i. 384. Sir G. Sitwell, *The First Whig* 36), and on a question of honesty simply the balance of probability might turn against them. But the supposition cannot be maintained. It was suggested at the time that, if the letters of the years 1673, 1674, 1675 contained such dangerous matter as appeared from their perusal, those of the three ensuing years must, had they been found, have revealed still more horrible schemes. But the force of this argument was not sufficient to afford a motive for taking the risk of detection (Ralph i. 412). And although the personality of Shaftesbury, by whom alone such a scheme could have been worked out, was of great potency in the committee of the House of Lords, he hardly dominated it so completely as to render the manœuvre practicable in the presence of such men as Lord Anglesey, the Marquis of Winchester, and the Bishop of Bath and Wells (House of Lords MSS. i.).

598 See above 312. 7 State Trials 59.

599 *Ibid.* 65.

600 L.C.J.: "If the cause did turn upon that matter, I would be well content to sit until the book were brought; but I doubt the cause will not stand on that foot; but if that were the case it would do you little good." 7 State Trials 65.

601 7 State Trials 71.

602 *Ibid.* 66–68. Besides this he said several other things, of which mention will be made later.

603 *Ibid.* 70.

604 *Ibid.* 78. Luttrell, *Brief Relation* i. 4. Burnet ii. 178.

605 Burnet ii. 113.

606 Evidence of Carstairs, 6 State Trials 1503.

607 Macaulay, *Hist. of England* i. 237. Lingard xiii. 107, 108.

608 Hist. MSS. Com. Rep. 14. Appendix ii. 361. See also Fairfax Correspondence. Civil Wars (ed. R. Bell) ii. 297. James Babington to Henry Lord Fairfax, November 20, 1678. "Staley, the goldsmith's son, was tried to-day at the King's Bench, and condemned."

609 Schwerin, *Briefe aus England* 356. On December 2 (n.s.) he notes: "Des Goldschmied's Sohn, von dessen unbesonnenen Reden ich bereits Mittheilung gemacht, ist gehangen und nachher geviertheilt worden. Man hatte sich vorher überzeugt, dass er gesagt, dass der König in England sei der grösste Ketzer und Schelm in der Welt. Darauf hat er mit der Hand auf die Brust geschlagen, mit den Füssen fünf bis sechsmal auf die Erde gestampft, und mit ausgestrecktem Arm gesagt. Dies ist die Hand, die ihn hätte umbringen sollen, der König und das Parlament glaubten, das alles gethan und vorbei sei, allein die Schelme wären betrogen." *Ibid.* 362. Barillon's testimony is on the same side: "Le témoin, sur la foi duquel Staley, fils d'un orrèvre, a été condamné, a accusé le Duc d'Hamilton." December 16/26, 1678. And Warner (MS. history 40): "Primus, qui Catholico sanguine Angliam rigavit, fuit Gulielmus Stalaeus, alterius Gulielmi auri fabri et trapazitae Londiniensis civis divitis filius." The act under which Staley was condemned is 13 Charles II cap. i.

610 House of Lords MSS. 77, 78.

611 Burnet (ii. 171) speaks of Staley as "the popish banker, who had been in great credit, but was then under some difficulties"; but this is one of the rare mistakes he makes in point of fact.

612 He disclaimed all such sentiments and did deny the words, but afterwards said that he had "never with intention, or any thought or ill-will, spake any word upon this matter." 6 State Trials 1506, 1508.

613 6 State Trials 1509. Lingard (xiii. 108) states on the authority of *Les Conspirations d'Angleterre* that Fromante, who is there called Firmin, was put into prison to prevent his appearance at the trial; but the work is by no means above suspicion, and is directly contradicted on the point. Large extracts from *Les Conspirations d'Angleterre*, which was published in 1681 and is now extremely rare, are quoted by Arnauld, *Œuvres* xiv. 515–535. Arnauld says in a note: "C'est M. Rocole, ancien chanoine de S. Benoit à Paris, qui en est l'auteur; mais l'avertissement qui le fait paraître Protestant, n'est pas de lui." There is among the State Papers an order in council for the arrest of Bartholemew Fermin for high treason on account of the Popish Plot, but without date. S.P. Dom. Charles II 408; i. 110.

614 6 State Trials 1511, 1512.

615 Foley v. 233, 234.

616 *Ibid.* v. 12. Lingard xiii. 64. *True Narrative of the Horrid Plot and Conspiracy,* lxxvii.

617 Foley v. 233, 244, 245.

618 *Ibid.* 223.

619 7 State Trials 91–101.

620 *Ibid.* 101–104.

621 *Ibid.* 105.

622 7 State Trials 105. L.C.J.; "You must be tried by the laws of England, which sends no piece of fact out of the country to be tried."

623 There is much evidence to show this. The following instances are from the same volume of the State Trials:—The Attorney-General not allowed to read a certificate against the accused 129. Whitebread not allowed to use Oates' *Narrative* 374. Fenwick, Whitebread, and Harcourt not allowed to use the report of Ireland's trial. Harcourt was, in fact, mistaken on the point for which he wished to refer to the report 360, 384–386. Lord Stafford not allowed to use the council book as evidence 1440. See also 451, 462, 467, 654.

624 7 State Trials 106–108.

625 On April 16, 1679. *Ibid.* 259–310, and see below.

626 7 State Trials 272, 295.

627 *Ibid.* 392.

628 *Ibid.* 117, 118. Sergeant Baldwin produced the letter, saying, "We do conceive a letter from one of that party, bearing date about the same time, concerning Mr. Whitebread's summons, who was then master of the company, is very good evidence against them."

The prosecution was forced to retract, and Mr. Finch, the junior, was made to eat his leader's words: "My Lord, it can affect no particular person, but we only use it in general."

629 7 State Trials 120.

630 7 State Trials 315–317.

631 Cf. Rookwood's case 1696. Powell, J.: "Certainly now the jury is charged, they must give a verdict either of acquittal or conviction." Sir T. Trevor, Att. Gen.: "I know what has been usually thought of Whitebread's case." And the trial of Cook, 1696. Powell, J.: "Whitebread's case was indeed held to be an extraordinary case." And see 7 State Trials 497–500 n, where many instances and opinions adverse to the decision of the court are collected.

632 Hale, P.C. ii. 294. "By the ancient law, if the jury sworn had been once particularly charged with a prisoner, it was commonly held they must give up their verdict, and they could not be discharged before their verdict was

given up.... But yet the contrary course hath for a long time obtained at Newgate, and nothing is more ordinary than after the jury is sworn and charged with a prisoner and evidence given, yet if it appears to the court that some of the evidence is kept back, or taken off, or that there may be a fuller discovery and the offence notorious, as murder or burglary, and that the evidence, though not sufficient to convict the prisoner, yet gives the court a great and strong suspicion of his guilt, the court may discharge the jury of the prisoner, and remit him to the gaol for further evidence; and accordingly it has been practised in most circuits of England, for otherwise many notorious murders and burglaries may pass unpunished, by the acquittal of a person probably guilty, where the full evidence is not searched out or given." "The whole law upon this subject," says Sir James Fitzjames Stephen, "was elaborately considered a few years ago in R. *v.* Winsor (L.R. 1 Q.B. 289), when it appeared, from many authorities, that the practice had fluctuated." *Hist. Crim. Law* i. 397.

633 7 State Trials 98.

634 7 State Trials 122–126.

635 *Ibid.* 121, 122.

636 *Ibid.* 124.

637 7 *Ibid.* 128.

638 10 State Trials 1243–1281.

639 7 State Trials 388–391.

640 *Ibid.* 132.

641 *Ibid.* 133–135.

642 Stephen i. 399.

643 7 State Trials 138–141.

644 7 State Trials 142–144. Klopp II. 464, app. IV.

645 Foley v. 58.

646 See "An impartial consideration of these speeches," etc., 1670, attributed to John Williams, D.D. "Animadversions on the last speeches of the Five Jesuits," etc., 1679. Printed 7 State Trials 543.

647 Burnet ii. 201.

648 Sidney, *Letters* 123, 124. The opinion of Ranke, who in his writings was neither Catholic nor Protestant, lies midway between these views:

"Grässlich ist die lange Reihe von Hinrichtungen Solcher, die nichts bekannten," v. 235.

649 "The examination of Captain William Bedloe deceased, taken in his last sickness by Sir Francis North, Chief Justice of the Court of Common Pleas." Printed 6 State Trials 1493–1498.

650 See Russell's written Speech, printed at length, Ralph i. 755–757.

651 Sitwell, *First Whig* 153–158. And see Stephen i. 408, 409.

652 Stephen i. 449. And see Burnet II. 303, 304.

653 Above 328.

654 See above 204–209.

655 Longleat MSS. Coventry Papers xi. 363. Order of the king in council, February 5, 1679.

656 7 State Trials 259, 287, 296.

657 *Ibid.* 287–289, 292.

658 So Bedloe swore 7 State Trials 271. Burnet (ii. 199) says that Bedloe made use of Reading's intrigue to cover his omission to swear against the Jesuits in the previous December. But Reading never denied the fact that Bedloe's account of this part of the transaction was correct.

659 Presumably, from the absence of any Christian name, Mr. George Speke of White Lackington, M.P. for Somersetshire, a more reputable person than his sons Hugh and Charles. George Speke had been a royalist and after the Restoration lived in retirement for many years, but, following the example of his son-in-law, John Trenchard, turned against the court and became a leader of the Whig interest in his part of the country. In 1680 he entertained Monmouth during his western progress. Fea, *King Monmouth* 96.

660 The date fixed first was March 28, and was afterwards altered. 7 State Trials 281.

661 Evidence of Bedloe, Speke, and Wiggins. *Ibid.* 270–286.

662 *Ibid.* 278, 279.

663 7 State Trials 310.

664 Colonel Mansell's *Exact and True Narrative of the late Popish Intrigue* 64.

665 See Ralph i. 431. Echard 970, 971. Danby, *Memoirs* 39, 40.

666 7 State Trials 763–812. An Exact and True Narrative of the Horrid Conspiracy of Thomas Knox, William Osborne, and John Lane to invalidate the testimonies of Dr. Oates and Mr. William Bedloe. London 1680.

667 See below.

668 Burnet ii. 200.

669 7 State Trials 881–926.

670 This was contradicted and his reputation much debated at the trial of Lord Stafford eighteen months later; but at the time it was believed to be the fact.

671 Thomas Whitebread, provincial; William Harcourt, rector of the London province; John Fenwick, procurator for the college at St. Omers; John Gavan, and Anthony Turner. 7 State Trials 311–418.

672 *Ibid.* 340, 1455. This was so far confirmed that Dugdale was proved to have spoken on Tuesday, October 15, 1678 of the death of a justice of the peace in Westminster, which does not go far. Dugdale also declared at Lord Stafford's trial that on Coleman's arrest the Duke of York sent to Newgate to ask if he had made disclosures to anybody, and when Coleman returned that he had done so only to Godfrey, the duke gave orders to have Godfrey killed. 7 State Trials 1316–1319. Burnet ii. 190, 191. And see above 153, n. Burnet says: "The Earl of Essex told me he swore it on his first examination, December 24, 1678, but since it was only on hearsay from Evers, and so was nothing in law, and yet would heighten the fury against the duke, the king charged Dugdale to say nothing of it." This is a mistake. Dugdale's first and second examinations, December 24 and 29, 1678. S.P. Dom. Charles II 408: II. 49, 22. Dugdale did formally tell the story in his information, but not until March 21, 1679. Fitzherbert MSS. 135.

673 Dugdale's evidence. 7 State Trials 334–342.

674 7 State Trials 343–349.

675 *Ibid.* 119, 355. House of Lords MSS. 15.

676 7 State Trials, 350–357.

677 7 State Trials 359–378.

678 "... Three of them, having been apprehended by Sir Will. Waller at their first coming, told him they were come to be witnesses, and being asked what they were to witness, they said they must know that from their superiors." Sidney, *Letters* 101.

679 Examination of Christopher Townley, April 28, 1679. Fitzherbert MSS. 151, 152.

680 7 State Trials 371. At the trial of Langhorn another witness was produced to explain this, but his testimony was unconvincing.

681 *Ibid.* 361, 364, 366. Information was also given that Gifford had admitted in conversation "that his Superior of the College at St. Omers had sent him over to swear on behalf of the Lords, and that he must obey, and would, right or wrong." Examinations of Chamberlayne and Gouddall. Fitzherbert MSS. 149.

682 Examinations of Coulster and Townley. Fitzherbert MSS 151, 152.

683 7 State Trials 396–403. North, *Examen* 239, 240. 10 State Trials 1183–1188. Smith, *Intrigues of the Popish Plot*. The evil reputation of these men was unknown at the time of the trial. See Burnet ii. 226.

684 7 State Trials 404–418.

685 At the time of the fire of London, Tillotson told Burnet a story of Langhorn's methods of business which is too ridiculous to be believed. Burnet i. 412.

686 *True Narrative* lxxxi.

687 7 State Trials 463–465, 470.

688 *Ibid.* 439.

689 7 State Trials 514.

690 *Ibid.* 172, 173.

691 Sidney, *Letters* 124. "Wakeman's trial is put off, as is believed, to avoid the indecency of the discourses that would have been made."

692 L.J. xiii. 388–392. C.J. November 28, 29, 1678. Ralph i. 397. James (Or. Mem.) i. 529.

693 Burnet ii. 231.

694 7 State Trials 602–618.

695 *Ibid.* 619–623.

696 *Ibid.* 624–641. Bedloe however gave no evidence against the prisoner Rumley.

697 7 State Trials 644–651. Sir J. F. Stephen has strangely missed the bearing of this evidence, and writes as if it had been decisive in favour of the prisoners. *Hist. Crim. Law* i. 391.

698 The first serious acquittal at least, for the trial of Atkins, after the conviction of Green, Berry, and Hill for the murder of Godfrey, was hardly more than formal.

699 7 State Trials 651–653.

700 Hatton Correspondence ii. 187. Charles Hatton to Lord Hatton, July 10, 1679. "Mr. Pepys and Sir Anthony Deane was bailed yesterday, and if my Lord Chief Justice hang five hundred Jesuits, he will not regain the opinion he thereby lost with the populace, to court whom he will not act against his conscience." Luttrell, *Brief Relation* i. 74.

701 Verney MSS. 474.

702 Burnet ii. 232. *The Narrative of Segnior Francisco de Faria*, 1680, 17, 18.

703 Deposition of F. de Faria, March 24, 1681. S.P. Dom. Charles II 415: 159. Verney MSS. 474. Luttrell, *Brief Relation* i. 17, 74.

704 Luttrell, *Brief Relation* i. 19.

705 8 State Trials 163–174. Hatton Correspondence ii. 220.

706 7 State Trials 702–706.

707 Hatton Correspondence ii. 191, 195, 207–210.

708 C.J. ix. 661, 688–692. L.J. xiii. 736–739. Luttrell, *Brief Relation* i. 64.

709 L.J. xiii. 752.

710 Luttrell, *Brief Relation* i. 74, 75.

711 See Burnet ii. 196. North, *Examen* 567, 568. *Lives of the Norths*, 195, 196. Hatton Correspondence, *passim*.

712 Burnet ii. 196. North, *Examen* 568.

713 Reresby, *Memoirs* 146. "Being with the king at the Duchess of Portsmouth's lodgings, my Lord Treasurer being also present, the king told me he took it (Oates' story) to be some artifice, and that he did not believe one word of the Plot." Reresby, though always well-informed, was never at this time in possession of real secrets.

Barillon, October 1/10, 1678. "Le Roi de la Grande Bretagne m'a dit qu'il ne croyait pas que cette accusation eût un veritable fondement."

Shaftesbury, *The present state of the Kingdom at the opening of the Parliament*, March 6, 1679. "As concerning the plot and the murder of Godfrey, the king's discourses and managing are new and extraordinary. No man can judge by them but that he is in the plot against his own life; and no man doubts but he is so far in as concerns us all." Printed Christie ii. 309.

714 Barillon, January 16/26, 1679. "Le Roi d'Angleterre ne me parle plus comme il a parlé jusqu'à present. Il me dit hier que la déposition d'un dernier témoin nommé Ducdale lui parassait si peu concertée et si pleine de faits vraisemblables qu'il ne pouvait plus s'empêcher de croire à une conspiration contre sa personne. Ce Prince me redit toutes les raisons qui lui ont fait croire qu'Oats et Benloi sont des parjures et des imposteurs, mais en même temps il me fit connaître que ce qu'ils avaient dit de faux n'empêchait pas qu'il n'y eût quelque chose de vrai qui servait pour fondement à tout ce qu'ils avaient pu inventer d'eux mêmes."

715 See the trials of Andrew Bromwich, 7 State Trials 715–726, Lionel Anderson and others, *ibid.* 729–750, Knox and Lane, *ibid.* 763–812, Lord Castlemaine, *ibid.* 1067–1112.

716 Luttrell, *Brief Relation* i. 34.

717 See *e.g.* his summing up at Lord Castlemaine's trial. 7 State Trials 1408–1412.

718 In spite of his own and his brother's assertions there cannot be the least doubt of this. North afterwards declared in his memoirs that he never believed in the Popish Plot, a statement which is belied by every action and word of his on the bench.

719 7 State Trials 218, at the trial of Green, Berry, and Hill.

720 7 State Trials 69.

721 *Ibid.* 133, 134.

722 *Ibid.* 218, 411, 642, 1102. 10 State Trials 1170. L.C.J.: "You may assure yourselves, I will remember whatsoever has been said on the one side and on t'other as well as I can; the gentlemen of the jury are men of understanding, and I see they take notes, and I'll give them what assistance I can." Instances might be multiplied. See Stephen i. 377, 566, 567.

723 6 State Trials 701–710. His trial was in 1665.

724 *Parl. Hist.* iv. 1088.

725 7 State Trials 134. *Absalom and Achitophel* 120.

726 7 State Trials 678–680. This is another fair specimen. "Never brag of your religion, for it is a foul one, and so contrary to Christ; it is easier to believe anything than to believe that an understanding man may be a papist."

727 These trials in their order of mention will be found:—7 State Trials 1043. *Ibid.* 959. 8 State Trials 502. 7 State Trials 1162. 8 State Trials 447. 7 State Trials 1067. 8 State Trials 243.

728 Reresby, *Memoirs* 194.

729 See Appendix E.

730 The proceedings in Parliament against the five popish lords are collected in 7 State Trials 1218–1292.

731 Reresby, *Memoirs* 193, 194, North, *Examen* 218.

732 Barillon, November 31/December 9, 1680. "Ce qui se passera dans ce procès est de grande consequence. Si le comte de Stafford était absous, la conjuration recevrait une grande atteinte, et quoique le peuple soit prévenu, il est néantmoins assujetti aux règles et aux lois, et ne s'en départ pas aisément."

733 *Secret Services of Charles II and James II* 24.

734 Barillon, December 6/16, 9/19, 1680. James i. 640.

735 7 State Trials 1298–1339.

736 Dugdale's evidence. 7 State Trials 1341–1347.

737 Oates' evidence. *Ibid.* 1347–1350.

738 Turbervile's evidence. *Ibid.* 1351–1355.

739 *Ibid.* 1394, 1395.

740 7 State Trials 1397–1400.

741 *Ibid.* 1388–1393.

742 *Ibid.* 1396–1406.

743 *Ibid.* 1407–1415.

744 7 State Trials 1415–1419.

745 Stafford admitted afterwards that in recent years he had constantly used a walking stick, "being lame with weariness." *Ibid.* 1478.

746 *Ibid.* 1419–1434.

747 7 State Trials 1437–1447.

748 *Ibid.* 1462, 1463.

749 *Ibid.* 1485–1492.

750 *Ibid.* 1486–1491.

751 6 State Trials 119.

752 7 State Trials 1519–1529.

753 *Ibid.* 1493–1515.

754 *Ibid.* 1544–1551.

755 Reresby thought that he acquitted himself well, but James said "it was always his misfortune to play his game worst when he had the best cards." James i. 637.

756 Barillon, December 16/26 1680.

757 Reresby, *Memoirs* 194.

758 Anglesey, *Memoirs* 9.

759 Barillon, November 21/December 1, 1680. "Ce Prince prend souvent la liberté de se moquer la conjuration, et ne se constraint pas d'appeller tout haut Oatz et Bedlow des coquins. Il a dit cependant que les preuves contre le Vicomte de Stafford étaient fortes, et qu'il pouvait bien n'être pas innocent."

760 Hatton Correspondence ii. 241.

761 Barillon, December 9/19 1680.

762 *Ibidem.*

763 The Earls of Carlisle, Berkshire, and Suffolk. The appearance of Lord Howard of Escrick on the same side is of no importance on account of his bad character.

764 Anglesey, *Memoirs* 9. James to Hyde. Clarendon Cor. i. 50. James to Col. Legge, Dartmouth MSS. 54. Barillon, December 19/29, 1680.

765 L.J. xiii. 724. C.J. December 23, 1680. *Parl. Hist.* iv. 1261. 7 State Trials 1562.

766 7 State Trials 1544, 1440–1447, 1342, 1343.

767 *Ibid.* 1564–1567.

768 Echard 997. Lingard xiii. 247–249.

769 Dispatch of Sarotti-Bignola, January 10, 1681. "Tanta è la impressione de' popoli della verità della congiura e della reità del conte (Stafford), che da pochi è stato compatito e molti lo hanno ingiurato con infami parole." Quoted Brosch 451. Dispatch of Thun, January 10, 1681. "Der Henker hat den kopf auf der Bühne herumgetragen und dem Volke gezeigt, welches darüber ein unausprechliches Freuden- und frohlockendes Geschrei hat erschallen lassen." Quoted Klopp II 473, app. XXII.

770 7 State Trials 1129–1162.

771 *Ibid.* 1162.

772 *Ibid.* 1133.

773 *Ibid.* 1161.

774 Evidence of Richmond and Bridges. *Ibid.* 1140, 1142.

775 Evidence of Arnold. 7 State Trials 1135–1137.

776 Evidence of Phillips. *Ibid.* 1138.

777 Evidence of Philpot. *Ibid.* 1145, 1146.

778 Evidence of Watkins, Richmond, and Powel. *Ibid.* 1139.

779 Evidence of H. Jones and J. Jones. *Ibid.* 1146, 1147.

780 Evidence of W. Richmond. 7 State Trials 1140, 1141, and evidence for the defence. *Ibid.* 1148–1151.

781 *Ibid.* 1152–1159.

782 *Ibid.* 1160. Luttrell, *Brief Relation* i. 53, 55. S.P. Dom. Charles II 414: 79. Petition of John Giles. Read in Council, 6 August 1680.

783 7 State Trials 1138, 1146.

784 It is evident that the writer was an agent employed by Jenkins for the purpose. Otherwise the secretary would certainly have noted from whom and the date on which he received the information. The style of the report is also evidence of this.

785 Stephen i. 393. Macaulay i. 234.

Milton Keynes UK
Ingram Content Group UK Ltd.
UKHW011123050624
443649UK00006B/519